Post-Pandemic Talent Management Models in Knowledge Organizations

Mohammad Rafiqul Islam Talukdar
American International University-Bangladesh, Bangladesh

Carmen Z. Lamagna
American International University-Bangladesh, Bangladesh

Charles Carillo Villanueva
American International University-Bangladesh, Bangladesh

Rezbin Nahar
American International University-Bangladesh, Bangladesh

Farheen Hassan
American International University-Bangladesh, Bangladesh

A volume in the Advances in Logistics, Operations, and Management Science (ALOMS) Book Series

IGI Global
PUBLISHER of TIMELY KNOWLEDGE

Published in the United States of America by
IGI Global
Business Science Reference (an imprint of IGI Global)
701 E. Chocolate Avenue
Hershey PA, USA 17033
Tel: 717-533-8845
Fax: 717-533-8661
E-mail: cust@igi-global.com
Web site: http://www.igi-global.com

Library of Congress Cataloging-in-Publication Data

Names: Talukdar, Mohammad Rafiqul Islam, 1978- editor.
Title: Post-pandemic talent management models in knowledge organizations / Mohammad Talukdar, Carmen Lamagna, Charles Villanueva, Rezbin Nahar, and Farheen Hassan, editors.
Description: Hershey, PA : Business Science Reference, [2023] | Includes bibliographical references and index. | Summary: "This book focuses on human capital management and talent management in a post-pandemic world, making a significant contribution to the literature on strategic human resource management, specifically talent management in post-modern knowledge-based organizations during the COVID-19 pandemic period and post-pandemic paradigm"-- Provided by publisher.
Identifiers: LCCN 2022008804 (print) | LCCN 2022008805 (ebook) | ISBN 9781668438947 (hardcover) | ISBN 9781668438954 (paperback) | ISBN 9781668438961 (ebook)
Subjects: LCSH: Personnel management. | Human capital--Management. | Manpower planning.
Classification: LCC HF5549 .H29767 2023 (print) | LCC HF5549 (ebook) | DDC 658.3--dc23/eng/20220223
LC record available at https://lccn.loc.gov/2022008804
LC ebook record available at https://lccn.loc.gov/2022008805

This book is published in the IGI Global book series Advances in Logistics, Operations, and Management Science (ALOMS) (ISSN: 2327-350X; eISSN: 2327-3518)

British Cataloguing in Publication Data
A Cataloguing in Publication record for this book is available from the British Library.

All work contributed to this book is new, previously-unpublished material.
The views expressed in this book are those of the authors, but not necessarily of the publisher.

For electronic access to this publication, please contact: eresources@igi-global.com.

Advances in Logistics, Operations, and Management Science (ALOMS) Book Series

John Wang
Montclair State University, USA

ISSN:2327-350X
EISSN:2327-3518

MISSION

Operations research and management science continue to influence business processes, administration, and management information systems, particularly in covering the application methods for decision-making processes. New case studies and applications on management science, operations management, social sciences, and other behavioral sciences have been incorporated into business and organizations real-world objectives.

The **Advances in Logistics, Operations, and Management Science** (ALOMS) Book Series provides a collection of reference publications on the current trends, applications, theories, and practices in the management science field. Providing relevant and current research, this series and its individual publications would be useful for academics, researchers, scholars, and practitioners interested in improving decision making models and business functions.

COVERAGE

- Operations Management
- Marketing engineering
- Political Science
- Information Management
- Decision analysis and decision support
- Computing and information technologies
- Finance
- Networks
- Risk Management
- Services management

IGI Global is currently accepting manuscripts for publication within this series. To submit a proposal for a volume in this series, please contact our Acquisition Editors at Acquisitions@igi-global.com or visit: http://www.igi-global.com/publish/.

The Advances in Logistics, Operations, and Management Science (ALOMS) Book Series (ISSN 2327-350X) is published by IGI Global, 701 E. Chocolate Avenue, Hershey, PA 17033-1240, USA, www.igi-global.com. This series is composed of titles available for purchase individually; each title is edited to be contextually exclusive from any other title within the series. For pricing and ordering information please visit http://www.igi-global.com/book-series/advances-logistics-operations-management-science/37170. Postmaster: Send all address changes to above address.

Titles in this Series

For a list of additional titles in this series, please visit: http://www.igi-global.com/book-series/

Considerations and Characteristics of the Millennial Leader in Today's Global Society
Tymon M. Graham (TMGraham Consulting, LLC, USA)
Business Science Reference • © 2023 • 300pp • H/C (ISBN: 9781668447116) • US $240.00

Moving From R&D Development to Production and Sales in Start-Up Companies Emerging Research and Opportunities
Amiram Porath (APC, Israel)
Business Science Reference • © 2022 • 300pp • H/C (ISBN: 9781799856856) • US $215.00

Advancing Interpersonal Emotion Regulation and Social Regulation
Donta S. Harper (Argosy University, USA)
Information Science Reference • © 2022 • 384pp • H/C (ISBN: 9781668424780) • US $215.00

Handbook of Research on Activating Middle Executives' Agency to Lead and Manage During Times of Crisis
Ann-Marie Wilmot (The University of the West Indies, Mona, Jamaica) and Canute Sylvester Thompson (The University of the West Indies, Mona, Jamaica)
Business Science Reference • © 2022 • 415pp • H/C (ISBN: 9781668443316) • US $325.00

Business Models to Promote Technology, Culture, and Leadership in Post-COVID-19 Organizations
Joseph Robert Heinzman (Western Governors University, USA) Debbie S. Judge (Western Governors University, USA) Vincent Franklin (Western Governors University, USA) and Jim A. McCleskey (Western Governors University, USA & Houston Community College System, USA)
Business Science Reference • © 2022 • 300pp • H/C (ISBN: 9781668443583) • US $250.00

Global Risk and Contingency Management Research in Times of Crisis
Narasimha Rao Vajjhala (University of New York Tirana, Tirana, Albania) and Kenneth David Strang (W3-Research, USA & RMIT University, Australia)
Business Science Reference • © 2022 • 356pp • H/C (ISBN: 9781668452790) • US $270.00

IGI Global
PUBLISHER of TIMELY KNOWLEDGE

701 East Chocolate Avenue, Hershey, PA 17033, USA
Tel: 717-533-8845 x100 • Fax: 717-533-8661
E-Mail: cust@igi-global.com • www.igi-global.com

Table of Contents

Detailed Table of Contents

The chapter builds on a conceptual and theoretical understanding of talent management. It documents the notions and essence of talent management in modern organizations, especially in modern knowledge-based organizations, and frames a theoretical framework for talent management at present. It explains the fundamental link between talent management and human capital theory and answers three featured questions: Why is talent management so crucial in 21st-century organizations? How can talent strategy be reinvented to support digitalization? What are the changing landscape and evolving concerns of talent management and their implications for knowledge organizations in the post-pandemic paradigm?

This chapter provides a journey to understand the origin of talent management along with the need for talent management. The chapter describes how talent management has evolved over the period to date. The chapter further states the process of talent management highlighting the prerequisites. This section also describes the framework of the talent management process and its connections with other disciplines. The chapter further elaborates on various challenges associated with talent management. There is a section that would help understand successful strategies adopted by the companies for enhanced performance. The chapter further states future trends to be followed for improved performance. The chapter states the scenario during the COVID-19 pandemic and concludes with successful talent management implementation examples.

The focus of this chapter is on the connection between good talent management and the development of sustainable competitive advantage in organizations. The resource-based view (RBV) of the firm is leveraged in analyzing that connection; RBV upholds that competitive advantage is closely related to an organization's internal characteristics. More specifically, if an organization owns and utilizes valuable, rare, inimitable, and non-substitutable resources and capabilities in its processes and operations, it will achieve superior performance and sustainable competitive advantage. A framework is developed that organizational leaders can use in facilitating conversations and developing talent management programs to ensure that their talent management processes are focused on honing the organization's core competencies that feed their sustainable competitive advantage and superior performance.

The chapter explored the evolution of human resources management to position strategic human resources management (SHRM), human capital development (HCD), and employee behavior, such as creative work behavior, as important variables required by organizations to survive in challenging environments. It argued that the alignment of the fits between SHRM and business strategy and between SHRM and HCD positions employees as sources of organizations' competitive advantage and drives positive and innovative employee behavior required in the business challenging environments faced by organizations. The chapter discussed a study done with samples from knowledge workers to establish the relationship between SHRM, HCD, and creative work behavior. Results showed that SHRM had a direct relationship with HCD and an indirect relationship with CWB through HCD. There was no direct relationship between SHRM and CWB. Implications of the study and future research were recommended.

A knowledge-based organization such as educational institutes, consultancy firms require certain skills from their employees. Among many, the prime duty of the department of human resource management (HRM) of an organization is to identify the required skills for a particular task or job. HRM searches those skills during the time of recruitment. However, skills are not constant; rather, they are dynamic. Different eras require different skills to perform any task successfully. During the post-pandemic period of COVID-19, usage of technology in educational institute for their regular tasks such as lecture delivery, online assessment, seminars, conducting workshops have increased rapidly. Unfortunately, the academicians in many cases are not trained to perform these tasks in an efficient manner. This is especially true for developing countries like Bangladesh, where the transition from an analog to a digital world is still in progress. The chapter focuses on how HRM in any knowledge-based organization can play a very crucial role to convert its human resources into human capital.

This literature-based chapter addresses the vital issues and challenges of KM in respect of knowledge transfer barriers and mechanisms of Hasnain, Jasimuddin, and Fuller-Love and makes an endeavor to materialize those with TM strategies mainly identified by Whelan and Carcary in the context of the COVID-19 pandemic. The contributions of talent management (TM) and knowledge management (KM) are undisputedly acknowledged by researchers and business organizations. Both TM researchers and KM researchers have hardly addressed the strategies of integrating TM and KM for implementing TM strategies against KM challenges in the context of the COVID-19 pandemic. Positioning and integrating appropriately the TM strategies against KM challenges could derive huge benefits for the organizations during hostilities. The COVID-19 pandemic has made the world environment volatile and complex. Therefore, numerous challenges of KM have emerged demanding TM strategies.

The authors highlight some of the aspects that contribute to the country's cyber vulnerabilities. Finally, several proposals are made to protect Bangladesh's cyberspace against harmful assaults.

Online transactions have increased abruptly during the COVID-19 pandemic. In recent years, the expansion of easy banking in Bangladesh has become necessary, particularly when banks do not have sufficient branches in Bangladesh's rural areas. This research provides a quick overview, a managerial framework of cybersecurity, and several potential threats that might significantly affect the security of online monetary transactions by giving some important ways. The authors explore contemporary scamming strategies used by cybercriminals and the impact of such scams on the financial sector. In addition, this chapter presents a way to mitigate these concerns by inflexible banking, provides a quick overview of the current automated teller machine (ATM) fraud, and offers potential solutions to avoid these attacks. Furthermore, the authors examine the consequences of banking fraud and identify possible research avenues where researchers could focus their efforts on benefit.

Agile leaders have the ability to think flexibly in changing environmental conditions to adapt an organization perfectly to these changes. These leaders can uncover the strengths of their employees, use their insights to transition the organization's intended change, and take advantage of the opportunities in change while trying to minimize their negative impact on the organization. Organizations that incorporate agile into their processes through agile leaders are better able to respond quickly to change and deliver superior business value to their stakeholders. With agile leadership, organizations will be in a better position to quickly detect developments in the business environment and achieve agility with few resources. As the volatility, uncertainty, complexity, and ambiguity (VUCA) of today's business world continues to pose great challenges for many organizations, this research examines the impact of agile leadership style on organizational performance from the perspective of VUCA world.

Preface

The world transformation from capitalism to a knowledge-based society took place in the early 21centuary. Over the past two decades, rapid digitalization has leveraged organizations to re-engineer the work style, workforce, and talent management. The global pandemic has inevitably intensified this process, radically altered the work and lifestyle, and heavily impacted knowledge and learning organizations. Despite being a serious challenge and expensive cost, most individuals and organizations accepted the changing reality of the paradigm shift caused by COVID-19. Yet the pandemic is fluctuating and going on, the time for adaptation is outmoded. The focus of both individuals and organizations has shifted now to the pandemic recovery, which is known as the post-pandemic paradigm shift.

This emerging paradigm requires a new set of work rules, patterns, and mind setup. Organizations also need to be altered their design and structure to make them fit and relevant to the new context keeping the structural contingency theory in mind. Business entities, particularly knowledge firms and learning organizations are more responsive to the internal and external stakeholders' concerns and brand image. Agile, talent, and impact-focused leadership are coupled to deal with the new workforce engagement and in attracting, developing, and retaining talent to encounter the multifaceted organizational needs today and to navigate the future sustained growth of the organizations through an integrated and technology-enabled approach.

The post-pandemic paradigm is setting three highest priorities for organizational development: Leveraging talent management, digitization in HR, and the future-impact focus and brand image of the work. In this context, the book is time worthy and valuable to advanced readers: Academics, researchers, professionals, policymakers, civil society representatives, and graduate and post-graduate university students of development studies, governance, public administration, public policy, and business schools. The book focuses on human capital theory and talent management in the pandemic and post-pandemic paradigms of the world and adds value to organizational change management, culture, and leadership.

The book ranked exceptional authors' diversity level in terms of gender, affiliations, and geographical positions in the globe. This splendid book is a 10-chapter edited monograph, published by the IGI Global, Hershey, US. The book is edited by a panel of distinguished scholars from a renowned business school titled "Faculty of Business Administration," American International University-Bangladesh (AIUB), Bangladesh. The diversity of the editorial team in terms of gender, expertise, and nationality is magnificent. The editorial team includes Professor Dr. Mohammad Rafiqul Islam Talukdar, Professor Dr. Carmen Z. Lamagna, Professor Dr. Charles Villanueva, Associate Professor Dr. Rezbin Nahar, and Professor Dr. Farheen Hassan.

Chapter 1 builds on a conceptual and theoretical understanding of talent management. It documents the notions and essence of talent management in modern organizations, especially in modern knowledge-based organizations, and frames a theoretical framework for talent management at present. It explains the fundamental link between talent management and human capital theory and answers three featured questions. Why is talent management so crucial in 21st-century organizations? How can talent strategy be reinvented to support digitalization? What are the changing landscape and evolving concerns of talent management and their implications for knowledge organizations in the post-pandemic paradigm?

Chapter 2 provides a journey to understand the origin of talent management and the need for talent management. The chapter analyses how talent management has evolved over the period to date and outlines the process of talent management, highlighting the prerequisites. It describes the framework of the talent management process and its connections with other disciplines. It elaborates on various challenges associated with talent management and outlines future trends to be followed for improved performance. The chapter also demonstrates the scenario during the COVID-19 pandemic and concludes with successful talent management implementation examples.

The focus of Chapter 3 is the connection between good talent management and the development of sustainable competitive advantage in organizations. The Resource-Based View (RBV) of the firm is leveraged in analyzing that connection; RBV upholds that competitive advantage is closely related to an organization's internal characteristics. More specifically, if an organization owns and utilizes valuable, rare, inimitable, and non-substitutable resources and capabilities in its processes and operations, it will achieve superior performance and a sustainable competitive advantage. A framework has been developed that organizational leaders can use in facilitating conversations and developing talent management programs to ensure that their talent management processes are focused on honing the organization's core competencies that feed their sustainable competitive advantage and superior performance.

Chapter 4 explores the evolution of human resources management to position Strategic Human Resources Management (SHRM), Human Capital Development (HCD), and employee behavior, such as creative work behavior, as important variables required by organizations to survive in challenging environments. It argues the alignment fit between SHRM and business strategy and between SHRM and HCD positions employees as sources of organizations' competitive advantage and drives positive and innovative employee behavior required in the challenging business environments faced by organizations. This chapter discusses a study done with samples from knowledge workers to establish the relationship between SHRM, HCD, and creative work behavior. The results reveal that SHRM holds a direct relationship with HCD and an indirect relationship with CWB through HCD. There is no direct relationship between SHRM and CWB.

Chapter 5 is about a knowledge-based organization, such as an educational institute or consultancy firm, that requires certain skills from its employees. Among many, the prime duty of the department of human resource management (HRM) of an organization is to identify the required skills for a particular task or job. HRM searches for those skills during the time of recruitment. However, skills are not constant, but rather they are dynamic. Different eras require different skills to perform any task successfully. During the post pandemic period of COVID-19, the usage of technology in educational institutions for their regular tasks such as lecture delivery, online assessment, seminars, and conducting workshops has increased rapidly. Unfortunately, academicians, in many cases, are not trained enough to perform these tasks in an efficient manner. In particular, this is true for developing countries like Bangladesh, where the transition from an analog to a digital world is still in progress. The chapter focuses on HRM in any knowledge-based organization that can play a very crucial role in converting its human resources into human capital.

Chapter 6 addresses the vital issues and challenges of KM in respect of knowledge transfer barriers and mechanisms and makes an endeavor to materialize those with TM strategies. The contributions of Talent Management (TM) and Knowledge Management (KM) are undisputedly acknowledged by researchers and business organizations. TM researchers and KM researchers have hardly addressed the strategies of integrating TM and KM for implementing TM strategies against KM challenges in the context of the COVID-19 Pandemic. Positioning and integrating TM strategies against KM challenges appropriately could result in significant benefits for organizations during hostilities. The global environment has become more volatile and complex as a result of the COVID-19 pandemic. Therefore, numerous challenges to KM have emerged, demanding TM strategies.

Chapter 7 focuses on the numerous, yet deceptively subtle differences between virtual and face-to-face communication that profoundly influence organizational performance, team interaction, and psychological well-being. This chapter identifies the "big 10" factors that affect human communication in virtual mediums: Mutual gaze; directional gaze; objective self-awareness; seating configurations; back-channel utterances; side conversations; touching; gesturing; collisions; and shared context. This chapter then examines each of these key factors, discusses how each affects virtual communication, and suggests best practices for overcoming and navigating these challenges.

Chapter 8 focuses on the COVID-19 pandemic and how consecutive lockdowns have made people dependent on the online environment and have made society compatible with virtual platforms. But the management of the electronic environment is not so easy but too crucial and vital, and it needs to be user-friendly. As a developing country, Bangladesh has welcomed digital changes. Unfortunately, threats and vulnerabilities have risen in lockstep with technological advancement. Businesses and educational institutions are now encountering cyber security concerns. Penetration Testing (Pen-Test) is a way of assessing the security of a web application, system, or network by systematically checking and confirming the efficacy of that system. The chapter discusses the purpose, classifications, and uses of penetration testing in Bangladesh's IT industries and demonstrates the present state of cyber security in Bangladesh.

Chapter 9 focuses on how online transactions have increased abruptly during the COVID-19 pandemic. In recent years, the expansion of easy banking in Bangladesh has become necessary, particularly when banks do not have sufficient branches in Bangladesh's rural areas. This research provides a quick overview, a managerial framework of cybersecurity, and several potential threats that might significantly affect the security of online monetary transactions in some important ways. The authors explore contemporary scamming strategies used by cybercriminals and the impact of such scams on the financial sector. Besides, this chapter presents a way to mitigate these concerns through inflexible banking, provides a quick overview of the current Automated Teller Machine (ATM) fraud, and offers potential solutions to avoid these attacks.

Chapter 10 investigates the impact of an agile leadership style on organizational performance in a VUCA world. The chapter explains how an agile leader can think flexibly in changing environmental conditions, allowing an organization to adapt to these changes perfectly. Such a leader can uncover the strengths and insights of the employees to transition the organization's intended change and take advantage of the opportunities in change while trying to minimize their negative impact on the organization. Organizations that incorporate agile approaches into their processes are better able to respond quickly to change and deliver superior business value to their stakeholders. With agile leadership, organizations can be in a better position to quickly detect developments in the business environment and achieve agility with few resources.

The editors are thankful to the chapter authors for their valuable academic contributions. The editors also acknowledge the advisory support of the Editorial Advisory Board. The editors show their sincere gratitude to the reviewers for their extensive reviews and feedback through the double-blind review process. The editorial panel is glad to the publisher – IGI Global, Hershey, US. Also, the editorial team's special thanks are due to two book project development representatives of IGI Global: Gianna Walker, Formerly Assistant Development Editor, Book Development IGI Global, and Angelina Olivas, Assistant Development Editor, Book Development IGI Global.

Mohammad Rafiqul Islam Talukdar
American International University-Bangladesh, Bangladesh

Carmen Z. Lamagna
American International University-Bangladesh, Bangladesh

Charles Carillo Villanueva
American International University-Bangladesh, Bangladesh

Rezbin Nahar
American International University-Bangladesh, Bangladesh

Farheen Hassan
American International University-Bangladesh, Bangladesh

Introduction

In an organization, talent management refers to the anticipation of the required level of human capital and strategic positioning to meet such a need, especially by attracting and retaining talented people and systematically transforming the organization's human resources into human capital. In a nutshell, talent management is building and maintaining a winning talented workforce to achieve organizational goals aligned with the vision and mission of the organization. Once an organization affords to set such a standard, it gains an advanced competitive advantage over the rival firms. Such affordability of an organization requires an agile and applied comprehensive approach grounded heavily on advanced theoretical and conceptual knowledge of organizational development and strategic human resource management (SHRM).

Talent management is not about HRM or people management of an organization. It is not an either-or proposition with human resource management, nor should it be. A modern open system organization deals with both regular workforce management and talent management within a comprehensive strategic human resource framework. According to Talukdar et al. (2022), an organization's regular operating objectives require a trained, engaged, and devoted staff; additionally, the organization requires a committed and talented workforce to set its strategic perspectives, construct successful strategies, frame effective business models, and propel the organization to new heights. The activities of an organization's talent leaders, as well as the culture of commitment, cooperation, engagement, learning, and talent appreciation, determine the organization's strength.

The responsibility of talent management does not go to the chief learning officer or people management leader alone; it also goes to the strategic apex of an organization. Organizations cannot manage their scholars in the same way they manage their other human resources. Managing talent means managing human capital. The first driving force behind retaining brilliant individuals is fostering a talent-friendly culture within the organization and addressing talent concerns about dignity and freedom. A talent-friendly culture refers to developing an innovative, agile, knowledge-building, and sharing culture.

From capitalism to a knowledge-based society, major world transformations were recognized by Peter Drucker in the early 1990s. These transformations were analyzed in terms of how they would have affected society, impacted economics, business, and politics, and how the dynamics of capitalist society, including capital, land, and labor, would have become submissive to the knowledge-based society. Drucker predicted in "Post-Capitalist Society" (1993), one of the most widely read and influential books of the time, that the post-capitalist world would have become neither socialist nor capitalist. The market norms of capitalism would have survived, but the society would have become a society of specialized organizations.

In the early twenty-first century, Drucker's assumption became a reality. Capital, land, and labor are no longer dominant factors in the success of a 21st-century organization. Human capital is now the most critical factor in an organization's success. Drucker proves how knowledge has become the new basis of wealth. Concerning this theory, one recent example is Professor Sarah Catherine Gilbert's contribution to the fight against the COVID-19 pandemic, which has propelled Oxford University to a new height.

A similar paradigm shift has significantly impacted leadership theory, namely the transformation of cost management or costs accounting-focused leadership to differentiation-focused or innovation-focused leadership, leading to impact-focused leadership. In a 2008 contribution to Harvard Business Review, Johnson et al. pointed out that when Apple introduced the iPod with the iTunes store in 2003, it revolutionized portable entertainment, created a new market, and increased the company's value. The iPod-iTunes combination generated nearly $10 billion in product sales within three years, accounting for almost half of Apple's revenue during the specified period. That wasn't the only thing. By late 2007, Apple's market capitalization had risen to more than $150 billion, up from around $1 billion in early 2003.

Talukdar (2020) provides two additional examples in this regard. First, in the early twenty-first century, Nokia was a market leader in mobile phone apparatuses. Suddenly, Samsung introduced touch-phone technology, and it eventually became the market leader in smartphone technology. Second, while many higher education institutions have failed to present a new strategic business model to deal with the COVID-19 pandemic situation, American International University-Bangladesh (AIUB), has emerged as a role model in Bangladesh by making strategic decisions within days of the country's initial COVID-19 outbreak.

The first is an example of technological innovation-focused leadership, and the second is management differentiation-focused leadership. Regardless of the context, each of the organizations referred to in the preceding examples highly values its talented employees by implementing robust talent management practices that are also somehow aligned with the agile management approach, particularly in a disruptive situation such as the COVID-19 pandemic.

Indeed, an agile management is a change management approach that values talent or human capital, communicates, and employs collaborative tools to make the organization resilient and adaptable to change through a flexible management style, increased delegation, and autonomy, and ensuring a safe environment to fail and learn quickly, as well as to become innovative. Both talent management and agile management require a mindset and a creative and iterative approach that is most likely to be suitable in modern open system-based and knowledge-based organizations, evolving business situations, and turbulent environments.

In the pandemic period, organizations focus on keeping their employees safe, virtually connected, and taking their care in stressful situations. To date, all employees have access to the remote working system. With the recent development in combating pandemics, organizations attempt to reintegrate remote workers into the office. Thus, the post-pandemic paradigm is getting started. In such a context, the critical concerns both organizational leaders and employees have faced throughout the pandemic period are leadership styles and management policies that help retain talented employees, bring on board high performers, and measure adaptive performance. The same concerns might be valid for the post-pandemic paradigm as well. Anecdotes support a blended mindset of talent management and agile management, and a creativity-friendly iterative approach would be most appropriate for the post-pandemic paradigm.

VALUE ADDITION

The book focuses on human capital theory and talent management in the pandemic and post-pandemic world. This book makes valuable contributions to the literature on strategic human resource management, specifically talent management in modern knowledge-based organizations during the COVID-19 pandemic period and post-pandemic paradigm.

It also adds value to organizational change management, organizational culture, human capital theory, organizational theory and development, and leadership theory. It recognizes the value of differentiation and innovation-focused leadership and how this helps shape the impact-focused leadership that is needed at this time. It also appreciates the fact that the highest priority for organizational development is leveraging talent management, increased digitalization, and the future orientation and brand image of the work.

TARGET READERS

This advanced book is tailored for academics, researchers, professionals, and postgraduates. Specifically, it aims at strategic human resource management experts, organizational theory and development scholars, leadership and strategic management fellows, management and human resource management practitioners, corporate and entrepreneurship leaders, policymakers and development partners, civil society representatives, graduate and post-graduate university students of development studies, and governance, public administration, public policy, and business schools, and interested advanced readers.

BOOK CHAPTERS

The book ranked exceptionally high in the authors' diversity level, which means male and female authors from different business schools and practitioner fields around the globe contributed significantly in theoretical, practical, and empirical perspectives. This is a 10-chapter edited monograph, published by IGI Global, Hershey, US. The editorial team includes five distinguished scholars from a renowned business school titled "Faculty of Business Administration" at American International University-Bangladesh (AIUB), Bangladesh.

Mohammad Rafiqul Islam Talukdar
American International University-Bangladesh, Bangladesh

REFERENCES

Drucker, P. (1993). *Post Capitalist Society*. Routledge.

Johnson, M. W., Christensen, C. M., & Kagermann, H. (2008). Reinventing Your Business Model: One secret to maintaining a thriving business is recognizing when it needs a fundamental change. *Harvard Business Review*. https://hbr.org/2008/12/reinventing-your-business-model

Talukdar, M.R.I (2020). The case-based pedagogy in business schools: Should it go alone? *AIUB Journal of Business and Economics, 17*(1), 159-176.

Talukdar, M. R. I., Lamagna, C. Z., & Lamagna, D. C. (2022). Modern Talent Management: Theoretical Framework. In M. R. I. Talukdar, C. Z. Lamagna, C. Villanueva, R. Nahar, & F. Hassan (Eds.), *Post-Pandemic Talent Management Models in Knowledge Organizations*. IGI Global.

Chapter 1
Modern Talent Management: Theoretical Framework

Mohammad Rafiqul Islam Talukdar
https://orcid.org/0000-0003-0507-1396
American International University-Bangladesh, Bangladesh

Carmen Z. Lamagna
American International University-Bangladesh, Bangladesh

Dulce Corazon Z. Lamagna
American International University-Bangladesh, Bangladesh

ABSTRACT

The chapter builds on a conceptual and theoretical understanding of talent management. It documents the notions and essence of talent management in modern organizations, especially in modern knowledge-based organizations, and frames a theoretical framework for talent management at present. It explains the fundamental link between talent management and human capital theory and answers three featured questions: Why is talent management so crucial in 21st-century organizations? How can talent strategy be reinvented to support digitalization? What are the changing landscape and evolving concerns of talent management and their implications for knowledge organizations in the post-pandemic paradigm?

DOI: 10.4018/978-1-6684-3894-7.ch001

INTRODUCTION

Organizations face evolving contexts beyond the competition with rivals, particularly the increased magnitude of globalization and environmental disruptions and advanced competency framework requirements due to rapid technological advancement and business paradigm-shifting. The latter is the outcome of human capital investment, disruptive innovations, and environmental destruction. Organizational leaders require organizations to focus on strategic and change management and future development. Human capital recognition and talent management are at the heart of this endeavor. While the demand for research on talent management is increasing, literature and experts on this subject are inadequate. This chapter intends to provide theoretical advancement to scholars and practitioners in this field with a theoretical framework based on talent management's conceptual and theoretical understanding.

It documents the notions and essence of talent management in modern organizations, especially in modern knowledge-based organizations. It answers the lead questions: Why is talent management so crucial in 21st-century organizations? How can talent strategy be reinvented to support digitalization? And, what are the changing landscape and evolving concerns of talent management and their implications for knowledge organizations in the post-pandemic paradigm?

The paper also explains the linking context of talent management with human capital theory. It shows how the theory and practice lead to the advancement of a modern organization and create a sustained competitive advantage for the organization and how their entwined approach plays a critical role in paradigm-shifting in the concerned domain of the organization. The paper makes a significant contribution by clearly depicting talent management's conceptual understanding and theoretical framework and documenting its importance concerning human capital appreciation in modern organizations' strategic and change management landscape.

METHOD AND TIMEFRAME

The paper employs a qualitative-focused synthesis research method while heavily based on a literature review.

Contemporary development of synthesis methods for qualitative research is seminal and has encompassed diverse custom-made approaches, e.g., meta-ethnography, grounded theory, thematic synthesis, textual narrative synthesis, meta-study, meta-synthesis, meta-narrative, critical interpretive synthesis, focused synthesis, ecological triangulation, framework synthesis, and "fledgling" approaches. (Talukdar et al., 2021:4).

However, this current study has applied a tailor-made qualitative focused synthesis method that implies collecting and documenting information and data from various sources, including literature review and participant observations (See "focused synthesis" in Talukdar, 2012, 2020, 2021).

The authors designed the study in December 2021, reviewed literature and collected data in January 2022, assessed the reviewed material and findings in February 2022, and thus, prepared the chapter.

CONCEPTUAL UNDERSTANDING

Peter Drucker reckoned a major world transformation, from capitalism to a knowledge-based society, was underway in the early 1990s. This transformation was examined in terms of how it would have affected society, how it would have affected economics, business, and politics, and how the dynamics of capitalist society, including capital, land, and labor, would have become subservient to a knowledge-based society.

Drucker predicted in 1993 that the post-capitalist world would become neither socialist nor capitalist. The market norms of capitalism would have survived, but society would have become a society of specialized organizations. In the early twenty-first century, Drucker's 1993 assumption, outlined in his "Post-Capitalist Society," one of the most widely read and influential books of the time, became a reality.

Capital, land, and labor are no longer dominant factors in the success of a 21st-century organization. Human capital is now the most important factor in an organization's success. Drucker (1993) proves how knowledge has become the new basis of wealth. Concerning this theory, one recent example is Professor Sarah Catherine Gilbert's contribution to the fight against the COVID-19 pandemic, which has propelled Oxford University to a new height. A similar paradigm shift in leadership theory has significantly impacted this research. Moreover, this is the transformation of cost management and cost-accounting-focused leadership to differentiation-focused and innovation-oriented leadership, leading to impact-focused leadership.

Johnson et al. (2008) pointed out in the Harvard Business Review that when Apple introduced the "iPod" with the iTunes store in 2003, it revolutionized portable entertainment, created a new market, and increased the company's value. The iPod-iTunes combination generated nearly $10 billion in product sales within three years, accounting for almost half of Apple's revenue during the specified period. That was not the only thing. By late 2007, Apple's market capitalization had risen to more than $150 billion, up from around $1 billion in early 2003.

A 1998 paper titled "The War for Talent" stated that talent would be the future's distinctive source for achieving competitive advantage (Chambers et al., 1998). Organizations attempt to invest in human capital through attracting, developing, and retaining people to attain industry leadership (Boxall & Steenveld, 1999). Scholars and practitioners began to focus on a talent management approach after an early definition of talent by the global management consulting firm "McKinsey & Company" in 1998 with the publication of "The War for Talent," which was authored by Chambers et al. (1998).

According to the Economist Intelligence Unit (2006), organizations are changing their focus from growth to sustainability. Thus, organizational leaders appreciate the strategic importance of talent management as a source of sustained competitive advantage. Talent management was identified as the most critical element of human resource management and competitive advantage by Boston Consulting Group (BCG) and the World Federation of People Management Association (WFPMA). (See reports in Boston Consulting Group, 2007; Boston Consulting Group and World Federation of People Management Association, 2010). The BCG is a global management consulting firm and a leading adviser on business strategy, and WFPMA is the world's largest global network of people management professionals.

The 2014 report of BCG and WFPMA identified that leadership and talent management are the highest priorities for organizations in various regions and industries, given the 27 HR subtopics, using the urgency metric.

Across industries and regions, most respondents identified leadership, talent management, behavior and culture, HR and people strategy, employee engagement, and strategic workforce planning as their organization's most urgently needed action. (Boston Consulting Group and World Federation of People Management Association, 2014:4)

The 2021 report of BCG and WFPMA is more comprehensive, with contributions from more than 6,600 respondents in 113 countries, along with in-depth interviews of more than 30 management leaders at organizations around the globe. The report classified the top 12 global priorities for organizations worldwide into three categories: Talent management, digitalization in HR, and the future of work. The top 12 priorities for organizations are selected from 32 people management topics considering the highest future importance and the lowest current capabilities (Boston Consulting Group and World Federation of People Management Association, 2021).

Figure 1 below shows the highest priority 12 topics for HR leaders in 3 broad classifications considering the highest future importance and the lowest current capabilities: talent, digitalization, and the future of work.

Figure 1. Highest priority 12 topics for HR leaders in 3 broad classifications
Source: Based on Boston Consulting Group and World Federation of People Management Association (2021)

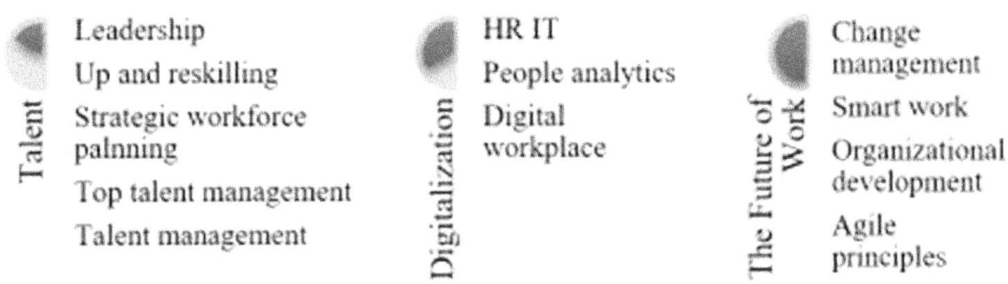

Given the 2021 report of BCG and WFPMA, table 1 below elaborates on the three broad categories with 12 priority topics: Talent management, digitization in HR, and the future of work.

Table 1. Three broad categories with 12 priority topics

Talent	Digitization	The Future of Work
A cutting-edge approach to discovering, developing, and cultivating high-potential employees is required in the war for talent, particularly digital talent. As the gig economy evolves, businesses must increasingly manage a mixed workforce of contractors, gig workers, temporary workers, and permanent employees. Simultaneously, HR must identify future talents that the company will require and devise strategies to address any gaps.	Human resources departments in most companies are having trouble digitizing. Employees are accustomed to having streamlined digital experiences and accessible interfaces in their personal technology, and they want the same in the workplace.	Because of COVID-19, businesses are putting pressure on HR to play a bigger role in redefining how and where work is done. The physical workplace will be redesigned, a new organizational structure will be established, and the facilitation of revolutionary change will be prioritized.

Content Source: Boston Consulting Group and World Federation of People Management Association (2021)

Furthermore, the report points out five key actions for people management leaders to take to step ahead with the evolution of HR in 2021 and beyond: Put employees at the center; Shape the future of work; Accelerate in digital; Set new paradigms for skills and employees; Transform the people management function (Ibid, 2021). The first essential action, titled "put employees at the center," is central to our current study on talent management. The report explains it more elaborately:

At the macro level, companies need to create personalized experiences in the form of more customized career paths for employees. At the micro-level, they need to move beyond rigid, one-size-fits-all processes and interactions to enable personalized solutions on a day-to-day basis. In our survey, 85% of respondents said that focusing on employee needs and expectations is the key success factor in the competition for talent—the highest level of consensus in the entire study. (Ibid, 2021:20).

Defining Talent Management

Meyers et al. (2013) defined talent as a concept of any or mix of five different traits—i.e., giftedness, strength, meta-competency, high potential, and high-performance orientation. Gallardo-Gallardo et al. (2013) framed all talent definitions in the academic literature within two broad spectrums: Object approach (i.e., characteristics-centric) and subject approach (i.e., people-centric). The object approach values "the ability, capacity, capability, commitment, competency, contribution, experience, knowledge, performance, and potential, patterns of thought, feelings, or behavior" (P.293) related to people's characteristics. The subject approach holds two perspectives: First, an inclusive or strengths-based perspective on talent management (i.e., considering and managing the potential talent of all employees); Second, an exclusive perspective on talent management (i.e., considering and managing the talents of high-potential, high-performing employees only) (Iles et al., 2010; Gallardo-Gallardo et al., 2013).

According to Ulrich (2007), talent is becoming a science for some HR experts and a passion for many line managers. Numerous programs and investments have been made to attract, retain, and enhance talent (para 3). "Talent equals competence times commitment times contribution" (para 4). Tansley et al. (2007:8) define "talent" as "consists of those individuals who can make a difference to organizational performance, either through their immediate contribution or in the longer term by demonstrating the highest levels of potential."

In general, "talent" refers to a person's abilities, skills, or artistic ability in a particular profession. It also refers to individuals with high potential, knowledge, and skills who can successfully lead the organization through transition and change. Such individuals are frequently in high demand in the market, and their contributions to the company's strategic or competitive posture bring immediate value. (Mngqibisa, 2017).

So how do we define talent management? Moczydowska (2012) opines that talent management (TM) is viewed as a modern and efficient method of executing personnel policies that help firms meet their strategic objectives by maximizing the potential of their employees. According to Mngqibisa (2017), in an organization, talent management refers to the specific processes taken to acquire, develop, and retain its talent pool. In most cases, the procedures taken should be innovative and free of bureaucracy. Talent management also refers to an organization's systematic strategy for attracting, retaining, motivating, and developing succession plans for employees with the aptitude and ability to satisfy present and future organizational needs.

Talent management (TM), according to Third Eye Blind Productions (2021), is the carefully managed, planned process of attracting the right people and aiding them in realizing their maximum potential while keeping the organization's goals in mind. Tetik (2016) describes "talent management" as identifying high-potential and high-performing individuals, building a talent pool, providing development techniques, and developing retention practices.

TM in Modern Organizations

Talent management has gained strategic importance due to demographic transitions and difficulties such as a shortage of a competent workforce, the war for talent, an aging workforce, declining birth rates, and cultural diversity (Benson & Brown, 2011; Chambers et al., 1998; Michaels et al., 2001). Organizations are currently confronted with evolving challenges because of increased globalization and environmental disruptions on the one hand and disruptive innovations that fuel business paradigm shifts on the other. All these together help frame the intangible value of human capital in a knowledge economy that creates the need for talent management.

Participant observations of the authors and literature in the preceding sub-chapters reveal that the transformation of workforce management systems, the demand for a new paradigm for skills, evolving organizational and HR functions, the uncertainty of future challenges, increased digitalization, granular employee perceptions, changing political landscape, reformed legal frameworks, and emerging economic pressure have relentlessly added new magnitudes to the significance of talent management (TM) in modern organizations.

Thc topic has been gaining the increasing attention of modern organizations since its inception in the early 21st century. Modern corporations, industries, enterprises, research institutions, consulting firms, universities, media, international development organizations, United Nations organizations, and other learning organizations have become concerned with the concept. Unlike other academic domains, many knowledge firms and people management associations have made significant contributions towards advancing the TM concept rather than individual academics and researchers. Among them, McKinsey & Co., the Boston Consulting Group (BCG), the World Federation of People Management Associations (WFPMA), the Chartered Institute of Personnel and Development (CIPD), the Society of Human Resource Management (SHRM), and more recently, Gartner's role are noteworthy.

TM Elements and Process

Competency focus, talent pooling, talent investment, and talent orientation are four unique attributes of human talent management that contribute to an organization's performance. These are important tools for managing human talent and creating value in the organization (Ganaie & Haque, 2017). This paper termed these attributes "elements of talent management." These elements are interconnected, and the connectivity process is illustrated in Figure 2.

Figure 2. Process of interconnected elements of talent management

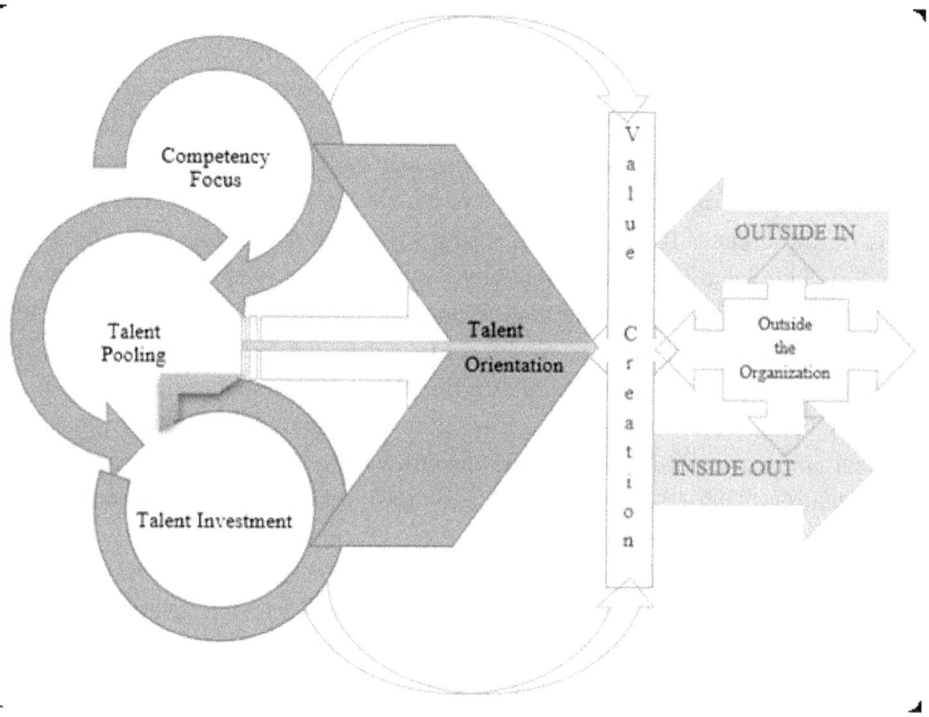

Talent commitment to competency development is increased by perceived talent management techniques (Khoreva et al., 2017). The phrase "pivotal competencies" refers to a collection of critical abilities that an organization can build among high-potential people to help the organization become a value-driven entity. Competence is one of the most important traits of a skilled employee (Gallardo-Gallardo et al., 2013; Ulrich et al., 2007), and it leads to great and exceptional job performance when developed appropriately (Gallardo-Gallardo et al., 2013). Competency mapping has been recognized as one of the essential tools for effective talent management practices such as succession planning, development, and retention (Nair, 2012).

Employees with great potential and high performance are critical to the success of any business. Talent pooling refers to gathering these high-potential and high-performing people who can be exposed to these critical abilities to fill the organization's current and future vital jobs. The primary practice of human talent management is creating a talent pool inside an organization. Obtaining essential competencies and assuming vital strategic positions in the future can develop value and business competitiveness, resulting in organizational success (Collings & Mellahi, 2009; Mellahi & Collings, 2010; Smilansky, 2006; Stahl et al., 2007).

When talent investments are aligned with business strategy, customer-focused, directed at motivating and valuing employees to perform and excel, and focused on increasing the capabilities and resources to get the best performance out of business, they add value to the business (Schiemann, 2006). HR must see human talent as a crucial source of value development for the firm and prioritize operations that coincide with the business model to get the most out of a company's investment in its people.

Participants' observations reveal that talent investment does not always produce optimal results; instead, success is dependent on understanding the importance of two things in one line: First, a skilled, engaged, and committed workforce to meet common operational objectives; Second, a committed as well as talented workforce to set strategic lenses, build winning strategies, and have a robust business model with competitive advantages. A talent investment policy focuses on achieving a balance between these two loops. Furthermore, it is critical to integrate business strategies into a business model, keeping brand image development and impact paradigm-shifting in mind.

Talent orientation refers to an individual's or an organization's desire to share knowledge, improve skills, and channel abilities through relationships to foster a culture of learning and creativity that leads to value construction (Ganaie & Haque, 2017). It is the exchange of complementary abilities and information between at least two people to enable reliant or interdependent work practice (Gold et al., 2016). Instead of talent orientation, Gold et al. (2016) used the term "talenting," while Ganaie & Haque (2017) used the term "talenting orientation."

Knowledge sharing is an important practice for employee commitment, value generation, and innovation at work. Organizational competitiveness is influenced by knowledge integration, which has been highlighted as a factor (Almaaitah et al., 2013). More crucially, the substance of external knowledge can be simplified only by a firm's talent orientation, which shows how a firm can coordinate a diverse group of human talent. One specialized group acquires external knowledge, and another group disseminates it (Whelan et al., 2010). When talented individuals' contributions are recognized and rewarded, they provide a source of incentive and dedication for others (Bolden et al., 2014). Swailes and Blackburn (2016) reveal that those not included in the talent pool feel unfairly treated and have lower expectations for their career advancement.

Individuals' knowledge-gaining expectations may be raised because of talent orientation, which might lessen feelings of unfairness. Appreciation of the practice of talent orientation adds value to a company, improves its competitiveness, and helps it succeed by focusing on social and organizational elements, including talent culture, networks and teams, and work routines (Iles et al., 2010; Ganaie & Haque, 2017). The processes that occur during talent orientation, such as knowledge and skill sharing, maintaining a clear information-sharing plan, building a suitable culture, using technology, and collecting exciting knowledge, are precious (Griffiths et al., 2016; Ganaie & Haque, 2017).

THEORETICAL ADVANCEMENT

A theory is a set of claims and principles intended to explain a collection of facts or occurrences, particularly one repeatedly tested or widely accepted, and can be used to forecast natural phenomena (Popper,1963). This idea is a positivist view based on "the idea of objective and absolute truth" (Popper, 1963:224). While it emphasizes the "correspondence to the facts" (1963:223), Popper (1972) claims that "satisfactory theories must, as a matter of principle, transcend the empirical instances which gave rise to them" (p. 355). Theories must be capable of being tested by experience. If a theory's essential propositions do not correlate with experience, it does not qualify as empirically scientific (Popper, 1968). Until the propositions are scientifically tested and proven, they are still hypotheses. Theories have certain conditions or assumptions. If a context or paradigm shift does not correspond to the pre-specified conditions of a theory, the theory becomes irrelevant there.

Theories and definitions seem to be identical, but they are different things. Theories have been characterized as analytical tools for understanding, explaining, and making predictions about a specific subject matter. At the same time, a definition reveals the meaning and a clear-cut synthesis of the conceptual understanding. A theoretical perspective on a 2020 literature definition is as follows:

A theoretical perspective is a set of assumptions about reality that inform the questions we ask and the kinds of answers we arrive at as a result. In this sense, a theoretical perspective can be understood as a lens through which we look, serving to focus or distort what we see. It can also be thought of as a frame, which serves to both include and exclude certain things from our view. (Crossman, 2020: Para1)

There has been a change to a learning perspective. Now people prefer employability, lifelong learning, and talent management over job security and lifelong employment (Nilsson & Ellström, 2012). In a competitive business environment, the effects of globalization, technological developments, and innovation are short-lived and imitable ingredients for gaining a competitive advantage (Barney, 1991). Firms should seek long-lived resources (Heinen & O'Neill, 2004; Mattone & Xavier, 2012). When human resources are transformed into human capital, it becomes a genuine, sturdy, and long-lived means of creating a sustained competitive advantage for the firm. This approach was supported by Mattone and Xavier (2012), who stated the importance of human capital for gaining market differentiation value, positive branding, superior execution, and operating success. These perspectives signify a paradigm shift in human resources with a strategic approach (Boudreau & Ramstad, 2005), i.e., human capital orientation.

The human capital orientation transformed enterprises and industrial societies from labor-based economies to knowledge-centric economies (Burton-Jones, 2001). Drucker (1993) defines knowledge as the primary resource for today's economies and a source of increasing productivity. This perspective divides the workforce into service workers and knowledge workers. Knowledge workers are the people who can create and acquire knowledge for their organizations (Davenport, 2005), and they are the capital assets of those organizations. Hence, the productivity of knowledge workers has become one of the main concerns of organizations (Drucker, 1999). Tetik (2016) refers to a 2005 Deloitte report on the global talent pulse survey to reveal that most organizations are shifting investments to address attracting and retaining talent. Earlier, global management consulting firm McKinsey & Company's *McKinsey Quarterly* published a highly influential research report titled "The War for Talent," authored by Chambers et al. (1998). The report reveals that talents seem to be the future's unique source for gaining competitive advantage. According to Boxall and Steenveld (1999), organizations strive to invest in human capital by attracting, developing, and retaining employees to gain industry leadership.

Theoretical Base

Talent management (TM) is practiced, measured, and studied based on several linked theoretical foundations. This statement is partly supported by Sparrow et al. (2014) and mostly by participant observations. The theoretical perspectives for talent management (TM) are based on the evolution of the human capital concept. The linking context of human capital thought with the conceptions of people management, open systems, sustained competitive advantage-based organizational development, sustainable development, and new institutionalism.

Clearly, the TM theoretical foundations include soft models of normative and strategic human resource management perspectives; human capital theory and sustained competitive advantage; resource-based view; organizational knowledge-based view or learning organizations and organizational learning perspective; agile management view for adaptation to disruptive innovation and disruptive environments; sustainable development and impact-leadership perspective; and distributive rationalism perspective-based rational choice institutionalism theory.

The resource-based view (Barney, 1991; Barney & Wright, 1998) is used in most talent management (TM) research to explore the role of human resources in obtaining competitive advantage. Those valuable, unique, non-substitutable, and unique human resources, according to Barney (1991) and Barney & Wright (1998), are a source of competitive advantage for the firm. Furthermore, according to Heinen & O'Neill (2004) and Mattone & Xavier (2012), those resources should be long-lasting and non-replicable to provide a sustained competitive advantage. According to Heinen & O'Neill (2004), talent-management methods such as attracting, developing, motivating, managing, rewarding, and retaining personnel can provide a long-term competitive edge.

Another influential theoretical foundation for gaining a competitive advantage is treating knowledge as a strategic resource, also known as the knowledge-based view (Grant, 1996). Grant emphasized the necessity of knowledge creation, transmission, and integration within the company. This necessity distinguishes knowledge firms and makes it difficult to mimic knowledge (Tetik, 2016). As a result, the knowledge that is difficult to mimic and socially complex is viewed as a source of competitive advantage (Felin & Hesterly, 2007). Although it is challenging to imitate firm-specific knowledge, it is not impossible. However, it is impossible to duplicate someone's abilities, experiences, skills, and knowledge (Spender, 1996).

The third principal theoretical basis is that the firm's specialized competencies may be improved to obtain a long-term competitive advantage (Lado and Wilson, 1994). The workforce's skills should contribute to achieving the organization's goals. Managing competencies and skills has been linked to firms' efforts to develop their staff to gain a competitive edge, innovate, and be more effective (Draganidis & Mentzas, 2006). A competency-based approach is defined as an effort to rebuild competencies in line with the organizations' strategic objectives (Tetik, 2016).

The distributive rationalism outlook-based rational choice institutionalism theory is the fourth crucial theoretical foundation for talent management (TM) practice and research. It derives from the limitations of the resource-based view. Tatoglu et al. (2016) point out that the resource-based view is insufficient for defining the motivations for TM and the nature of its practice. People are treated as economic assets in the resource-based view, but the social capital perspective is overlooked. In this stance, the motives behind TM and its implementation are revealed by utilizing diverse viewpoints of new institutional theory. The motives are assessed as strategic and tactical to understand the nature of TM practice.

This paper reveals that the stated motives are related to a new institutionalism theory—i.e., Voeten's (2019) distributive rationalism-based rational choice institutionalism. According to Voeten (2019), there are two types of rational choice scholarship on institutions: rational functionalism and distributive rationalism. Organizations are seen as functionally optimal solutions to collective issues by the former, but organizations are seen as an outcome of actors' individual and collective aspirations by the latter.

Theoretical Framework

A theoretical framework is a set of interconnected theories. A broad assumption about nature and phenomena explains why things are the way they are based on theories (Kombo & Tromp, 2006). The academic field of talent management (TM) is marked by a lack of a solid theoretical framework (Lewis & Heckman, 2006; Scullion et al., 2010; Sparrow et al., 2014). Thus, TM is studied and evaluated based on numerous theoretical foundations due to the lack of a comprehensive theoretical framework. It is assessed as an anchor with several linked theoretical perspectives (Sparrow et al., 2014).

Figure 3. The comprehensive theoretical framework of talent management

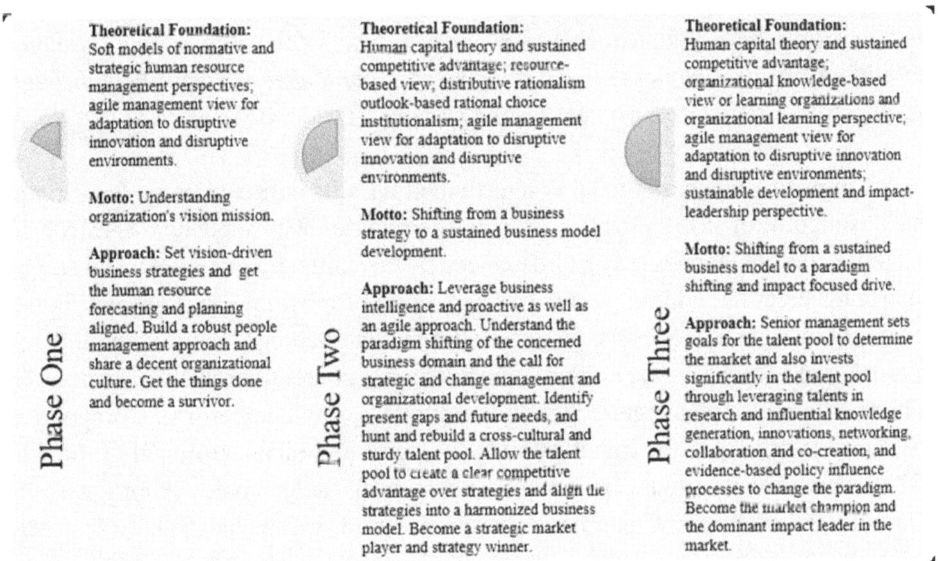

This paper further stresses that TM practices, assessment approaches, and studies are based on several linked theoretical grounds. However, the dominant one is the human capital theory, as discussed in the preceding sub-chapter titled "theoretical base." Without a robust theoretical framework, the paper develops a comprehensive theoretical framework to create the basis for talent management studies, assessments, and practices (see figure 3).

In business, strategies combine deliberations based on new ideas and emerging conditions and boldness built on experience and actions. As a result, businesses adjust their existing strategies by considering the changing facts and contingency aspects and the knowledge of their executives. Whatever the basis, corporate strategies frequently strive to build advantages, with each advantage requiring consideration of a potential downside (Jofre, 2011). Setting direction, focusing effort, defining the organization, and creating consistency are the four main advantages of corporate strategy. However, an organization may assess a potential disadvantage for each strategic advantage to be accomplished (Mintzberg et al. 1998).

A business model explains how an organization generates, delivers, and captures value, while the term "business model canvas" refers to a tool for describing, analyzing, and developing business models (Osterwalder & Pigneur, 2010). Rather than the usual complex business plan, a business model canvas allows organizations to have structured, quantifiable, and strategic conversations about new or current enterprises (Osterwalder, 2013).

We believe a business model can best be described through nine basic building blocks that show the logic of how a company intends to make money. The nine blocks cover the four main areas of a business: Customers, offers, infrastructure, and financial viability. A business model is like a blueprint for implementing a strategy through organizational structures, processes, and systems. (Osterwalder & Pigneur, 2010)

A company's business model is intertwined with its entire strategy. It is, in the end, an outcome of an organization's business strategies. The opposite is also true, in that organizational tactics may be influenced by the company model. It is the design criteria for creating, adding, and delivering value propositions and generating the necessary income to pay costs, generate a profit, and keep growing. It emphasizes internal and external stakeholders' involvement, contentment, and admiration. When necessary, it also regenerates and reinvests to stay competitive. Competitive advantage is critical to the organization's strategies and business model (Talukdar, 2021). The business model framework is shown in Table 2 below, along with its four essential elements: Customer value proposition, value chain, profit formula, and competitive strategy.

Table 2. The frame of a business model

Core elements	Analysis
Customer value proposition	A customer value proposition describes how a company or institution is likely to focus on and address a customer's demands through a product or service.
Value chain	To experience the value proposition, a value chain refers to shaping processes, innovation, technology intervention, other resources, partners, and interaction with the value network.
Profit formula	A profit formula is a formula or plan that outlines how an organization or institution can earn enough money to cover costs, turn a profit, and continue to develop.
Competitive strategy	A competitive strategy outlines how an organization or institution can gain a competitive advantage and become a champion in a specific area by focusing on innovation, technological intervention, cost management, and leadership focus while competing with competitors and defending its position in the value network.

Source: Talukdar (2021)

The final concern is about paradigm-shifting and its impact-focused drive. Thomas Kuhn, an American philosopher, created the term "paradigm shift" in his seminal work, "The Structure of Scientific Revolutions," published in 1962. A paradigm theory is a generic theory that aids scientists working in a specific field develop their broad theoretical framework—what Kuhn refers to as their "conceptual scheme" in a specific regime. It lays forth their fundamental assumptions, core concepts, and approach. It establishes their research's broad direction and objectives (Khun, 1962; Westacott, 2019).

The term "pattern" is a synonym for "paradigm." Pattern development is a part of making meaning of our lives (Ausubel, 1968). The pattern is used to understand situations, ask questions, create connections, and predict outcomes (Jacobs & Farrell, 2001). When we experience a paradigm shift, we see things from a different viewpoint as we focus on different aspects of life's events (Berman, 1981; Capra, 1983; Merchant, 1992).

Organizations face their greatest business challenge, i.e., "change." Moreover, today's executives must have a solid awareness of the changing conditions they face and how to adapt to them efficiently (Bersin by Deloitte, 2017). Effective leadership talent is scarce in organizations according to the High-Impact Leadership Research 2016 published by Bersin and Deloitte (2017); 60% of organizational leaders are perceived to have commercial acumen and business judgment, 48% are driving change and innovation, and only 44% are developing talent for competitive advantage.

Leadership abilities have received much attention. However, what does it take to lead companies equally concerned with the effects of their efforts on social and environmental change and profit? These are exceptional organizations. They face a changing corporate climate in which firms are shifting their focus from profit to multi-stakeholder appreciation and social and environmental impact. They plan to pursue both impact and profit as primary objectives that complement and support one another (Jorch, 2019).

EVOLVING CONCERNS

The fundamental concerns that arise include how we manage the next generation of people and what individuals expect from their jobs. The current generation of employees, it appears, does not subscribe to the adage to stay around until organizations need them. They are more ambitious and willing to take risks in their careers; they are more accepting of failures and prepare to deal with them. People these days prefer flat hierarchies, job-based careers, and a well-defined performance management system. Work-life balance challenges and employment flexibility issues all necessitate the renewal of the social contract with employees. More importantly, there is no room for complacency in talent management in its current framework. Thus, evolution is necessary (Juneja, n.d.).

This section of the paper answers three featured research questions: Why does talent management matter so much in 21st-century organizations? How can talent strategy be reinvented to support digitalization? And what are the changing landscape and evolving concerns of talent management and their implications for knowledge organizations in the post-pandemic paradigm?

Why Does Talent Management Matter So Much In 21st-Century Organizations?

Talent management is crucial for hiring the right individuals for the job who fit an organization's needs and deciding when to hire them (Juneja, n.d.). In a turbulent economy, one of the most dynamic functions for businesses is talent management (Dries, 2013). Academics and practitioners also agree that one of the most forward-thinking strategies is talent management (Boston Consulting Group and World Federation of People Management Associations, 2010).

Talent management (TM) is viewed as a modern and efficient method of enacting personnel policies that enable firms to achieve their strategic objectives by maximizing the potential of their employees (Moczydowska, 2012). Talent management is a strong predictor of employee value proposition, which leads to lower staff turnover and discontent (Tajuddin, Ali, & Kamaruddin, 2015). In a dynamic and volatile market, it also revitalizes talent by ensuring a healthy emotional and work-life balance (Ganaie & Haque, 2017).

In a 2014 write-up, Ariss, Cascio, and Paauwe foresaw a trend that has now become true. According to Ariss et al. (2014), on a local level, a scarcity of talent may intensify due to a lack of young people and an increase in the number of elderly individuals, many of whom are approaching retirement age. National demographic contexts are meant to play a role in this. There may be more similarities (e.g., the desire for respect, supportive employers, and competent and trustworthy leaders) and differences between work generations. New ways of working and new relationships between users and suppliers of talent could be a reality. More diverse, remote, and virtual workforces with varying attitudes toward work would be evident. These may require new ways of working and building new partnerships between users and talent suppliers.

According to the Boston Consulting Group and the World Federation of People Management Associations (2021), the top 12 topics for HR leaders are divided into three categories, with the highest future importance and the lowest current capabilities: Talent, Digitalization, and the Future of Work (see Figure 1 under the sub-chapter "Conceptual Understanding"). Table 3 below exhibits five key recommended actions decision-makers take in 2021 and beyond (Ibid).

Table 3. Five key actions for people management leaders to take in 2021 and beyond

Put employees at the center.	Listen to and collect input from employees regularly to focus HR efforts on what they genuinely require; enhance employee experiences; organize HR procedures from their perspective; and personalize career paths and learning opportunities.
Shape the future of work.	To motivate employees, develop an intelligent work plan, rethink employment possibilities and workforce structure, and create connection by sharpening the organization's purpose and culture.
Accelerate in digital.	Improve people analytics maturity by getting the IT basics right and focusing on digital priorities that matter to employees.
Set new paradigms for skills and employees.	Build a learning organization, dynamically plan the workforce for the future, and improve HR expertise.
Transform the people management function.	Rethink the target HR business partner and transform managers into actual people leaders by developing and following a clear HR and people management strategy with defined values and priorities.

Content Source: Boston Consulting Group and World Federation of People Management Association (2021)

How Can Talent Strategy Be Reinvented to Support Digitalization?

Eighty-seven percent of senior enterprise leaders think digitization is a priority. They are looking to HR professionals to help them build the digital skills they will need to achieve their goals. However, as HR leaders attempt to realize the promise of digitization, many encounter skills gaps in their workforce today. HR's long-standing strategies for attracting and retaining people are beginning to fail. Only 21% of HR executives believe that current build-and-buy processes are assisting them in meeting their objectives. HR professionals spend more money, time, and effort on seemingly ineffective tactics as skill gaps widen and hiring costs and time to fill them rise. HR needs a more efficient method of employee development as well as a talent acquisition strategy that is receptive to the continuously changing needs of the digital era. A strategic plan is also required to foster innovation in driving digital business performance (Gartner, 2019).

According to Gartner's research (2019), there are new and more successful approaches to developing and acquiring talent as well as stimulating innovation. Combining these strategies forms an agile and scalable digital-age approach that creates enterprise value now while preparing the company for the future (see Gartner, 2019). Table 4 below, based on Gartner's research, sketches what it means to reinvent talent strategy to support digitalization in modern organizations.

Table 4. Reinvent talent strategy to support digitalization

Strategic means	Imperative	Action	Benefits	Example
Reskill the workforce.	***Maintain a constant awareness of changing skill requirements.*** Are your employees equipped with the skills they will need in their current jobs and future careers?	Build a connected peer learning approach.	Higher performance and engagement because of increased skill readiness.	Citi encourages self-improvement through micro-actions.
Adopt an agile recruiting model.	***Be more than a staffing agency or a hiring service.*** Business planning no longer happens regularly when entire industries and business models are disrupted, and every organization is in a race to compete — and business executives do not always know what their talent needs will be.	Lead enterprise talent acquisition process.	Reduced hiring costs and time to fill and increased recruiter productivity.	Philips provides advice to the business based on talent analytics.
Foster innovation.	***To innovate at a large scale, use networks.*** Where does your company rank on the innovation effectiveness (IE) scale? To put it another way, how good is it at spotting new opportunities, deciding which ones to follow, and altering company processes to take advantage of them?	To improve innovation effectiveness, use network-based tactics.	Improved digital business performance through increased innovation efficacy.	IBM encourages creative thinking through crowdsourcing.
Leverage analytics.	***Provide talent advice to the company.*** To take advantage of big data's predictive capability, organizations must accomplish two things: 1. Improve the HR function's analytics capability to increase business impact; 2. Train recruiters to use labor-market analytics to act as talent counselors.	To manage labor market data, use the 9-step process (see 9-step toolkits in Gartner, 2019:21)	Better talent decisions and an adequate talent pool.	Big data enables more strategic talent sourcing.

Content Source: Gartner (2019)

What are the Changing Landscape and Evolving Concerns of Talent Management and Their Implications for Knowledge Organizations in the Post-Pandemic Paradigm?

Despite the growing interest in this field among practitioners and academics, research in this domain is still in its early phase (Dries, 2013). While talent is the single largest overhead expense and the most significant competitive advantage for most firms, optimizing their talent strategy is crucial. To make better talent decisions, HR must use analytics (Gartner, 2019).

In 2019, HR leaders ranked planning for future talent needs as their top priority (Gartner, n.d.). COVID-19 has altered the landscape, resulting in new workforce trends, ramifications, and regulations. HR leaders must embrace real-time talent analytics and rethink their planning, development, and buying decisions to traverse these paradigm shifts in the new unbounded workforce successfully (Gartner, n.d.a).

Hybrid and virtual teams have long been a component of the workforce. However, they have become the primary mode of operation during the global pandemic, while investing in rising leaders in this area has proven highly rewarding. Modeling and encouraging resilience behaviors, developing equitable and inclusive virtual teams, and offering access to leadership development are three methods that talent leaders may use to assist emerging leaders in managing the challenges of virtual leadership. The greater the number of young people equipped to lead worldwide, the better our chances of creating a healthy global community devoted to growth, equity, and impact for all (Flink et al., 2022).

2020 and 2021 seem to be regarded as the years when the world's organizations underwent rapid operational changes. Businesses made quick adjustments to prioritize employee safety and adapt day-to-day operations to new remote-friendly working methods. While some of the new ways of working were startling at first, others were long overdue modifications that will undoubtedly become standard in post-pandemic operations (DocuSign, n.d.).

Prospective employees are increasingly interested in sustainability initiatives, and firms are responding by recruiting the finest personnel. This change is especially true for the generation of millennials. According to a Deloitte survey, 81 percent of millennials are concerned about climate change, and 88 percent believe businesses have a responsibility to tackle the issue. Nearly half of millennial employees believe that working for a firm with sustainability and/or climate goals is vital (DocuSign, n.d.; RE100, 2020).

Moreover, 4.5 million Americans left their jobs in November 2021. In October, another 4.2 million people left their jobs there. In just two months, that accounted for roughly 6% of the whole workforce of the United States. In total, in 2021, over 38 million people resigned from their occupations there, with no signs of this trend decreasing. How can organizations keep their people from succumbing to the Great Resignation? Create an environment where employees feel compelled to contribute to a greater purpose in line with their values. (Real, 2022).

Beyond these, the featured research question concerning the implications of talent management for knowledge organizations in the post-pandemic paradigm raises additional concerns that the authors of the current study put forward for the next round of talent management studies. These include questions: How can knowledge organizations enable and empower a talented workforce in post-pandemic recovery? How could knowledge organizations prepare and retain a talented workforce to meet the challenges of the post-pandemic paradigm? How could knowledge-based firms identify cost-saving opportunities by appropriately using remote, contingent, and a blended workforce? How can a transition from a role-based to a skills-based planning strategy improve workforce planning activities, broaden talent pools, and meet talent needs?

Furthermore, how can knowledge organizations build a workforce equipped to address digital transformation and future needs? What kind of leadership matters most for knowledge organizations in the new context? What sort of organizational culture is needed for knowledge organizations in the new paradigm? What are the gaps between theory, perceptions, and practices evident for contemporary talent management in knowledge-based firms?

CONCLUSION

A skilled, engaged, and committed workforce is required for an organization to meet its regular operational objectives. However, it also requires a committed and talented workforce to set strategic lenses, build winning strategies, frame a robust business model, and propel the organization to new heights. An organization's strength is determined by the shoulders of its talent leaders and utilizing a culture of commitment, cooperation, engagement, learning, and talent appreciation.

Talent management aids organizations in maximizing employee value (VALAMIS, 2021). Effective organizations are defined by the value of their "ends" and "means" business partners and by a sustainable enterprise growth orientation. The latter promotes the shareholders' interest. The committed, engaged, talented workforce and the winning HR business partner are the means-business partners, while the end-business partners are the clients.

Brian Kropp, a Vice President of the Gartner Group, in Gartner (2019:24) opined that when it comes to how HR reinvents itself in the digital age, HR's role is to address the problem that their CEOs are asking about, not just to recruit, retain, and develop digital talent. What CEOs want to know is how to boost their firms' inventive effectiveness in the digital age.

REFERENCES

Almaaitah, M. A., Al-Shalabi, F. S., & Aljamal, W. H. (2013). Talent management and competitive advantage: The moderating effect of knowledge integration. *International Journal of Computer Applications*, *66*(11), 19-27. https://research.ijcaonline.org/volume66/number11/pxc3886202.pdf

Ariss, A. A., Cascio, W. F., & Paauwe, J. (2014). Talent management: Current theories and future research directions. *Journal of World Business, 49*(2), 173–179. doi:10.1016/j.jwb.2013.11.001

Ausubel, D. P. (1968). *Educational psychology: a cognitive view*. Holt, Rinehart and Winston.

Barney, J. (1991). Firm Resources and Sustained Competitive Advantage. *Journal of Management, 17*(1), 99–120. doi:10.1177/014920639101700108

Barney, J. B. and Wright, P. M. (1998). On becoming a strategic partner: The role of human resources in gaining competitive advantage. *Human Resource Management, 37*(1), 31–46. doi:10.1002/(SICI)1099-050X(199821)37:1<31::AID-HRM4>3.0.CO;2-W

Benson, J., & Brown, M. (2011). Generations at work: are there differences and do they matter? *The International Journal of Human Resource Management, 22*(9), 1843-1865. doi:10.1080/09585192.2011.573966

Berman, M. (1981). *The re-enchantment of the world*. Cornell University Press.

Bersin by Deloitte. (2017). *High-Impact Leadership: The New Leadership Maturity Model.* Retrieved on February 2, 2021, from https://www2.deloitte.com/content/dam/Deloitte/ca/Documents/audit/ca-audit-abm-scotia-high-impact-leadership.pdf

Bolden, R., Gosling, J., & O'Brien, A. (2014). Citizens of the academic community? A societal perspective on leadership in UK higher education. *Studies in Higher Education, 39*(5), 754-770. doi:10.1080/03075079.2012.754855

Boston Consulting Group. (2007). *Aligning Talent for Global Advantage: How top companies develop the right talent in the right places.* Author.

Boston Consulting Group & World Federation of People Management Association. (2010). *Creating People Advantage 2010: How companies can adapt their HR practices for volatile times.* Author.

Boston Consulting Group & World Federation of People Management Association. (2014). Creating people advantage 2014-2015: How to set up great HR functions - Connect, prioritize, impact. Author.

Boston Consulting Group and World Federation of People Management Association. (2021). *Creating People Advantage 2021: The Future of People Management Priorities.* Author.

Boudreau, J. W., & Ramstad, P. M. (2005). Talentship, talent segmentation, and sustainability: A new HR decision science paradigm for a new strategy definition. *Human Resource Management, 44*(2), 129-136. doi:10.1002/hrm.20054

Boxall, P., Steenveld, M. (1999). Human Resource Strategy and Competitive Advantage: A Longitudinal Study of Engineering Consultancies. *Journal of Management Studies, 36*(4), 443–463.

Burton-Jones, A. (2001). The Knowledge Supply Model: A Framework for Education and Training in the New Economy. *Education and Training, 43*(4-5), 225-232. https://eric.ed.gov/?id=EJ630485

Capra, F. (1983). *The turning point: Science, society, and the rising culture.* Bantam Books.

Chambers, E. G., Foulon, M., Handfield-jones, H., Hankin, S. M., & Michaels, E. G. (1998). The War for Talent. *McKinsey Quarterly, 3*(3). 44-57. https://www.researchgate.net/publication/284689712_The_War_for_Talent

Collings, D.G., & Mellahi, K. (2009). Strategic talent management: A review and research agenda. *Human Resource Management Review, 19*(4), 304-313. doi:10.1016/j.hrmr.2009.04.001

Crossman, A. (2020). *The Major Theoretical Perspectives of Sociology: An Overview of Four Key Perspectives.* Posted in ThoughtCo on January 22, 2020. Retrieved on February 6, 2022, from https://www.thoughtco.com/theoretical-perspectives-3026716

Davenport, T. H. (2005). *Thinking for a living: how to get better performance and results from knowledge workers.* Harvard Business Publishing.

Deloitte. (2005). *Becoming a Magnet for Talent.* Global Talent Pulse Survey Results.

DocuSign (n.d.). *Building Sustainability into the Modern Business: Landscape Reducing waste and emissions with powerful digital workflows.* DocuSign eBook.

Draganidis, F., & Mentzas, G. (2006). Competency Based Management: a review of systems and approaches. *Information Management & Computer Security, 14*(1), 51-64. doi:10.1108/09685220610648373

Dries, N. (2013). The psychology of talent management: A review and research agenda. *Human Resource Management Review, 23*(4), 272-285. doi:10.1016/j.hrmr.2013.05.001

Drucker, P. (1993). *Post Capitalist Society*. Routledge.

Drucker, P. (1999). Knowledge-Worker Productivity: The Biggest Challenge. *California Management Review, 41*(2), 79-94. doi:10.2307/41165987

Economist Intelligence Unit. (2006). The CEO 's role in talent management: How top executives from ten countries are nurturing the leaders of tomorrow. *The Economist.* http://graphics.eiu.com/files/ad_pdfs/eiu_DDI_talent_Management_WP.pdf

Felin, T., & Hesterly, W. S. (2007). The Knowledge-Based View, Nested Heterogeneity, and New Value Creation: Philosophical Considerations on the Locus of Knowledge. *The Academy of Management Review, 32*(1), 195-218. doi:10.5465/amr.2007.23464020

Flink, C., Leslie, J., & Mehta, S. (2022). *Talent leaders can help emerging leaders manage the challenges of virtual leadership with three key tools.* Retrieved on February 4, 2022, from https://www.talentmgt.com/articles/2022/01/31/equipping-emerging-leaders-for-success-in-a-virtual-world/

Gallardo-Gallardo, E., Dries, N., & González-Cruz, T. F. (2013). What is the meaning of 'talent' in the world of work? *Human Resource Management Review, 23*(4), 290–300. doi:10.1016/j.hrmr.2013.05.002

Ganaie, M. U., & Haque, M. I. (2017). Talent management and value creation: A conceptual framework. *Academy of Strategic Management Journal, 16*(2), 1-9.

Gartner. (2019). *Gartner for HR - Reinvent Talent Strategies: The digital-age mandate for HR.* https://www.gartner.com/en/confirmation/human-resources/trends/reinvent-talent-strategies?msclkid=75a00348645716bee27862bc54bbe601

Gartner. (n.d.). *3 Workforce-Planning Imperatives That Drive Business Outcomes.* Retrieved on February 4, 2022, from https://www.gartner.com/en/human-resources/research/talentneuron/3-key-hr-workforce-planning-challenges

Gartner. (n.d.a). *The Unbounded Workforce: Design a data-driven talent strategy that aligns with today's shifting workforce trends.* Retrieved on February 3, 2022, from https://www.gartner.com/en/human-resources/research/talentneuron/unbounded-workforce-ebook?

Gold, J., Oldroyd, T., Chesters, E., Booth, A., & Waugh, A. (2016). Exploring talenting: Talent management as a collective endeavor. *European Journal of Training and Development, 40*(7), 513-533. https://www.emerald.com/insight/content/doi/10.1108/EJTD-11-2015-0091/full/html

Grant, R. M. (1996). Toward a knowledge-based theory of the firm. *Strategic Management Journal, 17*(S2), 109-122. doi:10.1002/smj.4250171110

Griffiths, K., Birdi, K., & Alsina, V. (2016). Knowledge sharing practices and issues in policing contexts: A systematic review of the literature. *European Journal of Policing Studies, 3*(3), 267–291. www.maklu-online.eu/en/tijdschrift/ejps/volume-3/issue-3/

Heinen, J. S., & O'Neill, C. (2004). Managing talent to maximize performance. *Employment Relations Today, 31*(2), 67–82. doi:10.1002/ert.20018

Iles, P., Preece, D., & Chuai, X. (2010). Talent management as a management fashion in HRD: Towards a research agenda. *Human Resource Development International, 13*(2), 125–145. doi:10.1080/13678861003703666

Jacobs, G. M., & Farrell, T. (2001). Paradigm shift: Understanding and implementing change in second language education. *TESL-EJ, 5*(1). https://files.eric.ed.gov/fulltext/ED574144.pdf

Jofre, S. (2011). *Strategic management: The theory and practice of strategy in (business) organizations.* DTU Management: Kgs. Lyngby. https://orbit.dtu.dk/en/publications/strategic-management-the-theory-and-practice-of-strategy-in-busin

Johnson, M. W., Christensen, C. M., & Kagermann, H. (2008). Reinventing Your Business Model: One secret to maintaining a thriving business is recognizing when it needs a fundamental change. *Harvard Business Review.* https://hbr.org/2008/12/reinventing-your-business-model

Jorch, U. (2019). *Develop these 6 skills for impactful leadership.* Posted in WorkAlchemy on November 12, 2019. Retrieved on February 2, 2021, from https://www.workalchemy.com/impactful-leadership-skills

Juneja, P. (n.d.). *Talent Management for the New Generation.* Retrieved on February 3, 2022, from https://www.managementstudyguide.com/talent-management-new-generation.htm

Khoreva, V., Vaiman, V., & VanZalk, M. (2017). Talent management practice effectiveness: investigating employee perspective. *Employee Relations, 39*(1), 19-33. https://www.emerald.com/insight/content/doi/10.1108/ER-01-2016-0005/full/html

Kombo, K. D., & Tromp, L. A. D. (2006). *Proposal and Thesis Writing: An Introduction.* Paulines Publications.

Kuhn, T. S. (1962). *The Structure of Scientific Revolutions*. University of Chicago Press.

Lado, A. A., & Wilson, M.C. (1994). Human Resource Systems and Sustained Competitive Advantage: A Competency-Based Perspective. *The Academy of Management Review, 19*(4), 699-727. doi:10.5465/amr.1994.9412190216

Lewis, R. E., & Heckman, R. J. (2006). Talent management: A critical review. *Human Resource Management Review, 16*(2), 139–154. doi:10.1016/j.hrmr.2006.03.001

Mattone, J., & Xavier, L. (2012). *Talent Leadership: A Proven Method for Identifying and Developing High-Potential Employees*. AMACOM.

Mellahi, K., & Collings, D.G. (2010). The barriers to effective global talent management: The example of corporate élites in MNEs. *Journal of World Business, 45*(2), 143-149. doi:10.1016/j.jwb.2009.09.018

Merchant, C. (1992). *Radical ecology: The search for a livable world.* Routledge.

Meyers, M. C., VanWoerkom, M., & Dries, N. (2013). Talent—innate or acquired? Theoretical considerations and their implications for talent management. *Human Resource Management Review, 23*(4), 305–321. https://www.sciencedirect.com/science/article/abs/pii/S1053482213000314

Michaels, E., Handfield-Jones, H., & Axelrod, B. (2001). *The War for Talent.* Harvard Business Press.

Mintzberg, H., Ahlstrand, B., & Lampel, J. (1998). *Strategy Safari: A Guided Tour through the Wilds of Strategic Management.* The Free Press.

Mngqibisa, S. (2017). Theoretical Framework of the Talent Management. *Talent Management.* Retrieved on January 30, 2022, from https://www.academia.edu/38102731/Chapter_1_THEORETICAL_FRAMEWORK_OF_TALENT_MANAGEMENT

Moczydłowska, J. (2012). Talent Management: Theory and Practice of Management - The Polish Experience. *International Journal of Bossiness Management and Economic Research, 3*(1), 432-438.

Nair, P. J. (2012). Is talent management accentuated by competency mapping? With special reference to educational sector. *International Journal of Social Science & Interdisciplinary Research, 1*(11), 132-147. www.indianresearchjournals.com/pdf/ijssir/2012/november/14.pdf

Nilsson, S., & Ellström, P. (2012). Employability and talent management: challenges for HRD practices. *European Journal of Training and Development, 36*(1), 26–45. doi:10.1108/03090591211192610

Osterwalder, A. (2013). *A Better Way to Think About Your Business Model.* Posted in Harvard Business Review on May 06, 2013. Retrieved on February 7, 2022, from https://hbr.org/2013/05/a-better-way-to-think-about-yo

Osterwalder, A., & Pigneur, Y. (2010). *Business Model Generation: A Handbook for Visionaries, Game Changers, and Challengers* (1st ed.). John Wiley & Sons.

Popper, K. (1963). *Conjectures and refutations.* Routledge & Kegan Paul.

Popper, K. (1968). *The Logic of Scientific Discovery.* Harper & Row.

Popper, K. (1972). *Objective knowledge: An evolutionary approach.* Oxford University Press.

RE100. (2020). *Growing renewable power: companies seizing leadership opportunities.* RE100 Annual Progress and Insights Report 2020, Released in December 2020 by RE100, a global initiative led by the Climate Group in partnership with CDP. Retrieved on February 5, 2022, from https://www.there100.org/growing-renewable-power-companies-seizing-leadership-opportunities

Real, A. D. (2022). *How to retain your top talent amid the Great Resignation.* Posted in TM on January 27, 2022. Retrieved on February 5, 2022, from https://www.talentmgt.com/articles/2022/01/27/how-to-retain-your-top-talent-amid-the-great-resignation/

Schiemann, W.A. (2006). People Equity: A New Paradigm for Measuring and Managing Human Capital. *Human Resource Planning, 29*(1), 34-44.

Scullion, H., Collings, D.G., & Caligiuri, P. (2010). Global talent management. *Journal of World Business, 45*(2), 105-108. doi:10.1016/j.jwb.2009.09.011

Smilansky, J. (2006). *Developing Executive Talent: Best Practices from Global Leaders.* John Wiley & Sons Ltd. https://onlinelibrary.wiley.com/doi/pdf/10.1002/9781119202370.fmatter

Sparrow, P., Scullion, H., & Tarique, I. (2014). Multiple lenses on talent management: Definitions and contours of the field. In P. Sparrow, H. Scullion, & I. Tarique (Eds.), *Strategic Talent Management*. Cambridge University Press. doi:10.1017/CBO9781139424585.004

Spender, J.C. (1996). Making knowledge the basis of a dynamic theory of the firm. *Strategic Management Journal, 17*(S2), 45–62. doi:10.1002/smj.4250171106

Stahl, G. K., Björkman, I., Farndale, E., Morris, S. S., Paauwe, J., Stiles, P., Trevor, J., & Wright, P. M. (2007). *Global Talent Management: How Leading Multinationals Build and Sustain Their Talent Pipeline*. INSEAD Working Paper Series, INSEAD. file:///C:/Users/Teacher/Downloads/Globaltalentmanagement.pdf

Swailes, S., & Blackburn, M. (2016). Employee reactions to talent pool membership. *Employee Relations, 38*(1), 112-128. doi:10.1108/ER-02-2015-0030

Tajuddin, D., Ali, R., & Kamaruddin, B.H. (2015). Developing Talent Management Crisis Model for Quality Life of Bank Employees in Malaysia. *Procedia-Social and Behavioral Sciences, 201*, 80-84. doi:10.1016/j.sbspro.2015.08.133

Talukdar, M. R. I. (2012). Mobile communications and fighting corruption. In V. Kumar & J. Sevensson (Eds.), *M4D 2012. Karlstad University Studies.*

Talukdar, M.R.I. (2020). Uncertain time calls for agile management and adaptation of contingency plan: Lessons from HEIs in Bangladesh. *AIUB Journal of Business and Economics, 17*(2), 219-238.

Talukdar, M.R.I. (2021). The emergence of new strategic business models for HEIs: Evidence from Bangladesh. *Academy of Entrepreneurship Journal, 27*(S2), 1-16.

Talukdar, M. R. I., Hassan, F., & Nahar, R. (2021). Virtual, Blended, and Dual System Teaching-Learning: Fitness and Relevance for Universities. In *Proceedings, AICBM-2021*. FBA-AIUB.

Tansley, C., Turner, P., Foster, C. J., Harris, L., Stewart, J., Sempik, A., & Williams, H. (2007). *Talent: strategy, management, measurement.* CIPD. http://hdl.handle.net/10545/621011

Tatoglu, E., Glaister, A.J., & Demirbag, M. (2016) Talent management motives and practices in an emerging market: A comparison between MNEs and local firms. *Journal of World Business, 51*(2), 278–293. doi:10.1016/j.jwb.2015.11.001

Tetik, S. (2016) Talent Management: A Review of Theoretical Perspectives and a Guideline for Practitioners. *Nile Journal of Business and Economics, 4*, 40-56. doi:10.20321/nilejbe.v2i4.77

Third Eye Blind Productions. (2021). *What is talent management and why is it important?* Posted in Talent Management on June 12, 2021. Retrieved on January 30, 2022, from https://thirdeyeblindproductions.com/what-is-talent-management-and-why-is-it-important/

Ulrich, D. (2007). *The Talent Trifecta.* Posted in workforce.com under Staffing Management on September 17, 2007. Retrieved on February 5, 2022, from https://workforce.com/news/the-talent-trifecta

Ulrich, D., Brockbank, W., Johnson, D., & Younger, J. (2007). Human resource competencies: Responding to increased expectations. *Employment Relations Today, 34*(3), 1-12. doi:10.1002/ert.20159

VALAMIS. (2021). *Talent Management.* Posted in valamis.com. on April 9, 2021. Retrieved on February 2, 2022, from https://www.valamis.com/hub/talent-management

Voeten, E. (2019). Making Sense of the Design of International Institutions. *Annual Review of Political Science, 22*, 147–163. doi:10.1146/annurev-polisci-041916-021108

Westacott, E. (2019). *What is a paradigm shift?* Posted in ThoughtCo on October 12, 2019. Retrieved on February 1, 2021, from https://www.thoughtco.com/what-is-a-paradigm-shift-2670671

Whelan, E., Collings, D. G., & Donnellan, B. (2010). Managing talent in knowledge-intensive settings. *Journal of Knowledge Management, 14*(3), 486-504. doi:10.1108/13673271011050175

KEY TERMS AND DEFINITIONS

Competitive Advantage: A competitive advantage is defined as the ability of a business entity to serve or produce something in a preferred manner and more effectively than competitors, resulting in higher brand value and profit margins.

Human Capital: Human capital is a combination of the experience, attitude, capability, and competence of the people of an organization in navigating the portfolio with technology, intelligence, innovation, and future orientation to build brand value.

Impact Leadership: Impact leadership is a leadership style that leverages talent leadership in the convergence of technology, innovation, impact investment, and committed culture to impact development, co-creation, networking, public-private partnerships, and valuation in emerging markets concerning the future sustainable growth of the organization and the wider context of the environment, society, and inclusive economies.

Knowledge Organizations: A knowledge organization is simply a knowledge generation and transformation and evidence-based policy influence firm. In such a firm, one group is known as knowledge workers, who develop original knowledge and transform it through seminars, symposiums, conferences, and/or teaching classes and influence national as well as international governance and development policies through research-based policy inputs. The other group serves as a service team that encapsulates, preserves, and archives generated knowledge; enables information communication technology to distribute and reuse the firm's generated knowledge; and supports the knowledge transformation and policy influence process. A knowledge organization is a learning organization, but not all learning organizations are necessarily knowledge organizations.

Modern Talent Management: Modern talent management is defined by a process that is strategically driven by the organization's vision orientation to encounter the complex needs of the organization today and navigate the future sustained growth with a high brand image of the business through an integrated and technology-enabled process that apparently covers attracting, developing, and retaining talent with an end-to-end process.

Theoretical Framework: A theoretical framework is a set of connected concepts and theories that a researcher frames into a structure to inform the research problem aligned with the theoretical basis and to compel the research findings in support or contrast of the dominant theory in the framework.

Value Creation: Value creation to date means turning the organization's resources into the capital to generate sustained results that add value to the key stakeholders of the organization, including shareholders, investors, general workforce, talent pool, talent leaders, and HR business partners. It also raises concerns about the sustainable development of the organization and its underlying impact on the external environment, society, and economies.

Chapter 2
Talent Management:
Conceptual and Theoretical Understanding

Shraddha Purandare
https://orcid.org/0000-0002-7914-2225
Dr. D. Y. Patil B-School, India

Aditi Vijaysingh Aljapurkar
https://orcid.org/0000-0001-8766-3111
Dr. D. Y. Patil B-School, India

ABSTRACT

This chapter provides a journey to understand the origin of talent management along with the need for talent management. The chapter describes how talent management has evolved over the period to date. The chapter further states the process of talent management highlighting the prerequisites. This section also describes the framework of the talent management process and its connections with other disciplines. The chapter further elaborates on various challenges associated with talent management. There is a section that would help understand successful strategies adopted by the companies for enhanced performance. The chapter further states future trends to be followed for improved performance. The chapter states the scenario during the COVID-19 pandemic and concludes with successful talent management implementation examples.

DOI: 10.4018/978-1-6684-3894-7.ch002

INTRODUCTION

In today's aggressive & cutthroat competitive environment, talent has become critical. Talent has become the crucial differentiator for human capital management and for leveraging competitive advantage. A company's ability to capture talent helps determine its success in the marketplace. Attracting and retaining great talent is becoming challenging day by day due to the inverse demand-supply ratio of highly skilled employees. Talent management has evolved over a period and is still evolving. Talent management has never been a strategy about building employees or generating succession plans, nor is it about achieving specific staff turnover rates or any other deliberate outcome. It happens naturally to strengthen the organization's global goals, which are essential measures in terms of profits generated. Talent has become a universal phenomenon, thus there is a pressing need to rethink the organizational strategies related to managing talent.

BACKGROUND & EVOLUTION OF TALENT MANAGEMENT

Talent management has become a buzzword in the 21st century. McKinsey & Company (1997) coined the term "the war for talent" on talent management practices and beliefs. McKinsey quoted "better talent is what will separate the winning companies from the rest". In the 21st Century, the war for talent has become a business reality. As defined by Gartner" Talent management is the attraction, selection, and retention of employees, which involves a combination of HR processes across the employee life cycle". DDI defines talent management "as a mission-critical process that ensures organizations have the quantity and quality of people in place to meet their current and future business priorities". Talent Management is a term that has quite a flexible definition, and that's important as it offers a chance for evolving the definition along with organizations. It means what talent management is today; was not the same 20 years ago. Thus, the concept is not confined to hiring the right person at the right time, but it goes beyond exploring the undetermined and outstanding abilities of employees, fostering, and developing them to attain the expected result.

Acquiring the best talent from the industry may be an immense concern for the organizations at present but retaining them and most importantly, helping their smooth transition according to the culture of the organization and motivating them to deliver their best performance is a more immense task. Harvard Business Review (2008) mentioned that Talent Management is a matter of forecasting the demand for human resources and then determining a strategic proposal to meet it. It is acknowledged as a much broader concept meant at attracting, retaining, creating, and developing talented employees. Many researchers through their research findings quoted that high potential employees of the company may leave the company when they notice a lack of overall development opportunities, lack of payment as per the market standards, and non-recognition. It has become critical for companies to attract a pool of talented employees for the company's success. Fundamentally, Talent Management promotes the management of skills, ability, and competency of employees within an organization. The focus of Talent management was always the most talented employees of the organization. Different approaches were adopted by the companies to identify the high potential candidates. One of the popular approaches was the implementation of management grids with 9-box which helps in the assessment of employees based on their potential and performance. Top to bottom order has the employees with the maximum performance and abilities at the top and lowest performers and potential employees at the bottom.

Over a period, Talent management became the management of all employees and not just limited to the high performers and high capabilities. This leads to better engagement levels which help employees to take a closer look at their careers and to take charge of their careers. Talent management has evolved over a period. Some of the stages of Talent Management are stated below

The very first phase of Talent Management involved the central concept of talent management rotating around the most talented employees i.e., the high potential employees of the company. This was a typical system of a normal distribution popularly known as a bell curve. It was observed that twenty percent of the employees were labeled as high potential based on their contribution and productivity. Around seventy percent were not considered to be high potential but productive which was still a vital number, and finally, the last ten percent were not considered to be good performers and could be separated from the organization.

The second phase focused on the organizational structure to understand the exact requirement of manpower and the number of employees to be hired. Priority was given to training highly productive employees who were the top contributors.

In the third phase, the talent management concept became wider. Organizations became global due to expansion, diversification, etc., and started hiring candidates from the global pool of talent. This trend has become more prevalent.

In the fourth & current phase, talent management has become more comprehensive which gives importance to the uniqueness of every individual. It is well-accepted fact that every employee is different and unique in his way of delivering and executing the task. A company's ability to capture talent helps determine its success in the marketplace. Attracting and retaining great talent is becoming challenging day by day due to the inverse demand-supply ratio of highly skilled employees. Organizations are now giving importance to developing and nurturing the talent of every employee. This is also in harmonization with providing equal work opportunities to all employees. In today's aggressive & cutthroat competitive environment, talent has become critical. Talent has become the crucial differentiator for human capital management and for leveraging competitive advantage. The primary benefit of this strategy is that the employees feel respected and valued and employees in return display better output. This phase of talent management is slowly gaining popularity as it helps in maintaining industrious and content staff. This shows that talent management has evolved over a period and is still evolving.

NEED FOR TALENT MANAGEMENT

Any organization can't do any wonders without the right talent managing it from behind the scenes. The right people can produce the right strategy, and the right procedures and in the end, embrace the right technology to boost their organization on the chosen path. Talent management is all about having the right person at the right place at the right time for the optimal time and at the right price.

Organizations now have re-conceptualized talent management to maintain their competitive advantage. Many companies have taken the rights steps & those were visible in the constant disruptions in the work environment highlighted by the recent Covid-19 pandemic. The Covid-19 pandemic has undoubtedly accelerated the pace of transformation. Its impact on international & national economies, establishments, and different categories of employees has stunned conventionally tested business structures and rudimentary practices worldwide. Organizations have now comprehended that people could be that critical distinguishing factor for them in the ever-increasingly competitive market. Talent management (TM) as an extensive HR process is crucial for all businesses, from brick-and-mortar to the sophisticated premium Industry 4.0 establishments that are embracing processes right from machine learning to artificial intelligence.

McKinsey & Company conducted a series of research on talent management practices and based on the overall findings concluded that the leaders should devise strategies to concentrate on attracting talent across all levels of their organizations. (McKinsey & Company,2001). As predicted by McKinsey over the period, the talent war has intensified and has become the top priority. Companies should highlight the different factors that motivate the top talent to choose their companies. Restructuring the talent acquisition strategies, generating ample growth & development opportunities, and implementing a robust performance evaluation system to identify their ace performers as well as less capable performers would help companies to sustain in long run. At the same time, it is essential to focus on enriching employee experience and invest in them to succeed in the current uncertainties. The widespread practice of poaching talent made it unrealistic for traditional employee retention practices to sustain. This highlighted the need for different thinking about cultivating talent and facing the opportunities and challenges within the transforming workplace and the emergent talent development practices

At present, artificial intelligence and emerging technologies have already disrupted the market. Within the next 5-10 years, we will see tenfold changes. Consumers are getting clever, and smart resulting in changing business models. This influences the style of our work and builds yields for the 21st century. These disruptions have foremost implications on talent, resulting in a shortage of skills, substantial learning gaps, leadership scarcity, and shifting workplace demographics.

PROCESS OF TALENT MANAGEMENT

Talent management in the general context includes all the processes involved in various HRM functions such as recruitment, employee learning & development, succession planning, career development, etc. When business needs and talent management systems are aligned, organizations can expect maximum benefits associated with it. Talent management being a continuous process helps in evaluating the manpower requirement. It covers the development of the employees who are contributing to the goals of the organization and creating value for the business. As talent management focuses on cultivating and developing people, an appropriate process should be in place. An important step in the process is to recognize the crucial employees. In an attempt at cost-cutting and downsizing, many organizations retrenched their valuable employees. Organizations forgot that these employees are the most valuable assets of their organization and hence the retention of the talent became a challenge for them. On the other hand, other organizations with the right vision and foresight took more innovative approaches which helped them gain a competitive edge over others by retaining talent. Thus, Talent management emphasizes that an organization must find the skills and abilities in the employees necessary for overall business success.

Box 1.

Prerequisites for Talent Management

i. Alignment of business goals with competencies of the existing pool of employees
ii. Talent requirement for achieving the set goals
iii. Comprehensive processes to spread the goals from top to bottom within the organization
iv. An estimation of opportunity costs to be incurred
v. Strategic plan to move to next stages

These prerequisites are crucial for designing the process of talent management. Considering the existing employees and their competencies organizations are expected to come up with SMART goals i.e. Specific, Measurable, Achievable, Relevant, and Time-bound goals. At the same time, it is essential to map the talent requirement that can act as input for manpower planning. Organizations also need to devise strategies for proper allotment of these goals among all levels. As hiring the right talent involves huge costs, estimation of this cost and strategic planning will enable organizations to execute the talent management process successfully.

Figure 1. Stages of Talent Management process

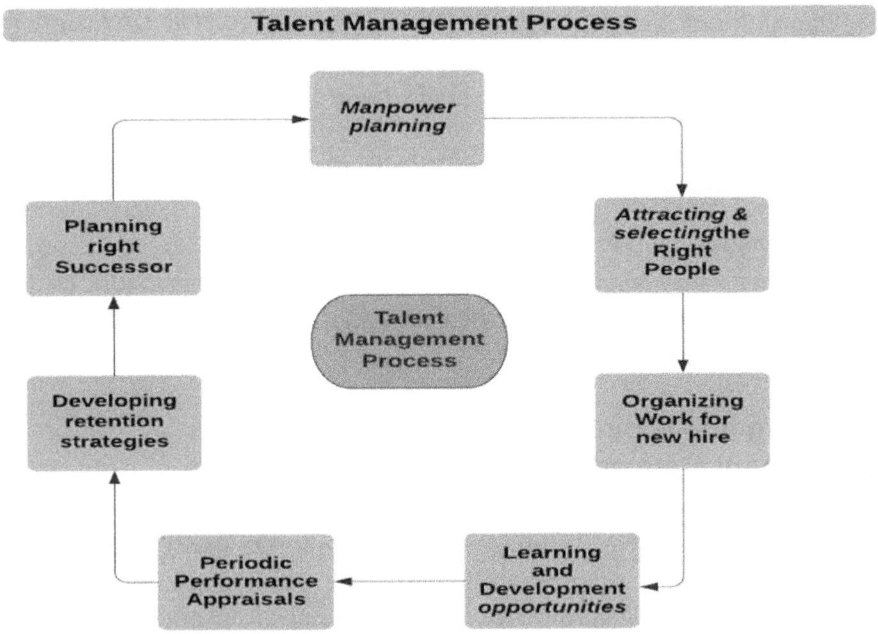

Manpower Planning

As a part of manpower planning, a company needs to determine the number of employees needed, the type of employees needed, and what requirements they should fill in. Other criteria like workforce diversity, succession planning, and business expansion strategies also need to be taken into consideration. The company also needs to list down the competencies of existing employees and check if by providing the training they can develop new skills among existing employees to avoid new hiring. Manpower planning also includes the identification of skills needed and proposed changes in the organization's structure if any.

Attracting & Selecting the Right People

One of the key areas for the organizations is to develop an HR brand that would help in attracting talent. Companies must develop the right set of HR policies & the best practices in the organization. If the right HR brand is created, it helps in attracting talent which is one of the critical areas in the talent management process. Attracting quality people is not sufficient but selecting the right talent for the right job is very important. The exact representation of role fitment would be a clear post-analysis of the job and matching that with the prospective candidate. For gaining a cutting-edge advantage over competitors it's essential to focus on this crucial stage. Planning interviews, placing experienced interviewers to conduct the interview & identifying the best person for the job is also important. This would help in hiring the right fit for the right job & avoiding selection errors.

Organizing Work for New Hires While Onboarding

Many organizations, fail to allocate work to employees post their orientation and onboarding. This may result in disengagement if employees remain idle. Hence, it is essential to allocate them the task, schedule training for them, and help them to settle down in the organization.

Organizing and providing Learning and Development Opportunities

It is always a better strategy to build the skills of employees rather than buying i.e., hiring new employees. Employee development may start immediately after joining the organization with job-specific training, training needs identification based on performance evaluation, and the development of new skills in alignment with business objectives. High potential candidates will always want to go through the process of learning and relearn as per the requirement of their roles. Hence, organizations should focus on creating appropriate platforms for the learning and development of the existing employees. To enhance their engagement level

Conducting Periodic Performance Appraisals

Monitoring employees' performances on regular basis would help organizations to check if employees are capable enough to handle additional responsibilities given to them. If HR conducts a competency mapping exercise, they will get a fair idea of the skills possessed by employees and whether they are matching with their requirements. This may save the cost of new hiring and create opportunities for the promotion of employees.

Developing Retention Strategies

The organization should not only focus on hiring but also on retaining their best talent by offering job satisfaction to employees through increments, promotions, rewards and recognition, a flexible working environment, providing learning and development opportunities, and giving a good employee experience with healthy and harmonious company culture. In the current context, employees select companies that have an amiable atmosphere and prefer to stay only if they get a desirable atmosphere. Employees not only leave the organizations but take away the valuable knowledge gained. Attrition is one of the obstacles which hampers the strategic plans & overall growth of the company. Therefore, it is essential to develop retention strategies. Employees need to be motivated and encouraged for learning. Proper financial assistance for undergoing training should be provided. Compensation should be aligned with performance evaluation and fulfillment of business goals. In absence of the above strategies, employees may tend to leave the organization.

Planning Right Successor

Effective leadership is of utmost importance to succeed in business. To avoid the last-minute hustle-bustle of hiring employees when a senior leader retires or leaves, it's always better to nurture and groom existing talented employees by way of succession planning. This creates a great sense of belongingness to the organization and employees contribute to the organization's goals with accountability. It also creates a learning opportunity for employees.

CURRENT STATUS OF TALENT MANAGEMENT

Globalization is a continuous ongoing process that will change the dynamics of industries in the BANI environment. Thanks to the COVID-19 pandemic that forced us to coin the new acronym BANI i.e. Brittle, Anxious, Non-linear, Incomprehensible. An extremely connected world will get easily impacted worldwide even by local failures or breakdowns making the systems fragile. Breakdown becomes easy, making people more anxious. At the same time, the world becomes too uncertain, and the incomprehensibility and unpredictability of the system increase resulting in inflations. Sustaining in such a challenging situation is a key to success.

Organizations need talented employees who are not only competent but are resilient, empathetic, agile, and adaptable. These requirements resulted in crucial demand for worldwide talent. Many countries across the globe are facing challenges in acquiring the right talent. A rapidly aging population, higher pay demands from the migrants, job market availability for college graduates, and shortage of skilled workers are some of the reasons contributing to the shortage of talented employees (OECD Report 2020) Organizations should realize that one size does not fit all & accordingly they need to come up with talent management strategies.

Talent has become a universal phenomenon, thus there is a pressing need to rethink the organizational strategies related to managing talent. (HBR, 2014) Considering the uncertainty of the demand, companies nowadays have started looking for innovative approaches to manage talent. There is a need to devise a strategy to balance the demand by way of build or buying. At the same time, considering the supply, there is a necessity to develop a plan to improve the return on investment on talent. This acts as a win-win situation for both company and employees and results in encouraging employees to be with the firm. (Peter Capelli, 2008)

In the current context, though talent management acts like a buzzword, still a lot needs to be done to address major gaps. The McLean and Company Trends Report (2021) stated below key disparities in talent management areas

Employee skills gap (24%),
Developing employees on new competencies (24%) and
Training new employees in specific new skills (21%)

Figure 2. SHRM Global skill-shortage survey, 2018
Source: SHRM," The Global skill-shortage survey (2018)

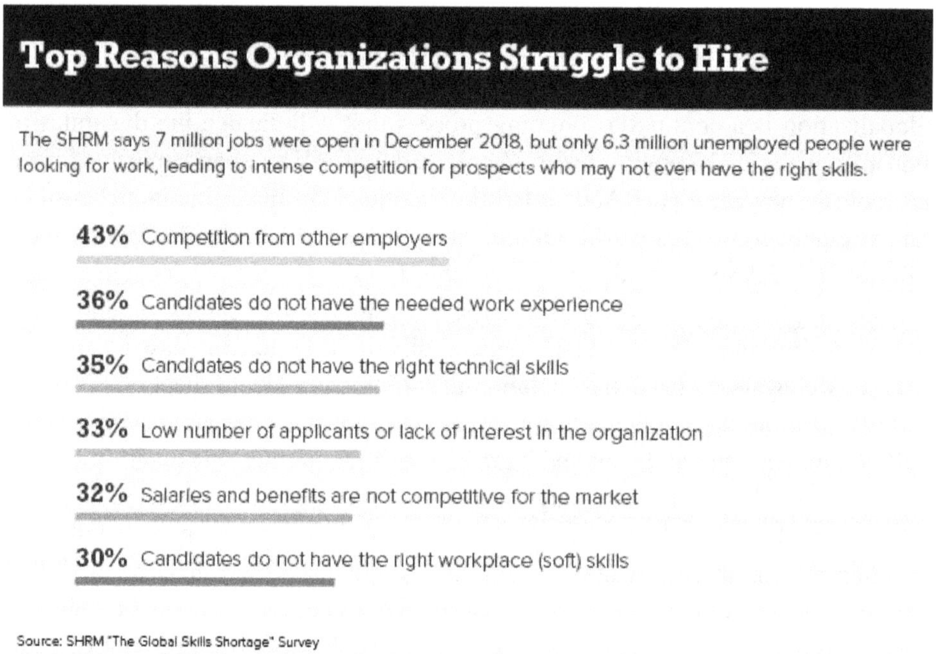

One of the prominent issues that many companies are facing today is that although organizations put enormous endeavors into inviting and attracting employees but devote very little time to developing strategies for retention. As it is a part of strategy not only HR, but the management should also participate in strategy development. The business strategy should involve all the managers and shoulder their responsibilities of them to develop the competencies of their subordinates. SHRM conducted a global survey in the year 2018 to understand the reasons behind organizations' struggle to hire talent. Below are the findings of their survey.

Box 2.

Talent Management at Starbucks
Starbucks as a company stand out in the human resources and the talent management practices that they have long believed and executed. From its inception in 1971 till 2017 under the abled leadership of Howard Schultz along these many years, it crafted HR policies and has always shown improvements. At Starbucks, HR management has rarely been an issue since the organization has always understood the role that its employees play in the company's success in the target market (Ogbu Edeh & Mlanga, 2019).

Employee empowerment:
The company is practiced collaborative work practices that help in empowering every employee. This is possible due to the provision of regular incentives and financial rewards as well as the support coming in the form of emotional encouragement. Staff members can focus on collaboration, which can be seen as the basis for the successful implementation of organizational goals (Uddin & Arif, 2016). One may see this model of collaboration be unhealthy in terms of competition, but then many organizational leaders and managers believe that a bit of rivalry is important for people to perform. Studies show that the introduction of a bit of rivalry into the workplace setting typically encourages employees to be more proactive and innovative (Kontoghiorghes, 2016).

Maintaining Turnover rate:
The company's turnover rate in the year 2018 was a whopping 65%. This figure is on a higher scale which may signal a less efficient approach to retention practices and strategies for reducing turnover. However, the specified statement could not be proved, as it has been established above since staff members were quite content with the current opportunities that the organization offered to them (Harkness, 2018). These figures when compared with other industries as the stress and workplace tension is less, can be validated as the customer response in the fast-food industry has to be prompt and that the negative feedback may be disproportionately huge compared to the reward. 2018 showed a whopping 140-150% of the turnover rate in the US and thus the company Starbucks stands good.:

Talent development:
Practices designed for 'employee well-being' keep a special focus on the 'health' under contingent situations. A policy that makes 'holiday a mandate' helps in resolving mental health concerns, reducing burnout, and lowering stress levels too. Also, practices of rest and replenishment would act as an appropriate tool for retention and engagement reducing the extent of turnover rates too. The company provides benefits like insurance options, but if the organization can include decent insurance options, staff members could still use a wider range of health management opportunities, which include treatment for anxiety, depression, workplace burnout, fatigue, and similar issues caused by the increasing workplace pressure (Akunda et al., 2018).

Starbucks ' corporate setting can be considered a perfect example of how the issue of HRM, namely, rewards and incentives, should be handled.

Despite such odd, certain companies managed to take care of their talent management process. Starbucks is one of them. At present date, when organizations are operating in an extremely volatile uncertain, and complicated business environment, sustainability in the market requires hugely improved skills and competencies to adjust to continual changes, be accommodating and act quickly. Thus, multifaceted, and challenging market surroundings have created a demand for exceptional and talented professionals. Starbucks with its established practices set an example for others on how to deal with this issue of critical prominence

Challenges Associated with Talent Management

Right Compensation

High potential candidates are aware of their skills, and competencies and expect organizations to pay the appropriate compensation that values their potential. Due to the availability of several companies, candidates expect to get desired compensation as per the market standards. Many companies are not willing to pay high compensation as an obstacle to getting the right talent on the job. One of the key reasons for high attrition in the workplace is not offering competitive salaries and benefits as per the market trends.

Job Engagement

Pay does not act as a motivational factor for every employee. Talented employees work for those organizations which offer them appropriate job roles matching their competencies and job expectations. Regular employees may get attracted by the pay packages but this strategy of paying higher packages does not attract all employees. Accordingly, companies need to come up with talent management strategies. Highly talented employees want to align their job expectations with the organizations that will keep them engaged, with interesting and challenging jobs. Jobs are no more looked up to as the means of earning bread and butter, but they are expected to be enjoyable with challenging roles. Unfortunately, many organizations fail to keep employees engaged and could meet their aspirations. Creating a culture of engagement to enhance the overall retention rate is the topmost talent management challenge.

Dealing With the Young Workforce

Gone are the days, when employees used to start their careers with the organization and used to leave the company at the age of superannuation. Organizations are witnessing radical changes in the thought process of the young workforce who are digital natives. The Channel of interaction with the world for this dynamic workforce is technology. They work under the leaders who are the baby boomers. Due to the major generation gap, it becomes difficult for them to communicate. The young want to work in the young culture only & they are certain of leaving the jobs even within a year if it does not fit with their ambitions. In this fast-changing world, it's difficult to gauge what is going on in the mind of the workforce. Due to this fundamental divergence in the thought process and style of operations, talented employees are not retained.

Creating a Dynamic Work Culture

The younger workforce can collaborate on the work and generate new ideas. With the help of technology, they showcase multiple skills and are also productive in the workplace. The pattern of their work and operation styles are different in comparison with baby boomers. They can be productive at midnight as well if any innovative idea strikes them. This workforce does not want to confine themselves to routine 8 hours of a shift. Their expectations are different. Be it related to work flexibility or dressing style. Workforces need proper attention and the right environment to work. It is a challenging task for organizations to create and maintain the level of employee experience that will cater to the needs of different generations with their needs & preferences. Creating the right value proposition for sustainability is the real challenge.

Attrition of Mid Management Employees

Technology is changing at a rapid speed every day with advanced features. It becomes difficult for Gen X to adjust to rapidly changing technology. People who are in their mid-career find it difficult to cope with the changes and leave the organizations. Till the time organizations have invested in these resources and they expect the Return on this investment. They look up to these resources as a future leader. Increasingly, the challenge of developing their competencies falls to the corporations. In such cases, there is a growing risk of failure in the entire talent management process.

Weak Hiring Policies

It is of utmost essential for the company to have a strong manpower plan. Many organizations fail to attract the right pool of talented employees. The major reason is too long and cumbersome hiring policies that result in candidates losing their job interests. At times responses are not received within a stipulated time.

New Forms of Talent Groups

Industry 4.0, and now the Covid-19 pandemic resulted in the formation of new talent groups. A different range of employees is getting into the workforce. Managing this diverse set of employees, therefore, has become very challenging. Considering the disruptions that happened to many business models, organizations now are struggling with issues like better functioning of hybrid teams, the need for new skills, and the future of the workforce broadly.

Figure 3. New forms of talent groups
Source: Created by Author

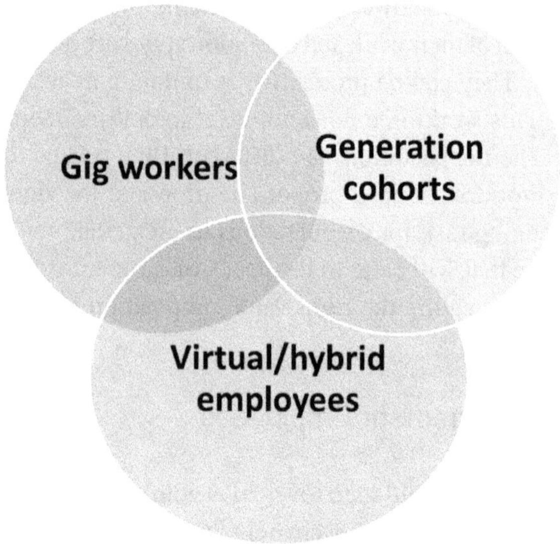

The workforce requirements have changed post-pandemic. They are completely different from the one with which the organization started. The structure of the workforce has also changed; the most noteworthy point is how organizations approach their employees & how they look up to the talent. Below talent groups, have emerged with specific characteristics

a. Generation cohorts
b. Virtual/hybrid employees
c. Gig workers

a. The Generational Cohorts:

Different employees belonging to different age groups working in the organization are termed generation cohorts. The average age of employees contributes to developing the organizational culture and in designing job roles, teams, etc. are taken into consideration. At present, four generations of employees are working that include the generation Z, millennial(Y), generation X & baby boomers. As per the report of SHRM, Baby Boomers are like a structured organization who are cautious about change. They are dedicated workers who value visibility. Generation X is termed to be independent, and flexible and wants to bring changes in the rules and look at change as an opportunity. Millennials (Y) have a cooperative and impact-oriented approach and more flexible work systems. They expect to set up their own rules with changes and upward progress. Finally, Generation Z employees are termed as an optimistic agile workforce who seek balanced rules, seeing change as simply reality. Managing this varied workforce having diverse characteristics is the major challenge for every organization

b. Virtual/ Hybrid Employees:

Technology has made this world flat. Of late, Covid-19 also played its role and forced organizations as well as employees to work virtually. The virtual workforce is certain for upcoming years too. To work virtually it is essential to get accustomed to the technology and work in synchronization with the teams. Some of the organizations moved to the hybrid model of working, where employees report to an office on a rotation basis. These virtual teams are located anywhere and everywhere. Managing the different employees of different generations working at different locations is a herculean challenge to all organizations. Data from Gartner also tells us that by 2030, the demand for remote work will increase by 30 percent, when "Gen Z" enters the workplace. Management should be conscious enough of this extension of the work and must take all essential actions to make sure that the parallel online workplace also is safe and free of any intended or unintended nuisance.

c. The GIG Workers:

According to the data provided by MasterCard, it is expected that the global gig economy will be worth almost 350 billion US dollars by 2021. The Global Gig Economy is expected to grow from $204 billion in 2018 to $455 billion in 2023, with a Compound Annual Growth Rate (CAGR) of 17.4%. It is also stated in the same report, that number of freelance workers is steadily increasing in the Western World. For example, the number of US freelancers is estimated to grow from 57 to 86 million by 2027 and the UK's gig economy workforce more than doubled from 2016-to 2019 as it accounts for 4.7 million people. A joint report by the Boston

Consulting Group and Michael & Susan Dell Foundation stated that the gig economy can service up to 90 million jobs in India's non-farm economy alone. This converts to over $250 billion in volume of work and may contribute an incremental 1.25% to India's GDP. By 2020, 50% of Indian workers are expected to go freelance. This will have an impact on the HR processes and manage the talent. As these are not a part of the full-time workforce of the company and prefer to work at their own pace. It is essential to have a completely flexible system in place to deal with them.

Over Application of 9 Box Grids

The nine-box matrix originated to judge the performance of business units. The organization can evaluate a unit by two factors the allure of the industry and the competitive power. Taking this model as a base, HR designed a model to evaluate the performance of their employees with consistent patterns. The main aim of the 9 Box Matrix was to come up with a classification of employees to decide upon promotion, retention, and learning development. These settings ultimately helped in performance appraisal & roll out of compensation. The management team executes a talent plan investing in the top performers. In addition, the plan also focuses on improving the performance of low-performing employees.

Figure 4. 9 Grid model of Talent Management
Source: McKinsey (1970)

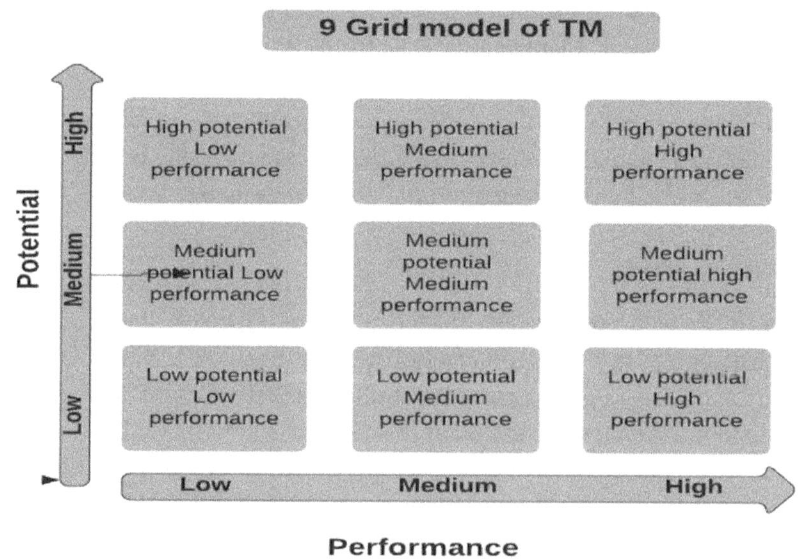

Unfortunately, the main issue with this 9-box system was its emphasis on retaining only the high performers and maximizing the performance of high potential employees. The entire emphasis is on the feedback provided by the managers. At times, it could be skewed based on association with different employees and tend to be biased. In an organization set up, the talent& competencies of every employee may not be recognized and remain untapped. Hence organizations need to develop strategies to take care of such hidden talent, and competencies of the diverse workforce.

FUTURE TRENDS TO FOLLOW IN TALENT MANAGEMENT

Considering the current unprecedented time, BANI environment, and associated challenges, it is of utmost essential to understand, predict the flow & come up with solutions to overcome the challenges. Below listed are some of the trends to follow for better talent management

Smart Hiring Strategies

Smart hiring strategies are company-specific customized strategies to get the best talent on board. Companies may use chatbots to screen and shortlist the candidates resulting in shortlisting exactly fit candidates and saving the time of the recruiter. A recruiter can utilize this time to develop a rapport with talented employees and attract them to their organization. According to the study by the Global Supply Chain Institute at the University of Tennessee, executives spot the warning signs as 91 percent of CEOs identified a need to change their strategy for inviting and hiring talent. Similarly, 61 percent claimed they have not taken the first step to do so. The key to the strategy is to think about talent with a clear vision. Wherever possible, an organization can introduce automation of the systems. It is also essential to make sure that talent continues & remains with the organization. The company also needs to devise strategies and come up with intelligent decisions on whether to buy the talent or build the talent by making talent a priority.

Talent Geographically Unleashed

Post pandemic also, employee preference would be working from remote locations. The talent is not confined by the borders in the current virtual world. Now the trend is to live at the location of one's choice and contribute to work. It's not only easy to follow this trend in the IT sector but also in banking and consumer goods. As the market is open, the best talent can be found anywhere in the world. As The Economist estimates, opening borders to free up talent would result in a $78 trillion increase in global GDP. If technology and a newly adopted organizational culture would enable employees to do their work from wherever they want, it would result in increased revenues for the organization. It was expected that recruiters need to be agile, but in a true sense, pandemics made the industry understand the importance of change and adaptability.

Contingent Hiring will be More Integrated

Steve Jobs once said that their top-secret achievement lies in the fact that his company has gone to extraordinary lengths to hire the best people in the world.

The rise of gig employees and freelance employees entering the workplace has made things challenging. Organizations need to devise strategies to integrate these employees into the workplace. The job roles need to be properly defined to understand the requirement of several employees and accordingly recruitment team need to act on them.

Hiring without College Degrees

Job-search site Glassdoor compiled a list of top employers who are intensifying their talent search wherein they would not rely on a college degree. Companies like Google, Apple, and IBM are some of those companies. This reinstates that global trend is changing and companies' expectations are also changing. Companies are no longer looking for degrees but candidates who are having hands-on experience through internships or the vocational class. This does not mean that candidates do not need to undergo formal education and still, would be hired but those who cannot afford to get an education but possess requisite skills and talent would get the job.

Maggie Stilwell, Ernst, and Young's managing partner for talent stated that Academic credentials will be a crucial factor while evaluating candidates but that no longer acts as an obstacle in getting a candidate.

Proactive Approach

The current workforce with an increasing number of millennials and upcoming generation z comprises a large set of employees who are independent, acting as freelancers and out-of-the-box thinkers. This shift forced HR professionals to change their approach toward workforce development. The company can hire the best of the talent but it is also essential to fit the talent in the right roles and assign them the right job duties. COVID-19 has changed the dynamics of the workplace and provided an opportunity to reconsider knowledge, skills, abilities, and other characteristics (KSAOs) for current roles and expected future roles. As per the HBR (2020), Gen

X and Boomers, who are leading many companies today, enjoy the separation that the physical workplace brings in their efforts to keep work and home a bit more separate. It is also vital to provide flexibility to employees to maintain the balance of professional & personal life.

Figure 5. Glassdoor survey results
Source: Glassdoor (2018)

15 Companies That Will Hire Candidates Without A College Degree As A Requirement
Apple
Bank of America
Chipotle
Cosco Wholesale
EY (UK)
Google
Hilton
Home Depot
IBM
Lowe's
Nordstrom
Penquin Random House
Publix
Starbucks
Whole Foods

Source: Glassdoor, August, 2018

Use of AI

Artificial intelligence (AI) has also contributed to the evolution of talent management stages into high-performing systems. The borders between in-house and external employees have distorted and extended an organization's talent pool. Though AI has numerous applications in the field of the human resources sector, the main areas where AI is involved first are recruitment and on-boarding of employees, followed by employee experience within the organization, overall process improvement, etc. Recruitment Chatbots help in the standardization of the processes. As per the Global Human Capital trends survey conducted by Deloitte (2019), it was observed that 81% of the respondents mentioned that the recruitment process was below standard. This highlights the need of using advanced technology like Chatbots which helps in screening and shortlisting the right candidates fitting into the requirement. This helps in increasing the speed of hiring. Though talent is geographically scattered, with the help of technology, organizations are expected to take their work to talented employees instead of asking them to work at a central location. In this way, the entire process of talent management can be executed right from developing the talent to retaining the talent which takes care of the end-to-end talent management process.

Alumni Programs for Employees

Many times employees leave the job due to personal reasons like relocation, marriage, higher studies, maternity break, ailing parents, etc. Many organizations do not hire back their employees who left them earlier. Considering the flat world, the organization should start cultivating and restoring the connection with ex-employees. They can establish an informal alumni network by regularly checking with ex-employees, by sharing relevant jobs with them. IT giant Oracle has successfully implemented this policy and is immensely benefited through this alumni network.

Leadership

Considering different talent groups working together, the right leader must lead and direct them. As baby boomers are being replaced by generation X, effort should be put into strengthening the relations with and among the talent groups. Working with a good leader and contributing to their vision & mission results in getting a greater amount of job satisfaction. Management needs to invest in developing the capabilities of leaders and giving them the responsibility of retaining the talent.

Career Opportunities & Career Support

Oracle with Workplace Intelligence has conducted a survey (2021) to understand employees' expectations for their futures, and what success means to them. Their findings stated that 85% of employees aren't satisfied with their employer's support of their careers. The same survey also stated that 88% of employees feel Work-life balance, mental health, and flexibility are now top priorities. As skills are becoming stale over a period, organizations should earnestly develop career progression strategies to take care of their talent and attract new talent else they would face the greater risk of losing their employees. In the same survey, 83% of people stated that they want to make career changes over the next year i.e. 2022. Pandemic has changed the mindset of employees and they are having a different set of priorities. Companies are facing a rising skills gap. It is up to organizations to be mindful of these changes & devise policies & offer proper tools to support their workforce growth well as a strong dedication towards workforce career development is crucial for business growth.

Box 3. Food for Thought

Importance of great employee experience: Research on "What workers want", was conducted by Becky Frankiewicz and Tomas Chamorro-Premuzic. In this research, Fortune 500 CEO was asked the question: "How do you possibly build culture when you don't sit together"? In nutshell, they responded that Culture doesn't exist within walls; it exists within people. They stressed building the culture through people, irrespective of whichever location they sit. This highlights the need to focus on giving the best employee experience through organization culture, job roles, best facilities, and good employee relations. Enhancing the employer-employee relationship is also essential. Many times employees leave organizations because of non-cordial relationships with bosses. It is crucial to look after this area and sensitize employees, especially in the managerial positions, considering gig employees, freelancers, and generations z are entering into the systems.

COVID-19 AND SUCCESSFUL TALENT MANAGEMENT IMPLEMENTATION

Covid-19 has badly impacted the lives of people. Pandemic forced people to reorganize their home and their work responsibilities. Due to lay off during the pandemic many employees lost their jobs. For the sake of survival, people responded to these challenges by starting their businesses. According to the Census Bureau, more than 4.4 million new businesses were created in the U.S. during 2020 — the highest total on record. People are enjoying their businesses and most importantly being their boss. 70% of the businesses which started during this period were digital firstborn out of technology. Not requiring any physical space or any equipment apart from mobile and laptop. Pandemic forced employees to work from remote locations. Initially, though it was difficult, it has its own set of advantages like self-care, work-life balance, and work flexibility. It is being observed that employees started enjoying work from remote locations. Manpower Group's global analysis showcased that, 8 out of 10 workers want more remote work to attain a healthier work-life fusion. Most employees do not have to want to return to the office full-time, and, by extension, be forced to live close to it.

In March 2020, only one in 67 paid US jobs on LinkedIn used to offer remote work, but now that number has increased and is up to nearly one in 6. The flexibility that remote work offers has been proclaimed as crucial to retaining employees, especially women and caregivers but can also be extended to all workers depending upon the nature of their job. Due to this shift in the overall psychology of people, retention became critical. Employers need to discover a variety of benefits that may work to retain employees and work pragmatically. Some of the key areas of talent management recognized for overall development by many organizations are as follows

- Leadership Development
- Succession Planning
- Performance Management
- High Potential Employee Development
- Learning and Training
- Retention

Box 4. CISCO: An example of a company driving positive talent transformation

✓ Business agility-being the prime focus
i. The company ventured into the usage of collaborative technological tools to empower employees and be agile in their response.
ii. The company changes the practices of hiring from outside for offices with immediate location
iii. The enhanced hiring decision for vendors and full-time employees is not restricted to a geographical area to have the best talent.
✓ Talent analytics
i. Pandemic increased the importance of data-driven HR processes and decision-making. The same goes with the company's approach is using talent analytics in sourcing, attracting, engaging, and retaining talent.
ii. The company's approach was to better understand the positioning as an employer for better talent attraction-talent retention. For this, the company was leveraging data for skills mapping, talent market availability, competitors, demand intelligence, and internal and external skill analysis
✓ Culture refined in new work structure
➢ Cisco had to revamp how employees were cared for, connected, and treated
➢ These include weekly check-ins from leadership across the entire ecosystem – full-time employees and contractors alike – to keep the teams informed and educated.
➢ Giving flexibility to employees when they are working from home.
➢ Taking care of corona-affected employees and family members.
➢ The care and connect practices went down from employees to vendors to customers too.
➢ Leadership was redefined in this pandemic period

Talent management with technological support.
With the hybrid model or even WFH (work from home) model, the human touch to processes is significant. For this Cisco leveraged HR technology by escalating WebEx usage. The company has conducted baby showers and happy hours, for example, to provide a chance for colleagues to connect beyond the regular work meetings. Live recruitment and internships (online mode) continued with the company.

Reassess upskilling priorities.
Uncertain times make the company rethink its priorities. Cisco as a company did this! It could analyze the in-demand skills required and decide to equip employees and contractual employees with them. Learning by doing at work was the strategy adopted. The focus was to support employees in their learning process. Here, weekly check-ins with managers proved very critical. During these meetings, employees were asked a certain set of questions like, if employees are fully making use of their strengths, and if their feeling towards contribution to the organization. These questions help understand the level of their engagement and help in identifying whether employees are benefited from new learning

As the COVID19 crisis has affected our lives, businesses have no alternative left but to adapt. Despite many obstacles, one can make constructive differences that may last after the pandemic. Cisco is an example of a company driving positive talent transformation. Kelly Jones, Cisco's Global Leader and Senior Talent Acquisition Director, mentioned how her company coordinated its personnel strategy to stay on top during a pandemic and ensure continued success

Box 5. Deloitte

Deloitte is one of those companies, that worked on the retention of employees during Covid-19. They put in efforts to retain the talent by restricting and redesigning their benefits The firm declared $1 billion as an added investment in compensation and benefits for their employees including expanded paid time off, mental health and wellbeing benefits, and remote-work subsidies. They also focused on upskilling their employees. According to a Deloitte report, 2021, "Younger generations especially are hungry for opportunities to learn." Investment in a career is also connected with feeling valued at work and that sense of belongingness. This factor is also associated with retention. As a part of the shift from the pandemic crisis & responding to changes, certain changes are introduced in Talent management practices like nonlinear career progression, career revolving around the portfolio, etc. This helped them to retain their talent.

Creating an environment of encouragement and aligning a financial reward enables employees to perform and enhances the outcome of the talent management strategy. An HR framework built upon this foundation would help in increasing performance quality, keeping performance rate consistent, and little deviation from required quality rates. In nutshell, the companies that are keen on managing and developing their talent, produce far better outcomes for their stakeholders. (HCI,2008) Organizations that understand the significance of talent management and are willing to plan talent management policies systematically deliver better shareholder benefits.

The implementation of talent management policies must start from the top management level. Enhancing the depth and strength of the talent pool must be considered one of the top priorities of senior leaders. Talented employees always look for opportunities to grow, and without such opportunities, they will tend to fade. Companies who tend to disregard & fail to prioritize talent management practices, end up paying the price. The entire process of talent management depends upon having the right talent in place else it would be termed impractical. Every employee plays a specific role in achieving the goals of the organization. Organizations need to understand their structure, and growth plans, and accordingly weave around the talent management policies. This in effect will increase the rate of retention of talented employees. In the current unprecedented times, employees' agility and adaptability are considered requisites skills to succeed. As technology is changing rapidly, candidates possessing niche skills are in demand. Rather demand for these candidates is higher than supply. Many organizations are facing challenges to onboard such employees. Hence organizations should redesign & improve their talent management strategies and maintain the talented pool of employees. In the highly competitive world and BANI environment that is the only strategy that organizations can rely upon.

CONCLUSION

Considering the BANI environment and ongoing demand for niche skills and competencies, Companies nowadays have started looking for groundbreaking approaches to attract, develop and retain talent. There is a need to revisit old strategies & devise a strategy to balance the demand in the uncertainty like Covid-19

Pandemic. Talent management has evolved over a period and is still evolving. In nutshell, Talent management is needed for

1. Aligning the workforce with the business needs
2. Engaging the workforce to maintain the highest level of productivity
3. Increasing the employee satisfaction
4. Succession planning leadership development
5. Balancing a diversified workforce enabling the maximum possible level of employee engagement

Companies must acknowledge the strategic position of talent and operate their businesses accordingly to obtain long-term benefits & rewards.

REFERENCES

Agrawal, De Smet, Lacroix, & Reich. (2020). To emerge stronger from the COVID-19 crisis, companies should start re-skilling their workforces now. *McKinsey Insights*. https://www.mckinsey.com/

Aguinis, H., & Burgi-Tian, J. (2021). Talent management challenges during COVID-19 and beyond: Performance management to the rescue. *BRQ Business Research Quarterly*, *24*(3), 233–240. doi:10.1177/23409444211009528

Akunda, D., Chen, Z., & Gikiri, S. N. (2018). Role of HRM in talent retention with evidence. *Journal of Management and Strategy*, *9*(2), 8–19. doi:10.5430/jms.v9n2p8

Margherita, A., Elia, G., & Klein, M. (2021). Managing the COVID-19 emergency: A coordination framework to enhance response practices and actions. *Technological Forecasting and Social Change*, *166*, 120656. doi:10.1016/j.techfore.2021.120656 PMID:33551496

Frankiewicz, B., & Chamorro-Premuzic, T. (2020). The Post-Pandemic Rules of Talent Management. *Harvard Business Review*.

Berger, L., & Berger, D. (2010). *The Talent Management Handbook: Creating a Sustainable Competitive Advantage by Selecting, Developing, and Promoting the Best People*. McGraw-Hill Publication.

Bhalla, A. (2020). *Talent Engineering For Tomorrow*. https://www.forbes.com/sites/forbestechcouncil/2020/12/14/talent-engineering-for-tomorrow/?sh=9449d75271c4

Ryder, B. (2021). *Solving Talent Management Challenges Today And For The Future*. https://www.forbes.com/sites/ryder/2021/06/01/solving-talent-management-challenges-today-and-for-the-future/?sh=3d094956739f

Cappelli, P. (2008). Talent Management for the Twenty-First Century. *Harvard Business Review, 86*(3), 74-81.

Lisbeth, C. (2019). HR disruption- Time already to reinvent talent management. *BRQ Business Research Quarterly, 22*(3), 207–215. doi:10.1016/j.brq.2019.04.002

Ready, D. A., Hill, L. A., & Thomas, R. J. (2014). Building a Game-Changing Talent Strategy. *Harvard Business Review*, (January–February), 2014.

Foote, E., Hancock, B., Jeffery, B., & Malan, R. (2021). *The key role of dynamic talent allocation in shaping the future of work*. https://www.mckinsey.com/

Tammy, E. (2008). Today's Top 10 Talent-Management Challenges. *Harvard Business Review*.

Loscos, F. (2022). *The 15 Big Challenges Facing Talent Management In 2022*. https://www.forbes.com/sites/esade/2022/01/10/the-15-big-challenges-facing-talent-management-in-2022/?sh=1b382c5d5d60

Lestrange, G. (2019). *The evolution of Talent Management*. HRD Connect. https://www.hrdconnect.com/2019/10/17/the-evolution-of-talent-management/

Ankur, G. (2021). *The 7 Steps to build a great Talent Management Process*. https://www.peoplestrong.com/

Mahapatra & Dash. (2022). Talent development in a changing world of work. *IIMB Management Review*.

Bersin, J., & Chamorro-Premuzic, T. (2019). New ways to gauge talent and potential. *MIT Sloan Management Review, 60*(2), 7–10.

Payal, J. (2019). Talent management: Opportunities & challenges for industry 4.0. *Journal of Management Development, 38*, 1–15.

Kontoghiorghes, C. (2016). Linking high-performance organizational culture and talent management: Satisfaction/motivation and organizational commitment as mediators. *International Journal of Human Resource Management, 27*(16), 1833–1853. doi:10.1080/09585192.2015.1075572

Mugayar-BaldocchM.SchaningerB.SharmaK. (2021). https://www.mckinsey.com/business-functions/people-and-organizational-performance/our-insights/the-organization-blog/the-future-of-work-the-now-the-how-and-the-why

McLean and Company HR Trends Report. (2021). https://hr.mcleanco.com/

Tuccio, M. (2020). *OECD Social, Employment and Migration Working Papers No. 229*. OECD Report. https://www.oecd-ilibrary.org/social-issues-migration-health/measuring-and-assessing-talent-attractiveness-in-oecd-countries_b4e677ca-en

Michaels, E., Handfield-Jones, H., & Axelrod, B. (2001). *The War for Talent*. Harvard Business School Press.

Ogbu Edeh, F., & Mlanga, S. (2019). Talent management and workers' commitment to oil & gas firms in Nigeria. *Journal of Management*, *2*(3), 1–15.

Rothwell, W. J. (2008). Next-generation talent management. *HRM Review*, *8*(10), 10–16.

Shukla, R. (2008). *Talent Management: Process of Developing and Integrating Skilled Workers*. Global India Publications.

Tammy. (2008). Today's Top 10 Talent-Management Challenges. *Harvard Business Review*, *86*.

Wall, T., & Knights, J. (2013). Leadership Assessment for Talent Development. Kogan Page.

Uddin, R., & Arif, A. A. (2016). Talent management and organizational performance: An empirical study in the retail sector in Sylhet City, Bangladesh. *IOSR Journal of Business and Management*, *18*(10), 11–18. doi:10.9790/487X-1810041118

Susanna, V. (2022). *Morning Brew*. Retrieved July 28, 2022, from https://www.morningbrew.com/series/the-years-ahead/stories/2022/01/05/happy-new-year-recruiting-and-retaining-employees-in-2022-won-t-get-any-%20easier?%2BUtm%2B_%2Bcampaign%2B=%2Bhrb%2B&%2Butm_medium=newsletter&utm_source=morning_brew&mid=8c47bac00786b49a5ebabb2258b3ae22%2B%5Baccessed%2Bon%2B15th%2BJan%2B2021%5D

Van Durme. (2019). *Talent mobility: Winning the war on the home front*. Global Human Capital Trends. https://www2.deloitte.com/us/en/insights/focus/human-capital-trends/2019/internal-talent-mobility.html

KEY TERMS AND DEFINITIONS

BANI: New acronym developed post COVID-19 pandemic. It stands for Brittle, Anxious, Non-linear, Incomprehensible. It describes multifaceted changes occurring due to unforeseen situations.

Gig Workers: Temporary workers working especially in the service sector as independent contractors or freelancers who have the liberty to set their work hours.

Globalization: A process or structure where people are connected, and goods can move easily through different borders.

Hybrid Employees: Employees have the liberty to work either from the office or partly from home.

Leadership Development: The act of leading a group of people in an organization. The development process enhances capabilities to lead in a disrupting situations within organization.

Succession Planning: Succession planning is the process of finding the critical positions within the organization and accordingly developing suitable action plans for creating future successors to undertake those positions.

Talent Groups: A small subset of candidates having similar characteristics within a large pool of Talent. These groups have formed to perform a specific set of tasks.

Chapter 3
Talent Management and Sustained Competitive Advantage

Emmanuel Ogbeide Imafidon
Pan Atlantic University, Nigeria

ABSTRACT

The focus of this chapter is on the connection between good talent management and the development of sustainable competitive advantage in organizations. The resource-based view (RBV) of the firm is leveraged in analyzing that connection; RBV upholds that competitive advantage is closely related to an organization's internal characteristics. More specifically, if an organization owns and utilizes valuable, rare, inimitable, and non-substitutable resources and capabilities in its processes and operations, it will achieve superior performance and sustainable competitive advantage. A framework is developed that organizational leaders can use in facilitating conversations and developing talent management programs to ensure that their talent management processes are focused on honing the organization's core competencies that feed their sustainable competitive advantage and superior performance.

INTRODUCTION

The nature of talent management in an organization is acknowledged as a predictor of the organization's sustainable competitive advantage. For practitioners and organizations, the imperative is to find out how to go about making talent management a source of sustainable competitive advantage. There is no shortage of studies on the

DOI: 10.4018/978-1-6684-3894-7.ch003

importance of talent management in organizational performance (Kabwe & Okorie, 2019; Mellahi & Collings, 2010; Skuza et al., 2013) and its criticality in developing an organization's sustainable competitive advantage (Ali, 2017, 2019; Fareed et al., 2016; Farndale et al., 2010; Latukha, 2015; Sikora et al., 2016). People, particularly in the knowledge economy era, are ever more viewed as the key catalyzing factor for competitive advantage in organizations; their capabilities impel success or failure for the organization. Therefore, it is imperative for organizations to develop a talent strategy that focuses on identifying the most critical features of the right talent that would enable the business success of that organization and ensure that resources are prioritized towards maximizing the effectiveness of that talent. This requires organizational leadership to understand where the organization is and where it is looking to be, where and how it competes for marketplace success and the required organizational capabilities that would be instrumental to that success.

Particular attention must be paid to the socio-technological trends that are shaping talent management practices in progressive organizations. These include hybridization of work, internal talent mobility imperatives, informal learning platforms, social learning, the "gig" workforce, multi-generational workforces, new employee experience necessities, deep adoption of data analytics capabilities, mainstreaming of diversity, equity, and inclusion issues, etc. These factors and more should be considered in framing the talent management efforts in contemporary organizations.

While focusing on the human capital (knowledge, skills, abilities, creativity, experience, resilience, etc.) that talent exerts in an organization's productive processes, attention must also be paid to the social capital of that talent. The justification for this comes from the Social Capital theory, which posits that good social relationships are resources that can lead to the development and accretion of human capital. This should be factored into the management of a firm's talent if an optimal output is to be obtained from talent's contribution to the organization's sustainable competitive advantage. Consequently, organizations cannot rely on securing smart talent alone for their competitive advantage; they also must ensure that such talent is relationally positioned to work cooperatively with other employees for superior results. This holds true in formal and informal labor markets as well as micro and macro-organizational settings (Ali, 2017, 2019).

Social capital would require such talent to have emotional intelligence and social intelligence skills. Emotional Intelligence as defined by the *American Psychological Association* is "a type of intelligence that involves the ability to process emotional information and use it in reasoning and other cognitive activities." It comprises attributes of self-awareness, self-management, social awareness, and relationship management. The *American Psychological Association* defines Social Intelligence as "the ability to understand people and effectively relate to them." It comprises attributes such as verbal and conversational abilities, understanding of norms of social interaction, listening abilities, self-efficacy, and impression management. Two forms of social capital are predominant in organizational literature: bonding and bridging social capital. "**Bonding social capital** brings together similar people (i.e., strong ties), and captures an individual's close network, in which existing skills and expertise are known. As such, individuals interact with others with whom they can identify easily. **Bridging social capital** provides connections between people with significant dissimilarities (i.e., weak ties), for example, in terms of beliefs and background" (Yoganathan et al., 2021, p. 51). A good social and harmonious relationship between employee and employer, as well as among employees, is imperative for employees' higher-level performance, motivation, happiness, and satisfaction (Hans, 2021).

SUSTAINABLE COMPETITIVE ADVANTAGE

An organization's competitive advantage refers to the factor(s) that allow the organization to have an edge over its rivals in the marketplace, helping it grow its market share by attracting more customers than its competition. "A firm is said to have a competitive advantage when it is implementing a value-creating strategy not simultaneously being implemented by any current or potential player" (Barney 1991, cited by Clulow et al., 2003, p. 221). Hence, competitive advantage is the leverage that an organization has over its competitors, enabling it to produce goods or services at a better quality and/or more cheaply than others. The study of this advantage has elicited considerable research interest, particularly sequel to the pivotal work by Michael Porter in 1990. Issues pertaining to organizational competitiveness have taken center stage in understanding the levers of organizational success. It is in this regard that studies have extended to the concept of sustainable competitive advantage as an indispensable element in business sustainability.

Sustainable competitive advantage is a long-term advantage that enables an organization to remain more successful than its competitors over the long term, as a consequence of the organization's ability to preserve its competitive edge over those rivals. It is built on truly differentiating capabilities. Research has identified certain factors that engender sustainable competitive advantage in organizations. These include cost leadership, quality, speed, innovation, human capital, outsourcing, strategic alliances, knowledge management, and a learning organization (Hanif et al., 2013; Khan et al., 2019; Latukha, 2018; Saravanan, 2017). Other factors that are often cited include branding/brand loyalty, the organization's distribution network, intellectual property, location, and customer service (Vinayan, et al., 2012; Leach, 2018; Srivastava et al., 2013).

The age of disruption that we are in has impelled a new dynamic in several of the factors that engender sustainable competitive advantage. In a 2019 article under the auspices of the World Economic Forum, Karthik Krishnan (2019), global CEO of Britannica Group declared, "the human race has seen more social and technological change in the past two decades than in all previous centuries combined." This change has been induced largely by rapid technological advancements marked by disruptive innovations, collaborative technologies, cloud computing, big data, mobility, ubiquitous high-speed mobile internet, robotics, Artificial Intelligence, and quantum automation. These developments were overlaid by extreme disruptions driven by the global pandemic of 2019–2022 that has led to changes in business models and consumer behavior, elevated e-commerce penetration, and the "delivery economy." These disruptions have inevitably affected the shelf life of the levers of sustainable competitive advantage. The general experience has been that digital technologies have, on the one hand, upended the stability of competitive advantage, while conversely enabling more sustainable competitive advantages (Ferreira et al., 2019; Knudsen et al., 2021; Sousa & Rocha, 2019).

As Michael Porter (1990) notes, "Ultimately, the only way to sustain a competitive advantage is to upgrade it—to move to more sophisticated types" (Porter, 1990, p. 75). With the resultant hyper-competition in the macro-environment arising from the speed of technological innovations, as well as the pandemic-induced disruptions, organizations have had to be eclectic in ensuring that their factors of competitive advantage are adjusted for sustainability in the circumstance.

Figure 1. The interplay of resources, capabilities, and core competencies in competitive advantage

Source: Author's adaptation of information gleaned from sources already cited in this chapter (e.g., Latukha, 2018; Saravanan, K. 2017 and Srivastava et al., 2013)

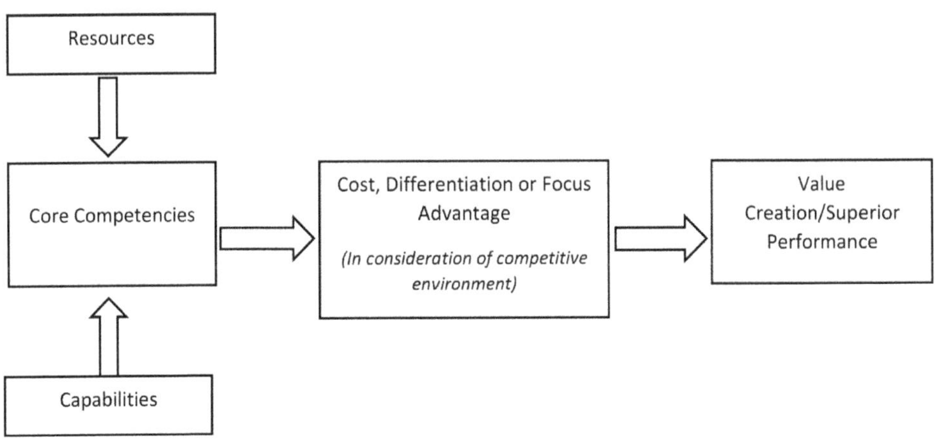

At an aggregate level, all the factors can be clustered into two buckets: **resources** (the organization's assets, knowledge, and skills) and **capabilities** (an organization's ability to effectively leverage its resources). These feed the development of the organization's core competencies, which it relies on to drive the strategic option of its choice (low cost, differentiation, or focus) for value creation/success. This flow is presented in Figure 1.

TALENT MANAGEMENT & SUSTAINABLE COMPETITIVE ADVANTAGE

Studies in strategic management affirm that good talent management is the common denominator in sustainable competitive advantage (Aggarwal, 2006; Collings & Mellahi, 2009; Farndale et al., 2010; Kazlauskaite & Buciuniene, 2008; Lawler, 2008; Lemerle et al., 2019; Lewis & Heckman, 2006). Good talent management plays a considerable role in determining a firm's sustainable competitive advantage and this role tends to flow from talent management's uniqueness and its not-so-easily replicable or imitable nature (Dewhurst et al., 2013; Khavul et al., 2010; Lemerle, et al., 2019). Competition is endemic and the playing field has been considerably leveled by the prevalence of technology that is converging and making it easier, cheaper, and faster to collect data, connect diverse data points, analyze them, and take action. The only true and dependable organizational performance differentiator, in the long run, is the firm's human capital.

The quality of human capital and how it is managed has also been cited as a factor in the competitiveness of nations. In his seminal work on the competitive advantage of nations, Michael Porter (1990) introduced the 'diamond of national competitiveness,' which had four elements that determine the competitive strengths and weaknesses of countries. These elements are factor conditions (among which are skilled human capital), demand conditions, related and supporting industries, firm strategy, structure, and rivalry. A lot of research work has been carried out on Porter's original output, and this has led to different observations on the diamond factors (Hanafi et al., 2017; Sigalas et al., 2013; Wilson et al., 2014; Yoyo et al., 2014). However, the role of skilled human capital as a factor in the competitiveness of nations has never been disputed by the different research efforts.

Coming back to organizations, if a firm's human capital is its most dependable organizational performance differentiator, how then do firms go about making talent management a source of sustainable competitive advantage in practical ways? The resource-based view (RBV) of competitive advantage provides a framework to analyze how firms leverage talent management as a source of sustainable competitive advantage. Underlining this approach is the imperative on the part of the firm to seek a thoughtful and in-depth understanding of its resources and capabilities so that it would pursue a strategy that exploits its core strengths and competencies as well as provide a basis for developing its resources and capabilities for long-term success. This is an internally focused strategy that must be used in conjunction with the externally focused competitive advantage strategic tools that have dominated organizational literature for quite some time—examples include Porter's Five Forces, PESTLE Analysis, and Value Chain Analysis. Donnellan and Rutledge (2019) note that in the last two decades, "The emphasis in the strategic management literature has shifted from viewing advantage as primarily determined by environmental (industry/market) factors to an RBV that highlights how the deployment of unique and idiosyncratic organizational resources and capabilities can result in sustained superior performance. Underlying this shift is the recognition that sustained competitive advantage grows out of those valuable, income-generating, firm-specific resources and capabilities that cannot easily be imitated or substituted." (p. 730). Strategic management studies are considerably aligned on the fact that an organization's sustained competitive advantage and performance over time draw from its exploitation of opportunities in its macro-environment, as well as leveraging the strength and quality of its internal resources and capabilities (David & David, 2015; Egbunike & Okerekeoti, 2018; Volberda et al., 2011; Purwanto, E., & Purwanto, A. D. B., 2020).

According to RBV, an organization's internal resources that are valuable, rare, inimitable, and non-substitutable (Barney, 1991) enable the organization to develop a sustainable competitive advantage that produces superior marketplace success. Resources are **valuable** when they improve the organization's efficiency and effectiveness, as well as reduce its competitive weaknesses; **rare** if they are unique and not easily available to other competing organizations; **inimitable** if they are hard to imitate or duplicate by competitors, and **non-substitutable** if they cannot be substituted by any other available, equivalent resources that are themselves not rare or imitable. The thought process underpinning the RBV's connection with a sustainable competitive advantage, which hinges on the firm's resources or capabilities being valuable, rare, inimitable, and non-substitutable, is depicted in Figure 2.

Collings and Mellahi (2009) state, "The resources and capabilities that underpin firms' competitive advantage are directly tied to the capabilities of talented individuals who make up the firm's human capital pool" (p. 305). So many research efforts have been directed at analyzing the nature of resources and capabilities in organizations (Edwards, 2014; Fung, 2019; Madhani, 2010; Simon & Bartle, 2012). Here, the author adopts the most general classification of ***tangibles*** (financial, physical, technological, organizational, etc.) and ***intangibles*** (human/talent, culture, innovation, reputational, etc.). Strategic talent management falls under the intangible category and, in consonance with RBV, can be approached to gain a competitive advantage (Boudreau, & Ramstad, 2005).

Figure 2. The valuable, rareness, inimitability, and non-substitutability framework of RBV
Source: Adapted from Donnellan & Rutledge, (2019, p. 731)

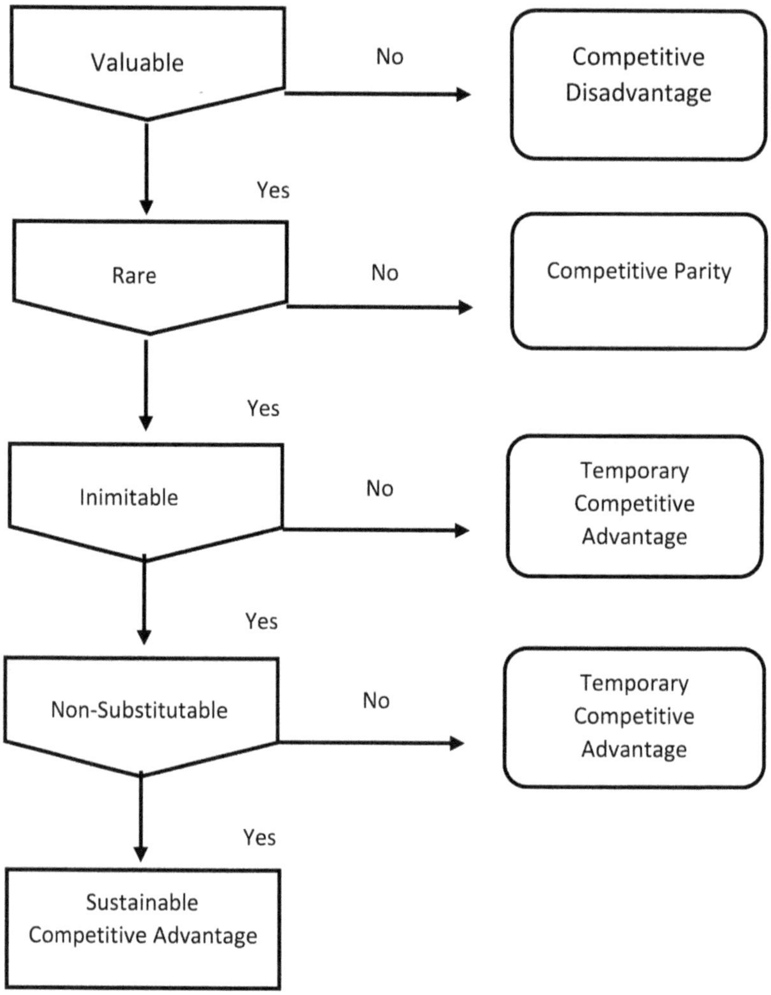

Leveraging the RBV framework, strategic talent management can be made to engender sustainable competitive advantage by ensuring that talent management, as a process, is constructed through the lenses of RBV's criteria: "*valuable, rare, inimitable and non-substitutable*" *(VRIN)*. Talent management needs to be construed and operationalized as a differentiating strategic capability that translates into a real and substantial competitive advantage. This starts with the organization identifying the core competencies that distinguish it in the marketplace and then lining up its

(VRIN) talent management process(es) for a sustainable competitive advantage. This thought process is represented in the framework shown in Figure 3.

In this framework, talent management is viewed both at the aggregate level and the sub-processes level. The goal is to have the organization's talent management process envisioned and operationalized based on how each of the sub-processes speaks to the RBV criteria (valuable, rare, inimitable, and non-substitutable) and in turn, continually strengthen the core competencies of the organization. This is therefore a generic framework that each organization would adapt to its peculiar circumstances in cognizance of the competitive factors at play in the organization's business and labor markets. Sustainable competitive advantage is required for enduring success in the marketplace and given the endemic nature of change and disruption in contemporary times, continuous improvement and innovation would be required in talent management systems for any competitive advantage to be preservable by organizations.

Figure 3. Strategic talent management as a source of sustainable competitive advantage

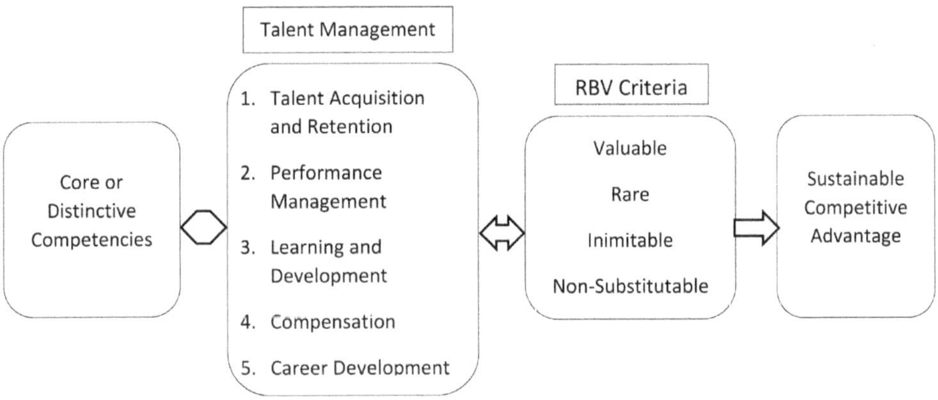

APPLYING THE FRAMEWORK TO YOUR ORGANIZATION

The goal here is to use the talent management framework shown in Figure 3 to facilitate conversations by organizational leadership in order to activate the kind of talent management contribution that will be instrumental to having and maintaining a sustainable competitive advantage, the utility of which is measured by superior performance in the marketplace. The approach adopted by the author is not to provide a prescriptive full-blown "workbook" or "template," but a tool for analysis, using questions to drill into the essence of each element. At a philosophical level of articulation, when examining talent management as a process relative to the RBV variables, there is a fundamental question that should be asked before getting into analysis at the sub-process level. This question is: "*Can strategic talent management be "valuable," "rare," "inimitable," and "non-substitutable?"* The answer is "yes," though the degree may vary from variable to variable, particularly in acknowledgment of the different dynamics at play in varying industries/sectors and labor markets (Elbanna & Abdel-Maksoud, 2020). A point to note however is that "The VRIN resource characteristics are individually necessary, but not sufficient for a sustained competitive advantage" (Srivastava et al., 2013). For a sustainable competitive advantage to occur, the organization's talent management process has to reflect a minimum combination of the variables. Talaja (2012) states, "The value and rarity of resources are necessary conditions for achieving competitive advantage; however, for achieving sustainable competitive advantage, resources also have to be imperfectly imitable and not substitutable" (p. 54).

Table 1 shows a sample of questions that organizational leaders can use in framing discussions on each talent management sub-process relative to the RBV (VRIN) criteria. A critical tool that would help in this analysis is Human Capital Analytics (HCA). HCA capability supported by digital technology will be required by leaders to be able to make better, faster, and more data-driven talent decisions that are in consonance with the business strategy. HCA enables the measurement of a spectrum of human capital metrics from which critical insights about an organization's talent, both on an as-is, as well as predictive bases, can be gleaned (Minbaeva, 2018; Schiemann et al., 2018; Stoian & Tohanean, 2019).

OBSTACLES AND CHALLENGES

In the age of disruption, there have been insinuations that no competitive advantage can actually be deemed sustainable given the challenges of maintaining such sustainability in the face of very dynamic, and sometimes, intractable factors. Many erstwhile big companies that had "sustainable competitive advantages" have disappeared due to unstoppable headwinds from competitors and new disruptive entrants. Key challenges in preserving an organization's competitive advantage in contemporary times include:

- The pace of technological evolution and adoption
- Evolving markets
- Well-informed buyers arising from the democratization of knowledge and information access
- Changing social norms

Table 1. Mapping of talent management processes to RBV and sustainable competitive advantage

Talent Management Process	Aspirational Goal of the Organization	RBV Criterion (VRIN) Implications	Resultant Activities	Sustainable Competitive Advantage Implication (Output, Outcome & Impact)
Talent Acquisition and Retention	What is the specific/unique goal that the organization needs to achieve in talent identification, acquisition, and retention, relative to the core competencies that the organization needs to have, consolidate or develop?	What does each of the following mean relative to the goal? • Valuable • Rare • Inimitable • Non-Substitutable	What Specific activities must the organization undertake to deliver on the goal? E.g.: • Defining the most valuable positions that influence competitive advantage. • Defining the skills (organizational, team and individual levels) that align with the organization's core competencies and culture. • Quality screening/Rigorous selection process, etc.	This is the "measurement & evaluation" aspect where organizational leadership gauges the results against goals/targets with respect to outputs, outcomes, and impact.
Performance Management (PM)	Identify the clear linkages between the organization's PM and - • Its core competencies/ capabilities? • Its core values and strategic business goals? • Employees' career development? • Engendering individual and group productivity? • Fostering communication between managers and employees?	To what extent can the organization's Performance Management practices outlined in the previous column be described as: • Valuable • Rare • Inimitable • Non-Substitutable	1. What specific ongoing activities must the organization be focusing on to ensure the goals in the linkages identified in column 2 are realized? 2. How do such activities continue to mature in quality, bearing the VRIN variables in column 3 in mind?	What output, outcomes, and impact measures will the organization adopt in ensuring an effective calibration of efforts and results with respect to the organization's performance management processes/practices contributing to its sustainable competitive advantage?
Learning and Development (L & D)	What is the specific/unique goal that the organization needs to achieve in talent development, relative to: a. The core competencies that the organization needs to have, consolidate, or develop? b. Delivery of the strategic business objectives? How does the organization ingrain a learning culture that helps employees keep their skills and knowledge at the edge of innovation in the industry?	To what extent are the organization's L & D strategies and tactics (from a process and outcomes point of view) characterized by the VRIN factors of: • Valuable • Rare • Inimitable • Non-Substitutable	What specific L & D processes and/or interventions, with appropriate resource allocation, should the organization be carrying out?	What output, outcomes and impact measures will the organization adopt in ensuring an effective calibration of efforts and results with respect to the organization's Learning and Development interventions and processes that feed its: • Sustainable competitive advantage? • Organizational performance? • Employee satisfaction?
Compensation	Identify the clear linkages between the organization's compensation strategy and - • Attraction and retention of the right employees? • Developing and entrenching its core competencies/ capabilities? • Its core values, culture, and strategic business goals? • Motivation towards higher individual and group productivity/ innovation?	To what extent are the organization's compensation strategies and tactics (from a process and outcomes point of view) characterized by the VRIN factors of: • Valuable • Rare • Inimitable • Non-Substitutable	What specific compensation policies, design, processes, and interventions should the organization be carrying out in consonance with its goal aspirations and VRIN characteristics?	What metrics will organizational leadership be tracking to ensure that its compensation strategy is enabling/ enhancing the development of the organization's core capabilities, attracting, motivating and retaining of talent, high productivity of employees, pay for performance, and return on investment in the marketplace.

continues on following page

Table 1. Continued

Talent Management Process	Aspirational Goal of the Organization	RBV Criterion (VRIN) Implications	Resultant Activities	Sustainable Competitive Advantage Implication (Output, Outcome & Impact)
Career Development	What is the organization's philosophy with regard to the career development of its employees? How are the career development processes and practices linked with developing the core competencies/ capabilities of the enterprise? How are the career development processes and practices geared towards harnessing employees' full potential as well as their retention?	What is the organization doing in career management/ development that can be said to be? • Valuable • Rare • Inimitable • Non-Substitutable	What specifically is the organization doing in properly calibrating potential? How are work, assignments, and learning balanced for optimal career development outcomes for employees?	Strategic career development focuses on ingraining resilience in the organization to enable it to survive in the age of high innovation, disruption, and change. What leading and lagging indicators will the organization track to ensure that career development practices in the organization are enabling business success as well as consolidating sustainable competitive advantage?
Succession Planning	Identify the clear linkages between the organization's succession management strategy and - • Assurance of the likelihood of the organization having a supply of appropriately qualified individuals (with right skills and motivation) for current and future job roles. • Enhancement of the organization's Employee Value Proposition • Improvement of business results and capacity to meet expansion and growth needs.	How do the succession management practices in the organization carry the qualities of: • Valuable • Rare • Inimitable • Non-Substitutable	Activities include position identification, identifying key role requirements, calibrating potential, matching talent to tasks/positions, cross-training employees and assessing progress, integrating of succession plans into hiring strategy.	What leading and lagging indicators will the organization track to ensure that succession management practices in the organization are enabling business success as well as consolidating sustainable competitive advantage? Organizations would consider indices like bench strength, diversity, and other program effectiveness indicators.

- Lack of differentiation in competencies, products, and services
- An increased potential of the emergence of a different and unique type of competition as a result of all or some of the factors above

This should not discourage organizational leaders from determining their core competencies and sources of competitive advantages, and exploiting them; the alternative will be extinction without trying. The author's advice for organizational leaders is to ensure that more rigor is applied in the organizations' strategy discussions and to also create a cadence of strategy sessions that enable the leadership to realistically interrogate on an ongoing basis, the internal and external data that feed the organization's sustainable competitive advantage strategies.

RECOMMENDATION

A key point to note is that excellence in talent management strategies and practices cannot be pursued in isolation from other Human Resource Management processes in the organization. Competitive success through people cannot be achieved by deepening an organization's fluency in talent management alone; on account of their interrelatedness, focus must be put on the entire ecosystem of people management practices. It is only by so doing that the advantage that good talent management strategies and processes give the organization in its quest for sustained competitive advantage can be realized and preserved. It is in this regard that the author would like to recommend the *Thirteen Practices for Managing People,* which Pfeffer (1995) laid out for organizations based on his extensive studies. These thirteen practices are summarized in Table 2.

Table 2. Thirteen practices for managing people

	Practice	Summary
1	Employment Security	An organization's enduring commitment to its workforce signals employment security, which elicits reciprocal loyalty from employees. The converse is also true.
2	Selectivity in Recruiting	Organizations should ensure effective recruitment processes so that the right talent is brought into the enterprise; thorough recruitment processes also have a signaling effect in terms of the seriousness of the company (For example, it signals expectation of high performance and that people matter in the company.).
3	High Wages	Pay is definitely a key consideration for people in accepting employment offers; though not absolutely, always necessary, high wages will attract more applicants to a hiring organization. High wages send a message about how the organization values its people.

continues on following page

Table 2. Continued

	Practice	Summary
4	Incentive Pay	Notwithstanding the tendency by some organizations to over-rely on money to solve human motivation problems, rewarding high performance with contingent compensation is advised in order to retain highly talented employees.
5	Employee Ownership	Employee ownership engenders alignment of the employees' interests with shareholders'; it also makes employees take a longer-term view of the firm.
6	Information Sharing	Access to information that is necessary to be successful must be made available to employees if they are to be truly a source of competitive advantage.
7	Participation and Empowerment	There is a need to encourage the decentralization of decision-making to enable broader employee participation in determining issues pertaining to their own work processes. Such participation elicits employee satisfaction and productivity.
8	Self-Managed Teams	Efforts must be made by organizations to effectively harness the energy of teamwork because of the value that peer monitoring and expectations of co-workers bring to bear on work outcomes.
9	Training and Skill Development	Organizations should not only be strategic and intentional in their training and development efforts but should also ensure that the structures and processes in the organization are not inimical to employees utilizing the skills they obtain from training and development programs.
10	Cross-Utilization and Cross-Training	Exposing employees to multiple competencies is motivational for them; moving them around to different jobs allows transparency in work processes and enables the potential for newcomers to a job to see improvement opportunities that experienced employees might not see.
11	Symbolic Egalitarianism	The counsel here is that organizations get the best out of their workforce when they reduce or eliminate symbols that separate people from one another. Their removal signals comparative equality within the workforce, moderates the "us" versus "them" thinking, and fosters mutuality in goal pursuit.
12	Wage Compression	Tasks in organizations are becoming more interdependent, thereby necessitating more cooperation in accomplishing work. Pay compression is advised because it helps to reduce interpersonal competition while enhancing cooperation, and in the process catalyzing efficiency gains.
13	Promotion from Within	This element is a necessary adjunct to many of the practices already described; when adopted, it binds workers and organizations, promoting trust across organizational strata.

Content Source: Pfeffer, J. Producing sustainable competitive advantage through the effective management of people (1995).

The thirteen described elements might not be exhaustive; the full definition/meaning or implication and relative importance of each may be debatable in different geographies and labor markets, but Pfeffer's (1995) effort is a good start. Further research can fine-tune the elements and add or eliminate some, depending on what further empirical data impels.

CONCLUSION

In this chapter, the author focused on how, in practical terms, organizations can leverage the Resource-Based View (a model that sees resources as crucial to superior firm performance) in deepening their talent management practices toward the development of sustainable competitive advantage for their organizations. A framework was recommended for organizational leadership to facilitate their conversations around building clear linkages among elements of their talent management practices, the organization's core capabilities/competencies, and its sustainable competitive advantage and superior performance. The measures of RBV's VRIN elements are not easily quantifiable, but qualitative descriptions are a good start in framing what is valuable, rare, inimitable, and non-substitutable. Exploration of my rigorous or standardized measures can be an area for further research.

REFERENCES

Aggarwal, D. (2006). *Strategic approach of HR – Managing the Talent Pipe line*. Netkode Solution Pvt. Ltd. https://ww.netkode.com/whitepapers/Strategic_Approach.pdf

Ali, M. M. (2017). Testing hypothesis on theory of social networking, community banking and empowerment of people: A conceptual view. *Psychology and Behavioral Sciences.*, *6*(5), 96–104. doi:10.11648/j.pbs.20170605.14

Ali, M. M. (2019). The Strategic Role of Human Resources Planning to Achieve Sustainable Competitive Advantage. *Електронно списание. Dialog*, (2), 1–13.

Barney, J. (1991). Firm resources and sustained competitive advantage. *Journal of Management, 17*(1), 99–120. doi:10.1177/014920639101700108

Boudreau, J. W., & Ramstad, P. M. (2005). Talentship, talent segmentation, and sustainability: A new HR decision science paradigm for a new strategy definition. *Human Resource Management, 44*(2), 129–136.

Clulow, V., Gerstman, J., & Barry, C. (2003). The resource-based view and sustainable competitive advantage: The case of a financial services firm. *Journal of European Industrial Training*, *27*(5), 220–232. doi:10.1108/03090590310469605

Collings, D. G., & Mellahi, K. (2009). Strategic talent management: A review and research agenda. *Human Resource Management Review*, *19*(4), 304–313. doi:10.1016/j.hrmr.2009.04.001

David, F. R., & David, F. R. (2015). Strategic Management: Concepts and Cases (15th ed.). Harlow.

Dewhurst, M., Hancock, B., & Ellsworth, D. (2013). Redesigning knowledge work: How to free-up high-end experts to do what they do best. *Harvard Business Review, 91*(1), 58–64.

Donnellan, J., & Rutledge, W. L. (2019). A case for resource-based view and competitive advantage in banking. *Managerial and Decision Economics, 40*(6), 728–737. doi:10.1002/mde.3041

Edwards, J. (2014). *Mastering Strategic Management*. BCcampus. https://opentextbc.ca/strategicmanagement/

Egbunike, C. F., & Okerekeoti, C. U. (2018). Macroeconomic factors, firm characteristics, and financial performance: A study of selected quoted manufacturing firms in Nigeria. *Asian Journal of Accounting Research, 3*(2), 142–168. doi:10.1108/AJAR-09-2018-0029

Elbanna, S., & Abdel-Maksoud, A. (2020). Organizational resources and performance: The case of an oil-rich country. *Public Performance & Management Review, 43*(3), 713–739. doi:10.1080/15309576.2019.1660187

Fareed, M., Noor, W. S., Isa, M. F., & Salleh, S. S. (2016). Developing human capital for sustainable competitive advantage: The roles of organizational culture and high-performance work system. *Journal of Economic & Management Perspectives, 10*(4), 655–673.

Farndale, E., Scullion, H., & Sparrow, P. (2010). The role of the corporate HR function in global talent management. *Journal of World Business, 45*(2), 161–168. doi:10.1016/j.jwb.2009.09.012

Ferreira, J. J., Fernandes, C. I., & Ferreira, F. A. (2019). To be or not to be digital, that is the question: Firm innovation and performance. *Journal of Business Research, 101*, 583–590. doi:10.1016/j.jbusres.2018.11.013

Fung, M. K. (2019). Fraudulent financial reporting and technological capability in the information technology sector: A resource-based perspective. *Journal of Business Ethics, 156*(2), 577–589. doi:10.100710551-017-3605-4

Hanafi, M., Wibisono, D., Mangkusubroto, K., Siallagan, M., & Badriyah, M. J. K. (2017). Modelling competitive advantage of nation: A literature review. *Competitiveness Review, 27*(4), 335–365. doi:10.1108/CR-06-2016-0031

Hanif, R., Masood, A., & Azhar, S. (2013). Strategic Talent Management as Source of Competitive Advantage Talent Competitiveness Framework. SSRN *2240400 Electronic Journal* doi:10.2139/ssrn.2240400

Hans, S. (2021). Strategic Human Resource Management and Employee Relationship Management: An Approach for Realizing Sustainable Competitive Advantage. *IUP Journal of Organizational Behavior, 20*(4).

Kabwe, C., & Okorie, C. (2019). The efficacy of talent management in international business: The case of European multinationals. *Thunderbird International Business Review, 61*(6), 857–872. doi:10.1002/tie.22090

Kazlauskaite, R., & Buciuniene, I. (2008). The role of human resources and their management in the establishment of sustainable competitive advantage. *Inžinerinė ekonomika*, (5), 78–84.

Khan, S. Z., Yang, Q., & Waheed, A. (2019). Investment in intangible resources and capabilities spurs sustainable competitive advantage and firm performance. *Corporate Social Responsibility and Environmental Management, 26*(2), 285–295. doi:10.1002/csr.1678

Khavul, S., Benson, G. S., & Datta, D. K. (2010). Is internationalization associated with investments in HRM? A study of entrepreneurial firms in emerging markets. *Human Resource Management, 49*(4), 693–713. doi:10.1002/hrm.20367

Knudsen, E. S., Lien, L. B., Timmermans, B., Belik, I., & Pandey, S. (2021). Stability in turbulent times? The effect of digitalization on the sustainability of competitive advantage. *Journal of Business Research, 128*, 360–369. doi:10.1016/j.jbusres.2021.02.008

Krishnan, K. (2019). *3 Vital Skills for the Age of Disruption.* World Economic Forum. https://www.weforum.org/agenda/2019/09/3-vital-skills-for-the-age-of-disruption/

Latukha, M. (2015). Talent management in Russian companies: Domestic challenges and international experience. *The International Journal of Human Resource Management, 26*(8), 1051–1075. doi:.2014.922598 doi:10.1080/09585192

Latukha, M. O. (2018). Can talent management practices be considered as a basis for sustainable competitive advantages in emerging-market firms? Evidence from Russia. *Thunderbird International Business Review, 60*(1), 69–87. doi:10.1002/tie.21778

Lawler, E. E. (2008). *Make human capital a source of competitive advantage.* Marshall School of Business Working Paper No. MOR, 16–09. doi:10.1016/j.orgdyn.2008.10.007

Leach, B. (2018). Sustainable competitive advantage and demographic change. *Canadian Manager*, *43*(2), 19–21.

Lemerle, M., Rudisuli, R., & Steinert, M. (2019). *Talent in wholesale banking: Building a sustainable competitive advantage*. McKinsey Insights. https://www.mckinsey.com/industries/ financial-services/our-insights/talent-in-wholesale-banking-building-a-sustainable-competitive-advantage

Lewis, R. E., & Heckman, R. J. (2006). Talent management: A critical review. *Human Resource Management Review*, *16*(2), 139–154. doi:10.1016/j.hrmr.2006.03.001

Madhani, P. M. (2010). *Resource based view of competitive advantage: an overview. ICFAI business school.* Icfai University Press. http://www.researchgate.net

Mellahi, K., & Collings, D. G. (2010). The barriers to effective global talent management: The example of corporate elites in MNEs. *Journal of World Business*, *45*(2), 143–149. doi:10.1016/j.jwb.2009.09.018

Minbaeva, D. B. (2018). Building credible human capital analytics for organizational competitive advantage. *Human Resource Management*, *57*(3), 701–713. doi:10.1002/hrm.21848

Pfeffer, J. (1995). Producing sustainable competitive advantage through the effective management of people. *Academy of Management Executive, 9*(1), 55–69. 10.5465/AME.2005.19417910

Porter, M. E. (1990). The Competitive Advantage of Nations. (Cover story). *Harvard Business Review*, *68*(2), 73–93.

Purwanto, E., & Purwanto, A. D. B. (2020). An investigative study on sustainable competitive advantage of manufacture companies in Indonesia. *Business: Theory and Practice*, *21*(2), 633–642. doi:10.3846/btp.2020.12256

Saravanan, K. (2017). Sources of Sustainable Competitive Advantage: A Study & Industry Outlook. *St. Theresa. Journal of the Humanities and Social Sciences*, *3*(1).

Schiemann, W. A., Seibert, J. H., & Blankenship, M. H. (2018). Putting human capital analytics to work: Predicting and driving business success. *Human Resource Management*, *57*(3), 795–807. doi:10.1002/hrm.21843

Sigalas, C., Economou, V. P., & Georgopoulos, N. B. (2013). Developing a measure of competitive advantage. *Journal of Strategy and Management*, *6*(4), 320–334. doi:10.1108/JSMA-03-2013-0015

Sikora, D. M., Thompson, K. W., Russell, Z. A., & Ferris, G. R. (2016). Reimagining overqualified human resources to promote organizational effectiveness and competitive advantage. *Journal of Organizational Effectiveness: People and Performance*, *3*(1), 23–42. doi:10.1108/JOEPP-03-2015-0012

Simon, A., & Bartle, C. (2012). Resources, Capabilities, and Business Success. In Service Science Research, Strategy and Innovation: Dynamic Knowledge Management Methods (pp. 304-324). IGI Global. doi:10.4018/978-1-4666-0077-5.ch018

Skuza, A., Scullion, H., & McDonnel, A. (2013). An analysis of the talent management challenges in a post-communist country: The case of Poland. *International Journal of Human Resource Management*, *24*(3), 453–470. doi:10.1080/09585192.2012.694111

Sousa, M. J., & Rocha, Á. (2019). Strategic knowledge management in the digital age: JBR special issue editorial. *Journal of Business Research, 94,* 223–226. 10.1016/j.jbusres.2018.10.016

Srivastava, M., Franklin, A., & Martinette, L. (2013). Building a sustainable competitive advantage. *Journal of Technology Management & Innovation*, *8*(2), 47–60. doi:10.4067/S0718-27242013000200004

Stoian, C. A., & Tohanean, D. (2019, November). BMI in the digital era: Competitive advantage through human capital analytics. In *ECMLG 2019 15th European Conference on Management, Leadership & Governance* (p. 366). Academic Conferences and Publishing Limited. 10.34190/MLG.19.075

Talaja, A. (2012). Testing VRIN framework: Resource value and rareness as sources of competitive advantage and above average performance. *Management*, *17*(2), 51–64.

Vinayan, G., Jayashree, S., & Marthandan, G. (2012). Critical success factors of sustainable competitive advantage: A study in Malaysian manufacturing industries. *International Journal of Business and Management*, *7*(22), 29–45. doi:10.5539/ijbm.v7n22p29

Volberda, H. W., Morgan, R. E., Reinmoeller, P., Hitt, M. A., Ireland, R. D., & Hoskisson, R. E. (2011). *Strategic Management: Competitiveness and Globalization (Concepts & Cases)*. Cengage Learning.

Wilson, T. L., Lindbergh, L., & Graff, J. (2014). The Competitive Advantage of Nations 20 Years Later: The Cases of Sweden, South Korea and the USA. *Competitiveness Review*, *24*(4), 306. doi:10.1108/CR-11-2012-0027

Yoganathan, V., Osburg, V. S., & Bartikowski, B. (2021). Building better employer brands through employee social media competence and online social capital. *Psychology and Marketing*, *38*(3), 524–536. doi:10.1002/mar.21451

Yoyo, T., Daryanto, A., Gumbira-Sa'id, E., & Hasan, M. F. (2014). Competitiveness model and gap analysis of Indonesian palm oil-based fatty acid and fatty alcohol industry. *Journal of Economics and Finance*, *6*(2), 218–225.

KEY TERMS AND DEFINITIONS

Capability: The power or ability of a person, group, or organization to do something.

Competitiveness: Possession of the desire and ability to outperform comparable people organizations.

Core Competencies: The capabilities that an organization develops and deploys exceptionally well to achieve competitive success.

Human Capital: The value accruing from the education, training, skills, experience, competencies, health, and positive attitudes of an organization's employees.

Human Capital Analytics: A methodology of generating insights on how human capital contributes to successful organizational outcomes.

Organizational Leadership: A strategy to direct and coordinate individuals and groups within an organization towards the attainment of its goals or mission.

Resource-Based View: A managerial framework that focuses on an organization's strategic resources which it can exploit towards sustainable competitive advantage.

Resources: The assets, processes, systems, attributes, and knowledge that a firm owns or to which it has access, for the framing and implementation of its competitive strategies.

Social Capital: The social relationships, networks, shared norms, and values that catalyze cooperation within or among groups for the economic growth of an organization.

Chapter 4
Strategic Human Resource Management:
Shaping Human Capital Development and Creative Work Behavior

Okechukwu Ethelbert Amah
Pan Atlantic University, Nigeria

ABSTRACT

The chapter explored the evolution of human resources management to position strategic human resources management (SHRM), human capital development (HCD), and employee behavior, such as creative work behavior, as important variables required by organizations to survive in challenging environments. It argued that the alignment of the fits between SHRM and business strategy and between SHRM and HCD positions employees as sources of organizations' competitive advantage and drives positive and innovative employee behavior required in the business challenging environments faced by organizations. The chapter discussed a study done with samples from knowledge workers to establish the relationship between SHRM, HCD, and creative work behavior. Results showed that SHRM had a direct relationship with HCD and an indirect relationship with CWB through HCD. There was no direct relationship between SHRM and CWB. Implications of the study and future research were recommended.

DOI: 10.4018/978-1-6684-3894-7.ch004

INTRODUCTION

Globalization and, lately, COVID-19 have created various challenges to organizations because of the frequency of changes involved (Wijenayaka, 2021). To handle these challenges, organizations must develop interesting business strategies and align them with their human resources strategies to build a sustainable competitive advantage that positions them above their peers (April & Chum, 2005). Business strategy is how an organization plans to be relevant in its environment. Thus, the link between business strategy and human resources strategy is developing a competitive advantage (Gunnigle & Moore, 1994).

Sustainable competitive advantage is long-term and enables the organization to stay above its peers. To achieve this, competitive advantage must satisfy four criteria: valuable, rare, inimitable, and non-substitutable (Ford, 2021). Resources and competencies are a broad category of organizational assets confer competitive advantage (Barney, 1991). However, for sustained competitive advantage, the resource-based value theory stipulates that the human capital available to the business confers this (Boudreau & Ramstad, 2005; Boxall & Purcell, 2003; Gratton et al., 2000). Since People handle the success of all aspects of the business strategy, they are essential in guaranteeing sustainable competitive advantage (Inyang, 2010; Khan, 2010). For example, Duke II and Udono (2012) posited that people set the directions for the organization and manage various resources to get to the direction set.

Terms that have appeared in the modern approach to managing human resources include human resources management (HRM), human capital development HCD), and strategic human resources management (SHRM). How these terms interact and affect the behavior and effectiveness of employees in driving business strategy and goals have taken the attention of researchers (Rotich, 2015). Hence, past studies have called for the review of the interaction among SHRM, HCD, and employee behavior, such as employee creative work behavior (CWB) (Emeagwal & Ogbonmwan, 2018; Hsu & Wang, 2012). Thus, the book chapter discussed an empirical study that used samples from knowledge workers to establish the link between SHRM and employee creative work behavior and the role that human capital development played in the link. The study used resource-based value, social exchange, and norm of reciprocity theories to justify the relationships stipulated. Before discussing the study, the book chapter reviewed the evolution of human resources management, terms SHRM, CWB, and HCD, to identify research gaps.

LITERATURE REVIEW

The Evolution of Human Resources Management

The essence of this section is not to go into the details of the evolution of HRM since this would involve describing the evolution of management thoughts. The section clearly shows how evolutionary trends revealed a link between the terms HRM, HCD, and SHRM used in the modern-day management of people in the organization. People management has passed through evolutionary trends (Manashree, 2021). In the 19th-century, the personnel department, whose responsibility was to determine and control the cost of the human side of the business, handled people management. Organizations evaluated personnel managers by how far they controlled cost and not how effectively they managed the performance of human resources. Organizations saw human resources as a factor of production like any other factor, but not as a factor that confers competitive advantage. Human resources took center stage in organizations during the human relations era in the 20th Century (Nankervis et al., 2007). Organizations realize human resources are the most important resources a business can have and deserve to be effectively managed. This gave rise to human resources management (HRM). HRM went beyond cost control into ascertaining what enhances the productivity of people and the provision of these. Guest (1987) saw personnel management as short-term/reactive, drives compliance, creates low trust environment, needs specialized people, and involves cost minimization, while HRM is long-term, proactive, drive commitment, creates high trust relationship, integrated into line management, and maximizes utilization of people. The HRM era saw the introduction of human capital development to manage the organization's human capital. This era showed the realization that the human capital in an organization is the totality of the assets of the employees of the organization. Human capital development became a means to ensure that all the assets possessed by the human capital are effectively managed and harnessed for the productivity of the individual and the organization. The infusion of HRM into the overall business strategy gave rise to strategic human resources management (SHRM). Rotich (2015) summarized the evolution of HRM as follows (p. 60):

- Stage one (1900–the mid-1970s): Administration stage and welfare stages (Personnel management)
- Stage two (the mid-1970s–late 1990s): Human resource management and human capital development Stage three (beyond the late 1990s): Strategic human resource management (SHRM) stage
- Stage four (Beyond 2000): SHRM into the future

Stage four concentrates on how infusing HRM into the business strategy (SHRM) drives the development of human capital and ultimately affects the behavior of employees and organizational productivity. Dowling and Roots (2009) saw the future of SHRM as how to improve optimization and performance using new thoughts in human capital development. This will entail that HR professionals must understand the business environment and the challenges their industries face and craft a strategy to develop human capital to drive consistent superior performance and sustain organizational competitive advantage (Holdsworth & Lundgaard, 2009; Wilson, 2009). Globalization has further complicated human resources management because, as Erwee (2003) and Dowling and Roots (2009) stated, SHRM must balance the organizations' global, local, and industry-specific needs.

Human Capital and Human Capital Development

Human capital (HC) is the economic value of workers' experiences, comprising education, training, intelligence, skills, health, loyalty, and punctuality" (Kenton, 2020, p.1). It is intangible and cannot be captured in the business's balance sheet. The higher the investment in HC, the better the HC and the more productive it becomes (Bruce-Lockhart, 2019). All the HC of an organization do not have the same quality and usefulness. It is possible to calculate HC's value, profit, and rate of return on investment (Sawalha, 2014). When there is no investment made to make HC relevant to the organization's current situation, it can depreciate. For example, when an organization adopts a digital strategy, an HC that could not upgrade becomes obsolete and depreciate. Organizations use their human capital development practices (HCD) to ensure the relevance of their HC in their environments.

Human Capital Development is a set of practices whose "goal is to achieve organizational competence for workforce acquisition, management, and optimization" (Ghosh, 2021, p.1). This definition highlights that HCD involves practices that organizations use to address their needs using the right competencies in their workforce. This definition infers the link between business strategy and HCD. HCD involves managing the employees of an organization to ensure they contribute to organizational productivity. It is how organizations treat their HC to make them effective in driving their goals. The known drives of HCD are practices in leadership, accessibility to knowledge, workforce optimization, and learning capacity. These practices add value to the HC of an organization to ensure they drive superior results.

Specific trends in the 21st Century and beyond can affect HCD, and organizations must factor them into their strategy (Wijenayaka, 2021). These are the existence of both human and non-human workers (presence of robots), the influence of artificial intelligence in HCD, the importance of HR analytics in determining the contribution of the HR function, the role of digital assistants in the organizational process, and increasing use of social media and mobile equipment in recruitment. Organizations approach HCD through the best practice or best-fit approach (Choden et al., 2021). The former approach believes in practices that universally apply to all organizations and in every situation. This is the idea of the practices referred to as high-performance work practices, such as "employment security, targeted selection, high pay contingent on performance, employee training, and business information sharing" (Lewin, 2001, p. 91). The latter approach believes in having practices aligned with the organizational strategy and situation. According to Boxall and Purcell (2003), the best-fit approach is better because it considers the current strategy and context of the organization. For example, only the best fit of HCD can ensure that HC changes with principles and evolution, that only relevant careers are in organizations, and that work meets the current reality of HC and the organization. The best-fit approach also addresses the need to align organizational and HCD strategies.

Creative Work Behavior

The challenges of COVID-19 caused employees must be creative in introducing new ideas to explore the many opportunities in such an environment (Amabile *et al.*, 2005; (Rogers, 2014). Creativity is about the "complex human capacity to produce novel ideas, generate new solutions, and express oneself in a unique way" (Abraham, 2015:1). In the organizational study, creativity is understood as either a personal characteristic or a process (Amabile, 1998). Creativity gives rise to products, ideas, or procedures satisfying two conditions (George & Zhou, 2002). These conditions are that creativity must be novel/original and apply to an organization's needs. There is considerable variation in the level and outcome of creativity among individuals (Abraham, 2015). Creativity must have both originality and relevance to be important. Relevance means that creativity performs pertinent functions as required by the organization. Creative work behaviors are products of individual capacity and intentional behaviors (West & Farr, 1989). Hence, individual characteristics and activities will form a significant determinant of the antecedents of IWB. For example, Scott and Bruce (1994) established that CWB is at the intersection of the individual, leader, workgroup, and organizational context. Past studies have explored the variation of creativity with gender (see Cheung & Lau, 2010; He & Wong, 2011; Sayed & Mohamed, 2013).

Organizational researchers have categorized creativity based on the location of the drivers of engagement (external/internal) and problem types (open/closed). In the external drivers of engagement, an outside force makes employees creative, and in the internal, the individual drives creativity. Open ideas come from individuals, while closed is presented to the individual. Hence, four types of creativity can be identified (Unsworth, 2001): responsive, expected, contributory, and proactive.

Unsworth (2001) identified the preference for proactive and contributory creativity (Unsworth, 2001). For example, in a constant-changing environment such as the COVID-19, proactive and contributory creativity see changes ahead and plan for the same. Recent studies have shown that organizational contextual factors encourage creativity (Rogers, 2014). These include goals, creativity expectations, social influence, relationships with supervisors, co-workers, and organizational setting.

Strategic Human Resources Management

The HR function was initially conceived as a transactional passive standalone role in human resources management but has become strategic to enhance organizational productivity and ensure HC's sustained competitive advantage (Sullivan, 2005). There is a fusion of the business strategy and HRM strategy to form Strategic Human Resources Management (SHRM) to drive positive employee behaviors and organizational performance (Schler & Jackson, 1989). Joy and Homes (2001, p. 170) postulated that SHRM results from the alignment of the traditional HRM function of delivering results through "having the best talent in the right place, cost, and time, and business desire to have the right product in the right place and time." HRM drives the HCD and HC of organizations, and the alignment of these to the business strategy gives rise to SHRM. For example, organizations achieve effectiveness in human resources management when the traditional HR function of human resources planning is aligned with the business strategy plan. SHRM focuses on how employees' behaviors drive firm performance by developing specific HCD practices and policies aligned with business strategy to drive performance (Liao, 2005). The concept of SHRM appeared in the 1970s through the merger of corporate study and HR policies (Jackson, 1978). SHRM is defined as "the organizations' actions to align human resources management with business strategy to achieve competitive advantage through skilled, committed, and motivated employees" (Wijenayaka, 2021, p. 5). Strategic Human Resources Management (SHRM) is the "pattern of planned human resources deployment and activities intended to enable the organization to achieve its goals" (Wright & McMahan, 1992, p. 298). SHRM is the branch of people management that links the HRM (HCD and HC) strategy to the entire organizational strategy (Truss & Gratton, 1994; Wijenayaka, 2021). It does this by linking the policies and practices in HCD to the organization's growth (Sinha, 2014). In this way, it simultaneously meets the needs of the employees and the organization. A firm's human resources can play a strategic role in achieving business strategy, which points to SHRM as the nexus between business strategy and HCD strategy (Boxall, 1998; Boxall & Purcell, 2001). There are two sets of fits involved in aligning SHRM and HCD (Boxall & Purcell, 2003). The vertical/external fit is between the business strategy and each HCD practice, while the horizontal/internal fit is between the HCD practices. Past studies have articulated that organizations must achieve both fits for employees to contribute adequately to the business goals (Conner & Ulrich, 1996; Fitz-enz, 2002; Mohrman, 2007).

The works of Peters and Waterman (1982) and Porter (1980) saw competitive advantage as based on external factors, while the resources-based value of the firm looked at a competitive advantage from the internal factor of the firm (Barney, 1991; Wernerfelt, 1980). This shift has led organizations to look for sustainable competitive advantage from their internal resources. Hence, SHRM focuses on how HCD strategy can be aligned, develop a competitive edge, and drive the goals in its business strategy. Apart from the various fits, the behavioral perspective of SHRM assumes that different firm strategies require different behaviors from employees (Jackson et al., 19890 and that the success in strategy will arise when employees' behavior is aligned with the strategic intent (Cappelli & Singh, 1992; Wright & Snell, 1998). This perspective differentiates skills and behavior of human capital, with skill being only necessary and not sufficient for behavior to be noticed.

SHRM operates at the macro-level involving organizational performance and challenges instead of the micro-level that considers individual variables considered by traditional HR functions (Wijenayaka, 2021). SHRM achieves micro-level outcomes through its influence on HCD. Hence, SHRM influences organizational performance and individual employee behaviors, such as creativity, attitude, and turnover (Azmi, 2011; Delery & Doty, 1996; Gahlawat & Kundu, 2019). Thus, SHRM enhances organizations' sustainable competitive advantage by the way it develops employees' skills and motivation that ultimately leads to the achievement of goals captured in the business strategy (Lee, 2015). This means that the SHRM must achieve effective alignment of HCD practices and business strategy in such a way as to ensure that HC has the skills and elicits the behavior to achieve organizational goals (April & Chum, 2005). For example, most merger and acquisitions strategies fail because the process followed did not align with the HCD strategy (Cartwright & Cooper, 2000; Habeck *et al.*, 2000). Hence, the link between SHRM and business performance and competitive advantage is mediated by employee behavior, such as CWB and HCD. It is also likely that the HCD strategy mediates the relationship between SHRM and CWB. These relationships are shown in figure 1. The figure is a comprehensive SHRM model that accounts for the relationship among HRM (HCD and HC), business strategy, business outcome, and employee behaviors. The follow-up study used empirical research to test a part of figure 1 involving SHRM, HCD, and CWB.

Figure 1. Strategic human resources management model
Source: Wijenayaka, G. A. U. (2021, p. 6). HR strategy is necessary to underline the interactive relationship between business strategy and human resource management. Academia Letters, Article 4316. https://doi.org/10.20935/AL4316.

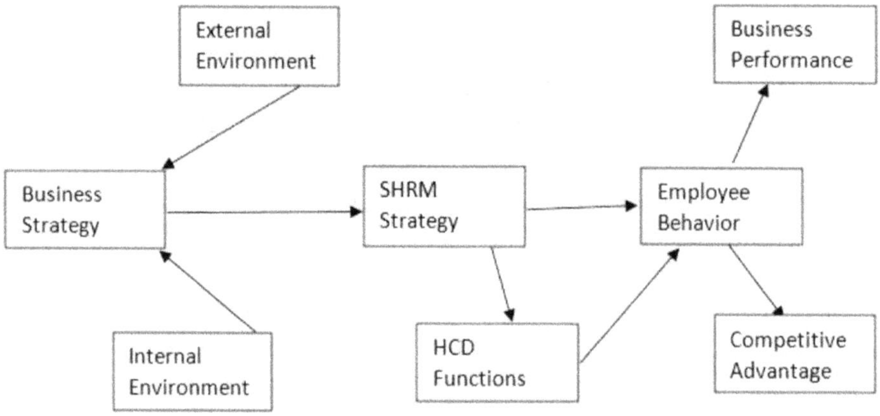

THE RELATIONSHIP BETWEEN STRATEGIC HUMAN RESOURCES MANAGEMENT AND CREATIVE WORK BEHAVIOR: THE MEDIATING ROLE OF HUMAN CAPITAL DEVELOPMENT

Background of The Study

The study was driven by the need to fill the gap identified in how SHRM plays a significant role in developing employees and ultimately enhances their behavior. SHRM, being a macro-level construct, affects the performance of the entire business and its competitive advantage (Lee, 2015). However, SHRM can also operate at the micro-level and affect employee behavior, performance (Gahlawat & Kundu, 2019), and creativity (Azmi, 2011, Delery & Doty, 1996). SHRM affects the quality of human capital because of the development policies adopted in organizations (Ahmad & Schroeder, 2003). SHRM aligns the HCD of the organization to the skills required by employees to drive business strategy (Hsu & Wang, 2012).

Theoretical Foundation and Hypotheses

The theoretical foundation for the study is the resource-based theory and social exchange theory. The resource-based view (RBV) reflects "how their resources are used and managed" in the organization (Zica, 2016, p. 435). Social exchange theory sees employees and their organization as being in a social exchange relationship. Each participant in the relationship must provide a social exchange currency that is exchanged to maintain the relationship (Blau, 1964). For example, the various components of SHRM and HCD make up social exchange currencies provided by the organization, which employees value; hence employees reciprocate with positive work behavior that enhances the organization's performance.

According to firms' resource-based theory, organizations with strategic resources that are rare, valuable, non-substitutable, and difficult to imitate can develop a sustainable competitive advantage over others. Strategic resources enhance organizational capability that can lead to superior performance. That SHRM provides a link between HRM and strategy, coupled with the fact that organizations place human resources as strategic resources, points to a link between SHRM and HCD and employee behavior represented as CWB in this study.

SHRM aims to encourage techniques that drive employee development and positive behavior (Jackson *et al.*, 2014). In HCD, the organizations provide training that enhances their skills, career planning, professional development, and competitive compensation and benefits, and this is done consistently through the plans that become SHRM. SHRM involves developing practices and implementing them to effect positive attitudes among employees (Emeagwal & Ogbonmwan, 2018). By providing skills and other desired individual benefits, SHRM creates a positive relationship between individuals who benefit from these and the organization based on the social exchange theory (Blau, 1964; Dessler, 2011; Mayhew, 2018).

Figure 2. Hypothesized model

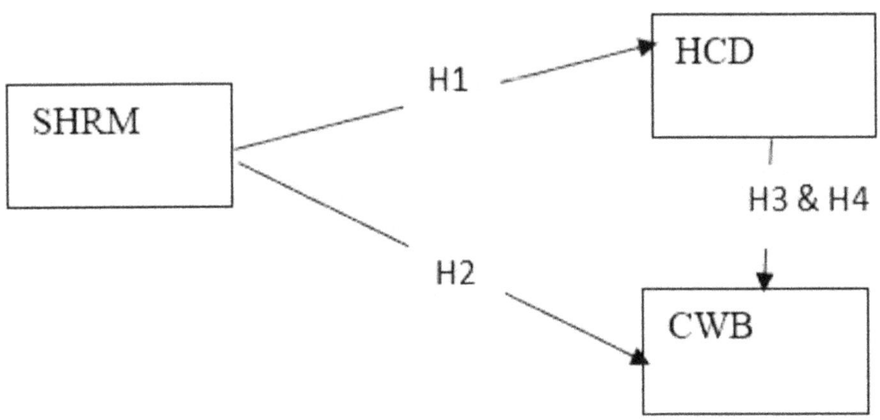

Hence, the following hypotheses are stated:

Hypothesis One: SHRM is positively related to HCD

Hypothesis Two: SHRM is positively related to CWB

Hypothesis Three: HCD is positively related to CWB

Hypothesis Four: HCD will moderate the relationship between SHRM and CWB

Method

The author invited participants in a seminar to take part in the study. The author explained the purpose of the study to the participants before agreeing to participate. The participants came from the Information technology, consulting, and online marketing areas. Because of the desire to minimize the use of papers, an online link was given to those who accepted and were instructed to fill out the same and provide the link to some of their colleagues. The questionnaire was in three parts. Part A contained instructions on the purpose of the study and for what it would be used. It also has an assurance that confidentiality would be guaranteed. Part B includes the demographic variables. These are variables found to affect the dependent variables in past studies. Part three contains 24 items that measured the study variables.

The total number of filled questionnaires received was 205. The usable questionnaires were 200. The demographic distribution of the participants is male (55%), the average age is between 31-40 years, and most are senior employees.

Measures

The study adopted already validated measures. All the variables were measured with a Likert scale of 1=strongly disagree to 5= strongly agree.

Strategic Human Resources Management:

This scale was taken from the work of Aryanto *et al.* (2015) and contained six items that captured the quality of the policies embedded in the SHRM. An example item is "The selection of an employee in my organization places priorities on the candidates' potential to learn" Cronbach's alpha in the past study is .86 compared to.70 got in this study.

Human Capital Development

HCD was measured with a scale taken from Kadir *et al.* (2018) and contains four items that captured the quality of development activities in the organization. An example item is "In my organization; employees are highly skilled" Cronbach's alpha in the past study was .80 compared to .90 in the current study.

Creative Work Behavior

CWB was measured with a scale taken from the work of Rice (2006) and contained seven items that measured the employees' creativity. An example item is "I transform innovative ideas into useful applications" Cronbach's alpha from the past study is .93 compared to .87 in the current study.

Control Variables

Three control variables found to affect the dependent variables were included. These are job status, gender, and age. Job-status categories included junior, senior, supervisor, and manager. Gender had male, female, and others, while age included under 30 years, 31-40 years, 41-50 years, and above 50 years.

RESULTS

The statistical analysis adopted the Statistical Package for Social Sciences (SPSS 23) and Analysis of Moment of Structures (AMOS 23) software. The fit of the models in the analysis was gauged using the goodness-of-fit index (GFI), comparative fit index (CFI), and root mean standard error of approximation (RMSEA). For the GFI and CFI, an effective model must have at least a value of 0.9, while the RMSEA value must fall between 0.05 and 0.08 (Hu and Bentler, 1999).

Preliminary Analysis

The KMO and Bartlett's test indicated the adequacy of the sampling method (.92 and 1090.71). An unrotated exploratory factor analysis (EFA) extracted three factors, with the first factor extracting only 20% of the variance compared to 75% of the variance extracted by all the factors. This is an acceptable common method variance level (Podsakoff & Organ, 1986). Confirmatory factor analysis (CFA) carried out before estimating the model showed that a three-factor model had the best for the data. All the items of the four factors loaded on their respective factors with no cross-loading. The fit indices for one, two, and three-factor models, coupled with the chi-square test, confirm that a three-factor model has the best fit ($\chi 2$= 22.35, p= .06; $\chi 2$/df = 1.596; GFI = 0.98; CFI = 0.99; RMSEA = .051). Three different statistical tests were used to gauge common method variance (see Eichhorn, 2014; Chang et al.,

2010; Podsakoff & Organ, 1986)). This was done because the cross-sectional method used is prone to common method variance. All the methods confirmed that the level of the common method variance was within the acceptable limit.

Construct, convergent, and discriminant validity was satisfied since factor loadings were above 0.5 cutoff point (Hair et al., 2010), Cronbach alpha was above 0.7and average variance extracted by each factor was more than the variance they share with other factors (Koufteros et al., 2002; Nunnally, 1978).

Regression Analysis

Table 1 contains the correlation among study variables, the Cronbach alpha (diagonal elements), and the mean and standard deviation of the study variables. Table 2 is the path estimate for the regression results, while Table 3 is the mediation estimate. The correlations presented in Table 1 show support for some hypotheses. For example, SHRM is positively correlated to HCD (.67, p=.000 and CWB (.47, p<.000). The Cronbach alphas are all greater than the .7 cutoff point. From the path estimates in Table 2 and Figure 3, SHRM is positively related to HCD (.66, p<.001), not related to CWB (.04, p<.54). Hence, hypothesis 1 is supported, while hypothesis 2 is not supported. HCD is positively related to CWB (.43, p<.001). Hence hypothesis 3 is supported. The indirect effect of SHRM on CWB through HCD is significant, as indicated by the effect size and LLCI and ULCI that did not contain zero (see Table 3). Hence, hypothesis 4 is supported. The total effect of the study variables on CWB is .32. The study variables accounted for .47 and .45 of the variances in HCD and CWB, respectively (see figure 2).

Table 1. Correlation, mean, SD, and Cronbach alpha

Variable	Mean	SD	1	2	3	4	5	6
1. Job-status								
2. Gender			.01					
3. Age			.48**	-.08				
4. SHRM	3.89	.90	.30**	.01	.16	**.70**		
5. HCD	4.03	.92	.32**	.01	.11	.67**	**.90**	
6. CWB	4.25	.65	.24**	-.11	.06	.47**	.65**	**.87**

Note. Bold diagonal items are Cronbach alpha
**, p <.001

Table 2. Path estimates

Variable	Estimates	SE	t	p
SHRM → HCD	.66	.07	10.02	.000
SHRM → HCD	.04	.06	.60	.540
SHRM → HCD	.43	.06	7.14	.000

Table 3. Mediation estimates

	Estimates	SE	LLCI	ULCI
Indirect Effect	.28	.07	.1411	.4419
Direct Effect	.04	.06	-.0547	.1585
Total Effect	.32	.05	.2095	.4263

Figure 3. Estimated model
Note: SHRM, Strategic human resources management; HCD, Human capital development; CWB, Creative work behavior

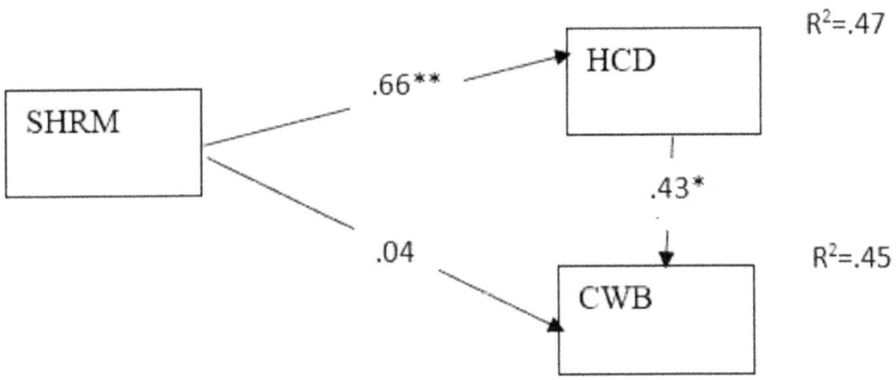

DISCUSSIONS

The book chapter starts from the premise that the HRM contains practices (HCD) aimed at developing the organization's human capital (HC). The alignment of these practices with the overall business strategy gives rise to the SHRM of an organization. The purpose of the book chapter was to establish how SHRM links with employee behavior, such as creativity which ultimately drives their performance. Past authors have proposed that to achieve positive employee behavior, SHRM must align appropriately with HCD practices and business strategy in such a way as to ensure that HC has the skills to drive business strategy (April & Chum, 2005). The book chapter proposed four hypotheses to explore the link between SHRM, HCD, and CWB. Three of the hypotheses were supported, while one was not supported. SHRM was found to affect HCD, as suggested by past researchers directly. However, the hypothesized direct relationship between SHRM and CWB was not positive. This agrees with the suggestion of Past studies that for employees to contribute adequately to the business goals, there must be a fit between SHRM and business strategy and between SHRM and HCD (Conner & Ulrich, 1996; Fitz-enz, 2002; Mohrman, 2007).

The hypothesized relationship between HCD and CWB was supported since there is a positive direct relationship between the two variables. HCD ensures employees have the necessary skills required to carry out assignments. Thus, HCD will directly influence positive behaviors by providing the essential skills required. For example, providing employees with the skills needed to think and act creatively will enhance their creative work behavior. SHRM focuses on how employees' behaviors drive firm performance, but it does this by developing specific HCD practices and policies aligned with business strategy to drive employee behavior (Liao, 2005).

IMPLICATIONS OF THE STUDY

The study highlights the importance of HCD in driving organizationally preferred employee behavior. For example, in the COVID environment, employee creativity is preferred because it helps employees identify and drive behaviors that solve unexpected challenges. Therefore, there must be alignment between SHRM and HCD such that required skills are provided to employees to be creative. Thus, organizations must achieve the alignment between SHRM and business strategy and between SHRM and HCD to ensure employees have these skills. Therefore competency-based training and development must be instituted in organizations to achieve synergy between training and skill development. Competency-based training must track skill requirements as organizational strategy changes.

FUTURE RESEARCH DIRECTIONS

The study tested only a section of the SHRM model in Figure 1. Hence, possible future research is to explore relationships in the model. This will involve reviewing how SHRM links with business strategy and how such links drive the relationships developed in this study. Future studies should also consider other essential behaviors, such as employee engagement.

CONCLUSION

Managing employees has progressed from the personnel management era to the era of linking human resources management to business strategy. The search for sustainable competitive advantage led to the emphasis placed on the quality of employees in the organization. The behavior of employees is critical in obtaining a competitive advantage from employees. Hence, there is a need to link SHRM to business strategy and allow this link to drive the practices permitted in the development of employees to acquire necessary skills that will position organizations above their peers. This study has started such exploration. Future studies must build on this to advance the understanding of the SHRM model in Figure 1 and translate such knowledge to position employees as the source of sustainable competitive advantage.

REFERENCES

Abraham, A. (2015). Gender & creativity: An overview of psychological and neuroscientific literature. *Brain Imaging and Behavior*. Advance online publication. doi:10.100711682-015-9410-8 PMID:26051636

Ahmad, S., & Schroeder, R. G. (2003). The impact of human resource management practices on operational performance: Recognizing country and industry differences. *Journal of Operations Management*, *21*(1), 19–43. doi:10.1016/S0272-6963(02)00056-6

Amabile, T. M., Barsade, S. G., Mueller, J. S., & Staw, B. M. (2005). Affect and creativity at work. *Administrative Science Quarterly*, *50*(3), 367–403. doi:10.2189/asqu.2005.50.3.367

April Chang, W., & Huang, C. T. (2005). Relationship between strategic human resource management and firm performance: A contingency perspective. *International Journal of Manpower*, *26*(5), 434–449. doi:10.1108/01437720510615125

Aryanto, R., Fontana, A., & Afiff, A. Z. (2015). Strategic human resource management, innovation Capability and performance: An empirical study in Indonesia software industry. *Procedia-Social and Behavioral Sciences*, *211*, 874-879. 10.1016/j.sbspro.2015.11.115

Azmi, F. (2011). Strategic human resource management and its linkage with HRM effectiveness and organizational performance: Evidence from India. *International Journal of Human Resource Management, 22*(18), 3888–3912. doi:10.1080/09585192.2011.561245

Barney, J. B. (1991). Firm resources and sustained competitive advantage. *Journal of Management, 17*(1), 99–120. doi:10.1177/014920639101700108

Barney, J. B. (2001). Is the Resource-Based 'View' A Useful Perspective for Strategic Management Research? Yes. *Academy of Management Review, 26*(1), 41–56. doi:10.2307/259393

Blau, P. M. (1986). *Exchange and Power in Social Life* (2nd ed.). Routledge.

Boudreau, J. W., & Ramstad, P. M. (2005). *Talentship, talent segmentation, and sustainability: A new HR decision science paradigm for a new strategy definition*. Human Resource.

Boxall, P. (1998). Achieving competitive advantage through human resource strategy: Towards a theory of industry dynamics. *Human Resource Management Review, 8*(3), 265–288. doi:10.1016/S1053-4822(98)90005-5

Boxall, P., & Purcell, J. (2000). Strategic human resource management: Where have we come from, and where should we be going? *International Journal of Management Reviews, 2*(2), 183–203. doi:10.1111/1468-2370.00037

Boxall, P., & Purcell, J. (2003). *Strategy and human resource management*. Palgrave Macmillan.

Bruce-Lockhart, A. (2021). What Is Human Capital? Everything You Need told. *Economic Forum*. https://www.weforum.org/agenda/2019/06/what-isital-know/

Cappelli, P., & Singh, H. (1992). Integrating strategic human resources and strategic management. In O. S. Mitchell & P. D. Sherer (Eds.), *Research frontiers in industrial relations and human resources* (pp. 165–192). IRRA.

Cartwright, S., & Cooper, C. L. (2002). *HR Know-how in mergers and acquisitions*. Cromwell Press.

Chang, S., Van Witteloostuijn, A., & Eden, L. (2010). Common method variance in international business research. *Journal of International Business Studies, 41*(2), 178–184. doi:10.1057/jibs.2009.88

Cheung, P. C., & Lau, S. (2010). Gender differences in the creativity of Hong Kong, school children: Comparison by using the new electronic Wallach–kogan creativity tests. *Creativity Research Journal*, *22*(2), 194–199. doi:10.1080/10400419.2010.481522

Choden, C., Zangmo, G., & Dem, K. (2021). Universalism in Human Resource Management. *Academia Letters. Article, 1580*. Advance online publication. doi:10.20935/AL1580

Conner, J., & Ulrich, D. (1996). Human resource roles: Creating value, not rhetoric. *Human Resource Planning*, *19*(3), 1–10.

Delery, J. E., & Doty, D. H. (1996). Theoretical frameworks in strategic human resource management: Universalistic, contingency, and configurational perspectives. *Academy of Management Journal*, *39*(4), 802–835.

Dessler, G. (2011). *Human resource management* (12th ed.). Pearson.

Dowling, P., & Roots, A. (2009). 'Review of Boudreau, P. and Ramstad, A. (2009) Beyond HR: The new science of human capital. In *Research and Practice in Human Resource Management* (p. 268). HBS Press.

Duke, I. I. J. II, & Udono, E. N. (2012). A new paradigm in traditional human resource management practices. *Journal of Management and Sustainability*, *2*(2), 146–159. doi:10.5539/jms.v2n2p158

Eichhorn, B. R. (2014). *Common method variance techniques*. https://www.lexjansen.com/mwsug/2014/AA/MWSUG-2014-AA11.pdf

Emeagwal, L., & Ogbonmwan, K. O. (2018). Mapping the perceived role of strategic human resource management practices in sustainable competitive advantage. *Academy of Strategic Management Journal*, *17*(2), 1–19.

Fitz-enz, J. (2002). *How to measure human resource selection* (3rd ed.). McGraw Hill.

Ford, J. (2021). *What are the four criteria of sustainable competitive advantage?* https://answerstoall.com/technolgownt-are-the-four-criteria-of-sustainable-

Gahlawat, N., & Kundu, S. (2019). Progressive human resource management and firm Performance. *The International Journal of Organizational Analysis*, *27*(3), 471–493. doi:10.1108/IJOA-05-2017-1159

George, J. M., & Zhou, J. (2002). Understanding when bad moods foster creativity and good ones do not: The role of context and clarity feelings. *The Journal of Applied Psychology*, *87*(4), 687–697. doi:10.1037/0021-9010.87.4.687 PMID:12184573

Ghosh, P. (2021). What is Human Capital Management (HCD)? Definition, Process, Platforms (tools) with Examples. *Performance Management*. https://www.toolbox.com/hr/performancemanagement/articles/what-is-human-capital-management/

Gratton, L., Hailey, V. H., & Truss, C. (2000). *Strategic human resource management*. Oxford University.

Guest, D. (1987). Human resource management and industrial relations. *Journal of Management Studies*, *24*(5), 503–521. doi:10.1111/j.1467-6486.1987.tb00460.x

Gunnigle, P., & Moore, S. (1994). Linking Business Strategy and Human Resource Management: Issues and Implications. *Personnel Review*, *23*(1), 63–84. doi:10.1108/00483489410053038

Habeck, M. M., Kroger, F., & Tram, M. R. (2000). *After The Merger. Seven Rules For Successful Post-Merger Integration*. Pearson Education Limited.

Hair, J. F. Jr, Black, W. C., & Babin, B. J. (2010). *Multivariate data analysis* (7th ed.). Pearson Prentice-Hall.

He, W., & Wong, W. (2011). Gender differences in creative thinking revisited: Findings from analysis of variability. *Personality and Individual Differences*, *51*(7), 807–811. doi:10.1016/j.paid.2011.06.027

Holdsworth, R., & Lundgaard, W. (2009). An HR intervention. *HR Monthly*, (May), 32.

Hsu, L. C., & Wang, C. H. (2012). Clarifying the effect of intellectual capital on performance: The mediating role of dynamic capability. *British Journal of Management*, *23*(2), 179–205. doi:10.1111/j.1467-8551.2010.00718.x

Hu, L. T., & Bentler, P. M. (1999). Cutoff criteria for fit indexes in covariance structure analysis: Conventional criteria versus new alternatives. *Structural Equation Modeling*, *6*(1), 1–55. doi:10.1080/10705519909540118

Huang, T. C. (2001). The effects of linkage between business and human resource management strategies. *Personnel Review*, *30*(2), 132–151. doi:10.1108/00483480110380316

Inyang, B. J. (2010). Strategic human resource management (SHRM): A paradigm shift for achieving sustained competitive advantage in an organization. *International Bulletin of Business Administration*, *7*(23), 215–243.

Jackson, S. E., Schuler, R. S., & Carlos Rivero, J. (1989). Organizational characteristics as to predictors of personnel practices. *Personnel Psychology*, *42*(4), 727–786. doi:10.1111/j.1744-6570.1989.tb00674.x

Jackson, S. E., Schuler, R. S., & Jiang, K. (2014). An aspirational framework for strategic human resource management. *The Academy of Management Annals*, *8*(1), 1–56. doi:10.5465/19416520.2014.872335

Joy, R. J., & Howes, P. (2001). Globalization and HR. In M. Effron, R. Gandossy, & M. Goldsmith (Eds.), *Human Resources in the 21st Century* (pp. 169–175). John Wiley & Sons Inc.

Kadir, A. R. A., Aminallah, A., Ibrahim, A., Sulaiman, J., Yusoff, M. F. M., Idris, M. M., Bahar, M. R., Hasanordin, R., Rahim, S. S. A., & Abd Malek, Z. (2018). The influence of intellectual capital and corporate entrepreneurship towards small and medium enterprises'(SMEs) sustainable competitive advantage: building a conceptual framework. *Proceedings of the 2nd Advances in Business Research International Conference*. 10.1007/978-981-10-6053-3_7

Kenton, W. (2020). Human capital. *Investopedia*. https://www.investopedia.com/terms/h/humancapital.asp

Khan, M. A. (2010). Effects of human resource management practices on organizational performance. An empirical study of the oil and gas industry in Pakistan. *European Journal of Economics, Financial and Administrative Sciences*, *24*(158), 1450–2275.

Koufteros, X. A., Vonderembse, M. A., & Doll, W. J. (2002). Examining the competitive capabilities of manufacturing firms. *Structural Equation Modeling*, *9*(2), 256–282. doi:10.1207/S15328007SEM0902_6

Lee, S. (2015). A concept analysis of 'meaning in work' and its implications for nursing. *Journal of Advanced Nursing*, *71*(10), 2258–2267. doi:10.1111/jan.12695 PMID:26010379

Lewin, D. (2001). Human resources management and performance: Lessons from the 21st Century. In M. Effron, R. Gandossy, & M. Goldsmith (Eds.), *Human Resources in the 21st Century* (pp. 91–98). John Wiley & Sons Inc.

Liao, Y. (2005). Business strategy and performance: The role of human resource management control. *Personnel Review*, *34*(3), 294–309. doi:10.1108/00483480510591444

Manashree, C. (2021). *Evolution of human resource management (HRM)*. https://www.economicsdiscussion.net/human-resource-management/evolution-of-human-resource-management-hrm/31460

Mayhew, R. (2018). *Employee turnover definitions & calculations*. Retrieved from https://smallbusiness.chron.com/employee-turnover-Definitions-calculations-11611.h

Mohrman, S. A. (2007). Designing organizations for growth: The human resource contribution. *Human Resource Planning*, *30*(4), 1–11.

Momtazian, M. (2021). What is talent management, and why is it important? *EXPERT360*. https://expert360.com/articles/talent-management-important

Nankervis, A., Chatterjee, S., & Coffey, J. (2007). *Perspectives of human resource management in the Asia Pacific*. Pearson Education Australia.

Nunnally, J. (1978). *Psychometric theory*. McGraw-Hill.

Peters, T. J., & Waterman, R. (1982). *In search of excellence*. Harper and Row.

Podsakoff, P. M., & Organ, D. W. (1986). Self-report in organizational research: Problems and Prospects. *Journal of Management*, *12*(4), 545–560. doi:10.1177/014920638601200408

Porter, M. E. (1980). *Competitive strategy*. New York Free Press.

Rice, G. (2006). Individual values, organizational context, and self-perceptions of employee creativity: Evidence from Egyptian organizations. *Journal of Business Research*, *59*(2), 233–241. doi:.jbusres.2005.08.001 doi:10.1016/j

Rogers, M. (2014). Job resources, employees' creativity, and firm performance of commercial Banks in Uganda. *International Journal of Economics, Commerce, and Management*, *11*(9), 1–14.

Rotich, K. J. (2015). History, evolution, and development of human resources management: A contemporary perspective. *Global Journal of Human Resource Management*, *3*(3), 58–73.

Sawalha, L. (2021). Measuring Human Capital: Why and How to Measure it. *Atman Co*. https://atmanco.com/resources/blog/measuring-human-capital/

Sayed, E. M., & Mohamed, A. H. H. (2013). Gender differences in divergent thinking: Use of the test of creative thinking-drawing production on an Egyptian sample. *Creativity Research Journal*, *25*(2), 222–227. doi:10.1080/10400419.2013.783760

Schuler, R. S., & Jackson, S. E. (1989). Determinants of human resource management priorities and implications for industrial relations. *Journal of Management*, *15*(1), 89–99. doi:10.1177/014920638901500108

Scott, S., & Palincsar, A. (2013). *Sociocultural theory*. http://dr-hatfield.com/theorists/resources/sociocultural_theory.pdf

Sinha, R. (2014). *What is strategic human resource management?* https://EzineArticles.com/expert

Sullivan, J. (2005). *Clarifying the strategic role of HR*. https//www.drjohnsullivan.com

Truss, C., & Gratton, L. (1994). Strategic human resource management: A conceptual approach. *International Journal of Human Resource Management*, *5*(3), 663–686. doi:10.1080/09585199400000053

Unsworth, K. (2001). Unpacking creativity. *Academy of Management Review*, *26*(2), 289–297. doi:10.5465/amr.2001.4378025

Wernerfelt, B. (1984). A resource-based view of the firm. *Strategic Management Journal*, *5*(2), 171–180. doi:10.1002mj.4250050207

West, M. A., & Farr, J. L. (1989). Innovation at Work: Psychological Perspectives. *Social Behaviour*, *4*, 15–30.

Wijenayaka, G. A. U. (2021). HR strategy is necessary to underline the interactive relationship between business strategy and human resource management. *Academia Letters*. Advance online publication. doi:10.20935/AL4316

Wilson, P. (2009). True north. *HR Monthly*, (May), 16–18.

Wright, P. M., & McMahan, G. C. (1992). Theoretical perspectives for strategic human resource management. *Journal of Management*, *18*(2), 295–320. doi:10.1177/014920639201800205

Wright, P. M., & Snell, S. A. (1998). Toward a unifying framework for exploring fit and flexibility in strategic human resources. *Academy of Management Review*, *23*(4), 756–772. doi:10.5465/amr.1998.1255637

Zica, R. M. F., Gonçalves, C. A., Cordeiro Martins, H., & Gonçalves, M. A. (2016). The resource-based theory and its adherence to a superior performance strategy: An analysis in small companies in Brazil. *Corporate Ownership & Control*, *13*(3-3), 434-444. . doi:10.22495/cocv13i3c3p2

KEY TERMS AND DEFINITIONS

Business Strategy: Business strategy is a clear set of plans, activities, and goals that outline how a business will compete in a market with a product or services.

Competencies: Competence is a collection of skills that improve job performance. Competencies aren't skills, despite similarities.

Competitive Advantage: A state of affairs or set of circumstances that places an organization in a more advantageous or dominant position in the marketplace.

Evolution of Human Resources Management: The concept of human resource management has evolved during the course of the Industrial Revolution, trade unions, scientific management, behavioral science, and human relations. As a result, the term Personnel Management has gradually been superseded by the notion HRM.

Globalization: The term "globalization" is used to refer to the increased interconnectedness and mutual dependence of people all over the world as a result of increased trade and technological development. The economic and social shifts brought on by globalization are encompassed by the term as well.

Personnel Management: Personnel management entails hiring and paying a company's personnel. It tries to recruit and retain a quality staff to satisfy an organization's goals.

Resources-Based Value: According to resource-based theory, an organization is in the best position for sustained success when its resources are high-quality, scarce, difficult to replicate, and non-substitutable. These strategic assets can serve as a springboard for building the kinds of in-house competencies that might pay dividends in sustained competitive advantage.

Chapter 5
Talent Management for Academic Institutions During the Post-Pandemic Paradigm

Humayra Ferdous
https://orcid.org/0000-0002-3227-4386
American International University-Bangladesh, Bangladesh

ABSTRACT

A knowledge-based organization such as educational institutes, consultancy firms require certain skills from their employees. Among many, the prime duty of the department of human resource management (HRM) of an organization is to identify the required skills for a particular task or job. HRM searches those skills during the time of recruitment. However, skills are not constant; rather, they are dynamic. Different eras require different skills to perform any task successfully. During the post-pandemic period of COVID-19, usage of technology in educational institute for their regular tasks such as lecture delivery, online assessment, seminars, conducting workshops have increased rapidly. Unfortunately, the academicians in many cases are not trained to perform these tasks in an efficient manner. This is especially true for developing countries like Bangladesh, where the transition from an analog to a digital world is still in progress. The chapter focuses on how HRM in any knowledge-based organization can play a very crucial role to convert its human resources into human capital.

DOI: 10.4018/978-1-6684-3894-7.ch005

INTRODUCTION

Knowledge-based organizations such as universities and research organizations are one of the significant components of any society. Here new knowledge has been created, and existing knowledge has been practiced and spread. People from various segments and classes come here or are admitted for learning. They study and nourish their hidden talent here and prepare themselves to contribute to society.

Moreover, people employed here are considered to have a certain level of talent and minimum skills to perform their tasks and responsibilities inefficient manner. But for the authorities, recruiting the right people at the right place is a constant challenging task.

Nonetheless, human resource management for academia is relatively a new concept in developing countries like Bangladesh, India etc. However, these countries have a rich heritage of educational institutions and knowledge-based organizations. But till today recruitment process and resourceful managing person remain not very well-structured. We must note that the duty of the department of human resource management never ends after completing the recruitment process; instead, it is only the beginning. It plays a role in enhancing entry-level, mid-level, and senior academicians.

However, attracting and retaining top talent is gradually emerging as a vital issue for university human resource management (Huisman et al., 2002; Metcalf et al., 2005; Kubler and DeLuca et al., 2006). Universities are certainly not the only employers competing for highly qualified employees. Several recent surveys suggest that academic disciplines are already suffering from a chronic shortage of talented people in some countries (Gilliot et al., 2002; van Balen & van den Besselaar et al., 2007; Lubbe and Larsen et al., 2008; Edwards and Smith et al., 2010). The composition and quality of academic staff are vitally important for the quality of education programmes and university research and the reputation and competitive position of universities and institutions in the academic community (Lorange, 2006).

Nonetheless, people run these organizations, and the talent of these people will determine their success; so, talent management is the foremost priority of the authority. (Husiman et al., 2002)

A survey shows that executives do not know some of their required talents for most basic and essential facts. Companies regularly mismanage talent development tasks. An employee value proposition can help management attract and retain the talent they need (Cliffe et al., 1998)

It is worth mentioning that Covid-19 brings more challenges for the educational institutes. Universities and schools had no other option but virtual classes. So, it is crucial to understand and assess the students' progress when academicians take virtual classes. Different skills are required in academicians to conduct such assessments.

Communication skills are needed to be enhanced. Programmes needed to be taken to increase the students' interpersonal skills, which indicates that the role of the department of human resources is no longer limited. It has been discussed elaborately in later parts of this chapter also.

BACKGROUND

The term talent management is being used to describe efficient and integrated human resources practices with the objectives of attracting and retaining the right individuals, for the correct positions, at the right time. (Mohaimen et al., 2013)

In today's world, all business entities face competition to improve their quality. Educational institutions and knowledge-based organizations also struggle to ensure their quality.

In this scenario, Mohaimen, in his research published in 2013, has shown that talent management begins with the recruiting process initially, where the decisions are taken to recruit a group of people who are asked to perform specific responsibilities. For those duties, different skills among the candidates are searched for.

In academia, the responsibilities include taking classes, conducting research activities, running projects, writing research papers, arranging, attending webinars, and attending seminars at regular intervals. Academicians must maintain a healthy environment among their colleagues and fellow researchers. Ethical practices are another key issue that needs to be scrutinized.

One of the significant tasks for academicians is to interact with people from different segments of society. It becomes even more challenging when a country like Bangladesh is going through an economic transition. However, guiding the young mind is one of the complex jobs that involves patience and outstanding communication skill.

Therefore, as mentioned earlier, identifying the most suitable people for the job requires a different level of talent management for the department of human resource management (HRM).

Thus Heinen (2004) pointed out that talent management processes include workforce planning, talent gap analysis, recruiting, staffing, education and development, retention, talent reviews, succession planning, and evaluation. To drive performance, deal with an increasingly rapid pace of change, and create sustainable success, a company must integrate and align these processes with its business strategies. Organizations can survive and thrive in today's increasingly competitive markets by assessing available talent and placing the right people in their best roles. Effective talent management becomes even more critical with the future talent shortage as many experienced leaders approach retirement. Internationally, fewer managers and professionals are ready to fill these leadership roles, and companies worldwide compete for a smaller talent pool. Businesses must have the ability to identify the most talented individuals, provide them with the necessary training and experiences, and retain valuable employees long term (William,2000).

Many developing nations aim to reach an optimum level of education by enacting several laws in this regard. For example, Bangladesh has taken several initiatives to enhance the quality of the academicians for preparing for the upcoming challenges. The Parliament of Bangladesh passed the Bangladesh Accreditation Council Bill in 2017, aiming to ensure quality higher education at both public and private universities. (Mahboob Ali, 2017). This law facilitated in establishment Bangladesh Accreditation Council (BAC), which provides accreditation for the activities of the higher educational institutions after monitoring and evaluating their performances. (Mahboob Ali, 2017).

This Council has the responsibility to ensure quality education, accrediting the higher educational institutions and their curriculum and programmes, forming separate accreditation committees for each discipline, and determine the condition of accreditation and confidence certificate.

However, the challenges come from the preparedness of academicians and knowledge-based institutions as it is hard to adapt an object-based teaching-learning system.

Previously no such steps are taken to introduce a ranking system for the universities in Bangladesh, like in other Asian countries and Australia. A participatory teaching-learning approach in higher education is essential for the teachers to create an engaging classroom atmosphere to transform students to make them employable that is work-ready for the real world. Effective communication of teachers with students has a positive influence on a good teaching-learning system, which further depends on the skill, knowledge, experience, and attitude. (Mahboob Ali, 2017)

Mahboob Ali et al. also mentioned a few very crucial factors, such as qualified staff, integration of information technology (IT), skill development mechanism, etc. for effective teaching-learning.

Therefore, a process is needed through students' involvement and engagement will be ensured via constructive feedback. So that teaching staff, university learning and teaching cell, department of human resource management can improve their recruitment process, contents, teaching methods, curriculum, pedagogy, assessment tasks and applying theory to real-life situations.

CASE STUDY OF SELF ASSESSED PROCESS

Self-assessment is a process where an individual or any organization goes through an evaluation process in different sectors to achieve its stated mission and vision successfully.

Nonetheless, shortcomings and scopes for improvement can be figured out conveniently through the self-assessment process. It also guides and directs to take corrective measures and necessary steps for the future. That is why when the internal human resource management department of any educational institute determines its own need and requirement, assesses its overall recruitment process through performance and acts; accordingly, it gives a better outcome.

This statement is supported by Mahboob Ali and Hasan's (2019) study where self-assessment operation has been conducted in one public-funded university and one private funded organization in Bangladesh. In the teaching-learning criteria of these two universities, it was found that the organization is asked to establish a "Human Resource Training Center" for developing the quality of the faculty members.

For process management and continuous development, the self-assessment report suggested developing a "Quality Improvement Plan" to enhance the standard of teaching and appoint research-based academicians for their better performances.

Hence it can be seen how crucial human resource management can be. Both the educational institutes are suggested to take a post-self-assessment improvement plan for the next couple of years.

These steps will not only benefit the students of two participating institutes, but such self-assessment will also shape the structure of the tertiary level education at the national level.

POST COVID-19 & PARADIGM SHIFT IN ACADEMIC INSTITUTION

Technology usage in the educational institute for academic activities has been alleviated rapidly. The increase rate becomes significant in post-Covid-19. In any knowledge-based organization or academia, the following techno-based tasks are performed regularly:

- Preparing lessons with animated content.
- Usage of audio-visual software
- Conduct online assessment
- Arrangement of Webinars
- Conducting Virtual Workshops etc.

However, in many cases, the academicians are not trained enough to perform these tasks in an efficient manner. Especially, this is true for developing countries like Bangladesh, where the transition from analogue to digital world is still in progress.

According to its vision of "Digital Bangladesh", it plans to operate all its daily activities with the involvement of technologies. Bangladesh has come a long way in this direction.

Digital Bangladesh was the first step towards a knowledge-based society. The core commitment of digital Bangladesh is to use digital tools to alleviate poverty, reduce corruption and establish a digital governance system.

However, "Digital Bangladesh" started through the introduction of the fourth generation (4G) mobile internet on February 19, 20218 ("Bangladesh enters 4G era, 2018"). Studies (Snug, 2018) described that the fourth industrial revolution (4IR) could help people from every sector of society, starting from farmers to students.

But the achievement will be slipped off if the academicians of the country do not get proper facilities to enhance their skills regularly.

There are cases where senior and mid-level teachers and veteran academicians require special training on developing technical skills, knowledge of the usage of contemporary software and designated computer programmes for research and data analysis. Undoubtedly these academicians are highly competitive and very experienced. Still, due to the lack of specific updated skills, they cannot channel their expertise for the betterment of any organization or the country.

It ultimately affects the students and learners as they are on the receiving end in any educational institute. Nonetheless, senior academicians would feel marginalized and isolated if they were not trained regularly. It will impact their performances severely.

On the other hand, entry-level academicians face severe challenges in the early days of their teaching career due to the lack of technical training and training on organizational structure. It leads to a scenario of loss of productivity.

Moreover, academicians with highly technical backgrounds also require training in developing practical human to human interaction skills, improved teaching techniques etc. In many cases, the researcher who spends most of the time in laboratories is required to develop law skills, legal frameworks on any topics, strategic issues, policy issues of society, etc. In this way, a knowledge-based institution can build a link to community. It would further influence policymakers to bring positive changes in any field.

Therefore, the department of HRM in any knowledge-based organization such as an educational institute may play a crucial role in this regard. This new talent management system would convert an organization's human resources into human capital to a great extent.

TALENT MANAGEMENT FOR ACADEMICIANS

There are different types of positions in academia, such as entry-level positions, mid-level, and senior-level positions. During the recruitment process, the human resource management (HRM) department and the interview board members predominantly selects the candidates based on their academic background. Their research activities are considered one of the critical criteria during recruitment. Working as a team member is also a criterion that should be pondered upon among the candidates.

In the popular culture of many developing countries like Bangladesh, the department of HRM does not get involved in the academic activities of the employees after the completion of the recruitment process. However, academicians have many other duties apart from teaching inside the classroom.

They must communicate with different sections such as students, parents, and other organizations to arrange various programmes and events. Academicians are also required to arrange several extracurricular activities for the betterment of the students. Therefore, developing communication skills is an integral part of an academician, which needs to be regularly evaluated by the department of HRM.

To improve the communication skills among the academics, HRM may categories their role for a different levels of academicians. The details are described in the following sections:

FOR ENTRY-LEVEL ACADEMICIANS

Authorities recruited academicians at different entry-level posts such as Junior lecturers, lecturers and senior lecturers for undergraduate studies. After recruitment, they are needed to be trained with the teaching style, content development for their classes and lecturer presentation, lecture delivery etc., i.e., an overall enhancement is required. The talent management for the beginners can be described as follows:

- Training on Capacity Buildup
- Training in Communication and Social Skills
- Training on Legislation for STEM
- Training to Prepare Post-Pandemic Paradigm

Discussion on each point is laid for the readers in the proceeding sections.

TRAINING ON CAPACITY BUILDUP

As mentioned above, it is necessary to conduct a training programme by the department of human resources and management for the capacity build-up of the beginners aiming to develop their lecture delivery and content development.

Of course, research activities carry one of the primary foci for knowledge-based educational institutions; nevertheless, generating existing knowledge for the freshers and learners requires equal attention. Otherwise, it will affect the young minds on the receiving end.

To enhance the capacity of entry-level academicians, the department of human resource management may actively coordinate training sessions with senior members of different disciplines. It may boost the confidence level of the beginners as well.

TRAINING IN COMMUNICATION AND SOCIAL SKILLS

As mentioned in previous sections, practical communication skills play a vital role in academics. Therefore duty comes on the shoulders of the human resources department to work in this direction.

It can engage communication experts to develop the skill among the academicians. Language experts can be involved for better language proficiency. As academicians are needed to work as a team, it is also vital to build up the skill that allows work collectively.

The written form of communication is an essential part of an academic career. So, the department of human resources and management can pay attention to developing the writing skill of its academics and officials.

Social skill is another one needed to interact with students to solve their problems, address their issues, and for many different purposes. So, training should be carried out for beginners so authorities can utilize their talent to the maximum extent.

TRAINING ON LEGISLATION FOR STEM

Academicians with science and engineering backgrounds play a distinct role in any knowledge-based organization or academic institution. Their research contributes to the development of the society and entire humankind. It is directly linked with a change of livelihood. However, it has been seen academicians with STEM backgrounds often struggle to understand organizational structures, different laws, policies, organizational strategies on specific issues, financial matters etc.

With the lack of knowledge in humanities and financial systems, academics cannot apply appropriate expertise in project planning, budget placement for further development, etc. The problem becomes acute for the countries like Bangladesh as here; students are divided into three streams (science, humanities and commerce) at a very early age. So, many students are not aware of social issues, political science and economics etc. So, when they enter into professional life, the struggle begins.

Therefore, this deficiency of understanding often creates grievances among the employees, i.e., it directly impacts the reputation of the institutions. The human resources and management department may take numerous initiatives to mitigate these problems. It can arrange a seminar regularly on different policies and strategies taken by the organizations. In the long run, it would narrow the gap between academic and non-academic staff of the organisation and increase its productivity.

TRAINING TO PREPARE POST-PANDEMIC PARADIGM

The responsibilities of the department of human resource management have increased during the post-Covid-19 period. As most educational institutes focus on virtual classes, academics were located at home. They are also required to conduct administrative activities online. It demands a distinct amount of skill with technical expertise. So those recruited in this period, especially in academia, should be trained adequately initially with the presence of senior members of the respective discipline. The human resource management department may keenly coordinate and monitor these capacity build-up issues and provide its assistance.

FOR MID-LEVEL ACADEMICIANS

In any academic institution, mid-level academicians have been employed in that organization for several years, are familiar with the norms, and already understand their duties and tasks. They play an instrumental role in running an inefficient organization manner. However, it is noticed that many mid-level academicians lose their momentum and motivation toward daily academic activities after a certain point. An inertness develops among them, which prevents them from further improvement.

However, we must also consider that these mid-level academicians are dealing with many family issues in their personal lives. Nonetheless, many times these issues are not very pleasant. Many struggles with the livelihood of their parents and taking care of children. Female employees remain in a more vulnerable position because of social pressure, pressure to the extent of their families, and alleviation of career, which ultimately put them behind in achieving leadership positions.

It ultimately causes a severe problem for the organization's growth as it is known that research is an integral part of academic institutions. But suppose the large segment of mid-level professionals does not find themselves in a comfortable zone for performing their duties, conducting largescale research projects. In that case, it will also see the diminishing effect extensively.

It would hurt the name of the organization outside as well.

Direct communication can be established between the department of human resources management and mid-level academicians to address these issues. Regular constructive dialogue can sort out many problems instantly. Training for leadership development skills and time management skills may improve the status of the mid-level professionals in different ways.

Authorities may reward, recognize, and provide monitory incentives based on performances as a form of encouragement. It would work as a motivation for mid-level academicians.

FOR SENIOR ACADEMICIANS

All academic institutions have senior faculty members who have experience of several decades in a specific field. It is a core responsibility of the department of HRM to get the benefit from such experiences. As people learn best from their own experiences, therefore, what the senior members have learnt from their lives and professional achievement can be disseminated to the young professionals or beginners.

So, the HRM department can arrange an idea exchange programme with the seniors at regular intervals. This would give the platform to be opened for the senior faculty members with their lifelong learnings and mistakes.

However, many senior members do not remain updated with new technologies. Many remain very rigid to being familiar with new tools for teaching. Nonetheless, Covid-19 worsens the situation. Usage of technology has increased due to the introduction of a home office.

In that case, trainings should be organized to bridge the gap. In this case, faculty members of science and engineering can contribute and be involved.

For veteran faculty members, health becomes an issue due to ageing. If they are not fit and healthy, they will not be able to take the classes with a substantial amount of effort, leading to less impactful lectures. Thus, continuous evaluation of their health condition should be put on the regular task list.

ORGANIZATIOAL DEVELOPMENT, PERFORMANCE EVALUATION & TALENT MANAGEMENT

The role in human resource management is broadening day by day. As academia needs to develop and nourish qualities such as oratory skills and collective efforts of the young minds; thus, it should focus on engaging academic people to lead the students. During the recruitment process, it can ask the already selected candidates about their interests and what qualities they possess or are good at other than their academic area; in other words, it may focus on identifying distinct talent among the faculty members.

Later, HRM can ask academicians to join clubs related to those activities. They can choose in their interest. In this way, students and learners involved in such clubs and entities can get guidance from the veteran faculty members and implement their advice in their lives, which will benefit them.

Moreover, these clubs may shape the opinion on different government policies, strategies taken by the policymakers and stances on various critical issues. Faculty members will get access to play a crucial role in framing other policies. Society will value their opinions also.

In the current practice, academicians in the knowledge-based organization do not get involved directly in various clubs, especially in Bangladesh, where academia remains streamed towards only regular activities if HRM takes initiatives in this direction.

Performance evaluation is another crucial feature that HRM performs in their routine task. Based on the talent and expertise of each resource person, HRM can evaluate their performance regularly.

Based on the performances, HRM can start providing rewards and recognize the contribution of its valuable resource persons.

STRUCTURAL REFORM FOR HUMAN RESOURCE MANAGEMENT IN ACADEMICA

Structural reform is required for the department of human resources and management of academic institutions to perform the tasks laid in the previous sections. This structure should be different from the existing one, where talent management is not on the priority list.

Figure-1 shows an organizational structure for the department of HRM. The wing of the talent management of HRM should be closely associated with the Institutional Quality Assurance Center [IQAC].

The close link between IQAC would allow both sides to enhance the organization's productivity. Regular monitoring and evaluation can identify the shortcomings; authorities can act in this direction.

Figure 1.

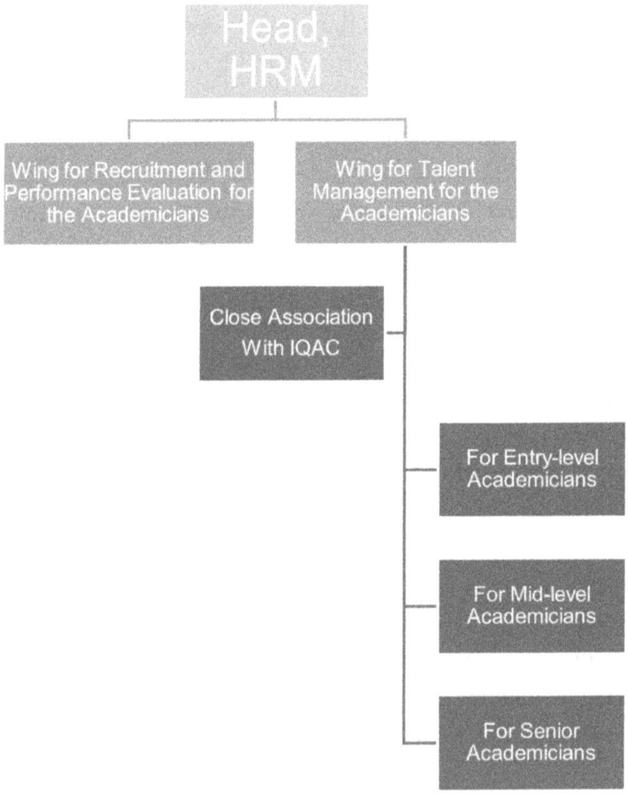

FUTURE RESEARCH DIRECTIONS

No policy reaches its goals and fulfils its objectives unless monitored and evaluated regularly. So how academic personnel are performing with efforts taken by the human resource and management department should be considered frequently. However, performance evaluation should be executed with the feedback from the young learners.

Proper documentation of the evaluated performances of the academicians would benefit the management in taking further decisions on quality improvement of the organizations.

The human resource management department can set the goals with a few specific "Key Performance Indicators (KPI)" with adequate communication with the faculty members at the beginning of the academic year. At the end of the year, the department shall prepare a report based on the KPIs, specifying achievements against the set goals. (Vincent, 2010).

The report may include a self-assessment appraisal from the academicians themselves and a superior evaluation (Vincent, 2010). Based on the findings of the assessment report human resource department can take further necessary steps to enhance quality.

CONCLUSION

From the discussion, it can be found that the human resource management department may put more effort than its current role. It should shift focus to identifying the talent for a particular academic task. Otherwise, it would lead to a position where talent will not be placed for the appropriate job; thus, human resources are not converted into human capital.

In 2015, United Nations adopted the charter with specific goals as a universal call to action to end poverty, protect the planet and ensure that by 2030 all people enjoy peace and prosperity. These are known as "the sustainable development goals" or "Global Goals". They recognize that action in one area will affect outcomes in others, and development must balance social, economic, and environmental sustainability. The SDGs are designed to end poverty, hunger, AIDS and discrimination against women and girls. The creativity, know-how, technology, and financial resources from all segments of society are necessary to achieve the SDG in every context.

By 2030, SDG also sets to increase the number of youth and adults with relevant skills, including technical and vocational skills for employment, decent jobs, and entrepreneurship.

Therefore, to achieve SDGs, more priority and emphasis must be given when managing knowledgeable personnel in academia.

REFERENCES

Ali, M. M. (2017). Quality Enhancement in Teaching-Learning Strategies of Bangladesh: A qualitative Assessment. *International Journal of Advanced Trends in Technology, Management & Applied Sciences, 3*(1), 121–147.

Ali, M. M. (2020). Digitization of Emerging Economy: An exploratory and explanatory case study. *Journal of Governance and Regulation*, *9*(4), 25–36. doi:10.22495/jgrv9i4art2

Ali, M. M., Rattanawiboonsom, V., & Hasan, F. (2018). Knowledge Management at Higher Educational Institutes in Bangladesh: The Case Study of Self-assessed Processes of Two Educational Institutes. *International Journal of Trade and Commerce-IIARTC*, *7*(2), 514–535.

Cliffe, S. (1998). Human resources: Winning the war for talent. *Harvard Business Review*, *76*(5), 18–19.

Edwards, D., & Smith, T. F. (2010). 'Supply issues for science academics in Australia: Now and in the future. *Higher Education*, *60*(1), 19–32. doi:10.100710734-009-9283-0

Gilliot, D., Overlaet, B., & Verdin, P. (2002). 'Managing academic personnel flow at universities. *Tertiary Education and Management*, *8*(4), 277–295. doi:10.1080/13583883.2002.9967085

Heinen, J. S., & O'Neill, C. (2004). Managing talent to maximize performance. *Employment Relations Today*, *31*(2), 67–82. doi:10.1002/ert.20018

Huisman, J., Weert, E., & Bartelse, J. (2002). Academic careers from a European perspective: The declining desirability of the faculty position. *The Journal of Higher Education*, *73*(1), 141–160. doi:10.1080/00221546.2002.11777134

Kubler, J., & DeLuca, C. (2006). *Trends in Academic Recruitment and Retention: A Commonwealth Perspective*. The Association of Commonwealth Universities.

Lorange, P. (2006). 'A performance based, minimalist human resource management approach in business schools. *Human Resource Management*, *45*(4), 649–658. doi:10.1002/hrm.20136

Lubbe, V., & Larsen, V. (2008). *Quick-Scan Jong Talent in De Wetenschap. Probleemanalyse Ten Behoeve Van Het Programma 'Loopbaanperspectief Jong Talent*. VSNU.

Metcalf, H., Rolfe, H., Stevens, P., & Weale, M. (2005). *Recruitment and Retention of Academic Staff in Higher Education*. National Institute of Economic and Social Research.

Mohaimein, M. A. (2013). Talent Management: Three new Perceptions intended for managing and retaining Talent in Bangladesh. *Asian Business Review*, *3*(5).

Van Balen, B., & van den Besselaar, P. (2007). Universitaire Onderzoeksloopbanen. Een Verkenning Van Problemen En Oplossingen [Academic Careers. An Exploration of Problems and Solutions]. Rathenau Instituut SciSa rapport 0702. Den Haag: Rathenau Instituut.

VincentN. (2010). A Constructive Model for Performance Evaluation in Higher Education Institutions. Available at https://ssrn.com/abstract=1877598 doi:10.2139/ssrn.1877598

Williams, M. (2000). *The war for talent: Getting the best from the best.* CIPD House.

KEY TERMS AND DEFINITIONS

Academic Institute: It refers to an organization which dismantle knowledges for the upcoming generations and create new knowledge through research and analysis for the betterment of the society.

Academician: In knowledge-based organizations, academicians are the professionals who are recruited by the authority for train up the future generations, generating knowledge among them. Their eligibility depends upon several factors such as academic performance, teaching experiences, research background etc. Authorities or recruiters set up different standard for entry, mid or senior most positions.

Human Capital: When the recruited employees are equipped with adequate trainings, enhanced with practical knowledge, and perform any task with highest level of efficiency then the employees are the human capital of that organization. This can be taken account for the broader picture of any country or society as well. If the citizen of any country is skilled and efficient, it will be considered as the human capital for that country too.

Human Resource Management (HRM): The department which is responsible to manage and take care of the human resources of any organization is known as the Department of Human Resource Management or commonly known as (HRM). Their responsibilities includes recruiting, screenings, training, rewarding and appraising.

Performance Evaluation: In every year or after a particular period the department of human resource management of any organization evaluates the performance of their employee. It is executed in the aim to understand how much goal the organization achieved or to what extent the organization reached in its vision and mission. This process is termed in this chapter as "Performance Evaluation".

Talent Management: In any knowledge-based organizations, employees generally are recruited with certain skills and criteria such as ability to take classes, delivering lectures, i.e. recruiters hires them with minimum level of talents. Therefore, to coordinate a group of talented individuals, extracts the maximum output from its employee require special managerial capacity. Here, it is referred as "Talent Management".

Technical Knowledge: To run a particular organization, specific skills and knowledges are required. It varies for organization to organizations. In addition, in the era of modern computers, certain knowledge based on computer software and hardware are also important. Overall, these skills for performing any tasks are referred as "Technical Knowledge".

Chapter 6
TM Strategies:
Panacea to KM Ills and Challenges - A Reference to COVID-19

Sheikh Shamim Hasnain
The British University in Egypt, Egypt

ABSTRACT

This literature-based chapter addresses the vital issues and challenges of KM in respect of knowledge transfer barriers and mechanisms of Hasnain, Jasimuddin, and Fuller-Love and makes an endeavor to materialize those with TM strategies mainly identified by Whelan and Carcary in the context of the COVID-19 pandemic. The contributions of talent management (TM) and knowledge management (KM) are undisputedly acknowledged by researchers and business organizations. Both TM researchers and KM researchers have hardly addressed the strategies of integrating TM and KM for implementing TM strategies against KM challenges in the context of the COVID-19 pandemic. Positioning and integrating appropriately the TM strategies against KM challenges could derive huge benefits for the organizations during hostilities. The COVID-19 pandemic has made the world environment volatile and complex. Therefore, numerous challenges of KM have emerged demanding TM strategies.

INTRODUCTION

Knowledge Management (KM) has been around since the 1990s. Talent Management (TM) has joined later, and if these two are positioned correctly, they could have synergistic effects. KM and TM both have their own knowledge transfer barriers and

DOI: 10.4018/978-1-6684-3894-7.ch006

strategies respectively. Selection and repair of knowledge transfer mechanisms and barriers necessitate TM strategies. KM has several challenges; yet, TM strategies may provide enterprises with answers to the COVID 19 pandemic. COVID19, which began in Wuhan, China in December 2019, will have both short- and long-term repercussions on the global economy (Ali, 2019).

Employees' skills, experiences, behavior, knowledge and cognitive abilities are identified as the talents in the organization (Al-Azzam & Al-Qura'an, 2018; Lewis & Hackman, 2006). Therefore, it is important to manage those talents. TM refers to the human procedures, practises, and methods used in HR-related activities, such as customer service, recruitment, selection and training, development, remuneration, and succession planning, as well as attraction, engagement, retention, and development of skilled personnel (Al-Azzam & Al-Qura'an, 2018). Both TM researchers and KM researchers have hardly addressed the strategies of integrating TM and KM for implementing TM strategies against KM challenges in the context of COVID 19 Pandemic. Positioning and integrating appropriately the TM strategies against KM challenges could derive huge benefits for the organizations. COVID 19 Pandemic has made the world environment volatile and complex (Ali, 2021; Kazemian and Grant, 2022). Numerous challenges of KM have emerged demanding TM strategies. Knowledge is transferred from one point to another through some vehicles. These vehicles are also called 'channels'. Knowledge transfer encounters a number of barriers. Therefore, this chapter addresses the vital issues and challenges of KM in respect of Knowledge Transfer barriers and mechanisms as identified by Hasnain, Jasimuddin & Fuller-Love (2016) and makes an endeavor to materialize those with TM strategies as narrated by Whelan & Carcary (2011). These may be put in the context of the COVID 19 pandemic. In the context of the COVID 19 pandemic, it is evident that KM and TM concerns are not sufficiently addressed in the literature. So this chapter sets the following objectives:

(i) To review the literature on KM, particularly, knowledge, knowledge transfer, its mechanisms, and barriers.
(ii) To develop TM strategies based on challenges in light of COVID19, with a reference to "Knowledge Transfer mechanisms" and "Knowledge transfer barriers".

Knowledge transfer between and within organizations appears to be at the heart of strategy creation and research (Chaturvedi and Singh, 2021; van Wijk, Jansen and Lyles, 2008). Knowledge transfer aids in the addition of force (Hall, 2001) and value (Hogberg and Edvinsson, 1998) to an organization's existing knowledge. Several scholars (Chowdhury, Butel, Eraslan and Bakan, 2009; Albino, Claudio and Schiuma,, 1999; Argote and Ingram, 2000) have identified knowledge transfer to be a strategic factor in competitive advantage. Knowledge Transfer is the subject of transmitting knowledge between the parties., like a badminton game, where one party sends the shuttlecock to other and vice versa. In Knowledge Transfer, the behavior of one party affects the other one (Argote & Ingram, 2000). This chapter is presenting the sections in the following order: (i) Introduction (ii) Literature Review (iii) Methodology/approach (iv) Conclusion (v) Recommendations.

LITERATURE REVIEW

Knowledge

Gettier's (1963) theory of knowledge, when articulated, overturns a thousand-year-old Aristotle's concept of knowledge, namely, 'justified true belief.' Gettier (1963) proposed that 'justified true belief' requires an extra element in order to acquire knowledge. Nonaka & Takeuchi (1995) reiterated this sentiment, stating that a false belief meeting these three characteristics cannot be considered knowledge. In addition, a dynamic human process of justifying personal conviction in the 'truth' is described (Nonaka & Takeuchi, 1995). It's worth noting that no universally agreed definition of knowledge exists (Hofer-Alfeis and Spek, 2002), owing to the difficulty of defining knowledge (Gamble and Black, 2001). However, philosophers will continue to argue about the concept for many years to come (Hislop, 2005; Jashapara). Davenport and Prusak (1998) made a comprehensive view of knowledge. They could reveal that Knowledge is a fluid combination of framed experience, values, contextual information, expert insider knowledge, and grounded intuition that creates a framework and environment for assessing and assimilating new experiences and information. They go on to say that it begins and ends in the brains of those who know. They discovered that it is often entrenched not just in papers or archives, but also in organizational routines, procedures, practices, and conventions in companies

Polanyi's (1962, 1966) theories were pioneers in the subject of knowledge management, and they are the foundations of a lot of widely used literature, including Nonaka and Takeuchi's (1995) SECI (Socialization, Externalization, Combination, and Internalization) model in the field of knowledge management. Polanyi finds that 'we can know more than we can convey' Humans can express part of their stored knowledge from the brain, allowing them to know more than they can tell, implying that 'can know' is larger than 'can tell.' Polanyi was a firm believer in the origins of all knowledge being tacit-type.

Sveiby (1996) find that true discovery, which cannot be explained by a set of explicit rules or algorithms, lies at the heart of Polanyi's idea. He said that knowledge is both public and, to a large part, personal, meaning that it is created by humans and hence contains emotions and 'passion.' All knowledge is either tacit or anchored in tacit knowledge; the knowledge that underpins explicit knowledge is more basic. In brief, according to Polanyi, knowledge is socially constructed, it is the experience of a person, highly tacit in nature, it is an activity, the process of knowing, and is a technique to obtain new knowledge. Indwelling, one of Polanyi's philosophies, was described by Gill (2000) as, immersion in the particulars of a subsidiary consciousness through embodied action until these particulars come together as a meaningful whole in an interactive act. Tacit knowledge is the foundation of all kinds of knowledge. Literature has recognized the important use of organizational knowledge. For example, Hasnain (2015) could identify that organizational knowledge is essential for (i) mobilization of resources (ii) capacity development (iii) strategic advantages (iv) responding to the changes of external environmental factors.

Knowledge Management (KM)

For the survival and growth of organizations, knowledge is an essential strategic resource (Hasnain, 2016; Prahalad and Hamel, 1990; Jasimuddin, Connell and Klein, 2005). "Knowledge itself is power" is the significant and appropriate claim made by Sir Francis Bacon (1564-1626). Organizational outputs are the outcome of knowledge use and transfer. So it is essential for the organizations to manage this valuable asset (knowledge).

Organizations have realized that making efficient use of their enormous and varied knowledge assets and resources allows them to innovate and respond to rapidly changing customer demands, therefore knowledge management (KM) has become increasingly vital (Sandhawalia and Dalcher, 2011). Both management philosophy and management tools are based on KM (Edvardsson, 2006). Knowledge management has received world recognition and value (Scharbrough, Robertson and Swan, 2005). The identification, organization, transfer, and use of knowledge are all elements/steps of the knowledge management process, according to Gamble and Blackwell (2001), while the collection, storage, and linking of knowledge are also elements of the knowledge transfer process, according to Zuckerman and Buell (1998). The steps of the knowledge management process, according to Jasimuddin, Connell, and Klein (2006), are: identifying, storing, retrieving, and transferring. The steps of the knowledge management process, according to Heavin and Neville (2006), are finding, capturing, storing, disseminating, and creating. These steps of KM can be divided into three categories: creation, storage, and transfer.

Knowledge Creation

Humans are the creators of new knowledge. In organizations, the generation of new tacit knowledge does not happen by itself. It requires collaboration, contact, and understanding among individuals participating in the development process (Balogun and Jenkins, 2003). It might also arise from outside sources. Knowledge development and application are mostly reliant on interactions with clients, suppliers, alliance members, and even rivals, in addition to internal ties (Dawson, 2000). As a result, knowledge formation is both a complicated internal process and the outcome of interactions between internal and external players.

Knowledge Storage

Knowledge storage is a critical component of the knowledge management process. It's similar to a bank where fresh knowledge is deposited and old knowledge is disbursed. Correct storage provides an up-to-date image of an organization's knowledge stock. It serves as the foundation for all strategic choices and has the potential to avert losses and knowledge gaps. Knowledge storage can be compared to physical storage in a warehouse. Physical products can be equated to an organization's knowledge in the case of knowledge storage. This asset's proper care and preservation allow the organization to reuse it in the future. Knowledge reuse is always cost-effective since it saves time, reduces communication costs, and allows businesses to grab opportunities.

Knowledge Transfer

Knowledge transfer is gaining a lot of attention (Argote et al., 2000; Chowdhury, 2009) since it is critical for an organization's survival and profitability (Wathne et al., 1996). These activities vary based on their goals and nature, as well as the changes and forces they face in the environment, which frequently necessitate the utilization of a variety of talents, ideas, and current and previous experiences from both inside and outside the businesses. The notion of knowledge transfer is necessary for learning and implementing others' experiences for societal and organizational gain. Mu *et al.* (2008) claim that the successful flow of knowledge across organizations promotes confidence and connections. This kind of trust assures that the beneficiaries of the knowledge will pass it on to others in the future. Organizational learning and innovations in new processes and practices may be aided by new knowledge, which may be incorporated into routines and culture (Darr and Kurtzberg, 2000). New knowledge helps to increase customer satisfaction (Goh, 2002). Furthermore, Knowledge transfer reduces productivity losses and increases organizational effectiveness (Argote and Ingram, 2000). Knowledge transfer aids in the addition of force (Hall, 2001) and value (Hogberg and Edvinsson, 1998) to an organization's existing knowledge. Knowledge transfer can take place between separate organizations (inter-organizational) or inside a single organization's sub-units (intra-organizational) (Darr, Argote and Epple, 1995; Albino, Garavelli and Schiuma, 1999). Knowledge transfer between and within organizations appears to be a source of strategy formulation and research (van Wijk, Jansen and Lyles, 2008). It's worth noting that, from a strategic standpoint, organizations don't share scarce and valuable knowledge with competitors, but they are interested in doing so with non-competitive enterprises (Bell et al., 2002). In reality, inter-organizational knowledge transfer choices are based on expected costs and benefits (Appleyard, 1996).

Knowledge Application

If the implementation stage fails, all of your knowledge management efforts will be for naught. This is the point when you put your plan into action. This is the practical phase in the decision-making process. The use of information technology may make the implementation process simpler (Ali, 2021). Human contributions to implementation, on the other hand, cannot be overlooked.

Talent Management (TM)

McKinsey consultants coined the expression "war for talent" in the late 1990s. At this moment, appropriate TM aids firms in attaining competitive advantages. Organizational strategies are provided by TM (Bayyoud & Sayyad, 2015; Ashton & Morton, 2005). According to numerous writers (Groves, 2007; Ringo et al. 2010), TM is engaged in defining strategy, recognizing talent shortages, succession planning, recruiting, selecting, training, motivating, and retaining great personnel through a variety of approaches.

This research borrowed the TM strategies from Whelan & Carcary (2011). Whelan and Carcary's (2011) studied on various literature and they suggest that using TM concepts can help with identifying important knowledge workers, knowledge generation, information sharing, improving knowledge competencies, and knowledge retention. Their focus group had the same viewpoints.

Al-Azzam and Al-Qura'n (2018) investigate the trend of TM strategies on customer satisfaction in the Jordanian banking sector. They carried out a quantitative study and found that Employee impressions of talent acquisition, development, succession planning, and, most importantly, talent retention techniques are critical contributors to TM strategies. They claim that with the advancements of KM, TM helps to expedite customer satisfaction.

Mohammad, Gururajan and Hafeez-Baig (2017) studied literature to examine the relationship between TM & KM in business environment. They discover that scholars are more interested in the processes of talent acquisition, development, and retention.

The most important phases in the KM process, on the other hand, are knowledge production, application, storage, transfer, and acquisition.

LITERATURE GAPS IDENTIFIED

Tome, Gromova, and Hatch (2021) examined COVID19's impact on organizations via the lens of knowledge management. COVID 19 arose as a result of a knowledge crisis, they concluded. They claim that pervasive knowledge failure is the source of the organizational crisis resulting from a lack of "social knowledge," which is connected to "organizational behavior." To deal with the challenge, they presented techniques including people, processes, and technology. Specific KM mechanisms, as well as barriers to knowledge transfer, are not examined. No TM strategy is suggested.

Chaturvedi and Singh (2021) presented a knowledge management framework to combat the COVID 19 pandemic in India. They propose three variables: critical areas that need to be addressed, suggesting methods based on technology and knowledge management, and collaboration and coordination. Though the model could highlight a few hurdles and mechanisms, no mention of TM strategies and their employment is made.

During the COVID 19 Pandemic in Bangladesh, Ali (2021) investigated the digital prospects in healthcare firms. He was able to discover that medical businesses are in terrible shape as a result of healthcare worker malfeasance and a lack of IT resources. He could make a number of recommendations, including increased investment in the medical sector, patient care, anti-corruption measures, ethical medical services, and ethical medical services through collaborative efforts of public, private, and foreign sectors. During the volatility of COVID19, his innovative recommendations of digitalization, medical robots, Artificial Intelligence, and blockchain technology (which typically does not allow alteration or manipulation of recorded data) might be effective knowledge transfer mechanisms. Ali (2021), on the other hand, made no mention of any KT barriers or TM strategies.

Tumiki and Jurcic (2021) looked at the impact of the COVID 19 crisis on KM practice in Oman. They noticed that organizations were utilizing an "inside-out" approach to KM during COVID 19. Companies began to move away from manual to computer-based knowledge management systems, depending mostly on internal knowledge sources. Businesses may benefit from improved employee motivation, engagement, development of job-related skills, knowledge-sharing culture, and other factors. Mechanisms, obstacles, and TM strategies were not discussed.

During the COVID-19 epidemic, Kazemian and Grant (2022) investigated the "content" aspects impacting consumption and contribution of Enterprise Social Networking (ESN) in UK higher education. This study examined interaction, information, and knowledge exchange using ESNs. Additionally, the study looked into how ESNs may assist knowledge seekers and suppliers in higher education before and during COVID-19. This study discovered motivators, impediments, and effects related to knowledge sharing on ESNs, as well as recommendations to improve academic staff utilization in higher education.

METHODOLOGY/APPROACH

The author examined the COVID 19 scenario attentively and noted the organizations' level of implementation of TM Strategies. The study analyzed a variety of online research publications such as books, magazines, organizational websites, newspapers, and other sources from 2019 to 2023."Knowledge," "Knowledge Management," "Knowledge Transfer Mechanisms," "Knowledge Transfer Barriers," "Knowledge Transfer Process," "Talent Management," "Talent Management Strategies," "Knowledge Management and COVID 19" were among the keywords utilized by the author in the search engine. Chartered Association of Business Schools ('ABS'), UK: journal rankings go from 4* (highest) to 1* (lowest) ranking pays special attention. However, indexed resources such as Google Scholar and Scopus are also considered. A few old journal articles and books were also evaluated, such as Gettier (1963), Grant (1997), Davenport & Prusak (1998), Appleyard (1996), Argote (1999), Whelan & Carcary (2011), Hasnain, *et al.* (2016) as these reading materials have worth and have commensuration with the requirements and objectives of this chapter. Data were recorded and cleaned as deemed appropriate as per the objectives of this study.

FINDINGS AND DISCUSSION: TM STRATEGIES DEVELOPED

This section focuses on the findings related to knowledge transfer mechanisms and barriers. Based on these it develops various TM strategies in the context of COVID 19.

Challenges and Strategies Related to Knowledge Transfer Mechanisms

The COVID 19 pandemic has complicated the global environment, making standard transfer mechanisms impossible to employ. As a result, everyone involved in the knowledge transfer process must choose the best mechanism for knowledge transmission.

Many researchers (Grant, 1996, 1997; Nonaka and Takeuchi, 1995; Davenport and Prusak, 2000; Darr, *et al.,* 1995; Connell,*et al.,* 2003; Jasimuddin, 2007; Argote *et al.*,2000; Dyer and Nobeoka, 2000) have emphasized on the importance of mechanism in ensuring a seamless and efficient knowledge transfer.

Different knowledge transfer mechanisms were outlined by Hasnain *et al.* (2016) in the context of Non-Governmental Organizations (NGOs) in Bangladesh, they also investigated the reasons and impediments to knowledge transfer between NGO personnel and beneficiaries. This study borrows the knowledge transfer mechanisms and barriers from Hasnain *et al.* (2016).

Argote (1999) finds, that training knowledge recipient organization's members, allowing them to see the performance of specialists at the donor organization, and offering possibilities for communication between members of both organizations (donors and recipients) are noteworthy mechanisms of knowledge transfer.

Additional mechanisms may be delivering records, plans, and explanations of the organization's structure to the receiver, as well as transferring experienced individuals, as part of the donor's expertise is entrenched in its technology, software, and products, transferring that knowledge to the receiving organization which facilitates (Argote, 1999).

Through his research on the Chinese-Singapore Suzhou Industrial Park (SIP) and the New United Motor Manufacturing, Inc. (NUMMI), Inkpen (2008) finds specific methods of knowledge transfer. In the case of the SIP and NUMMI joint venture, he discovered that personnel transfers, training programs, executive visits, the establishment of a coordinating office, leadership commitments to learning, and the building of a network were successful knowledge transfer channels. In any situation, successful knowledge transfer demands appropriate mechanisms (Jasimuddin, 2007; Davenport and Prusak, 2000; Pan and Scharbrough, 1999; Hansen *et al.,* 1999; Easterby-Smith, Lyles and Tsang, 2008; Hislop, 2005; Appleyard, 1996). For example, delivering papers, blueprints, or hardware that represent knowledge to the recipient organization, planning social events, transferring experienced employees, and supplying documents, blueprints, or hardware to the recipient organization (Easterby-Smith, et al., 2008). Organizational learning, rules, instructions, and routines (Grants, 1996, 1997; Dyer and Nobeoka, 2000). Rules, directives, routines (Grants, 1996, 1997; Dyer and Nobeoka, 2000), organizational learning (Richter and Vettel, 1995), training (Thompson, Gentner and Lowenstein, 2000), Information and Communication Technology (ICT) (Scarbrough *et al.*, 1999; Alavi and Leidner, 2001; Huber, 2001), discussions and meetings are also noteworthy mechanisms in transferring knowledge. However, question remains, how do we apply these mechanisms during the crisis time of COVID 19 Pandemic? Some important mechanisms and their counter TM strategies, of them, are in line with Welan and Carcary (2011).

In this era, internet-based social media has become an integral part of people's life, and many individuals communicate with one another via Facebook, Whatsapp, LinkedIn, blogs, and other social media platforms (Marbun, Juliandi, & Effendi, 2020). Social media works as an effective mechanism of knowledge transfer. During COVID 19 outbreak, knowledge transfer became very difficult. Customers, institutes, and organizations were stuck and people were confined to their homes. Social media worked as a common platform among all the stakeholders.

Strategy: Appleyard (2007) identifies that in terms of knowledge access and usage, the telephone serves as a private and unconstrained device. A telephone is useful during COVID 19 Pandemic.

However, Jasimuddin (2007) put the use of the telephone as a knowledge transfer mechanism on the basis of strong personal ties between the actors, distant location of the actors and personalization strategies.

Simple, readable, and understandable reading materials help the readers to absorb knowledge easily; hence, knowledge is also transferred through books, pamphlets, and other reading materials. *Strategy:* In the pandemic of COVID 19 time, maximum use of online library services may be helpful. Soft copies of the books are beneficial during the COVID 19-curfew time. Mobile library services and delivery services of hard copies of the book are useful. Courier and postal services for hardcopy books may be considered during COVID 19 outbreak.

Wathne *et al.* (1996) identify face-to-face as the richest vehicle for transfer. Appleyard (1996) and Hislop (2005) find face-to-face meetings are frequently used as a method of knowledge sharing. Davenport and Prusak (2000) also find that Face-to-face communication is frequently the most effective mode of knowledge transmission, hence knowledge transmission through face-to-face interactions and tales, in addition to more formal forms, may be strongly promoted (Davenport and Prusak, 2000). Face-to-face communication helps actors to explain and learn complicated knowledge from one another. It also allows contributors and receivers to freely and openly express thoughts, opinions, and ideas. *TM Strategy:* In the COVID 19 situation, outsourcing certain operations in a less spread area may be fruitful. Talented employees should be identified in the organization and a reshuffling of the employees may be carried out. Telephone and online activities are effective.

Appleyard (1996) identifies 'Conference' as a tool for opening knowledge to the public from an access point of view and allowing unfettered use of the knowledge.

Strategy: Maximum academic conferences (e.g. The British Academy of Management) have gone online during COVID 19. These virtual conferences could achieve their objectives of knowledge transfer in this turbulent time.

Strategy: Signboards, banners, and posters are the media for knowledge transfer. These mechanisms may be used to inform about the products and services of the organizations, and to aware people of the danger of the Pandemic.

From ancient Greek and Roman thinkers to current playwrights, dramas have been used to mirror and investigate the human predicament (George, *et al.,* 1998). George, *et al.* (1998) divides drama-based training into three categories: low-impact training, which focuses on the topic for a broad audience that is unfamiliar with the subject, moderate-impact training, which involves more audience participation and invites audience members to question the actors after the performance, and high-impact training, which is staged by the trainees and is contextual, such as a flight simulator where the trainee is the actor. *Strategy:* Though staging plays is one of the techniques for knowledge transfer, it is not recommended to gather people and produce drama during COVID 19. Instead, video snippets, YouTube, online films, and other similar resources could be beneficial.

Challenges and Strategies Related to Knowledge Transfer Barriers

The elements that promote or obstruct knowledge transmission may generally be divided into three groups. First, elements relating to the point of knowledge transmission; second, factors relating to the type of knowledge, medium, channels, context, and environment; and third, factors relating to the point of knowledge reception. An important topic of research is determining which variables obstruct knowledge transmission. (van den Hoff and van Weenen, 2004). Many researchers (Argote, 1999; Davenport and Prusak, 2000; Grant, 1996; van Wijk *et al.*, 2008; Osterloh and Frey, 2000; Hendriks, 1999; Szulanski, 2000; Kalling, 2003; Argote and Ingram, 2000; Easterby-Smith *et al.*, 2008; Liu and Liu, 2008; Hansen, 1999; Stenmark, 2000; Inkpen, 2007; Haldin-Herrgard, 2000; Barachini, 2009) have added numerous contributing factors influencing knowledge transfer to the literature of knowledge management. Argote (1999) identifies superordinate relationship, physical location, size, and the success of the organization s, chain and network relationships, characteristics of the recipient organizations, motivation, learning mechanisms, codifying knowledge in artifacts or routines, and rich communication mechanisms as important factors influencing knowledge transfer. Here certain fundamental factors influencing the transfer are noted.

Polanyi (1966) and Nonaka (1994) showed the two dimensions of knowledge, tacit and explicit, and how they generate value. The inherent characteristics of tacit knowledge, such as non-codification (Hu, 1995; Nonaka and Konno, 1998), difficulty in articulation (Spender, 1996), communication difficulties (Ambrosini and Bowman, 2001), and warehousing complications (Hensen, Nohria, and Tierney, 1999), act as catalysts to the transfer process's barriers. Stenmark (2000) discovered that tacit knowledge is difficult to come by consistently emphasizing that (i) we are not always conscious of our tacit knowledge, (ii) we do not need to make it explicit in order to utilize it on a personal level, and (iii) we may not want to give up a key competitive advantage as challenges and reasons for the externalization process' failure. Perception, language, time, value, and distance are obstacles, according to Haldin-Herrgard (2000). For example, community members of developing countries seldom know that they have enough indigenous knowledge, so they are in confusion about 'what to share?' Tacit knowledge is invisible and inaudible and resides in the human brain. Language is also a barrier to transfer in two different cultures between the donors and the recipients.

A strained connection between the source and the recipient makes it more difficult to resolve transfer-related issues (Szulanski, 2000) and the recipient's trust, authority, and prestige are all important factors in the relationship (Ipe, 2003). The degree of knowledge transfer is influenced by the type of social network. (Argote and Ingram, 2000). According to research, the number of relationships with other organizations and units enhances the likelihood of gaining access to important knowledge. (van Wijk *et al.,* 2008) and more, it enables them to learn from one another. (Hogberg and Edvinsson, 1998).

Strategy: In the outbreak of COVID19, frequent virtual meetings may improve the relationship and help transfer more knowledge.

Talukdar, Hasan, & Nahar (2021) revealed that the universities in Bangladesh had been facing actuate problems in teaching and learning during COVID 19. *Strategy:* They suggested blended learning techniques for all higher education institutes.

Extending the notions of motivation of Hendriks (1999) and Szulanski (2000), Ipe (2003) informs, internal variables include the perceived power of knowledge and the reciprocity that occurs as a result of sharing. Relationships with the receiver and benefits of sharing are examples of external variables. However, with a dissenting voice, Barachini (2009) claimed, Individuals do not freely share their knowledge; hence, knowledge transfer might be considered a business transaction. However, highly motivated workers transfer knowledge to their colleagues for the development of the latter spontaneously. During the outbreak of COVID 19, a line survey to measure the motivational level of the employees may be carried out. Short-term goals and objectives may be set. Need to share information as a team in the organization. Employee morale should be kept high. *TM Strategy:* (i)Reward and recognition programs (ii) Engaging Knowledge transfer mentoring. Further, a most appropriate employee should occupy a deserving position and, if additional employees are required, virtual recruitment and selection may be conducted (Whelan & Carcary, 2011).

Increased intra- and inter-organizational knowledge transfer necessitate the use of the absorptive ability (van Wijk *et al.,* 2008). Knowledge absorption is dependent on the recipient's capacity to add new knowledge to current knowledge at both the individual and organizational levels (Grant, 1996). However, if the receiver does not assimilate the knowledge, it has not been transferred (Davenport and Prusak, 2000), and the primary goal of knowledge transfer is compromised. *TM Strategy:* Competency-based training may be arranged (Whelan & Carcary, 2011) during the outbreak of COVID 19. However, these pieces of training, all should be virtual. There should be proper succession planning in the organization.

Several researchers (Davenport and Prusak 2000; Ardichvili, Maurer, Li, Wentling and Stuedemann, 2006; Sun and Scott, 2005; Lam, 2005) have demonstrated the impact of culture on knowledge transmission. Davenport and Prusak (2000) find that Lack of trust, different cultures, vocabularies, frames of reference, giving status and rewards to knowledge owners, treating knowledge as a prerogative of particular groups, lack of time and meeting places, a narrow idea of productive work, and other cultural factors could slow or prevent knowledge transfer and erode some of it as it moves through the organization. *TM Strategy:* People that have a common work culture are more likely to communicate efficiently, resulting in more effective knowledge transfer.(Davenport and Prusak, 2000).

The exchange of knowledge across teams is facilitated by trust (Goh, 2002). It is one of the most important success elements for successful transfer (Nahapiet and Ghoshal, 1998). Mutual trust gives actors the confidence and security to open out to one another (Wang *et al.,* 2006). On the other side, a lack of trust is a barrier to knowledge transfer since it creates uncertainty and risk. (Hislop, 2005). The information transfer network is built on mutual trust amongst the people involved in knowledge exchange. Over time, trust develops as a result of interactions (Dawson, 2000). When the parties' trust grows, so does their confidence in the future's certainty (Aadne, von Krogh and Roos, 1996). Lack of trust, on the other side, has a negative impact on organizational performance. (Debowski, 2006) and presents a long-term impediment to knowledge transmission. *TM Strategy:* Establish a relationship between the employer and employees, network mentoring, and socialization.

Hsiao and Ormerod (1999) suggest the main three ways of overcoming the barriers to knowledge transfer, by identifying a practitioner-oriented approach using advanced information technology and groupware, electronic product definition or data warehousing, a better mechanism approach such as the normative transfer process, and the knowledge spiral framework of Nonaka and Takeuchi, (1995), to enable the creation of knowledge, and motivational factors, particularly trust.

This corresponds with the views of Ali (2021).

Goh (2002) argues that leadership, the willingness of the leader to share knowledge, problem-solving/seeking behavior with all employees to be encouraged to be involved in knowledge transfer activities are important, along with a supportive structure in technology, training and skill development, and reward and organizational design. Additionally, he mentioned absorptive and retentive capacity and a knowledge base for all parties, and understanding between the parties. He also stated that the type of knowledge, which should match the process of transfer, is an important factor. Singh (2008) finds that consulting and delegating style of leadership has a significant positive impact on managing knowledge (knowledge transfer) in IT firms. *TM Strategy:* Leadership-based training.

Factors influencing transfer include collaborative know-how, learning capacity, alliance duration, training, knowledgeable personnel transfer, knowledge generation through know-how transfer, a focus on tacit knowledge, addressing assumptions about contextually, and the incorporation of knowledge in equipment or tools (Connell, Klein and Powell, 2003). Connell, Klein and Powell, 2003) also show the importance of similarities between the organizations engaged in the smooth flow of knowledge. Darr and Kurtzberg (2000) find that strategic similarities between the firms in the same industry allowed more knowledge transfer than that of customer or location similarities of firms.

Miscellaneous Barriers to Knowledge Transfer and Strategies

Davenport and Prusak (2000) chalked down a list of knowledge transfer barriers. A close study on these barriers, reveals that these barriers also fit in the COVID 19 Pandemic situation (Table-1).

The barriers and possible TM strategies in the light of COVID 19 are shown in Table-1. In COVID 19 situation, there may be a lack of trust between knowledge transferors and the recipients. *TM Strategy:* Frequent online meetings may eradicate this problem. Different cultural issues may be removed through team-building training or job rotation. It is not possible to arrange a physical meeting. *TM Strategy:* This problem may be solved through training employing Facebook, Microsoft team, Zoom, brainstorming on the issues in the organization, and online conferences. Rewards should be given to the maximum online users. 'Lack of absorptive capacity in recipients' is a frequent problem in knowledge transfer. COVID 19 has reinforced this problem. Online communication and the use of social media may create a misinterpretation of knowledge between the knowledge players. *TM Strategy:* Online competency-based training, Online Seminars, and short online training courses may be conducted. Knowledge may be confined to the hands of a particular group and position (s). *TM Strategy:* In such cases, the higher management of the organization should encourage a nonhierarchical attitude to knowledge, with the quality of ideas taking precedence above the source's rank. Disseminating knowledge using internet channels may be useful. Identifying the knowledge talents is a challenging task for the organizations. *TM Strategy:* Reviewing Annual reports, recruiting talents, IT experts, and Chief Knowledge Officer/ Coordinator may be fruitful strategies for it.

Table 1. Barriers to knowledge transfer and possible Strategies

Sl.	Knowledge Transfer Barriers	Possible TM Strategies/initiatives in light with COVID 19
1.	Lack of trust (lack of faith between the knowledge transferor and the knowledge recipient)	Frequent online face-to-face meetings help to build connections and trust.
2.	Diverse cultures, vocabularies, frames of reference	Educate, discuss, publish, team up, and rotate jobs to find common ground.
3.	Lack of time and meeting places; the narrow idea of productive work	Training: Facebook, Microsoft team, Zoom, brainstorming on the issues in the organization, Online conferences.
4.	Status and rewards go to the knowledge owners	Reward and recognition programs, the reward for engaging in online activities. Knowledge Transfer mentoring
5.	Lack of absorptive capacity in recipients	Online competency-based training, Online Seminars, short online courses,
6.	The belief that knowledge is the prerogative of particular groups, not-invented-here syndrome	Encourage a nonhierarchical attitude to knowledge, with the quality of ideas taking precedence above the source's rank. Disseminate information using internet channels.
7.	Identifying Knowledge Talents	Review Annual report, Recruit talents and IT expert Chief Knowledge Officer/ Coordinator.

Source: *Modified from Davenport and Prusak, 2000, p. 97; Whelan and Carcary, 2011*

A general discussion: There is no denying the fact that knowledge is a strategic resource for every firm. For every company, knowledge is a valuable asset. In a context, justified True Belief is knowledge (Gettier, 1963). Human brains are the source of all knowledge, as well as the place where knowledge is formed and conveyed. Tacit and explicit knowledge are the two most basic forms of knowledge. Tacit knowledge is stored in human brains and becomes explicit knowledge when it is released in any way (Nonaka and Takeuchi, 1995).

By utilizing this rich resource, businesses may gain a competitive advantage (Hasnain, 2015). Knowledge Management is concerned with how this precious resource may be best preserved inside the company. The art of recognizing, obtaining, storing, managing, transferring, and using the knowledge in an organization is known as knowledge management (Jasimuddin *et al.*, 2006).

Knowledge transfer may be the most important of these phases, as it is impossible for organizations to live and thrive without it (Argote *et al.*, 2000). A company may approach a standstill if knowledge is not transferred among personnel, and there will be a scarcity of fresh knowledge. As a result, competitive advantages, productivity, and innovativeness are lost. Any business that wants to avoid unanticipated events has to have a good knowledge management strategy in place.

Talent Management (TM) and Knowledge Management (KM) are sibling fields of study that go hand in hand. The goal of TM is to create strategies. TM searches for talent requirements in businesses. TM implements training and development programs. Their (TM) strategies include succession planning and talent retention measures (Whelan and Carcary, 2011). According to the findings, TM develops strategies and ensures client happiness.

The vehicles via which knowledge is moved from one place to another are known as knowledge transfer mechanisms (Davenport and Prusak, 2000). These are the channels via which is sent and received. It's critical to pick the right knowledge transfer mechanisms. Mechanisms are chosen based on the situation (Jasimuddin, 2007). Knowledge transfer mechanisms include training, social activities, the transfer of experienced personnel, documents, blueprints, hardware, books, leaflets, reading materials, social media, face-to-face meetings, conferences, signboards, banners, posters, staging dramas, and telephones, among others (Hasnain, et al., 2016). The COVID 19 epidemic has thrown the globe into disarray (Ali, 2021), and many knowledge transfer mechanisms are broken or ineffective.

IMPLICATIONS FOR THEORY AND PRACTICE

In a dynamic circumstance like COVID 19, understanding how to design and present TM strategies related to KM problems is crucial. This chapter has the potential to make a variety of theoretical and practical contributions. *Implications for business organizations*: This chapter outlines the steps that businesses may take to develop TM strategies that address KM concerns in a chaotic environment. Unexpected environmental circumstances can be accommodated by business entities. *Implications for academic institutions:* COVID 19 has created significant impediments to knowledge transmission and research in academia. Smart institutes might learn how to maintain their campuses open in the face of disasters. *Implications for state governments*: TM strategies may be used correctly by state governments throughout any crisis (s).

CONCLUSION

KM may get international attention as it has the potential to provide a lot of benefits to businesses. Knowledge identification, knowledge generation, knowledge storage, knowledge transfer, and knowledge application are all part of the KM process. Knowledge transfer might be one of the most important among them, as it is impossible to develop new and creative knowledge- applications without it. To transfer knowledge between the knowledge transferors and the knowledge recipients, media (channels) are required. The focus of Talent Management (TM) is on TM strategy, talent shortages, succession planning, recruiting, training, motivating, and retaining the essential individuals in businesses. In the context of the COVID 19 Pandemic, there are a number of KM difficulties related to knowledge transfer methods and impediments that necessitate TM techniques, which are developed from the literature. Many websites, academic publications, and books proved to be valuable resources. Knowledge transfer became difficult as a result of the COVID 19 Pandemic, and human physical presence may have exacerbated the problem. During the COVID 19 Pandemic, a phone comes in handy. On the other hand, the usage of the telephone as a knowledge transfer medium depends on strong personal links between the players, their remote location, and personalization methods. Knowledge absorption and obtaining tangible copies of books become difficult as a result of the COVID 19 Pandemic. During the COVID 19 epidemic, making full use of online library resources may be beneficial. During the COVID 19-curfew period, soft copies of the books are useful. Mobile library services and hard copy book distribution services are both beneficial. During the COVID 19 outbreak, courier and postal services for hardcopy publications may be considered. Academic conferences facilitate networking and knowledge transfer among academics. During COVID 19, the majority of academic conferences (for example, the British Academy of Management) went online. In this tumultuous period, these virtual conferences may be able to fulfill their knowledge transfer goals.

The medium for knowledge dissemination is signboards, banners, and posters. These tools might be utilized to inform people about the organizations' products and services, as well as to raise awareness about the COVID 19 Pandemic. Though staging plays is one of the methods for knowledge transfer, it is not advisable to gather people and stage theatre during COVID 19. Video clips, YouTube, online films, and other comparable tools, on the other hand, maybe advantageous.

The sort of social network has an impact on the degree of knowledge transfer. Physical presence is not permitted during COVID 19. In the event of a COVID19 epidemic, regular virtual meetings may build relationships and aid knowledge sharing. During COVID 19, higher education institutions faced significant challenges in teaching and learning. Blended learning techniques at all higher education institutions may be a solution. During the COVID 19 epidemic, a line survey to assess staff motivation may be conducted. It is possible to set short-term goals and objectives.

It is critical for the organization's team to exchange expertise. Employee morale should be maintained at a high level. It's possible that reward and recognition systems will be implemented. Mentoring for knowledge transfer may be beneficial. Furthermore, a deserving employee should hold a deserving job, and virtual recruiting and selection may be undertaken if extra employees are necessary. Competency-based training is useful in increasing the knowledge absorption capacity of employees during the COVID 19 epidemic. These components of training, on the other hand, should all be virtual. This issue might be resolved by training on, Facebook, Microsoft's team, Zoom etc. The largest number of internet users should be rewarded. In the organization, adequate succession planning is required. Establishing a relationship between the employer and employees, network mentoring, and socialization may be a good strategy for strengthening the trust among them. Employees in companies may have a shared culture. People that have a shared work culture are more likely to communicate effectively, resulting in more effective knowledge transfer during COVID 19. It is critical to developing a relationship between the company and workers, as well as network mentorship and socializing, in order to build strong employee trust.

Due to the possibility of a leadership crisis in the company as a result of COVID 19's mass hospitalization, leadership-based training should be provided to all levels of employees. Knowledge may be restricted to members of a specific group or position. In such instances, the organization's top management should promote a non-hierarchical approach to knowledge, with the quality of ideas taking precedence over the source's status. Organizations face a difficult problem in identifying knowledge skills. Reviewing annual reports, acquiring talent, IT expertise, and appointing a Chief Knowledge Officer/Coordinator might all be effective tactics.

RECOMMENDATIONS

It may be recommended, that maximum knowledge transfer mechanisms' alternatives are the IT/internet/related mechanisms, while people are confined at home. Ali (2020, 2021) finds, that during the COVID19 volatility, digitalization innovation, robots, AI (Artificial Intelligence), and blockchain technology might be useful knowledge transfer mechanisms. There are a number of knowledge transfer barriers identified as well. Knowledge transfer is hampered by a strained connection between the source and the recipient. Due to COVID 19 pandemic, frequent online meetings may improve the relationship between them. Lack of motivation is hindering knowledge transfer. Reward and recognition programs may help in the situation of COVID 19.

Knowledge transfer is hampered by receivers' inability to absorb knowledge. Hence, online competency-based training, online seminars, and short online training courses may be helpful during COVID 19 Pandemic. Knowledge transfer is hampered by cultural variations between senders and receivers. Both the parties should be careful and honor their respective cultures. For MNC, online training may be arranged for the expatriates. However, advanced information technology could be fruitful in this situation of the COVID 19 pandemic. Identifying knowledge talents is a struggle. Examining the annual report may be a helpful instrument. Highly qualified and skilled personnel should be placed in the proper position. Online recruitment may be carried out. Employment of a Chief Knowledge Officer/Coordinator may be advantageous during this COVID 19 Pandemic. There should be contingency Talent Management Strategies for any adverse situation. Necessary help may be taken from the World Bank as along with other supports it also shares knowledge with the public and private sectors of the partner countries (Talukdar, 2018).

REFERENCES

Aadne, J., Krogh, G., & Roos, J. (1996). Representationism: The traditional approach to cooperative strategies. In G. Krogh & J. Roos (Eds.), *Managing Knowledge: Perspectives on Cooperation and Competition* (pp. 9–31). Sage Publications. doi:10.4135/9781446280195.n2

Al-Azzam, Z.F., & Al-Qura'a. (2018). How knowledge management mediates the strategic role of talent management in enhancing customer satisfaction. *Pacific Business Review, 11*(1), 30-42. https://ssrn.com/abstract=3364693

Alavi, M., & Leidner, D. E. (2001). Knowledge management and knowledge management systems: Conceptual foundations and research issues. *Management Information Systems Quarterly*, *25*(1), 107–136. doi:10.2307/3250961

Albino, V., Claudio, G. A., & Schiuma, G. (1999). Knowledge transfer and inter-firm relationships in industrial districts: The role of the leader firm. *Technovation, 19*(1), 53–63. doi:10.1016/S0166-4972(98)00078-9

Ali, M. M. (2019). Grim situation of the world due to COVID19: economic perspective. *Geopolitics under Globalization, 3*(1), 24-29. . doi:10.21511/gg.03(1).2020.03

Ali, M. M. (2020). Digitization of the emerging economy: An exploratory and explanatory case study. *Journal of Governance & Regulation*, *9*(4), 25–36. doi:10.22495/jgrv9i4art2

Ali, M. M. (2021). Digital opportunities in the healthcare enterprises during COVID-19: An empirical analysis of the developing country. *Corporate Governance and Organizational Behavior Review*, *5*(2), 44–55. doi:10.22495/cgobrv5i2p4

Ambrosini, V., & Bowman, C. (2001). Tacit knowledge: Some suggestions for operationalisation. *Journal of Management Studies*, *38*(6), 811–829. doi:10.1111/1467-6486.00260

Appleyard, M. M. (1996). How does Knowledge flow? Interfirm patterns in the semiconductor industry. *Strategic Management Journal*, *17*, 137-154. https://www.jstor.org/stable/2486996

Ardichvili, A., Maurer, M., Li, W., Wentling, T., & Stuedemann, R. (2006). Cultural influences on knowledge sharing through online communities of practice. *Journal of Knowledge Management*, *10*(1), 94–107. doi:10.1108/13673270610650139

Argote, L. (1999). *Organizational Learning: Creating, Retaining and Transferring Knowledge*. Kluwer Academic Publishers.

Argote, L., & Ingram, P. (2000). Knowledge transfer: A basis for competitive advantage in Firms. *Organizational Behavior and Human Decision Processes*, *82*(1), 150–169. doi:10.1006/obhd.2000.2893

Argote, L., Ingram, P., Levine, J. M., & Moreland, R. L. (2000). Knowledge transfer in organizationns: Learning from the experience of others. *Organizational Behavior and Human Decision Processes*, *82*(1), 1–8. doi:10.1006/obhd.2000.2883

Argote, L., McEvily, B., & Reagans, R. (2003). Managing knowledge in organizations: An integrative framework and review of emerging themes. *Management Science*, *49*(4), 571–582. doi:10.1287/mnsc.49.4.571.14424

Barachini, F. (2009). Cultural and social issues for knowledge sharing. *Journal of Knowledge Management*, *13*(1), 98–110. doi:10.1108/13673270910931198

Bayyoud, M., & Sayyad, N. (2015). The role of talent management on companies' performance listed in Palestine: Literature Review. *American Journal of Business, Economics and Management*, *3*(4), 234-240. http://www.openscienceonline.com/journal/archive2?journalId=709&paperId=2470

Bell, D. G., Giordano, R., & Putz, P. (2002). Inter-firm sharing of process knowledge: Exploring knowledge markets. *Knowledge and Process Management*, *9*(1), 12–22. doi:10.1002/kpm.131

Chaturvedi, S., & Singh, T. (2021). Knowledge Management Initiatives for Tackling th COVID19Pandemic.*Metamorphosis*,*20*(1),25–34.doi:10.1177/09726225211023677

Chowdhury, D. (2009). *The Determinants of Knowledge Transfer in Turkish Textile Apparel Industry* (PhD Thesis). University of Plymouth.

Chowdhury, D., & Butel, L. (2007). Knowledge transfer-A network approach to Turkey's Small and Medium Sized Enterprises (SMEs). *Journal of Global Strategy Management, 1*(2), 142–151. doi:10.20460/JGSM.2007118707

Chowdhury, D., Butel, L., Hakki, E., & Ismail, B. (2009). Knowledge transfer (KT) practices in Small and Medium Enterprises (SME's) of Turkish textile and apparel industry. *Journal of Global Strategy Management, JSGM-6*(3), 52–66. doi:10.20460/JGSM.2009318460

Connell, N. A. D., Klein, J. H., & Powell, P. L. (2003). It's tacit knowledge but not as we know it: Redirecting the search for knowledge. *The Journal of the Operational Research Society, 54*(2), 140–152. doi:10.1057/palgrave.jors.2601444

Darr, E. D., Argote, L., & Epple, D. (1995). The acquisition, transfer and deprecation of knowledge in service organization s: Productivity in franchises. *Management Science, 41*(11), 1750–1762. https://www.jstor.org/stable/2632871. doi:10.1287/mnsc.41.11.1750

Darr, E. D., & Kurtzberg, T. R. (2000). An investigation of partner similarity dimensions of knowledge transfer. *Organizational Behavior and Human Decision Processes, 82*(1), 28–44. doi:10.1006/obhd.2000.2885 PMID:10631067

Davenport, T. H., & Prusak, L. (1998). *Working Knowledge: How Organizations Manage What They Know*. Harvard Business School Press.

Davenport, T. H., & Prusak, L. (2000). *Working Knowledge: How Organizations Manage What They Know*. Harvard Business School Press.

Dawson, R. (2000). *Developing Knowledge-Based Client Relationships: The Future of Professional Services*. Butterworth-Heinemann.

Debowski, S. (2006). *Knowledge Management*. John Wiley & Sons Australia Ltd.

Dyer, J. H., & Nobeoka, K. (2000). Creating and managing a high performance knowledge sharing network: The Toyota case. *Strategic Management Journal, 21*(3), 345–367. doi:10.1002/(SICI)1097-0266(200003)21:3<345::AID-SMJ96>3.0.CO;2-N

Easterby-Smith, M., Lyles, M. A., & Tsang, E. W. K. (2008). Inter-organizational knowledge transfer: Current themes and future prospects. *Journal of Management Studies, 45*(4), 677–690. doi:10.1111/j.1467-6486.2008.00773.x

Easterby-Smith, M., Thorpe, R., & Lowe, A. (2002). *Management Research: An Introduction*. Sage Publications.

Edvardsson, I. R. (2006). Knowledge management and SMEs: The case of Icelandic firms. *Knowledge Management Research and Practice*, *4*(4), 275–282. doi:10.1057/palgrave.kmrp.8500111

Gamble, P., & Blackwell, J. (2001). *Knowledge Management: A State of the Art Guide*. Kogan Page Limited.

Garaventa, E. (1998). Drama: A tool for teaching business ethics. *Business Ethics Quarterly*, *8*(3), 535–545. doi:10.2307/3857436

George, J. S., Schwager, S., & Canavan, F. (1998). A guide to drama-based training. *Employment Relations Today*, *25*(4), 15–19. doi:10.1002/ert.3910250408

Gettier, E. L. (1963). Is justified true belief knowledge? *Analysis*, *23*(6), 121–123. doi:10.1093/analys/23.6.121

Goh, S. C. (2002). Managing effective knowledge transfer: An integrative framework and some practice implications. *Journal of Knowledge Management*, *6*(1), 23–30. doi:10.1108/13673270210417664

Grant, R.M. (1996). Toward a knowledge-based theory of the firm. *Strategic Management Journal*, *17*, 109-112. . doi:10.1002/smj.4250171110

Grant, R. M. (1997). The knowledge-based view of the firm: Implications for management practice. *Long Range Planning*, *30*(3), 450–454. https://www.jstor.org/stable/2486994. doi:10.1016/S0024-6301(97)00025-3

Groves, K. S. (2007). Integrating leadership development and succession planning best practices. *Journal of Management Development*, *26*(3), 239–260. doi:10.1108/02621710710732146

Haldin-Herrgard, T. (2000). Difficulties in diffusion of tacit knowledge in organizations. *Journal of Intellectual Capital*, *1*(4), 357–365. https://doi.org/10.1108/14691930010359252

Hall, B. P. (2001). Values development and learning organization s of knowledge. *Journal of Management*, *1*(5), 19–32. doi:10.1108/13673270110384374

Hansen, M. T., Nohria, N., & Tierney, T. (1999). What's your strategy for managing knowledge? *Harvard Business Review*, (March-April), 106–116.

Hasnain, S. S. (2015). Organizational knowledge: The Panacea to NGO-operations. *Procedia: Social and Behavioral Sciences*, *195*, 197–201. https://doi.org/10.1016/j.sbspro.2015.06.350

Hasnain, S. S. (2016). *Knowledge Management: Towards a New Horizon*. IISTE.

Hasnain, S. S., Jasimuddin, S. M., & Fuller-Love, N. (2016). Exploring causes, taxonomies, mechanisms and barriers influencing knowledge transfer: Empirical studies in NGOs. *Information Resources Management Journal*, *29*(1), 39–56. doi:10.4018/IRMJ.2016010103

Heavin, C., & Neville, K. (2006). Mentoring knowledge workers. In D. G. Schwartz (Ed.), *Encyclopedia of Knowledge Management* (pp. 621–626). Idea Group Reference.

Hendriks, P. H. J. (1999). Why share knowledge? The influence of ICT on the motivation for knowledge sharing. *Knowledge and Process Management*, *6*(2), 91–100. https://doi.org/10.1002/(SICI)1099-1441(199906)6:2%3C91::AID-KPM54%3E3.0.CO;2-M

Hislop, D. (2005). *Knowledge Management in Organizations-A Critical Introduction*. Oxford University Press.

Hofer-Alfeis, J., & van der Spek, R. (2002). The knowledge strategy process: An Instrument for business owners. In T. H. Davenport & G. J. B. Probst (Eds.), *Knowledge Management Case Book: Siemens Best Practices* (pp. 24–39). Policies Corporate Publishing & John Wiley & Sons.

Hogberg, C., & Edvinsson, L. (1998). A design for futurizing knowledge networking. *Journal of Knowledge Management*, *2*(2), 81–92. https://doi.org/10.1108/13673279810249404

Hsiao, R., & Ormerod, R. (1999). *The dynamics of knowledge transfer: a discovery-oriented framework*. Warwick Business School Research Paper, No.307.

Hu, Y. (1995). The international transferability of the firm's advantage. *California Management Review*, *37*, 73–88. https://doi.org/10.2307%2F41165811

Huber, G. (2001). Transfer of knowledge in knowledge management systems: Unexplored issues and suggested studies. *European Journal of Information Systems*, *10*, 72–79. https://doi.org/10.1057/palgrave.ejis.3000399

Inkpen, A. C. (1998). Learning and knowledge acquisition through international strategic alliances. *Academy of Management Executives*, *12*(4), 69-80. https://www.jstor.org/stable/4165495

Ipe, M. (2003). Knowledge sharing in organizations: A conceptual framework. *Human Resource Development Review*, *2*(4), 337–359. https://doi.org/10.1177%2F1534484303257985

Jashapara, A. (2004). *Knowledge Management-An Integrated Approach*. Pearson Education Limited.

Jasimuddin, S. M. (2007). Exploring knowledge transfer mechanisms: The case of a UK-based group within a high-tech global corporation. *International Journal of Information Management*, *27*, 294–300. https://doi.org/10.1016/j.ijinfomgt.2007.03.003

Jasimuddin, S. M., Connell, N. A. D., & Klein, J. H. (2005). The paradox of using tacit and explicit knowledge: Strategies to face dilemmas. *Management Decision*, *43*(1), 102–112. https://doi.org/10.1108/00251740510572515

Jasimuddin, S. M., Connell, N. A. D., & Klein, J. H. (2006). Understanding organizational memory. In D. G. Schwartz (Ed.), *Encyclopedia of Knowledge Management* (pp. 870–875). Idea Group Reference.

Kalling, T. (2003). Organization-internal transfer of knowledge and the role of motivation: A qualitative case study. *Knowledge and Process Management*, *10*(2), 115–126. https://doi.org/10.1002/kpm.170

Kazemian, S., & Grant, S. B. (2022). The impact of the COVID-19 pandemic on knowledge sharing in UK higher education. *VINE Journal of Information and Knowledge Management Systems*. doi:10.1108/VJIKMS-06-2021-0096

Lam, W. (2005). Successful knowledge management requires a knowledge culture: A case study. *Knowledge Management Research and Practice*, *3*, 206–217. https://doi.org/10.1057/palgrave.kmrp.8500068

Lewis, R. E., & Heckman, R. J. (2006). Talent Management: A critical review. *Human Resource Management Review*, *16*, 139–154. https://doi.org/10.1016/j.hrmr.2006.03.001

Marbun, D. S., Juliandi, A., & Effendi, S. (2020). The effect of social media culture and knowledge transfer on performance. *BIRCI Journal, 3*(3), 2513-2530. doi:10.33258/birci.v3i3.1234

Marquardt, M. J. (1996). *Building the Learning Organization: A Systems Approach to Quantum Improvement and Global Success*. McGraw-Hill.

Mohammad, A. A., Gururajan, R., & Hafeez-Baig. (2017). Knowledge Management in Business Environment. *Proceeding WI '17*.

Moton, L., & Ashton, C. (2005). Managing talent for competitive advantage. *Strategic HR Review*, *5*(4), 28–31. https://doi.org/10.1108/14754390580000819

Mu, J., Peng, G., & Love, E. (2008). Interfirm networks, social capital, and knowledge flow. *Journal of Knowledge Management*, *12*(4), 86–100. https://dx.doi.org/10.1108/13673270810884273

Nahapiet, J., & Ghosal, S. (1998). Social capital, intellectual capital, and the organizational advantage. *Academy of Management Review*, *23*(2), 242–266. https://doi.org/10.2307/259373

Nonaka, I. (1994). A dynamic theory of organizational knowledge creation. *Organization Science*, *5*(1), 14–37.

Nonaka, I., & Konno, N. (1998). The concept of "Ba": Building a foundation for knowledge creation. *California Management Review*, *40*(3), 40–45. https://doi.org/10.2307%2F41165942

Nonaka, I., & Takeuchi, H. (1995). *The Knowledge Creating Company*. Oxford University Press.

Pan, S. L., & Scarbrough, H. (1998). A Socio-technical view of knowledge-sharing at Buckman Laboratories. *Journal of Knowledge Management*, *2*(1), 55–66. https://doi.org/10.1108/EUM0000000004607

Polanyi, M. (1962). *Personal Knowledge: Towards a Post-Critical Philosophy*. University of Chicago Press.

Polanyi, M. (1966). *The Tacit Dimension*. Routledge.

Prahalad, C. K., & Hamel, G. (1990). The core competition of the corporation. *Harvard Business Review*, *68*(3), 79–91.

Ringo, T., Schweyer, A., DeMarco, M., Jones, R., & Lesser, E. (2010). *Integrating talent management-turning talent management into a competitive advantage-an industry view*. IBM Global Business Services.

Sandhawalia, B. S., & Dalcher, D. (2011). Developing knowledge management capabilities: A structured approach. *Journal of Knowledge Management*, *15*(2), 313–328. https://doi.org/10.1108/13673271111119718

Scarbrough, H., Robertson, M., & Swan, J. (2005). Professional media and management fashion: The case of knowledge management. *Scandinavian Journal of Management*, *2*(21), 197–208. https://doi.org/10.1016/j.scaman.2005.02.011

Singh, S. K. (2008). Role of leadership in knowledge management. *Journal of Knowledge Management, 12*(4), 1367–3270. https://doi.org/10.1108/13673270810884219

Spender, J. C. (1996). Making knowledge the basis of a dynamic theory of the firm. *Strategic Management Journal, 17*, 45-62. doi:10.1002/smj.4250171106

Stenmark, D. (2000). Leveraging tacit Organizational knowledge. *Journal of Management Information Systems, 17*(3), 9–24. https://doi.org/10.1080/07421222.2000.11045655

Sun, P. Y., & Scott, J. L. (2005). An investigation of barriers to knowledge transfer. *Journal of Knowledge Management, 9*(2), 75–90. https://doi.org/10.1108/13673270510590236

Sveiby, K. E. (1996). Transfer of knowledge and information processing professions. *European Management Journal, 14*(4), 379–388. https://doi.org/10.1016/0263-2373(96)00025-4

Szulanski, G. (1996). Exploring internal stickiness: Impediments to the transfer of best practice within the firm. *Strategic Management Journal, 17*, 27-43. doi:10.1002/smj.4250171105

Szulanski, G. (2000). The process of knowledge transfer: A diachronic analysis of stickiness. *Organizational Behavior and Human Decision Processes, 82*(1), 9–27. https://doi.org/10.1006/obhd.2000.2884

Talukdar, M. R. I. (2018). Partners and priorities for Bangladesh: Development aid effectiveness. *The International Journal of Social Sciences (Islamabad), 7*(4), 435–446. https://doi.org/10.34190/ejkm.19.3.2102

Talukdar, M. R. I., Hasan, F., & Nahar, R. (2021). Necessity of blended learning Bangladesh's higher education institutions, *The Independent*, 1.

Thumiki, V. R. R., & Jurcic, A. (2021). Impact of COVID-19 Crisis on Knowledge Management Practices in Sultanate of Oman. *Electronic Journal of Knowledge Management, 19*(3), 213–225. https://doi.org/10.34190/ejkm.19.3.2102

Tome, E., Gromara, E., & Hatch, A. (2021). Knowledge management and COVID 19. *Knowledge and Process Management, 29*, 70–78. https://doi.org/10.1002/kpm.1699

Van Wijk, R., Jansen, J. J. P., & Lyles, M. A. (2008). Inter- and intra-organizational knowledge transfer: A meta-analytic review and assessment of its antecedents and consequences. *Journal of Management Studies, 45*(4), 830–853. https://doi.org/10.1111/j.1467-6486.2008.00771.x

Wang, J., Ashleigh, M., & Meyer, E. (2006). Knowledge sharing and team trustworthiness: It's all about social ties. *Knowledge Management Research and Practice*, *4*, 175–186. https://doi.org/10.1057/palgrave.kmrp.8500098

Wathne, K., Roos, J., & von Krogh, G. (1996). Towards a theory of knowledge transfer in cooperative context. In G. Krogh & J. Roos (Eds.), *Managing Knowledge: Perspectives on Cooperation and Competition* (pp. 55–81). SAGE Publications Ltd.

Whelan, E., & Carcary, M. (2011). Integrating talent and knowledge management: Where are the benefits? *Journal of Knowledge Management*, *15*(4), 675–687. https://ssrn.com/abstract=1694455

KEY TERMS AND DEFINITIONS

Barriers to Knowledge Transfer: The barriers that prevent knowledge transfer from knowledge donors to knowledge receivers.

Knowledge: Experiences, ideas, skills, values, information in possession of any individual or organization.

Knowledge Management: An art of managing knowledge tactfully in the organizations.

Knowledge Management Process: A series of steps consists of identifying, acquiring, creating, storing, maintaining, transferring, and application of knowledge.

Knowledge Transfer/Transmission: Diffusing experiences, ideas, values, and information from the knowers to the not-knowers.

Mechanisms of Knowledge Transfer: The vehicles/channels by which knowledge is transferred between contributors and receivers of knowledge.

Talent Management: Attractions, identification, engagement, retention, and development of experienced and skilled individuals.

Talent Management Strategies: The art of managing the talents in the organizations.

Talents: Skillful and knowledgeable persons in the organizations who are capable of providing strategies.

Chapter 7
Virtual Intelligence in the Post-Pandemic Era:
Human Communication Challenges and Best Practices

Leigh Thompson
Northwestern University, USA

ABSTRACT

Numerous yet deceptively subtle differences between virtual and face-to-face communication profoundly influence organizational performance, team interaction, and psychological well-being. This chapter identifies the "Big 10" factors that affect human communication in virtual mediums: (1) mutual gaze, (2) directional gaze, (3) objective self-awareness, (4) seating configurations, (5) back-channel utterances, (6) side conversations, (7) touching, (8) gesturing, (9) collisions (unplanned face to face encounters between colleagues), and (10) shared context. This chapter then examines research on each of these key factors, discusses how each affects virtual communication, and suggests best practices for overcoming and navigating these challenges.

INTRODUCTION

The Covid19 crisis ushered in the most significant over-night organizational restructure that businesses ever faced. There was no time to prepare and most businesses did not have a playbook of scientifically-tested best practices for navigating the new virtual landscape. So began a large field experiment in virtual communication. Business

DOI: 10.4018/978-1-6684-3894-7.ch007

people adopted one of three mindsets: (a) wait-it-out, avoid virtual communication and plan to return to normal face to face communication; (b) engage in virtual communication, but use the same strategies and practices as used in traditional face to face communication, or (c) make a significant investment in learning new communication skills anticipating a new era of virtual business.

Many business people opted for *plan b*, assuming the pandemic would run its course in a few weeks or month and assumed that the strategies and best practices that worked in traditional face to face interaction would translate to virtual interactions. However, as the pandemic and its many variants wreaked havoc, many people made permanent changes in their personal lives and work. This means that the virtual-hybrid communication era is here to stay. Prior to the pandemic, less than 7% of team leaders reported that they worked in or led virtual teams; within 3 months following the pandemic, this increased nearly five-fold with over 33% reported working in virtual teams (Thompson, 2022). Before the pandemic, WFH (work-from-home) accounted for 5% of paid full work days in the United States; but over 40% since May 2021 (Fox, 2022).

VIRTUAL COMMUNICATION INTELLIGENCE (VCQ)

Virtual Communication intelligence, or VCQ, is *the ability to communicate and navigate relationships and achieve business goals when engaging with others who are not physically co-present.* When we speak of Virtual Communication Intelligence or VCQ, the focus is <u>not</u> on the technical, programming and computer-science skills and savvy that may be involved in learning and using new communication platforms, but instead, the cognitive, emotional, and social-behavioral skills necessary to be effective when using whatever technology might be involved. In this sense, our focus is on the personal challenges of the leader, not the larger organizational challenges. To be sure, someone who is resistant to learning and using the relevant software or hardware systems to conduct a virtual meeting would hardly be displaying virtual communication intelligence. However, someone who might have an advanced programming degree, possess state-of-the-art technical equipment, and have expertise in using the latest virtual platforms does not necessarily guarantee that they are exhibiting virtual *communication* intelligence. Thus, VCQ does not refer to one's *technical* skills, but rather the *social-cognitive communication* skills used within technology-based platforms. In this article, VCQ refers to the emotional, cognitive, social and motivational skills that are used to communicate with others in non-face to face modalities.

IS VCQ THE SAME AS EQ?

Certainly, some of the social-cognitive skills involved in effective virtual communication might seem reminiscent of the classic emotional intelligence skills as articulated by Daniel Goleman and his colleagues (Goleman, Boyatis, & McKee, 2013) and also Peter Salovey and colleagues (Salovey & Mayer, 1990). However, the use of classic "EQ" skills requires modification in a virtual medium. Traditional EQ (emotional intelligence) skills are not sufficient to communicate effectively in the new virtual communication era, ushered in by the Covid19 pandemic.

Prior to the global Covid19 pandemic, people skills were considered essential "table stakes" for effective leadership. Managers, leaders, and business executives were evaluated not simply on their substantive knowledge and decision-making, but also in terms of their emotional intelligence, including self-awareness, empathy, self-management and relationship management. Yet, when the global Covid19 pandemic ushered in an era of prolific virtual communication across a variety of platforms, this presented new challenges for managers and leaders. Overnight, managers and leaders were expected to motivate and lead their teams, negotiate with customers and clients, and collaborate across geographies and cultures, from using virtual communication platforms, all without physical copresence. Many of these leaders and managers did not have time to hone, much less perfect their virtual communication skills and instead, used what worked in the past or engaged in trial and error. Some grew increasingly frustrated and exited; others committed organizationally-fatal errors (including indecent exposure, failing to realize that one's audio was on, etc.), and some found a new energy and flourished in the novel virtual landscape. For example, Chris Hyams, CEO of Indeed.com made the decision that 70% of his 11,000 employees could permanently continue working from home.

DOES ADVANCED TECHNOLOGY LEAD TO GREATER VCQ?

It could be argued that advances in communication technology, such as high-definition video, state of the art audio and other virtual medium features would create near-perfect conditions for effective human virtual communication, thereby minimizing the need for any special consideration of virtual communication skills. As rational as this argument appears to be, virtual communication presents profound communication challenges that defy the fidelity of the technical systems, and require that communicators, intent upon being their best virtual selves identify and thoughtfully navigate.

RESEARCH ON VIRTUAL INTELLIGENCE

The concept of "virtual intelligence" has been identified by both researchers and practitioners as a critical management skill, even prior to the pandemic. Some of these approaches emphasize the need for individuals to train and develop skills for successful virtual work (Makarius & Larson, 2017). For example, one investigation found that in a work simulation of 57 virtual teams, emotional intelligence was associated with greater team viability (Pitts, Wright, & Harkabus, 2012). Some of these treatments have examined gaming behavior, focusing on MMOGs (massive multiplayer online games) and find a relationship between emotional intelligence and transformational leadership on team effectiveness (Mysirlaki & Paraskeva, 2020). Still other treatments have focused on emotions and emotional expressions in virtual contexts. For example, de Mio defined virtual emotional intelligence as virtual teams who "are aware of emotions and able to regulate them and this awareness and regulation both inward and outward via the virtual channels in the virtual space" (de Mio, 2002).

Given the omnipresence of the Covid19 pandemic and the extreme proliferation and utilization of virtual meeting platforms, the concept of virtual intelligence encompasses more than emotional skills and team management skills. In this chapter, I outline five essential skills for effective communication with others, both in and outside of one's own team or company in a non-face to face mediums: nonverbal expression (aka body language); verbal-conversational skills, emotional-empathic skills; group and meeting management; and situational awareness. I review the scientific research on each of these skills and provide illustrative examples. First, let's examine the advantages and disadvantages of virtual communication.

ADVANTAGES AND DISADVANTAGES OF VIRTUAL COMMUNICATION

There are numerous, yet deceptively subtle differences between virtual and face to face communication that profoundly affect objective performance as well as overall subjective well-being. Whereas it may be tempting to conclude that virtual communication is *always* inferior to traditional face to face communication, that assumption is not supported by research. In fact, virtual communication offers many advantages, in addition to the obvious convenience and efficiency arguments. For example, people are more likely to assume that the behavior of a group is driven by a common goal for physically distant groups, presumably because common goals would be the only means by which they are united (Henderson, 2009), *(see Table 1)*. Moreover, virtual communication can have a positive effect on team creativity

(Thompson, 2021). One research investigation found that remote meetings are more conducive to the evaluation of creative ideas. In particular, 745 pairs of engineers in five different countries brainstormed ideas for using a Frisbee or bubble wrap. The remote meeting participants generated fewer ideas but, when it was time to evaluate the options, the remote meeting engineers selected the better choice, as judged by a team of outside experts (Brucks & Levav, 2022).

Yet, it is true that the disadvantages of virtual communication may indeed collectively outweigh the advantages *(see Table 1)*. Yet, at the same time, virtual communication sets the stage for some unexpected and valuable benefits, particularly regarding teamwork.

CHALLENGES OF VIRTUAL COMMUNICATION

Zoom fatigue is a concept that was introduced early in the pandemic. Whereas it may seem that back-to-back zoom (or other virtual meeting platforms) sessions would lead to physical exhaustion, the construct of zoom fatigue refers to mental fatigue, induced because the cues and signals that people normally monitor to guide behavior in social situations are absent or are obscured in virtual meetings (Wiederhold, 2020). For this reason, managers who lack knowledge of human communication cues and processes are likely to feel exhausted and depleted. When managers are depleted and exasperated with virtual communication, despite their good-faith efforts and high motivation levels, they often blame themselves.

What's most perplexing and haunting about virtual communication challenges is that they are not immediately obvious to most managers and leaders, because many of them involve the <u>absence</u> of a stimulus or input that was previously present (in pre-pandemic face-to-face communication). Therefore, when virtual meetings and online conversations are clumsy, awkward and frustrating, managers often conclude that either they or others are at fault and this faulty attribution exacts a psychological (and often economic) toll for the manager. We've interviewed dozens of high-level leaders about their online virtual meetings and many of them declare that "something is missing but it is not clear what it is". Communicators often believe that there is something amiss with their own energy levels, speaking ability, and conversational skills when the interaction does not result in a positive outcome.

In this chapter, we do not attempt to outline an exhaustive list of the key social-cognitive differences between traditional face to face communication and virtual. Instead, we identify the "big 10" factors that affect human communication in virtual mediums: (1) mutual gaze; (2) directional gaze; (3) objective self-awareness; (4) seating configurations, (5) back-channel utterances; (6) side conversations; (7) touching; (8) gesturing; (9) collisions (unplanned face to face encounters between colleagues), and (10) shared context *(see Table 2)*. We examine the research on each of these key factors and discuss how their absence or presence affects virtual communication. We then present implications and suggest best practices for overcoming and navigating these challenges.

MUTUAL GAZE

In a face to face setting, conversational interactants lock eyes with others several times during a meeting or conversation. These fleeting, but powerful experiences are known as "mutual gaze." Technically, it is only possible for two people to lock eyes or experience mutual gaze at any given moment. Scientifically speaking, mutual gaze lasts for a mere microsecond for optimal interaction. Longer gazes signal aggression and dominance; shorter gazes signal disinterest or fear. In a virtual meeting, mutual gaze is impossible. Communicators may stare at an image of their colleague on a screen, but locking eyes with a particular person is not possible. What is the impact of loss of mutual gaze?

Interaction Quality

A systematic review of 29 research studies revealed that eye gaze facilitates several important human communication processes, including: turn-yielding, speech monitoring, prevention and repair of conversational breakdowns, and facilitates speech interruption (Degutyte & Astell, 2021). Mutual eye gaze enriches people's feelings of social presence, fun and human experience; conversely absence of mutual eye gaze dramatically hinders the quality of interaction (Shahid, Krahmer, & Swerts, 2012).

Mutual Gaze and Oxytocin

When face to face communicators lock eyes, however briefly, there is an immediate release of oxytocin, the bonding hormone. This leads people to feel positively about the other party and paves the foundation for trust. The release of oxytocin is rewarding and energizing; yet, it is absent in most virtual meetings, thereby contributing to mental fatigue and loss of connection. Because people feel less social connection in virtual meetings, they often experience the online disinhibition effect, or *ODE*, which leads to more acting out, aggressive, and confrontational behavior (Suler, 2004).

Willingness to Engage in Mutual Glances

Mutual gaze is not solely the responsibility of one person; it requires two people to quickly and preconsciously negotiate mutual gaze. Willingness to engage in mutual glances is a means of establishing union with others (Simmel, 1969). Indeed, long-term relationship partners are characterized by relatively greater amounts of mutual looks (Rubin, 1970). However, there is a fine line between a mutual glance and a mutual stare. A prolonged glance elicits a threat response; and a power contest, such that the first person who breaks the mutual glance is regarded to be socially subordinate (Edelman, Omark, & Freedman, 1973); while the one who looks steadily at another in silence is perceived to be more dominant (Thayer, 1969).

Benefits of Avoiding Mutual Gaze

Thus far, it may seem that mutual gaze is uniformly beneficial for interactants, particularly team members. Given all the benefits of mutual gaze, it may seem hard to believe that averting gaze from an interlocutor can have some unintended creative benefits. In one series of studies, people who maintained eye contact with another person disrupted their accurate imagination of a visual stimulus; but those who averted their gaze were not disrupted (Markson & Paterson, 2009). This suggests that when the goal of the virtual meeting is to generate ideas or creatively brainstorm, gaze aversion may serve benefits because it removes visual attention from irrelevant visual information and interrupts social interaction processes. One highly impactful communication coach instructs participants to turn their cameras off when listening to leadership stories voluntarily shared by team members. This achieves two critical outcomes: first and foremost, it reduces evaluation apprehension on the part of the story-teller; second, the listeners can focus on the story, independent of the visual stimuli that might create distraction.

Implications for VCQ

In the absence of mutual gaze, our brain is not operating the same way as when we communicate face to face. This suggests that one critical element of VQ is to create and foster conditions that allow for the development of trust and goodwill, that are not naturally evoked.

DIRECTIONAL GAZE

In a face to face meeting, people are aware of the direction of gaze of the interactants. For example, we can tell if someone is staring at the clock, looking out the window, looking at their boss, or looking at us. The direction of other's gaze provides valuable information about the emotional and cognitive state of others. Moreover, gaze direction plays crucial function in regulating conversations and providing critical social information (Shahid, Krahmer, & Swerts, 2012). For example, professors in a physical classroom can determine if their students are disinterested and bored. Speakers in a conference room can often ascertain high-status members, merely by noting how many people are looking at that person. Indeed, high-status people are gazed at more often and gaze less than others.

Conversational Turn-Taking

Directional gaze is the key means in which conversational interactants negotiate speaking turns. Specifically, near the end of an utterance, the floor-holder (speaker) briefly gazes at the person who desires to speak (the interlocutor) to prepare to transfer control of floor. The interlocutor, who is gazed at, has the advantage of taking the floor because that person infers that the speaker has conceded the floor to them (Beattie, Webster, & Ross, 2010). Conversational turn-taking happens much like a highly choreographed dance in face-to-face meetings, and involves a mutual gaze break in which the speaker looks toward the listener, and they share a very brief mutual gaze, after which the listener breaks the mutual gaze and begins to speak. In fact, 42% of conversational turns follow this pattern (Novick, Hansen & Ward, 1996). Directional gaze cues are not present in virtual meetings and therefore, speakers and listeners experience ambiguity and anxiety about conversational turns. It is for this reason that simply turning on one's camera does not have a measurable effect on group synchrony and collective intelligence; in fact, teams without visual cues are more successful in synchronizing their vocal cues and speaking turns (Tomprou, Kim, Chikersal, Williams Wooley, & Dabbish, 2021).

Dominance Perception

Directional gaze also signals who has status or dominance in a face-to-face meeting. Specifically, people who are dominant exhibit a greater ratio of proportion of time spent looking while speaking to the proportion of looking while listening (Exline, Ellyson, & Long, 1975). Moreover, people who exhibit a high look-speak versus look-listen ratio are rated by others as being more powerful (Dovidio & Ellyson, 1982). Stated simply, the more a person looks while speaking, the more powerful they are seen by others; but the more they look while listening, the less powerful they are viewed. These visual cues are not present in virtual communication, and therefore, status cues are often obscured.

Augmented Gaze

When gaze direction is blocked or absent among virtual team members conversational turn-taking is less efficient, resulting in more stumbles, over-speaking, and interpersonal frustration. For these reasons, some computer science research has experimented with "augmented gaze", using 3D avatars to provide valuable information to conversational interactants about where others are focusing their attention (Bailenson, Beall, Loomis, Blascovich, & Turk, 2005). Unlike videoconference platforms, which transmit direct video streams, immersive CVE (collaborative virtual environments) track the movement of interactants in three-dimensional virtual space using avatars. When using "augmented gaze" people are more persuasive because the recipients of the persuasive message perceive that the speaker is gazing only at them (Bailenson, Beall, Loomis, Blascovich, & Turk, 2005).

Avoiding Turn-Taking

A key question concerns when gaze-selected next speakers do not take their turn. A speaker who is gaze-selected by the previous speaker can either pass on the turn to a third participant by gazing at them or they can reject the turn by "gazing away" or "dissolving the mutual gaze" (Weiss, 2018). This has the effect of opening the conversational floor for other participants to self-select.

Implications for VCQ

Given the loss of directional gaze cues, a key element of VQ is to navigate smooth turn-taking in virtual conversations. In multi-person virtual meetings, it is imperative that people have a clear means of establishing who is talking to whom. This is rather easy to determine in face to face meetings because conversational partners can track gaze direction. Gaze is an excellent predictor of conversational attention in multiparty conversations (Vertegall, Slagter, van der Veer, & Nijholt, 2001).

SELF-AWARENESS

One distinct feature of most virtual communication platforms is the presence of one's own image. Unlike a face to face meeting, wherein people do not have access to their own image, in a typical virtual meeting, one's face is omnipresent on the screen. What is the impact of the presence of one's own image in virtual meetings?

Heightened Self-Awareness

One implication of looking at one's own image is a distinct rise in objective self-awareness (Silvia & Duval, 2001). People who are made to be more aware of themselves, through the use of mirrors and images are more likely to be thoughtful and considerate as well as even more ethical (Reynolds, Knighten, & Conway, 2019). For these reasons, heighted self-awareness may act as a positive stimulus for inducting leaders and team members to be more reflective and thoughtful in their communication.

A potential disadvantage is that self-awareness may induce greater self-absorption, such that communicators are focused more on their own image and self-presentation than that of others. Indeed, one CEO we interviewed admitted that they spend "too much time looking at themselves" during a virtual meeting. The CEO went on to explain that this excessive self-focus produced negative feelings and self-criticism. Moreover, facial feedback theory suggests that when people communicate in a fashion that they can see themselves (e.g., with mirror or video), they are more self-critical and ethical in their communication. In addition, their emotions often are consistent with their facial features, such as when they see themselves frowning, they feel more angry; when they see a smile on their face, they feel happier (Buck, 1980).

Implications for VCQ

Objective self-awareness, or the ability to constantly see oneself in the virtual meeting may not be a strict liability for the communicator. Ideally, managers should maintain focus on the group members and occasionally monitor their own image. Excessive self-focus can come at the expense of reading-the-room.

SEATING CONFIGURATIONS

People can choose their seat at the table in face to face meetings, but virtual meetings are largely random. Moreover, there is no "head of the table" in virtual meetings. In face to face meetings, people who sit at the head of a table often assert more power and influence than others, even if they do not actually have more organizational status. Moreover, people who sit on the side of the table with the fewest number of people are more likely to be viewed as leaders as compared to people who sit on the side of the table with more interactants, because they are more likely to be gazed at (Pellegrini, 1971). Moreover, seating configurations in face to face interaction signal attraction (liking), as people tend to sit near others who they feel aligned with. In a virtual meeting, people cannot choose their seats and so, many traditional relationship network cues (as well as organizational status cues) are missing.

In many ways, the absence of status cues may promote greater equality among virtual interactants. With no one at the head of the table, people who otherwise might self-censor may feel more free to speak up. *Psychological safety* is the means by which group leaders create environments in which people feel comfortable speaking up and in many cases, disagreeing with others, for the purpose of making informed, and principled decisions (Edmondson, 1999).

Implications for VCQ

The loss of deliberate seating configurations may promote more egalitarian relationships among virtual interactants.

BACK-CHANNEL UTTERANCES

In face to face meetings, much of the auditory signals are not strictly limited to conversational speech. In face-to-face conversations, human communication is a collaborative process supported by back-channel responses. Back-channel responses refer to the hearer's use of peripheral utterances, such as "uh huh" or "right" or "uhm" to provide feedback that the utterance (by the speaker) is being understood and to coordinate turn-taking. Back-channel utterances represent a shockingly large proportion of conversations – at least 19% (Lee, Regan, & Young, 2009). Paralinguistic cues, including throat-clearing, taking in of breath, such as might occur prior to a person's verbal speech turn, uhm, uhs, and the like punctuate the conversation. People use both verbal (lexical and prosodic cues) as well as nonverbal cues (facial expression, eye gaze, hand gesture and body position) to manage floor control in conversations.

Back-channel utterances can also take the form of pauses, intonation, gestures and facial expression and support "grounding". Grounding is the development of a shared context that supports joint understanding and the timing of interactions.

Implications for VCQ

In virtual meetings, perceiving back-channel utterances is difficult. By the time a hearer perceives an audio signal, the location of that utterance is often not obvious.

The virtually intelligent group leader should articulate how conversational turns should occur in the meeting.

SIDE CONVERSATIONS

In addition to back-channel utterances, another type of communication that occurs in face to face meetings (but not in virtual meetings) are side conversations. In a typical group or team meeting, people often sit near colleagues that they like and engage in private conversations, also known as "side conversations". These side conversations serve serval important functions, including clarifying (e.g., "did they really say we are downsizing?") and evaluating (e.g., "I think that is a bad idea"). In a face to face meeting, people can adjust the volume of their speech so as to ensure that their side communication is only heard by the intended person (such as by using a whisper). In virtual meetings, impromptu side conversations are not possible. To be sure, people can privately "chat" with certain others. However, people may not be aware that another is sending a private chat.

Side conversations are not limited to verbal exchanges. Nudging someone's arm, playing footsie under the table, or writing a note on a pad of paper visible to one's colleague, are means by which people engage in surreptitious communication in the presence of a larger meeting. Presumably when playing competitive card games, such as in bridge or other games, interactants would benefit by communicating with others in the room in way that is undetectable to others. Known as the *multiple audience problem*, this type of surreptitious communication improves the relationship between the interactants because it is considered clandestine (Fleming, Darley, Hilton, & Kojetin, 1990).

Implications for VCQ

Side conversations are how people establish a shared reality or shared mental model of situations. Metaphorically speaking, side conversations are much like the *Emperor's New Clothes*, allowing people to check their assumptions. Moreover, conversations between two people are low risk because conversational interactants can quickly monitor and manage communication; conversely conversations among a larger group are distinctly higher risk for communicators.

TOUCHING

It is often surprising to learn how much people touch others, such as clients and colleagues when engaging in face to face interaction. When we refer to touch, we are not focusing on inappropriate, unwanted physical advances, but instead, to gestures such as handshakes and other mutual displays of appreciation and engagement, such as friendly mutual hugs.

In general, appropriate touch has benefits. In one study, opponent negotiators shook hands prior to a high-stakes business negotiation, whereas others did not; otherwise, the situation was the same. The opponents who shook hands prior to the negotiation experienced a release of oxytocin, the human bonding hormone, that was associated with the development of more mutually-profitable business deals (Schroeder, Risen, Gino, & Norton, 2019).

Implications for VCQ

The key benefits of handshakes and wanted physical greetings are primarily affective, producing positive emotion. Establishing positive emotion is a key challenge for virtual teams and therefore, the meeting manager needs to be proactive about introducing methods to establish positive affect. Humor and laughter are a key means by which subjective well-being is induced. One study used a digital, interactive adaptive mirror interface to induce positive emotion (Shahid, Krahmer, Neerincx, & Swerts, 2013). Participants engaged in virtual communication felt more positive, particularly when one colleague was physically co-present.

GESTURING

Thus far, we have been referring to visual cues, such as eye gaze. However, people use other types of nonverbal cues to control conversations, including hand gestures, postural shifts, and lower body adjustments (Chen & Harper, 2009). Known as "floor control shifts", people who want to speak in face to face meetings may adjust their posture and use their hands in gesture. The other conversational partners typically have full access to view other parties. If a person desires to keep speaking in a face to face meeting, they continue to gesture (and move their body), signaling to others that a turn transition is not forthcoming. Conversely, on most virtual meeting platforms, our visual cues of other people are restricted to a small area, from the neck up. Moreover, names and affiliations often block up to 5% of our visual field. For this reason, turn-taking, and conversational shifts are more awkward and frustrating for conversational interactants.

Benefits of Gesture for Communicators

Gaze and gesture are intimately related in human communication. One study measured the effect of gazing of speakers on their own gestures and on the gestures of others, and found that when interlocutors gaze back at speakers, gestural alignment between speakers and interlocutors is enhanced (Oben & Brone, 2015). Other research has found that gesturing not only serves to aid the listener or recipient of communication, it also helps the speaker communicate. In one intriguing study, blind children gestured while speaking to both sighted and blind recipients, suggesting that gesture helps the communicator formulate thoughts necessary for communication (Iverson & Goldin-Meadow, 1998).

Thin Slices

It may seem startling to learn how much of our impressions of others, in terms of business competence and interpersonal warmth is determined by nonverbal social signals. For example, in one investigation, people were able to predict which executives would win a business pitch competition solely on the basis of the nonverbal social signals they sent, including tone of voice, bodily gesticulation, and proximity to the speaker (Pentland, 2008). Research on "thin slices of behavior" reveals that people often form immediate judgments on the basis of nonverbal information (Borkenau, Mauer, Reimann, Spinath, & Angleitner, 2004).

Implications for VCQ

People who are high in virtual communication intelligence are self-aware of their own gestures and those of others. They consciously adjust their own gesticulations to communicate more effectively.

COLLISIONS

Perhaps of all the shortcomings of virtual communication that subtly rob the humanity of the experience and lead to less than rewarding emotional states, the absence of collisions is most starkly missed. Collisions are unplanned face to face encounters between colleagues, such as might occur in the coffee break area, elevator, or entering and exiting a building. Collisions have a dramatic positive effect on people's subjective well-being as well as economic profits. The late CEO of Zappos, Tony Hsieh, knew the importance of collisions when he launched the "downtown project" in which the goal was to create 100,000 collisionable hours per acre within Zappos, or every 2.3 square feet per year (Burke, 2013). At one call center, the company expanded the breakout rooms and gave sales representatives more time to gather there and productivity dramatically increased. Similarly, one pharmaceutical company invested several thousand dollars to remove several small coffee machines and build fewer, larger coffee machine stations. The effect was to increase collisions between different people and groups and their sales rose by 20% or $200M (Waber, Magnolfi, & Lindsay, 2014).

Virtual Distance

Virtual distance is the feeling of separation caused by a lack of face-to-face communication (Lojeski, Reilly, & Dominick, 2007). For example, people who have never met their work team in person may experience more virtual distance than those who shared history of face to face meetings.

Virtual Handshake

One possible solution for bridging virtual distance is the virtual handshake, in which interactants attempt to humanize or personalize their communication partners (Tenten & Allen, 2005). In one research study, conducted prior to the pandemic, managers negotiated with someone in either an existing or new relationship. The entire interaction was conducted via email and participants had different stakes regarding an important business interaction. Some people were told to engage in a 5-minute, non-business personal phone call prior to the online business interaction. Others did not engage in this pre-negotiation call. Otherwise everything was the same. The results were dramatic, particularly for those in new relationships: "schmoozing" (engaging in small talk, however brief) led to dramatic differences in deal closings (increased by over 15%, from 78% to over 95%). Moreover, the economic quality of the agreed-upon deals dramatically improved when the managers schmoozed, increasing from less than $12.5M to nearly $14M (Morris, Nadler, Kurtzberg, & Thompson, 2002).

Implications for VCQ

Because most virtual meeting platforms required scheduling, collisions (impromptu meetings) are impossible. However, the virtually intelligent manager can create virtual collisions by opening virtual meetings early, building in optional breaks during meetings, and lingering following meetings.

SHARED CONTEXT

People communicating virtually are located in different physical locations. Therefore, unlike a face to face meeting wherein everyone shares the same physical space and has access to the same situational cues (e.g., the sound of a door opening, noise in the hallway outside, and the scent of coffee brewing, etc.), people in virtual settings do not share a common context. When people share the same context, they subconsciously adapt and adjust their communication which has the benefit of reducing stress and building shared cohesion.

Conversely, the distinct absence of shared context creates communication challenges. To illustrate how people in a shared context subconsciously adapt, one study examined how people communicate when they share the same context (such as being in a car together in heavy traffic); other people did not share the same context (e.g., one person was in a car in heavy traffic and talking to someone who was not physically present). People who shared the same context (i.e., both in the car together) ceased conversation when a sudden move, such as a lane change or traffic signal occurred, thereby relieving stress. However, when people did not share the same context, the person attempting to have the conversation with the non-present other was under distinctly more stress (Lee, Regan, & Young, 2008). In short, face-to-face conversations allow interactants to accommodate some of the demands on the speaker by adjusting their engagement that support the changing context.

High- Versus Low-Context Cultures

Social-situational awareness may have some profound cultural differences. In one study, US and Chinese participants were shown a photo of a sheep standing in a lobby in a professional business building. Eye gaze and brain scans of U.S. and Chinese participants were examined. U.S. participants were highly object-focused and looked primarily at the sheep. Conversely, Chinese participants looked at the figure and the ground (i.e., the sheep and the lobby). Because of the incongruence involved, the Chinese participants experienced more emotional anxiety (Brett, 2014). The implication is that some cultures are more context-dependent and that incongruence between the background and the focal speaker can be upsetting. Similarly, a study of teamwork between US (low-context) and Chinese (high-context) team members revealed that understanding nonverbal cues is less culturally normative for US than Chinese employees, but the US employees who do pay attention and understand nonverbal cues report more successful cross-cultural relationship building (Buchan, Chen, Zhang, & Adair, 2021).

Implications for VCQ

One aspect of context is real and virtual backgrounds. One study found that students in a learning context preferred real versus virtual backgrounds (Goethe, Sørum, & Johansen, 2022). Another study examined three types of backgrounds: natural setting, urban setting or a plain grey background. The natural background facilitated more creative idea generation compared to urban or plain backgrounds (Palanica & Fossat, 2022). Another research study finds that ideal backgrounds are dependent upon the appearance of the users themselves (Anku & Farnand, 2021).

In sum, profound differences exist between face to face communication and virtual communication. Many conversational interactants are unaware of how much they rely on gaze direction, back-channel utterances, and shared context to regulate not only the content but also the tone of their communication. Many business professionals, high in emotional intelligence can make micro-adjustments to their communication when in a face to face context. However, these same business professionals might be flummoxed in a virtual context because social cues are missing or obscured. A person who is normally perceived as an empathic, sensitive, socially-adept manager in a face-to-face meeting may be regarded as insensitive, uncaring, and brusque in a virtual meeting. For this reason, it behooves managers and leaders to carefully examine their own virtual communication style and learn to rely upon a different set of cues and build in feedback mechanisms so that they can optimize their communication in virtual meetings. The ability to identify, leverage, and create effective communications in non-face to face media is the cornerstone of virtual communication intelligence.

VIRTUAL COMMUNICATION INTELLIGENCE IN THE POST-PANDEMIC ERA

The Coronavirus Covid19 pandemic proved to defy a known endpoint. As the pandemic raged, people and organizations alike pivoted to a new normal. With the realization that there is no return to the pre-pandemic business practices, managers and businesses must learn to sustain and flourish amidst the threat of an ever-present pandemic. Given the vast and profound differences between face to face and virtual communication, how can managers and leaders optimize the experience for their teams, relationships, and business partners? Simply being empathic, understanding, and positive are not sufficient to create a rewarding and sustainable virtual experience. Moreover, acquiring state of the art technology replete with technical support is not sufficient to produce a successful and rewarding virtual meeting.

The first step in leading and managing with VCQ (Virtual Communication Intelligence) is to understand the ten key factors involved. The next step is to modify, adjust, add, and remove elements from one's own communication repertoire to set the stage for rewarding virtual communication. Our focus now will be on how to begin to identify and use certain skills.

NONVERBAL BODY LANGUAGE

One of the key modifications that effective virtual communicators make involves body language or nonverbal adjustments. There are two key aspects involved: effective transmission and accurate perception.

Transmission

The virtually intelligent manager needs to be self-aware of their own facial expressions, as well as socially aware of others. Moreover, it behooves communicators to consciously move much of their body language to the shoulders, face, and arms – which are part of the visual picture. One method by which managers can transmit is through the use of *mirroring*. The *chameleon effect* refers to mirroring another person's body language, and often has a positive effect. Even when people are aware that their conversational partner is mirroring their body language, they like that person more (Chartrand & Bargh, 1999). To be sure, mirroring (also known as mimicking) is more difficult on virtual communication platforms. However, it is achievable. One study found that even when people are interacting with an artificial intelligence agent (non-human), they were more receptive when the AI agent mirrored their head movements (Bailenson & Yee, 2005).

Perception

Prior to the pandemic, much nonverbal research focused on the ability to detect emotion in facial expressions and detect deception based upon body language (Ekman & Friesen, 2003). To be sure, the accurate detection of emotion in others would seem to be an advantage in business relationships so as to properly adjust or modify one's message. Many lay people assume that the accurate detection of emotion is revealed primarily through facial expressions. However, emotion can be revealed through more than just the face and include posture and other full-body expressions. In one meeting of 27 people, a team member slumped over while the leader was speaking. However, the leader was unaware of this, presumably because they were focused on the densely-packed PowerPoint graphs on their shared screen.

Other team members began a string of urgent chat messages amongst each other because they did not want to risk interrupting the leader, who was actively speaking. Finally, the program assistant moved herself and the slumped-over team member into a private breakout room and used her voice to wake up the team member, who had fallen asleep because of the boring presentation. The remaining team members had difficulty focusing on the content of the leader's message because they were agitated about the slumped-over team member. Due to the absence of psychological safety, members self-censored.

VERBAL CONVERSATIONAL

It is not sufficient for managers to simply adjust their own body language and monitor others. The virtually intelligent communicator needs to also adjust their words and utterances (Glaser, 2014). Communicators who are high in virtual intelligence are aware of the pitfalls of *communication bravado*, in which speakers are under the faulty illusion that they are clearer and more effective than others regard them to be (Quintanilla & Mallard, 2008).

Lexical Cuing and Prosodic Cuing

One of the most profound and significant ways that leaders can bring virtual intelligence to meetings is to create conditions for smooth conversational turns using two types of cues, lexical and prosodic. *Lexical cuing* refers to short speech acts that cue or guide others to contribute (e.g., "any suggestions?"). *Prosodic cueing* refers to everything about a communicator's speech except the words themselves, such as rises and falls in intonation, final lengthening, wherein the communicator places an extra drawl on the final syllable to signal their conversational turn is ending) and energy tapering (to signal that they have communicated the most important aspect of their message and are now relinquishing the floor).

Gaze Captioning

Gaze captioning refers to a speaker's utterance about the direction and object of their gaze (e.g., "I'm looking at Greta now because her smile indicates that she has some insight into the problem we are faced with"). Gaze captioning allows for the smooth transition of conversational turns.

With two persons in a virtual meeting, smooth TCUs are not particularly problematic. However, as the number of meeting attendees increases, speak-overs, and late-starts increase exponentially. As noted, clumsy conversational turns exert a significant negative effect on group rapport and trust. For this reason, speakers who are high in virtual intelligence modify their own behavior so as to decrease communication apprehension (in others) and increase smooth TCUs (turn constructional units).

Leaders high in VQ try to minimize communication apprehension in others. Virtually intelligent communicators strive to be good turn-takers (via using head nods) and turn-giving (my changing their vocal intonation, signaling the end of their verbal communication turn). Communicators who are high in virtual intelligence use above-the shoulder gestures while speaking (to signal that they are not ready to transition) and then reduce or eliminate gestures to signal that they have reached then of their turn.

To be sure, many, if not most virtual communication platforms offer participants a variety of emojis, such as hand-raises that substitute or act as a proxy for lexical and prosodic cuing. However, participants vary in terms of their comfort with using such emblems and speakers often do not see the emblem, which can result in the want-to-be-speaker feeling disenfranchised. Moreover, when the group is intimately sized, such as 10 or fewer people, many members are reluctant to use emblems. Yet, the research indicates dramatic differences in conversational participation even in groups of less than 10 people (Wheelan, 2009).

EMOTION AND EMPATHY

Effective managers need to foster positive affect within the virtual meeting. Whereas traditional face to face meetings involve many elements, such as appropriate touching (e.g., handshakes and collisions) that naturally produce oxytocin, thereby stimulating positive affect, trust, and rapport, this is not the default in virtual meetings. For this reason, the manager needs to be proactive in setting stage for trust and positive emotion.

Trust is difficult to establish in virtual relationships because of the absence of shared social cues. Trust in virtual relationships takes a different route than does trust in traditional, face to face relationships. Initially, trust in virtual relationships is based on our evaluation of people's cognitive abilities or competence, such as their knowledge of the subject matter under discussion (e.g., "*I trusted Pat because they were very prepared for the meeting, having read the report thoroughly*"). Conversely, trust in traditional relationships is based on our evaluation of their similarity to us and people's benevolence, also known as affect-based trust (e.g., "*I trusted Jamie once I learned that she is also passionate about cycling*"). Overtime, cognitive and affective trust emerge as separate components in our overall level of trust.

Turn on the Camera

One of the simplest, yet most powerful ways to enhance human interaction is to simply turn on the camera. If cameras are inconvenient, then it is important to place a still photo of oneself on the screen. In one study, some people had access to a still photo, whereas other did not. Then, interactants engaged in a high-stakes mixed-motive decision making task. The results revealed that those who had access to the photo of their opponent were over five times more likely to avoid a costly impasse (no deal) and created more economically-valuable business deals (increasing from $12.24M to a joint $13.92M; Moore, Kurtzberg, Thompson, & Morris, 1999).

Socialize Before Business

People communicating virtually are more task focused. This has efficiencies, but can actually be a disadvantage when it comes to building collaboration and trust. For this reason, virtual groups are advised to socialize before getting down to business. Even five minutes of small talk can build trust and enhance cohesion (Morris, Nadler, Kurtzberg, & Thompson, 2002).

Self-Disclosure

One study found that virtual teams improve their connection and performance when they voluntarily share personal, and even sad experiences (Eadeh, Ostrowski, & Woolley, 2021). Pairs of people collaborated via videoconference and those who exchanged responses about sad experiences demonstrated more connection and better performance than those who exchanged responses about calm or neutral experiences.

To neutralize and perhaps even reverse the ODE (online disinhibition effect), managers should take proactive steps to humanize members and make connections. This can be partly achieved by socializing, turning on cameras, and calling people by name. In fact, one research program developed a large, teddy-bear like robot who would give reciprocal hugs to people and found that when people were hugged by the robot, they engaged in more prosocial behaviors (Shiomi, Nakata, Kanbara, & Hagita, 2017).

GROUP NORMS AND MEETING MANAGEMENT

Group dynamics are more complex in virtual meetings, and for this reason, managers high in virtual communication intelligence build in greater structure to the meeting. It is a bitter irony that managers often remove structure from virtual meetings, falsely believing that this will create psychological safety and full participation, but it often has the opposite effect. To neutralize the pernicious uneven communication effect, managers should proactively manage the speaking turns in virtual conversations.

An inevitable aspect of teams and certainly virtual teams is conflict. Most people find conflict uncomfortable and so they often avoid it. However, highly effective teams engage in conflict. For this reason, the virtually intelligent team leader should establish norms for the expression of differences.

Good Norm / Bad Norm

In one virtual meeting, the leader suggested that to establish clear norms for the virtual meeting that the group do an impromptu roleplay by engaging in "bad norms" for 3 minutes and then "effective norms" for 3 minutes. During the three minutes of "bad norms", several members turned off their cameras, some put a strange view angle on their camera (such as pointing at the ceiling or floor); yet others turned their microphones either too low or too high a volume; several people played annoying sounds in the background and verbally they interrupted one another. Because this was a role-play, there was much laughter. The team leader then artfully asked the group members to name each ineffective norm and summarized on a shared whiteboard. This discussion was followed by a 3-minute impromptu roleplay focused on "effective norms". Immediately everyone sat up, centering their face in their camera, several waved at the group, and began using TV-newscaster type of verbalizations to signal turns ("That's all for me. Back over to you, Janine...").

The group leader then asked the group to reflect on what was particularly effective during the impromptu role-play, again summarizing key points. The point of this demo was that the group felt ownership of their virtual communication process and established a non-threatening means to discuss their group communication. This meeting became a blueprint for their subsequent virtual meetings.

SOCIAL SITUATIONAL AWARENESS

Social Presence Theory

Social presence theory refers to the degree to which communication media permits communicators to experience others as being psychologically present (Fulk, Steinfield, Schmitz, & Power, 1987). For example, when communicating face to face, receivers need to listen and look for verbal and nonverbal cues, unlike in virtual contexts.

Group Rapport

Group rapport is a constellation of three interrelated components: mutual attentiveness, positivity and coordination (Tickle-Degnen & Rosenthal, 1990). The virtually-intelligent leader needs to set the stage for all three of these elements to occur in the virtual meeting space.

Contextual Empathy

Contextual empathy refers to communicator's ability to understand and proactively adapt to a partner's context. For example, when people meet face to face, a conversational partner might pause if the other party's phone rings or if there is a knock on the door. However, this pause would not be offered in a virtual meeting space, which produces more anxiety and stress for the communicator. To combat the lack of shared context, virtually-intelligent communications may often reference their physical environments. In one business meeting, a participant announced that their children would be soon invading the kitchen and that this would hinder their ability to keep the microphone on. In another group meeting, one participant apologized to the group for not turning on their camera, explaining that they were sole-parenting their special-needs child. In yet a different meeting, a participant noticed a guitar in the background of another particularly quiet member, and asked to hear the story of how they happened to have it. This had the positive effect of making the reserved team member feel both comfortable and affirmed.

Table 1. Virtual communication: Advantages and disadvantages

Advantages	Disadvantages
1. Task-focus (people get down to business) 2. Goal focus (people believe in common group goal) 3. Weak-get-Strong-effect (reduced status differences) 4. Persuasion and influence (substance more impactful than style) 5. Equalization of participation 6. Less inhibition 7. Less conformity 8. Provides buffer (when relationships are extremely contentious) 9. Buys time (when someone is in power-down position in business negotiations)	1. Zoom fatigue (cognitive, affective and emotional depletion) 2. ODE (online disinhibition effect): more aggressive, confrontational behavior 3. Irony Poisoning: lose ability to understand nuance, humor, sarcasm vs. sincerity 4. Greater risk-taking 5. Less trust and rapport 6. More relationship conflict and conflict escalation 7. More misunderstandings 8. Less efficient (increased time to make decisions, but not increased volume of information exchange) 9. Information suppression: less communication; lower frequency of communication

Status Updates

One method of enhancing situation awareness is using proactive status updates. In one investigation, group members played the role of doctors, nurses or specialists with the task of accurately diagnosing a patient (Haines, Kramer, & Vehring, 2011). Teams that could see automatically generated status updates from their teammates such as, "reading email"; and "composing message" felt greater team loyalty and congeniality, which were associated with better team performance.

Table 2. Key challenges of virtual communication

Key Challenge	Description	Virtual Communication Implications
Mutual Gaze	Sustained eye contact between two people	Impossible on most virtual meeting platforms; inhibits development of trust and positive affect
Directional Gaze	Ability to determine where others are looking	Impossible on most virtual meeting platforms; disturbs natural conversational turn-taking
Objective Self-Awareness	One's own image (face) is omnipresent during virtual meetings, producing heightened self-awareness	Creates heightened self-awareness and self-focus; may induce more generosity and moral decision making
Seating Configurations	Ability to choose seating, which can signal alliances and status	May have beneficial implications for encouraging otherwise lower-status people to speak up, because traditional status cues are absent
Back-Channel utterances	Words and gestures that signal to speaker understanding of their message	Not possible to detect in virtual meetings; and difficult to locate the source
Sidebar conversations	Impromptu conversations between subset of group members	Not possible to initiate, except with the use of private chat
Touching	Often a handshake, tap on shoulder	Not possible
Gesturing	Gesture helps the speaker and the hearer and often involves full-body posture	Virtual communicators lose many of the important gestural signals that regulate conversation
Collisions	Unplanned face to face encounters, usually in public space	People are more task-focused and do not engage in purely social communication, unless specifically prompted
Shared context	Communication between people in shared space	Lack of shared context prevents contextual empathy

THE FUTURE OF VIRTUAL COMMUNICATION INTELLIGENCE

In October of 2021, CEO Mark Zuckerberg announced that Facebook's new name would be "*Meta*", explaining that "we are a company that builds technology to connect" (Lyons, 2021). The launch of *Meta* clearly suggests that the future of virtual meetings will be conducted in a rich metaverse, in which social interactants may have more ability to engage in mutual gaze, directional gaze, touch, and full-body gesture. At the core of meta is the simple idea that people are at the center of technology. The virtually intelligent leader will be in a position to shape the metaverse in ways that lead to more profitable virtual teamwork and more fulfilling and rewarding relationships.

REFERENCES

Anku, A., & Farnand, S. P. (2021). Preferred white balance for applications using virtual backgrounds. *Color Research and Application*, *46*(6), 1227–1244. doi:10.1002/col.22694

Bailenson, J. N., Beall, A. C., Loomis, J., Blascovich, J., & Turk, M. (2005). Transformed social interaction, augmented gaze, and social influence in immersive virtual environments. *Human Communication Research*, *31*(4), 511–537. doi:10.1111/j.1468-2958.2005.tb00881.x

Bailenson, J. N., & Yee, N. (2005). Digital chameleons: Automatic assimilation of nonverbal gestures in immersive virtual environments. *Psychological Science*, *16*(10), 814–819. doi:10.1111/j.1467-9280.2005.01619.x PMID:16181445

Beattie, G., Webster, K., & Ross, J. (2010). The fixation and processing of the iconic gestures that accompany talk. *Journal of Language and Social Psychology*, *29*(2), 194–213. doi:10.1177/0261927X09359589

Borkenau, P., Mauer, N., Riemann, R., Spinath, F. M., & Angleitner, A. (2004). Thin slices of behavior as cues of personality and intelligence. *Journal of Personality and Social Psychology*, *86*(4), 599–614. doi:10.1037/0022-3514.86.4.599 PMID:15053708

Brett, J. (2014). *Negotiating globally: How to negotiate deals, resolve disputes, and make decisions across cultural boundaries* (3rd ed.). John Wiley & Sons.

Brucks, M. S., & Levav, J. (2022, April 27). Virtual communication curbs creative idea generation. *Nature*, *605*(7908), 108–112. doi:10.103841586-022-04643-y PMID:35477754

Buchan, N. R., Chen, X.-P., Zhang, Y., & Adair, W. L. (2021). *Teamwork during a global pandemic* [Manuscript in preparation]. CIBER, University of South Carolina.

Buck, R. (1980). Nonverbal behavior and the theory of emotion: The facial feedback hypothesis. *Journal of Personality and Social Psychology, 38*(5), 811–824. doi:10.1037/0022-3514.38.5.811 PMID:7381683

Burke, A. (2013, November 15). Why Zappos CEO Hsieh wants to enable more collisions in Vegas. *Forbes.*

Chartrand, T. L., & Bargh, J. A. (1999). The chameleon effect: The perception-behavior link and social interaction. *Journal of Personality and Social Psychology, 76*(6), 893–910. doi:10.1037/0022-3514.76.6.893 PMID:10402679

Chen, L., & Harper, M. P. (2009, November 2-4). Multimodal floor control shift detection. *Proceedings of the 2009 International Conference on Multimodal Interfaces*, 15-22.

de Mio, R. R. (2002, June 6-8). *On defining virtual emotion intelligence* [Conference session]. European Conference on Information Systems, Gdansk, Poland.

Degutyte, Z., & Astell, A. (2021). The role of eye gaze in regulating turn taking in conversations: A systematized review of methods and findings. *Frontiers in Psychology, 12*, 616471. doi:10.3389/fpsyg.2021.616471 PMID:33897526

Dovidio, J. F., & Ellyson, S. L. (1982). Decoding visual dominance: Attributions of power based on relative percentages of looking while speaking and looking while listening. *Social Psychology Quarterly, 45*(2), 106–113. doi:10.2307/3033933

Eadeh, F., Ostrowski, B., & Woolley, A.W. (2021, October). *Misery loves company: The implications of mood for affiliation and collective intelligence in remote collaboration* [Paper presentation]. Interdisciplinary Network for Group Research (INGRoup) Virtual Conference.

Edelman, M. S., Omark, D. R., & Freedman, D. G. (1973). Dominance hierarchies in young children. *Social Sciences Information. Information Sur les Sciences Sociales, 12*(1), 103–110. doi:10.1177/053901847301200105

Edmondson, A. (1999). Psychological safety and learning behavior in work teams. *Administrative Science Quarterly, 44*(2), 350–383. doi:10.2307/2666999

Ekman, P., & Friesen, W. V. (2003). *Unmasking the face: A guide to recognizing emotions from facial clues*. Malor Books.

Exline, R. V., Ellyson, S. L., & Long, B. (1975). Visual behavior as an aspect of power role relationships. In P. Pliner, L. Krames, & T. Alloway (Eds.), *Nonverbal communication of aggression: Advances in the study of communication and affect* (Vol. 2, pp. 21–52). Springer. doi:10.1007/978-1-4684-2835-3_2

Fleming, J. H., Darley, J. M., Hilton, J. L., & Kojetin, B. A. (1990). Multiple audience problem: A strategic communication perspective on social perception. *Journal of Personality and Social Psychology*, *58*(4), 593–609. doi:10.1037/0022-3514.58.4.593 PMID:2348361

Fox, J. (2022, January 18). Work from home is becoming a permanent part of how jobs are done. *Bloomberg Businessweek*. https://www.bloomberg.com/news/articles/2022-01-18/work-from-home-is-becoming-a-permanent-part-of-how-jobs-are-done

Fulk, J., Steinfield, C. W., Schmitz, J., & Power, J. G. (1987, October). A social information processing model of media use in organizations. *Communication Research*, *14*(5), 529–552. doi:10.1177/009365087014005005

Glaser, J. E. (2014). *Conversational intelligence: How great leaders build trust & get extraordinary results*. Taylor and Francis Group.

Goethe, O., Sørum, H., & Johansen, J. (2022). The effect or non-effect of virtual versus non-virtual backgrounds in digital learning. In T. Ahram, & R. Taiar (Eds.), *IHIET 2021: Human Interaction, Emerging Technologies and Future Systems V* (Vol. 319, pp. 274-281). Springer.

Goleman, D., Boyatis, R., & McKee, A. (2013). *Primal leadership: Unleashing the power of emotional intelligence*. Harvard Business Review Press.

Haines, R., Kramer, M., & Vehring, N. (2011). Activity awareness as a means to promote connectedness, willingness to do additional work, and congeniality: An experimental study. *Proceedings of the 32nd International Conference on Information Systems*.

Henderson, H. (2009). *Encyclopedia of computer science and technology*. Infobase Publishing.

Iverson, J. M., & Goldin-Meadow, S. (1998, November 19). Why people gesture when they speak. *Nature*, *396*(6708), 228. doi:10.1038/24300 PMID:9834030

Lee, J. D., Regan, M. A., & Young, K. L. (2009). What drives distraction? Distraction as a breakdown of multilevel control. In M.A. Regan, J.D. Lee, & K. Young (Eds.), Driver distraction: Theory, effects, and mitigation (1st ed., pp. 41-56). CRC Press, Taylor and Francis Group.

Lojeski, K. S., Reilly, R., & Dominick, P. (2007, January 3-6). *Multitasking and innovation in virtual teams* [Conference session]. 2007 40th Annual Hawaii International Conference on System Sciences, Waikoloa, HI, United States.

Lyons, K. (2021). *Facebook just revealed its new name: Meta.* The Verge.

Makarius, E. E., & Larson, B. Z. (2017). Changing the perspective of virtual work: Building virtual intelligence at the individual level. *The Academy of Management Perspectives*, *31*(2), 159–178. doi:10.5465/amp.2014.0120

Markson, L., & Paterson, K. B. (2009). Effects of gaze-aversion on visual-spatial imagination. *British Journal of Psychology*, *100*(3), 553–563. doi:10.1348/000712608X371762 PMID:19021925

Moore, D. A., Kurtzberg, T. R., Thompson, L. L., & Morris, M. W. (1999). Long and short routes to success in electronically mediated negotiations: Group affiliations and good vibrations. *Organizational Behavior and Human Decision Processes*, *77*(1), 22–43. doi:10.1006/obhd.1998.2814 PMID:9924140

Morris, M., Nadler, J., Kurtzberg, T., & Thompson, L. (2002). Schmooze or lose: Social friction and lubrication in e-mail negotiations. *Group Dynamics*, *6*(1), 89–100. doi:10.1037/1089-2699.6.1.89

Mysirlaki, S., & Paraskeva, E. (2020). Emotional intelligence and transformational leadership in virtual teams: Lessons from MMOGs. *Leadership and Organization Development Journal*, *41*(4), 551–566. doi:10.1108/LODJ-01-2019-0035

Novick, D. G., Hansen, B., & Ward, K. (1996, October 3-6). *Coordinating turn-taking with gaze* [Conference session]. Fourth International Conference on Spoken Language Processing, ICSLOP, Philadelphia, PA, United States.

Oben, B., & Brone, G. (2015). What you see if what you do: On the relationship between gaze and gesture in multimodal alignment. *Language and Cognition*, *7*(4), 546–562. doi:10.1017/langcog.2015.22

Palanica, A., & Fossat, Y. (2022). Effects of nature virtual background on creativity during videoconferencing. *Thinking Skills and Creativity*, *43*, 100976. doi:10.1016/j.tsc.2021.100976

Pellegrini, R. J. (1971). Some effects of seating position on social perception. *Psychological Reports, 28*(3), 887–893. doi:10.2466/pr0.1971.28.3.887

Pentland, A. (2008). *Honest signals: How they shape our world.* MIT Press. doi:10.7551/mitpress/8022.001.0001

Pitts, V. E., Wright, N. A., & Harkabus, L. C. (2012). Communication in virtual teams. The role of emotional intelligence. *Journal of Organizational Psychology, 12*(3/4), 21–34.

Quintanilla, K., & Mallard, J. (2008). Understanding the role of communication bravado: An important issue for trainers/educators. *Texas Speech Communication Journal, 33*(1), 44–49.

Reynolds, C. J., Knighten, K. R., & Conway, P. (2019). Mirror, mirror, on the wall, who is deontological? Completing moral dilemmas in front of mirrors increases deontological but not utilitarian response tendencies. *Cognition, 192*, 103993. doi:10.1016/j.cognition.2019.06.005 PMID:31229738

Rubin, Z. (1970). Measurement of romantic love. *Journal of Personality and Social Psychology, 16*(2), 265–273. doi:10.1037/h0029841 PMID:5479131

Salovey, P., & Mayer, J. (1990). Emotional Intelligence. *Imagination, Cognition and Personality, 9*(3), 185–211. doi:10.2190/DUGG-P24E-52WK-6CDG

Schroeder, J., Risen, J., Gino, F., & Norton, M. I. (2019). Handshaking promotes deal-making by signaling cooperative intent. *Journal of Personality and Social Psychology: Interpersonal Relations and Group Processes, 116*(5), 743–768. doi:10.1037/pspi0000157 PMID:30550327

Shahid, S., Krahmer, E., Neerincx, M. A., & Swerts, M. (2013). Positive affective interactions: The role of repeated exposure and presence. *IEEE Transactions on Affective Computing, PP, 4*(99), 1–13. doi:10.1109/T-AFFC.2012.39

Shahid, S., Krahmer, E., & Swerts, M. (2012). Video-mediated and co-present gameplay: Effects of mutual gaze on game experience, expressiveness and perceived social presence. *Interacting with Computers, 24*(4), 292–305. doi:10.1016/j.intcom.2012.04.006

Shiomi, M., Nakata, A., Kanbara, M., & Hagita, N. (2017, August 28 – September 1). *A hug from a robot encourages prosocial behavior* [Paper presentation]. *26th IEEE International Symposium on Robot and Human Interactive Communication*, Lisbon, Portugal.

Short, J., Williams, E., & Christie, B. (1976). *The social psychology of telecommunications*. John Wiley & Sons.

Silvia, P. J., & Duval, T. S. (2001). Objective self-awareness theory: Recent progress and enduring problems. *Personality and Social Psychology Review*, *5*(3), 230–241. doi:10.1207/S15327957PSPR0503_4

Simmel, G. (1969). Soziologie der Geselligkeit. In Deutscher Soziologentag" Wege und Ziele der Soziologie" (pp. 1-16). Sauer u. Auvermann.

Suler, J. (2004). The online disinhibition effect. *Cyberpsychology & Behavior*, *7*(3), 321–326. doi:10.1089/1094931041291295 PMID:15257832

Tenten, D., & Allen, S. (2005). *The virtual handshake: Opening doors and closing deals online*. American Management Association.

Thayer, S. (1969). The effect of interpersonal looking duration on dominance judgments. *The Journal of Social Psychology*, *79*(2), 285–286. doi:10.1080/00224545.1969.9922427 PMID:5810641

Thompson, L. (2021, December). Virtual collaboration won't be the death of creativity. *MIT Sloan Management Review*, *62*(2), 42–46.

Thompson, L. (2022). *Leading High Impact Teams* [Executive Education program]. Kellogg School of Management.

Tickle-Degnen, L., & Rosenthal, R. (1990). The nature of rapport and its nonverbal correlates. *Psychological Inquiry*, *1*(4), 285–293. doi:10.120715327965pli0104_1

Tomprou, M., Kim, Y. J., Chikersal, P., Williams Wooley, A., & Dabbish, L. A. (2021). Speaking out of turn: How video conferencing reduces vocal synchrony and collective intelligence. *PLoS One*, *16*(3), e0247655. doi:10.1371/journal.pone.0247655 PMID:33735258

Vertegaal, R., Slagter, R., van der Veer, G., & Nijholt, A. (2001, March 31 – April 5th). Eye gaze patterns in conversations: There is more to conversational agents than meets the eyes. *Proceedings of the SIGCHI Conference on Human Factors on Computing Systems*.

Waber, B., Magnolfi, J., & Lindsay, G. (2014). Workspaces that move people. *Harvard Business Review*, *92*(10), 68–77. PMID:25509577

Weiss, C. (2018). When gaze-selected next speakers do not take the turn. *Journal of Pragmatics*, *133*, 28–44. doi:10.1016/j.pragma.2018.05.016

Wheelan, S. A. (2009). Group size, group development, and group productivity. *Small Group Research*, *40*(2), 247–262. doi:10.1177/1046496408328703

Wiederhold, B. K. (2020, July). Connecting through technology during the Coronavirus disease 2019 pandemic: Avoiding "Zoom Fatigue". *Cyberpsychology, Behavior, and Social Networking*, *23*(7), 437–438. doi:10.1089/cyber.2020.29188.bkw PMID:32551981

KEY TERMS AND DEFINITIONS

Chameleon Effect: The nonconscious mimicry of the postures, mannerisms, facial expressions, and other behaviors to mirror those of one's interaction partner.

Collisions: Unplanned face to face encounters between colleagues, such as might occur in the coffee break area, elevator, or entering and exiting a building.

Communication Bravado: A psychological effect where a speaker is under the faulty illusion that they are clearer and more effective than others regard them to be.

Conversational Turn-Taking: A cue near the end of an utterance where the floor-holder (speaker) briefly gazes at the person who desires to speak (the interlocutor) to prepare to transfer control of floor.

Lexical Cuing: Short speech acts that cue or guide others to contribute.

Mutual Gaze: In a face-to-face setting, conversational interactants lock eyes with others several times during a meeting or conversation. These fleeting, but powerful experiences are known as "mutual gaze."

Prosodic Cueing: Refers to everything about a communicator's speech except the words themselves, such as rises and falls in intonation, final lengthening, and energy tapering.

Psychological Safety: The means by which group leaders create environments in which people feel comfortable speaking up and in many cases, disagreeing with others, for the purpose of making informed, and principled decisions.

Virtual Communication Intelligence (aka VCQ): The ability to communicate and navigate relationships and achieve business goals when engaging with others who are not physically co-present.

Virtual Distance: The feeling of separation caused by a lack of face-to-face communication.

Zoom Fatigue: Mental fatigue, induced because the cues and signals that people normally monitor to guide behavior in social situations are absent or are obscured in virtual meetings.

Chapter 8
Penetration Testing and Cyber Security Studies in Bangladesh:
Post-COVID-19 Managerial Issues

Shahadat Hossain
City University, Bangladesh

Lamiya Rahman
https://orcid.org/0000-0003-1274-2776
American International University-Bangladesh, Bangladesh

Rafat Azad
American International University-Bangladesh, Bangladesh

Md. Manzurul Hasan
American International University-Bangladesh, Bangladesh

Mehenaj Jebin
American International University-Bangladesh, Bangladesh

Md. Siam Mahmud
American International University-Bangladesh, Bangladesh

Md. Sadman Sakib
American International University-Bangladesh, Bangladesh

ABSTRACT

The COVID-19 pandemic and consecutive lockdowns have made people dependent on the online environment and have made society compatible with virtual platforms. But the management of the electronic environment is not so easy but too crucial and vital as well as needs to be user-friendly. As a developing country, Bangladesh has

DOI: 10.4018/978-1-6684-3894-7.ch008

welcomed digital changes. Unfortunately, threats and vulnerabilities have risen in lockstep with technological advancement. To deal with this issue, businesses and educational institutions are turning to cyber security. Penetration testing (Pen-Test) is a way of assessing the security of a web application, system, or network by systematically checking and confirming the efficacy of that system. The purpose, classifications, and uses of penetration testing in Bangladesh's IT industries are discussed in this chapter and depict the present state of cyber security in Bangladesh. The authors highlight some of the aspects that contribute to the country's cyber vulnerabilities. Finally, several proposals are made to protect Bangladesh's cyberspace against harmful assaults.

INTRODUCTION

Covid-19 came to the world as a galloping horse. It has been taking a number of lives of important citizens in society, such as engineers, doctors, police, bankers, etc. People faced a boring life during the lockdown periods. Many people have been converted from rich to poor even sometimes it became so hard to maintain their regular lives. People came to know how to struggle with the online platform rather than physical ones. Top to bottom, i.e., from children to senior citizens, top to the bottom became habituated with electronic and online tools at every sphere of life, such as banking transactions, telecommunications, electronic-online-Facebook markets, the education management system, virtual chatting, etc. The most fundamental tool is the internet and electronic devices in all cases. The rising popularity of the internet is remolding the earth into a global village. The internet has enabled the world to connect effortlessly with the press of a button. Organizations can now conduct their day-to-day business over the internet in seconds. With the growth of digitization, Bangladesh's information technology (IT) industry is becoming vital for the economic development and growth of the country. More and more companies are emerging in this sector. Alongside, the number of internet users is also escalating swiftly. Unfortunately, this brings about the risk of cyber-attacks. Hackers threaten valuable data worth millions of dollars. Security of data is one of the leading problems of digitization.

The importance of Cyber Security is growing with the rise in digitization (Moşteanu, N. R. 2020). Organizations invest more in cyber security to protect their data and system from cyber threats. As a result, the need for cyber security experts is soaring. Governments worldwide are emphasizing the practice of safe cyberspace (Fielder, A. et al., 2016). Bangladesh's government has always prioritized the development of the ICT sector through incentives. Both public and private organizations are instructed to evolve and involve technology. However, this also compromises the organizations, making them vulnerable to cyber-attacks. The government enacted the "The National Cyber-Security Strategy of Bangladesh" (Azmi, R., Tibben, W., & Win, K., 2016). Apart from the government, different organizations resort to private cyber security teams to conduct penetration testing and vulnerability assessment on their system. Both the government and the organizations are implementing different cyber security techniques to ensure the security and integrity of valuable data. This paper discusses the cyber security techniques, mainly penetration testing and vulnerability assessment, and how they are utilized in a developing country like Bangladesh. We also explore the strengths and weaknesses in the cyber security sector of Bangladesh.

Numerous researches have been conducted on cyber security, discussed in Section 2 of this paper. Section 3 explains penetration testing in detail. Section 4 and 5 continue to explore the benefits and drawbacks and the working procedure of penetration testing. Section 6 illustrates a detailed picture of Web application penetration testing. Section 7 talks about a few open-source penetration testing tools and operating systems. Section 8 is the essential portion of the paper where Bangladesh's current cyber security readiness is depicted. Finally, section 9 gives the conclusion and future directions regarding this paper.

BACKGROUND

As a developing country, the Government of Bangladesh has taken advantage of the rapid digitization to help with the growth and development of the economy. However, this also invites unsolicited threats from cybercriminals. It is becoming essential to acknowledge those threats and build up a strategy to prevent them. Numerous researches are being conducted on this topic as it becomes increasingly important to tackle these threats. Muller discussed the vulnerabilities and challenges developing countries face against cyber-attacks in this article (Muller, L., 2015). The author also suggested how to build up a strategy to fight back. Brechbühl advised developing countries on strategizing information security policies based on his studies (Brechbühl, H. et al., 2010). Finally, Kortjan depicted a comparison between two developed countries against South Africa (a developing country) based on their cyber security readiness, especially from an educational and awareness perspective (Kortjan, N., & Solms, R., 2012).

Several researchers have acknowledged the need for a more effective cyber security strategy in Bangladesh. Haque highlighted the necessity for a cyber security strategy and data protection policy in Bangladesh while pointing out the vulnerabilities in the sector (Haque, A., 2019). Maruf defined legal remedies against the transpiring cyber-attack (Maruf, A. et al., 2010). Ahmed conveyed a thorough survey of the awareness of cyber-related crimes in Bangladesh and suggested improving the cyber-security strategies (Ahmed, N. et al., 2017). Alam tested SQL injection penetration testing for an education-based website and a financial web application in Bangladesh (Farah, T. et al., 2015). Jagamogan et al. examined the existing and planned penetration testing methodologies and tools for content management systems (CMS) (Jagamogan, R. S., 2021). The matrix is divided into categories based on whether the approaches involve using machine learning algorithms or other methods such as essential penetration tools such as SQL Injection or Cross-site scripting (XSS). Hossain, M. et al. gave an overview of the state of the art in penetration testing, including the most often used tools and approaches, their comparison, and the most serious online application vulnerabilities (Hossain, M., 2021). An actual penetration test of the web application produced by VTXRM – Software Factory (Accipiens) will be discussed with the purpose of building a generic security testing technique applicable to any Web application. The Offensive Web Application Security Framework (OWSAF) is a comprehensive offensive security framework that aids in the detection of vulnerabilities in web applications and aids in real-time security evaluation, which may be used to detect security glitches (Agrawal, A. M. K., 2021).

PENETRATION TESTING

Penetration testing involves an individual or a team performing attacks on a system or network to check its vulnerabilities. In other words, it is an attempted break into it to secure that company or system (Office of CIO, 2018). However, unlike hacking, it has to be legal and ethical, which means before performing the attack, a pen tester or the team needs to take official permission from that particular company (Bishop, M., 2007 and Arkin, B. et al., 2005). A penetration test can be performed automatically or manually. However, a successful penetration is usually performed by professionals called pen-testers or ethical hackers (Whitaker, A., & Newman, D., 2005). The types of penetration testing performed are determined by the business goals. Penetration tester differs both in approaches and the weaknesses, which they attempt to utilize. All necessary information provided to pen-testers includes their approaches and the scope of the project. For example, will the pen tester know the network mapping, or are they required to uncover this information on their own? The different approaches of penetration testing include black box, gray box, and white box testing. Besides, different types of penetration testing include:

- Network Services
- Web Application

- Clint Side
- Wireless
- Physical
- Social Engineering

Figure 1. Total number of internet users around the world

Because of technological advancements, the number of internet users is rising by the day. Furthermore, we are currently entering the fourth industrial revolution in information technology. In this sense, the internet is widely available all over the world. Some data analyses reveal that the population of any country is also accountable for internet usage. Figure 1 depicts demographic data obtained from Kaggle (Prabhu, T. N., 2018), an open-source repository (The Citizen, 2018). To mention that we have given visual representation concerning the dataset. We can see that China has the most internet users among the other nations, with 765, 367, 947 individuals, while Ascension has the fewest, with only 361 online users. Penetration testing is both required and is in high demand to provide better secure internet experiences to users in every country.

BENEFITS AND DRAWBACKS

There are some benefits and drawbacks of pen-test. The benefits of pen-testing are given below.

- As penetration testing is done from the hackers' perspective, it helps us find our system's vulnerabilities.
- Penetration testing helps us to gain valuable insights into our system.

- We can impede the vulnerabilities before they are exploited through penetration testing. In addition, it helps us maintain a good relationship with the clients.
- By discovering the system's weaknesses, pen-testing shows the system's overall security posture and how to modify it.

Some drawbacks of pen-testing are as follows.

- We expose the system to many of the same potential consequences of real hacks by simulating a cyber-attack.
- If the test is not conducted smoothly, it can damage a lot, like exposing crucial information, crashing the servers, etc.
- The test results may be misled if we do not apply realistic test conditions.
- If the tester you hired is not trusted, your security attempts may backfire badly.

PENETRATION TESTING WORKING PROCEDURE

Penetration testing is operated in five main steps. The steps are the same for all kinds of penetration testing (Epling, L. et al., 2015). However, different tools and techniques are utilized depending on the purpose of the test. The five steps are described below.

- **Information Gathering:** This step defines the foundation of penetration testing. Gathering more information about the target means the tester can identify more vulnerabilities. There are three different approaches to information gathering:
    - **Black box testing:** Attacker or Operator has minimal internal knowledge about that system or network.
    - **Gray box testing:** Operator performed from the position of a user, which means he has access of the system or network, including elevated privileges.
    - **White box testing:** In this case, the Operator has access to the source code and architecture documents, which means he can perform from an IT user or administration position.
- **Scanning:** Scanning includes different targets, ports, websites, systems or networks, open ports, open services numbers, and versions. Different tools can automate Scanning (Hasan, A. et al., 2018). A penetration tester can buy those tools or can make them by himself. Also, there are some solid open-

source scanning tools available. The goal of the scanning phase is to detect the vulnerability to exploit it.

- **Vulnerabilities Assessment:** After the scanning phase, the vulnerabilities are analyzed. For example, an open port 21 is found, running a service called FTP with a *VSFTPD 2.3.4* version. Further analysis can find details like the FTP service version may contain a backdoor where an intruder might have created the backdoor (Epling, L. et al., 2015). The developers can use this information to solve the vulnerability.
- **Exploitation:** Exploitation is the last step of the technical process in pen-testing. It is the final ethical hacking step. Here a pen-tester exploits the vulnerabilities which have been found on the step (Shah, S. et al., 2015). In the previous example, we found a vulnerability called *VSFTPS 2.3.4*. So, this vulnerability will be exploited by pen-tester. These are the technical part of penetration testing, which leads to the final step, which is reporting.
- **Reporting:** After the Scanning and Exploitation, a report is created by the penetration tester to give a complete review on the penetration testing with recommendations. This report is usually written in a non-technical language (Shravan, K. et al., 2014). However, because the company or any non-technical person should understand the report and adopt the recommendations, the report should contain guidelines and instructions about reducing risk and taking necessary steps for security. Besides, *Kali* has some default options to generate a report after ethical hacking or penetration testing.

PENETRATION TESTING VS. VULNERABILITY ASSESSMENT

Penetration Test simulates an attack on the system or network to show how vulnerable the system is to outside attacks. In contrast, vulnerability assessment determines the weakness or flaws in a system. Table 1 depicts the significant differences between Penetration Testing and Vulnerability Testing (Ten, C.W., Liu, C.C., & Manimaran, G., 2008).

PENETRATION TESTING ROLES IN THE IT SECTOR

Penetration testing is used by various divisions in the IT sector. This differs depending on the tester's role and responsibilities. Table 2 lists the different roles in the IT sector practicing penetration testing.

Table 1. Difference between Penetration Testing and Vulnerability Assessment

	Penetration Testing	Vulnerability Assessment
Process	It is a two-step process: find and exploit the vulnerability.	It is a steps process: find the vulnerability
Type	It uses one solution for multiple vulnerabilities testing. &	It is a hybrid solution
Focus	On depth over breadth	On breadth over depth
Cost	High	Low to moderate
Working on	Discover and exploit vulnerabilities.	Discover unknown problems in the system
Defense	High	Medium
Control	Preventative control	Detective control
Performer	Attacker, pentester	In house staff

Table 2. Different Roles of Penetration Testing in the IT Sector

Roles	Details
Business contact	This role acts as the business contact for the project and assists in handling various tasks supporting the project, such as executing legal contracts, project invoicing, and scheduling.
Technical contract structure	Technical contracts provide the relevant information required for testing (IP addresses, URLs, compromise goals, etc.) In the project. In some cases, technical contracts act like business contact. It depends on the organization.
Account manager	In a project, the account manager assists with executing legal contracts, invoicing, and scheduling.
Lead engineer	The lead engineer is a technical point of a contract and an emergency contract for a project. Therefore, they have to be active 24/7 during the engagement.
Quality assurance/support engineer	In a project, the engineers validate and ensure the technical accuracy of all findings as part of our quality assurance process. They also assist on some active testing parts to ensure a comprehensive test is performed during the allotted time window.

DIFFERENT TYPES OF PENETRATION TESTING IN THE IT SECTOR

The web vulnerability is a weakness of a website that allows an attacker to harm the website. The attacker may gain some level of control of the website and possibly the hosting server. Here are some of the most common vulnerabilities that websites contain nowadays.

- SQL injection
- Cross-Site Scripting (XSS)
- Broken Authentication and Session Management
- Insecure Direct Object References
- Cross-Site Request Forgery (CSRF)
- Inadequate Transport Layer Protection
- Insecure Cryptography Storage

SQL Injection (SQLi)

SQL injection or SQLi is a web security vulnerability where the attacker bypasses the authentication to gain unauthorized access to the web application's database. Firewall and intrusion detection at the network layer can do little against such attacks since they are executed at the application level (Halfond, W. et al., 2006). The following pseudo-code is an example of a malicious SQL statement. By concatenating "OR 1=1", using URL or HTML form, the attacker alters the authentication query and gains unwarranted access to the database and web application.

```
username = request.POST('admin');
password = request.POST('adminpassword');
query = SELECT id FROM users WHERE username='admin' AND
password='adminpassword' OR 1=1;
```

Cross-Site Scripting (XSS)

Cross-Site Scripting or XSS is another web security vulnerability. It is a client-side code injection technique where the attacker injects malicious script into the victim's browser through a trusted web page. The attack is triggered when the user visits the web page and executes the script. This attack is used to deface a website by changing the content (Wassermann, G., & Su, Z., 2008).

```
print "<html>"
print "<h1>Recently Added Item</h1>"
print db.lastedAddedItem
print "</html>"
```

For example, the above code displays the most recent item added to a website. If a web application is vulnerable to XSS, an attacker can pass a malicious script through the last added item. Therefore, when a victim visits the website to check the last added item, he will unintentionally trigger the script.

```
<html>
<h1>Recently Added Item</h1>
<script>doSomethingMalicious();</script>
</html>
```

Cross-Site Request Forgery (CSRF)

Cross-Site Request Forgery or CSRF attack tricks the victim into executing actions unconsciously on an authorized web application. The attacker utilizes social engineering (sending links via email, chat, or pop-up ads that the victim might be interested in) to force the victim to perform an action planned by the attacker (Jovanovic, N., Kirda, E., & Kruegel, C., 2006). As a result, the attacker can accomplish dreadful tasks like transferring funds, changing account credentials, sending unauthorized messages through email and chat.

```
http://bankxyz.com/send?amount=1000&account=Victim
&receiver=Attacker&Auth=true
```

For example, the attacker wants to transfer 1000 units from the victim's account to his account. The above URL triggers this transfer. The attacker hides this GET request and provokes the victim to trigger it. When the victim loads the page, the request is triggered, and the fund is transferred to the attacker from the victims' account.

```
<img src="http://bankxyz.com/send?amount=1000&account=
Victim&receiver=Attacker&Auth=true">
```

WEB APPLICATIONS' PENETRATION TESTING TOOLS

Table 3 enlists some of the popularly used web applications in penetration testing tools in the industry. The table also provides a short description of the mentioned tools.

OPEN-SOURCE TESTING TOOLS

The term open source is used to refer to open-source software. This software is released under a license that grants users permission to freely modify and use the software and its source code. The approach of the open-source term is built on the values of collaboration, transparency, and community-oriented development. The open-source concept is becoming more familiar to the people with the growing popularity of open-source projects like chromium and firefox (Chromium, 2021 and Firefox: About your rights. Mozilla, 2021). Recent reports claim that the open-source market stands at around $21.6 billion in 2020 and can surge by 30 percent by the end of 2021, to reach $33 billion (Liu, S., 2019).

Table 3. Different Web Application Penetration Testing Tools

Categories	Tools	Descriptions
Service fingerprinting	NMAP	It is a well-known tool to check networks. It is free and genuine software through which anyone can check the port status and the host and server details of a system or network.
	Unicornscan	It helps introduce a stimulus, information gathering and correlation engine and measuring the response from a TCP/IP device.
	Dmitry (Deepmagic Information Gathering Tool)	It's a Linux command line application and coded in C language.
	GFI Languard 2014	It provides a comprehensive overview of network security through patch management, vulnerability assessment and network and software.
Vulnerability Scanner	Nessus	Nessus is one of the most used and popular tools for vulnerability assessment. It is partially accessible.
	Burp Suite	It is a paid tool but very efficient. It is used for intercepting proxy, web scanning and so on.
	OpenVAS (Open Vulnerability Assessment System)	A free, comprehensive and powerful vulnerability scanner and vulnerability management solution
	Metasploit	It is one of the famous penetration testing tools now.
	Wireshark	This tool is used to penetrate down into your everyday TCP/IP connection problems.

Open-Source Tools

There are thousands of open-source tools available for cyber security operations like penetration testing and digital forensic. It performs as expected and gives the security team or a third-party software developer the ability to modify the programming code to meet the specific needs and requirements. Mid- to small-sized companies use free and paid open-source tools to improve their organization's security and modify the solution to protect their digital assets and networks according to their unique business operation needs.

Numerous Linux distributions, based on Ubuntu or Debian, are primarily designed for cyber security operations. Some of the popular operating systems are listed below.

- Kali Linux
- Parrot OS
- BackBox
- BlackArch
- Fedora Security Lab

These operating systems come equipped with all the necessary tools required for penetration testing and vulnerability assessment. Kali Linux houses over 600 pre-installed penetration-testing programs, whereas BackBox Linux has over 70 valuable programs. The enlisted tools are some of the most used penetration testing tools:

- OWASP ZAP (Zed Attack Proxy)
- Burp Suite
- Scapy
- BeEF
- Sqlmap
- Kali Linux NetHunter

Open-Source Testing Tools Examples

The following code shows how python and its libraries have made it easy for programmers and professional cyber-security experts to create their testing tools. The functionality of this script is to identify the devices connected to the target network. Thus, this script can be used during the first step of penetration testing, the information-gathering phase.

```
from scapy.all import Ether, ARP, srp, conf
import sys
import time

def arp_scan(iface, ip_range):
    print("[+] Scanning ", ip_range)
    curr_time = time.time()
    print("[+] Scan started at ", time.ctime(curr_time))
    conf.verb = 0
    broadcast = "ff:ff:ff:ff:ff:ff"
    ether_layer = Ether(dst=broadcast)
```

```
    arp_layer = ARP(pdst=ip_range)

    packet = ether_layer/arp_layer

    ans, unans = srp(packet, iface=iface, timeout=2, inter=0.1)

    for snd, rcv in ans:
        ip = rcv[ARP].psrc
        mac = rcv[Ether].src
        print(ip, mac)
    duration = time.time() - curr_time
    print("[+] Scan completed, Duration: ", duration)

if __name__ == "__main__":
    iface = sys.argv[1]
    ip_range = sys.argv[2]
    arp_scan(iface, ip_range)
```

BANGLADESH AND CYBER SECURITY

Cyber Security and Cyber Crime

Cyber security protects systems, networks, programs, devices, and data from cyber threats (Goutam, R. K., 2015). Averting cyber assaults and unauthorized exploitation of systems, networks, and technology is its goal. There are five types of cyber security.

- Critical infrastructure cyber security
- Network security
- Cloud security
- IoT (Internet of Things) security
- Application security

Cybercrime is described as "any illegal conduct that involves the use of a computer, communication device, or computer network to commit or enable the commission of a crime. (Bossler, A. M. et al., 2019)" The majority of cybercrime comes into two broad categories:

- **Criminal activities that targets computers**
    - DDoS (distributed denial-of-service) assaults, in which servers, systems, and networks are flooded with traffic in order to bring them down.
    - Formjacking is when malicious code is inserted into internet forms.
    - Cryptojacking, which involves the installation of unauthorized bitcoin mining software.
- **Criminal activities that use computers**
    - Ransomware, botnet software, RATs (remote access Trojans), rootkits and bootkits, spyware, Trojans, viruses, and worms are all examples of malware.
    - Remote access using backdoors.
    - DNS (domain name system) poisoning attacks, in which the DNS is compromised and traffic is redirected to hostile websites.

Cyber Security in Developed Countries

Soldiers, guns, and other physical structures are the terms that are thought to be used for a country's security. However, security evolved to mean information security with the advent of computers. Today, a country is not secure if it cannot control its cyber assets. According to the "International Telecommunication Union," the United States of America, United Kingdom, Saudi Arabia, Estonia, South Korea, Singapore, Spain, Russia, United Arab Emirates, and Malaysia are the top-ranked countries in the Global Cyber security index (Global cybersecurity index, 2020). These countries have taken many measures to reach the top of the index. They provide security studies from the root level. They have the best cyber security courses in schools and universities and offer some of the most competitive bachelor and masters programs in cyber and information security. Thus, their students get involved with cyber security from an early age. Boston University (USA), University of Oxford (UK), Carnegie Mellon University (USA), Imperial College London (UK), George Washington University (USA) are some of the top universities for cybersecurity-related studies. They provide programs like Security and Cryptography, Design and analysis of algorithms, Ethical Hacking, Penetration Testing, Computer Network Defense, Advanced software paradigms, Malware Analysis, Wire-less, and mobile security, Internet and online law for security managers, Cyber data analytics, Cyber risk management, Security Engineering, Network Security and many more. They also offer several research opportunities for undergraduates who are interested in specializing in cyber security. These universities also have several significant links in the industry. They are also producing high-caliber graduates with impressive starting salaries. The starting salary in Cyber Security ranges from $50,000 to $100,000 annually (Home Indeed.com, 2021).

The most important thing is that they provide cyber security courses for school students. Their governments have taken many initiatives aimed at younger students with interest in cyber security. Many children are also being exposed to basic coding as young as 7 or 8 years. They provide short courses like Adventurers, Defenders, Trailblazers, Futures, and Advanced, introducing young people to the various aspects of cyber defense. They also arrange a half-day event for a two-week course of fun and interactive sessions. Also, there are many famous Capture-the-Flag challenges with attractive prizes. Thus, they succeed in growing their young generation's interest in this field by providing enough opportunities. All this is redirecting the enthusiast to the cyber security field. Thus, they are getting more and more cyber security experts.

Necessity of Cyber Security Bangladesh

The government of Bangladesh has been giving the utmost importance to the information and communication technology (ICT) industry to build an entirely digitized Bangladesh. It has brought about a wave of transformation in every sector of Bangladesh. Organizations are shifting their day-to-day activities to digital platforms. As a result, the influence of data rose. However, this also put the country in a state of vulnerability. The rate of cybercrime started to escalate as well. Therefore, the need for securing digital data and electronic transactions has become inevitable. Besides, Bangladesh had to learn this fact through a series of unfortunate events. On February 4, 2016, Bangladesh Bank, the central bank of Bangladesh, was the victim of one of the most horrific cyber-attacks in history (Fielder, A. et al., 2016). An international hacker group managed to transfer around $200 million to the several Philippines and Sri Lanka accounts. They did this by using malware to target a vulnerability in the SWIFT network (Alam, M., 2012). Their goal was to extract $1 billion from Bangladesh Bank. However, a transaction of $850 million to The Federal Reserve Bank of New York triggered suspicion. As a result, the whole transfer was blocked and reported, making Bangladesh Bank aware of this situation. This event warned the whole country about the magnitude of damage a cyber-attack can inflict on a country (Bukth, T., & Huda, S., 2017).

In the June of 2019, Dutch Bangla Bank was victim to a cyber-attack originating from Cyprus, Russia, and Ukraine. The hacker group stole around \$1.4 million from the Bank (Joveda, N. et al., 2019). Furthermore, a country-wide alert warned the banks about an upcoming cyber-attack from a North Korean Hacker group named Beagle Boys. As a result, all the atm transactions were suspended for a day (Dhaka Tribune., 2020). Furthermore, according to a report published by Bangladesh Government's e-Government Computer Incident Response Team (BD-CIRT) published in April 2021, a Chinese hacker group named HAFNIUM exploits vulnerabilities in Microsoft Exchange Server and email servers of government entities, financial institutions, and business organizations, including the Army, Banks, Telecommunication regulatory commission, Gas company, finance of Bangladesh (Cyber threat report, 2021).

Apart from the financial organizations, the other sectors are also vulnerable to cyber-attacks. It is because the organizations can lose valuable information to the attackers. BD-CIRT posts regular statistics about the cyber-attacks in Bangladesh. Figure 2 shows the reported incidents each month. We can notice that there was a surge in cybercrime in 2020. Similarly, Figure 3 illustrates the number of incidents reported each year

Figure 2. Registered incidents by month

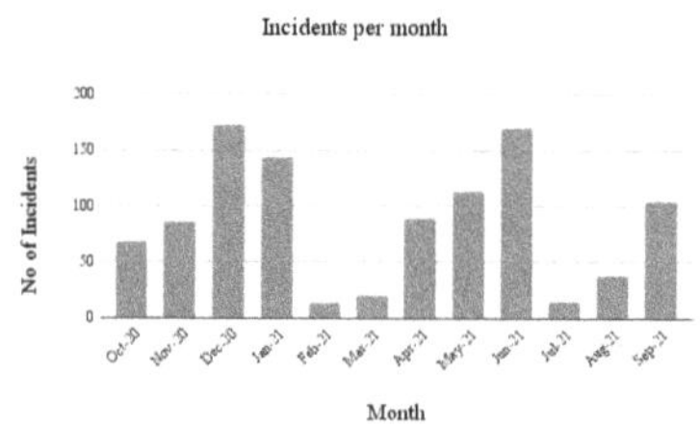

Figure 3. Registered incidents by year

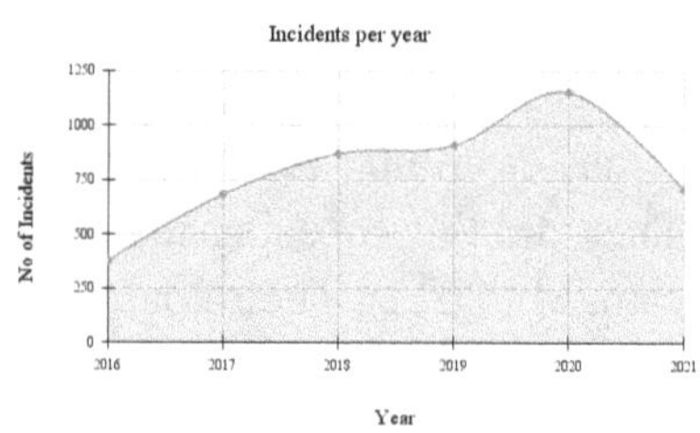

Figure 4. Classification of reported incidents

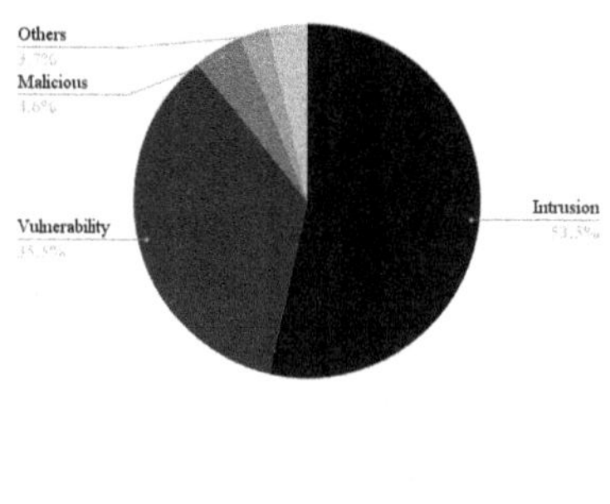

Figure 4 classifies the incidents. The lion's share of the incidents involved intrusion attempts, vulnerability exploitation, and Malicious scripts (Cyber threat report, 2021). It suggests that there is an urgent need for cyber security in the various sectors of Bangladesh.

Security Service Providers in Bangladesh

With the emergence of cyber-security, many companies offer security services in risk assessment, security strategy, policy development, penetration testing, and consultancy. Even though it is a comparatively new field, new companies and experts are offering their services. Some of the companies providing security services are listed below:

- Eicra Soft Ltd
- Pentester Space
- Bugsbd
- DataSec
- Cybersec Technology LTD
- EC-Council Global Services (EGS)

Cyber Security Challenges in Bangladesh

Organizations and companies in Bangladesh are avid practitioners of cyber-security techniques. However, a loophole still exists in the system. A large portion of the population of Bangladesh is not aware of the term "cyber-security." Enthusiastic learners are resorting to various free and paid courses online. However, schools are not teaching the students about the importance of cyber security. Most of the top universities in Bangladesh do not offer advanced cyber security and ethical hacking courses. Regular researches are not being conducted on this topic. Bangladesh University of Engineering and Technology (BUET), American International University-Bangladesh (AIUB), and Bangladesh University of Professionals (BUP) are some of the few institutes exploring the field of cyber security. BUP, along with some other universities, also provides a master's program in Information Security (Masters in Information Systems Security (MISS), BUP, 2021). Apart from that, the only way to become an expert and certified professional is by traveling abroad for an expensive degree and certificate in cyber-security. Despite being interested in pursuing a career in cyber security, most students cannot afford this career path.

Every IT company should have a security team, but in Bangladesh, a few companies may follow this or less than a few. Most companies in Bangladesh, especially those dealing with information technology, do not have a dedicated cyber security team.

BD CIRT (Bangladesh Government's e-Government Computer Incident Response Team) actively builds awareness among these companies to prevent attacks. They regularly provide security guidelines (Team, C. I. R. T. (n.d.), 2019). Despite their effort, Bangladesh is struggling to fight back against these attacks. According to the Kaspersky Security Bulletin 2020, Bangladesh is the top country to be affected by ransomware Trojan attacks, 8th in the list of countries where users faced the most significant risk of online infection, and 7th in the list for the level of risk of local infection (Amr, Galov, D. et al.,2020). A test conducted by Bangladesh Computer Council in 2020 indicated over 34552 infected IPs in Bangladesh. IPs of renowned companies like Grameenphone, Banglalink, and Link3 were also mentioned in that list. A study in 2019 published a list of websites in Bangladesh and their vulnerability against six attack vectors (BGD e-GOV CIRT, 2019). Table 4 shows the list of 10 websites that were tested for vulnerability in 2019 (Moniruzzaman, M. et al., 2019). These vulnerabilities were detected using various penetration testing tools like OWASP, SQLMap, BOLT, Burp, TLSSLed, Unicornscan, and many more. Some websites have addressed this issue and recently updated their security policy (Al Shebli et al., 2018). Additionally, to mention that Compliance with IT policies should be zero tolerance even in negligence.

Table 4. Vulnerability of websites in Bangladesh

Websites	SQLi	XSS	BAS	CSRF	Unusual ports	TLS
Bangladesh Bank	Secure	Secure	Not Applicable	Not Applicable	None	Secure
Dbbl	Secure	Secure	Secure	Secure	None	Secure
Prime Minister's Office	Vulnerable	Vulnerable	Not Applicable	Not Applicable	None	Vulnerable
Ministry of Home Affairs	Vulnerable	Vulnerable	Not Applicable	Not Applicable	None	Vulnerable
ICT Division	Vulnerable	Vulnerable	Not Applicable	Not Applicable	None	Vulnerable
Bangladesh Police	Vulnerable	Vulnerable	Vulnerable	Vulnerable	None	Vulnerable
Dhaka Stock-Exchange	Vulnerable	Vulnerable	Vulnerable	Not Applicable	None	Secure
Prothom-Alo	Secure	Secure	Secure	Secure	None	Secure
Kaler-Kantho	Secure	Secure	Not Applicable	Not Applicable	None	Secure
Daraz Bd	Secure	Secure	Secure	Secure	None	Secure

Progress in the Field of Cyber Security

Bangladesh is a newcomer in the field of cyber security. Despite struggling to cope up with the increasing demand for security strategies, Bangladesh has managed to turn around over the past few months. The recent National Cyber Security Index prepared by the Estonia-based e-Governance Academy Foundation ranked Bangladesh in 36th place out of 180 countries. It is an excellent accomplishment for Bangladesh as they leaped from the 85th position last year, indicating that Bangladesh is already growing in cyber security. Moreover, Bangladesh's government is drafting the first data protection acts or law, which is an excellent start towards ensuring cyber security (Mahmood, B. S., 2021). With more awareness and opportunities for newcomers, Bangladesh can establish itself as a leader in cyber security.

Recommendations

Bangladesh needs to prioritize the security of information and system against cyber-attacks, alongside the country's digitization. Therefore, there should be more investment in the field of cyber security. The Bangladesh government has invested around 400 million BDT in developing the cyber security branch in the ICT division. However, the private sector should also consider strengthening its security. Even though Bangladesh has the Information and Communication Technology (ICT) Act, 2006, and the Digital Security Act (DSA), 2018, there is no dedicated cyber security law. The existing law addresses data protection, data integrity, and confidentiality. However, in the era of cybercrime, a significant amendment is required to the existing laws. Therefore, the government needs to form a commission dedicated to its cyber security and its people. Cyber security is not only a global concern but also a national concern a more, even with respect to a 3rd world country like Bangladesh. It is to mention that we are in 3rd world country are sometimes more whimsical than that of a 1st and 2nd world countries. We should be more cautious about the policy guidelines and there need more training and practices in this regard. Otherwise, there may be a high possibility to fall in a vulnerable IT infrastructure.

Lastly, the government and organizations should work together to raise awareness regarding cyber security. Both public and private organizations should assess the vulnerabilities in their system regularly and practice strict security policies. A national cyber security strategy should be followed to ensure security for the organizations. Furthermore, educational institutes should emphasize training more cyber security professionals as the demand for experts in this field increases. Workshops and seminars on the career prospect of cyber security experts can guide the student and enthusiasts to pursue a career in this sector.

FUTURE WORK DIRECTION AND CONCLUSION

The authorities must take some critical initiatives to ensure that future generations are well-equipped to deal with cyber threats. Our research serves as a springboard for future work related to our topic. We have conducted penetration testing across the globe and in Bangladesh. Still, we should engage in industry-academic partnership, negotiation, and a memorandum of understanding to guide future research from a practical perspective. Additional assessments of the policies and guidelines governing cyber forensics and security systems are required, as they may illuminate certain avenues for preventing penetration and cyber-attacks.

Cyber-attacks have undoubtedly become a severe issue for emerging countries such as Bangladesh. Bangladesh's government should move quickly to prepare the country for cyber threats and criminality. It is possible to do this by raising public and organizational awareness. To improve cyber security, govt must establish strict regulations and policies. Furthermore, public and private enterprises must be given comprehensive rules to prevent cyber assaults. Finally, to solve the shortage of professionals in this sector, institutes must teach cyber security specialists. As a method of cyber security, this article has addressed penetration testing and vulnerability assessment. Other valuable technologies and approaches are used across the world to strengthen the system and network security. Our work has introduced such tools and linked their potential applications in Bangladesh's cyber security industry.

REFERENCES

Azmi, R., Tibben, W., & Win, K. (2016). Motives behind Cyber Security Strategy Development: A Literature Review of National Cyber Security Strategy. *Australasian Conference on Information Systems.*

Alam, M. (2012). E-governance in Bangladesh: Present problems and possible suggestions for future development. *International Journal of Applied Information Systems*, *4*(8), 21–25. doi:10.5120/ijais12-450804

Agrawal, A. M. K., Bolli, D. B., Teja, C., Budhwani, T. P., Sehgal, L., Dharia, J. N., & Aggarwal, A. (2021). Offensive Web Application Security Framework. *Design Engineering (London)*, (9), 17334–17342.

Ahmed, N., Kulsum, U., Azad, I., Momtaz, A., Haque, M., & Rahman, M. (2017). *Cybersecurity awareness survey: An analysis from Bangladesh perspective. 2017 IEEE Region 10 Humanitarian Technology Conference (R10-HTC).*

Arkin, B., Stender, S., & McGraw, G. (2005). Software penetration testing. *IEEE Security and Privacy*, *3*(1), 84–87. doi:10.1109/MSP.2005.23

Al Shebli, H., & Beheshti, B. (2018). A study on penetration testing process and tools. In *2018 IEEE Long Island Systems, Applications and Technology Conference (LISAT)* (pp. 1–7). 10.1109/LISAT.2018.8378035

Amr, G. (2020). Kaspersky security. *Bulletin*.

Brechbühl, H., Bruce, R., Dynes, S., & Johnson, M. (2010). Protecting critical information infrastructure: Developing cybersecurity policy. *Information Technology for Development*, *20*(2), 122–139. doi:10.1002/itdj.20096

Bukth, T., & Huda, S. (2017). *The soft threat: The story of the Bangladesh bank reserve heist*. SAGE Publications.

Bishop, M. (2007). About penetration testing. *IEEE Security and Privacy*, *5*(6), 84–87. doi:10.1109/MSP.2007.159

BGD e-GOV CIRT | Bangladesh e-Government Computer Incident Response Team. (n.d.). *Statistics development – BGD e-GOV CIRT: Bangladesh e-government computer incident response team*. BGD eGOV CIRT Bangladesh eGovernment Computer Incident Response Team. Retrieved October 13, 2021, from https://www.cirt.gov.bd/statistics-development/

Bossler, A. M., & Berenblum, T. (2019). Introduction: New directions in cybercrime research. *Journal of Criminal Justice*, *42*(5), 495–499.

Chromium. The Chromium Projects. (n.d.). Retrieved October 13, 2021, from https://www.chromium.org/Home

Cyber threat report - cirt.gov.bd. (n.d.). Retrieved October 13, 2021, from https://www.cirt.gov.bd/wp-content/uploads/2021/04/HAFNIUM.pdf

Epling, L., Hinkel, B., & Hu, Y. (2015, October). Penetration testing in a box. In *Proceedings of the 2015 information security curriculum development conference* (pp. 1-4). Academic Press.

Fielder, A., Panaousis, E., Malacaria, P., Hankin, C., & Smeraldi, F. (2016). Decision support approaches for cyber security investment. *Decision Support Systems*, *86*, 13–23.

Farah, T., Alam, D., Kabir, M., & Bhuiyan, T. (2015). SQLi penetration testing of financial Web applications: Investigation of Bangladesh region. In *2015 World Congress on Internet Security (WorldCIS)* (pp. 146–151). Academic Press.

Firefox: About your rights. Mozilla. (n.d.). Retrieved October 13, 2021, from https://www.mozilla.org/en-US/about/legal/terms/firefox/

Global cybersecurity index 2020. My ITU. (n.d.). Retrieved October 13, 2021, from https://www.itu.int/en/myitu/Publications/2021/06/28/13/22/Global-Cybersecurity-Index-2020

Goutam, R. K. (2015). Importance of cyber security. *International Journal of Computers and Applications*, *111*(7).

Halfond, W., Viegas, J., Orso, A., & ... (2006). A classification of SQL-injection attacks and countermeasures. In *Proceedings of the IEEE international symposium on secure software engineering* (pp. 13–15). IEEE.

Hacking alert: Banks in Bangladesh limit atms, cards and online transactions to avoid risks. Dhaka Tribune. (2020, September 7). Retrieved October 13, 2021, from https://www.dhakatribune.com/business/banks/2020/09/07/hacking-alert-banks-in-bangladesh-limit-atms-cards-and-online-transactions-to-avoid-risks

Haque, A. (2019). *Need for Critical Cyber Defence, Security Strategy and Privacy Policy in Bangladesh–Hype or Reality? International Journal of Managing Information Technology*, 11.

Hasan, A., & Meva, D. (2018). Web application safety by penetration testing. *International Journal of Advanced Studies of Scientific Research*, *3*(9).

Home. Indeed.com. (n.d.). Retrieved October 13, 2021, from https://www.indeed.com/career/salaries/Cyber%20Security

Hossain, M., Hassan, R., Amjad, M., & Rahman, M. (2021). Web Performance Analysis: An Empirical Analysis of E-Commerce Sites in Bangladesh. *International Journal of Information Engineering & Electronic Business*, *13*(4).

Jagamogan, R. S., Ismail, S. A., Hafizah, N., & Abas, H. H. (2021, October). A Review: Penetration Testing Approaches on Content Management System (CMS). In *2021 7th International Conference on Research and Innovation in Information Systems (ICRIIS)* (pp. 1-6). IEEE.

Jovanovic, N., Kirda, E., & Kruegel, C. (2006). Preventing cross site request forgery attacks. In 2006 Securecomm and Workshops. Academic Press.

Joveda, N., Khan, M., Pathak, A., & Chattogram, B. (2019). Cyber laundering: a threat to banking industries in bangladesh: in quest of effective legal framework and cyber security of financial information. *International Journal of Economics and Finance*, *11*(10), 54–65.

Kortjan, N., & Solms, R. (2012). Cyber security education in developing countries: A South African perspective. In *International conference on e-Infrastructure and e-Services for developing countries* (pp. 289–297). Academic Press.

Liu, S. (2019, September 13). *Open-Source Services Market Revenue Worldwide 2017-2022*. Statista. Retrieved October 13, 2021, from https://www.statista.com/statistics/270805/projected-revenue-of-open-source-software-since-2008/

Maruf, A., Islam, M., & Ahamed, B. (2010). Emerging Cyber Threats in Bangladesh: In quest of effective legal remedies. *Northern University Journal of Law*, *1*, 112–124.

Moşteanu, N. R. (2020). Challenges for Organizational Structure and design as a result of digitalization and cybersecurity. *The Business & Management Review*, *11*(1), 278–286.

Muller, L. (2015). *Cyber security capacity building in developing countries: Challenges and opportunities*. Norwegian Institute of International Affairs.

Masters in Information Systems Security (MISS). Bangladesh University of Professionals (BUP). (n.d.). Retrieved October 13, 2021, from https://bup.edu.bd/programs/22/details-academics?department_id=17%7D%2C+journal

Mahmood, B. S. (2021, September 13). Bangladesh's New Data Protection Act: Brittle shield or blunt sword? *The Daily Star*. Retrieved October 13, 2021, from https://www.thedailystar.net/views/in-focus/news/bangladeshs-new-data-protection-act-brittle-shield-or-blunt-sword-2174371

Moniruzzaman, M., Chowdhury, F., & Ferdous, M. (2019). Measuring vulnerabilities of Bangladeshi websites. In *2019 International Conference on Electrical, Computer and Communication Engineering (ECCE)* (pp. 1–7). Academic Press.

Penetration Testing. (2018). *Office of Chief Information Officer, U.S. Department of the Interior*. Retrieved December 18, 2018. https://www.doi.gov/ocio/customers/penetration-testing

Prabhu, T. N. (2019, August 10). *List of countries by number of internet users*. Kaggle. Retrieved April 14, 2022, from https://www.kaggle.com/datasets/tanuprabhu/list-of-countries-by-number-of-internet-users

Shah, S., & Mehtre, B. M. (2015). An overview of vulnerability assessment and penetration testing techniques. *Journal of Computer Virology and Hacking Techniques*, *11*(1), 27–49.

Shravan, K., Neha, B., & Pawan, B. (2014). Penetration testing: A Review. *Compusoft*, *3*(4), 752.

Team, C. I. R. T. (n.d.). *Common vulnerabilities in cyber space of Bangladesh.* BGD e-GOV CIRT |Bangladesh e-Government Computer Incident Response Team. Retrieved October 13, 2021, from https://www.cirt.gov.bd/common-vulnerabilities-in-cyber-space-of-bangladesh/

Ten, C. W., Liu, C. C., & Manimaran, G. (2008). Vulnerability assessment of cybersecurity for SCADA systems. *IEEE Transactions on Power Systems, 23*(4), 1836–1846.

The Citizen. (2018, October 17). *Analysis: Data breaches compromised 4.5bn records in half year 2018 - gemalto - thecitizen - it's all about you.* TheCitizen. Retrieved April 14, 2022, from https://thecitizenng.com/analysis-data-breaches-compromised-4-5bn-records-in-half-year-2018-gemalto/ [Accessed 11 October 2021].

Wassermann, G., & Su, Z. (2008). Static detection of cross-site scripting vulnerabilities. In *2008 ACM/IEEE 30th International Conference on Software Engineering* (pp. 171–180). ACM.

Whitaker, A., & Newman, D. (2005). *Penetration Testing and Network Defense: Penetration Testing*. Cisco Press.

KEY TERMS AND DEFINITIONS

Cybercrime: Cybercrime is defined as any criminal activity involving a computer, networked device, or network. While most cybercrimes are committed to generate profit for the perpetrators, some cybercrimes are committed against computers or devices directly in order to damage or disable them.

Cybersecurity: The protection of internet-connected systems, including their hardware, software, and data, against malicious cyberattacks is referred to as cybersecurity. To prevent unwanted access to data centers and other computerized systems, people and businesses alike engage in the practice of using two-factor authentication (2FA).

Education: Education is both teaching and learning. Education refers to schooling, instruction, and teaching as a whole.

Network Security: Our network and its data will be safe from invasions, breaches, and other dangers if we have adequate network security. This is a broad and all-encompassing phrase that refers to the many hardware and software solutions, as well as the procedures, policies, and settings that are associated with the usage of networks, accessibility, and overall protection against threats.

OWASP: OWASP means Open Web Application Security Project. The OWASP Top 10 is a document that serves as a benchmark for raising awareness among developers and online application security professionals. It exemplifies the widespread agreement among security experts on the most serious threats posed to web applications. Generally acknowledged as the first step towards better secure programming anywhere in the world.

Penetration Testing: A penetration test, also known as a pen test, is a simulation of an authorized attack that is carried out on a computer system in order to assess the system's level of security. To uncover vulnerabilities in a system and explain how such vulnerabilities may affect a company's operations, professionals known as penetration testers use the same kinds of tools, methods, and procedures that are utilized by attackers.

Threats and Risk: Even more simply, a threat is the potential damage to an asset (the item you're attempting to safeguard) that is present. The probability that the damage will be realized is known as risk. The asset's vulnerability is the point at which the damage may reach it.

Chapter 9
Contemporary Security Threats:
Some Proposals for Banking Networks in Bangladesh

Md. Manzurul Hasan
American International University-Bangladesh, Bangladesh

Shahadat Hossain
City University, Bangladesh

Prioty Saha Trisha
American International University-Bangladesh, Bangladesh

Md. Mohsin Hossain
American International University-Bangladesh, Bangladesh

Abu Saleh Mohammad Rajuwan
American International University-Bangladesh, Bangladesh

Md. Hasibur Rahman
American International University-Bangladesh, Bangladesh

ABSTRACT

Online transactions have increased abruptly during the COVID-19 pandemic. In recent years, the expansion of easy banking in Bangladesh has become necessary, particularly when banks do not have sufficient branches in Bangladesh's rural areas. This research provides a quick overview, a managerial framework of cybersecurity, and several potential threats that might significantly affect the security of online monetary transactions by giving some important ways. The authors explore contemporary scamming strategies used by cybercriminals and the impact of such scams on the financial sector. In addition, this chapter presents a way to mitigate these concerns by inflexible banking, provides a quick overview of the current automated teller machine (ATM) fraud, and offers potential solutions to avoid these attacks. Furthermore, the authors examine the consequences of banking fraud and identify possible research avenues where researchers could focus their efforts on benefit.

DOI: 10.4018/978-1-6684-3894-7.ch009

INTRODUCTION

Covid-19 is not only a pandemic but also a lesson to us. We should be cautious and sensitive regarding any further epidemics. Covid-19 and its consecutive lockdowns worldwide have taught us how to be dependent on online and electronic platforms. Newborn to old, all utilize the best use of virtual communications and tools at every limb in the skeleton of a nation like finance, agriculture, communication, etc. However, most of the population in Bangladesh is illiterate, and there is a lack of awareness regarding digital transactions among the people (Rahman, S., 2016). Bangladesh Bank is the country's highest banking body, in charge of banking regulation and transaction monitoring. This regulatory body has a broad range of monetary legislation for Bangladesh to grasp essential security components. Several pieces support this system. First, online transactions should be completed to instils trust among the users. Second, several ATM distortions have happened in this region and throughout the past. It culminated in billions of dollars in losses. This article discusses an observation on ATM usage and scamming strategies, particularly in Bangladesh. This research work identifies the usual ATM scams in the context of how, when, and where these types of fraud are rapidly increasing and subsequently enlightens the necessity of security traits that should follow. Identifying those threats to the banking sector and all online transaction methods is necessary. Several ATM scams have occurred in Bangladeshi banks, including Pubali Bank and the Dutch Bangla Bank (Shaw, L., 2016). Online banking is growing popular, and it provides a variety of security safeguards for its users. However, scammers are modifying their methods to avoid banks' security management detection. Money-related organizations transfer a massive proportion of organizations to buyers and associations, with trillions of dollars trading hands daily to keep the globe afloat. These businesses rely on technologies, regulations, and security measures.

Any disruption in the bank's security system might lead to sabotage and robbery. As a result, it disrupts the financial system and causes clients' money hijacking and reputations to be lost. In Bangladesh, the value of online transactions ranges from \$1 to \$12 million. This sum increased to five times its original value, which was \$5 million to \$25 million, between January 2013 and February 2015 (Rahman, S., 2016). The national and cybersecurity systems use specialized methods to protect the security of online transactions. This research demonstrates specific security methods that are excellent practices in online transaction security. To begin, undertake risk assessment by understanding the estimates of security measures. Second, physical security measures include stakes in organizations, work zones, and bank lockers. Third, human resource security procedures in which the worker should be checked appropriately with authentic confirmation. Fourth, create and test data recovery backups from fortifications. Finally, retain security patches and upgrades inside businesses, such as worker rotation, client confirmations, and system security approaches and frameworks. Finally, it should be mandatory use of the intranet (not the internet) among different branches of financial organizations.

Furthermore, the governing board should guarantee that access to critical areas of the organization is restricted. Routine tests and establishing a plan of action have a considerably more significant influence on security measures. This strategy includes a network monitoring system and well-defined analytic and management tools. Updating the versions of equipment such as switches, routers, firewalls, and other security appliances can help to reduce the likelihood of being scammed. The organization should use encryption in all aspects of internet data transactions, including official and promotional emails. Anti-malware and antivirus software may be used to implement a complete endpoint security solution. Finally, training programs for both employees and users of online systems can significantly raise scam awareness. The primary goal of the research is to learn about current security threats to Bangladeshi financial institutions and how we can detect or identify them more easily. Our main objectives for the research work are as follows.

- To explain certain security threats at Bangladeshi banking networks
- To develop a management framework for banking security
- To provide potential cyber-attack prevention methods and recommendations
- To present various online scams as well as a timeline of cyber-attacks

BACKGROUND

Maria et al. (Hofileña et al., 2017) stated numerous money laundering and banking legislation. The term “absolute” is deceptive in Philippine financial law because Section 2 of the bill offers exceptions to the absolute rule. The law states that the Government of the Philippines’ investments in bonds may not be examined, inquired about, or investigated by any person, government official, agency, or office except with the depositor’s written permission, or in cases of impeachment or if there is bribery or dereliction of duty by public officials. At the court’s discretion, the regulation punishes guilty offenders with a maximum sentence of five years in jail or a maximum fine of P20,000 or both. Most businesses have moved their operations online, commonly referred to as e-commerce. Nurudeen et al. (Nurudeen et al., 2012) introduced new technology that provides most companies with a more extensive market reach and rapid marketing. Still, it has also highlighted trust between business owners and consumers (Hossain et al. 2020). Passive attacks seek information from a network system without changing it in transit or place. This type of attack is complicated because no data is changed, and everything seems normal.

South African President Jacob Zuma has established a National Cybersecurity and Data Protection Framework (NCPF) to protect data privacy (Sutherland, E., 2020). The NCPF was slow, not helped by President Zuma's movement of responsibility between Cabinet "clusters" and departments nor by his rapid turnover of ministers. It requires extensive coordination across the Government, with the lead assigned to the Justice, Crime Prevention, and Security Cluster of Ministers. According to a global study of financial institutions, financial institutions are under a significant threat from cyberattacks (Saha, A. R., & Rahman, M. M., 2018). Cybercrime is a technological disease spreading at an alarming rate in the modern era.

Financial institutes must pay attention to their security and improve internal security. In addition, organizations should recruit cybersecurity experts to prevent cybercrimes. High-tech crime has facilitated and impeded the investigation of crimes, particularly high-tech crimes involving computing and communications technologies. Smith (Smith, R. G., 2004) identified several impediments to the effective investigation of high-tech crime across borders and offered some solutions that could be used to streamline future cyberspace investigations. The answers lie in harmonizing laws and procedures globally, improving the technical capabilities of investigators, and sharing information between public and private sector investigators (Fatima, A., 2011). Blockchain technology changes society by allowing new intensely scrutinized digital platforms (Mattila, J., 2016). It may be used to generate distributed recordings of any material that is immutable and resistant to censorship. Inter-mediators can be irrelevant by providing a technical solution for digital interaction in which innocent counterparties are not required. It might potentially result in new financial services based on this technology. Siddique (Siddique et al., 2019) proposed a cybersecurity framework to mitigate cyber risks because a business organization requires proper security management to safeguard its financial or customer data.

Research questionnaire responses from 30 banks out of 63 and 34 NBFIs by email, phone, and other colleagues' testimonials were collected from sampling the participants. He suggested that investment in new technology could avoid frequent attacks like phishing or malware attacks. The main goal of this research was to find out the current perspective of cybersecurity in Bangladesh among financial organizations. Multiple choice questions from the four different sections were later reviewed to gather the views and insights of the participants regarding cybersecurity. The author has used Interpretive Structural Modeling (ISM) and MicMac analysis to summarize the results based on the survey analysis and suggest necessary improvements. The Automated Teller Machine (ATM) Card is now one of the most widely used payment methods (Saha, et al., 2018). The ATM fraud issue in recent times has been widely spread in the country and over the world. Rumman et al. (2015) identified common ATM frauds and when, where, and how those frauds are preserved. Hasan et al. established the current state of e-banking and banking in

Bangladesh while demonstrating the scope and benefits of e-banking in comparison to the existing system (Hasan, A. S., 2010). This article addressed considerable knowledge gaps about online banking and its landscape. They attempted to portray the current state of e-banking in Bangladesh from a marketing perspective.

A secure three-layer electronic transaction mechanism for ATMs was developed to prevent ATM fraud in this chapter. The first tier was bio-metric authentication using fingerprints. The second tier is QR code authentication using GSM smartphones as scanners, and the third tier is PIN authentication using a mobile phone with a chip. We want to ensure that networks are secure so that if one ATM is hacked, fraudsters cannot infect the entire ATM network. Rumman et al. (2020) conducted an empirical study in Dhaka, Bangladesh, selecting eight ATM locations for the four banks. Most respondents used the machine for various purposes, citing convenience, quick fund transfer, and time savings as critical advantages. Despite some challenges and imperfections, many customers have access to the machines and are thus using them for multi-purpose transactions.

TIMELINE OF ATTACKS

The research is conducted on purpose, with eight ATM sites chosen for the four banks in Dhaka, Bangladesh. According to the data, most respondents utilized the machine for various functions, citing convenience, rapid cash transfer, and time savings as essential benefits. We do this research in four strategically chosen sites in Dhaka with a high concentration of commercial banks. According to 2006 estimates, the city has a cosmopolitan population of around 3,800,000 people (NPC and ICF Macro 2009). In each location, at least forty-six (46) respondents were chosen for the survey and twelve (12) for in-depth interviews, respectively (Hole, K. J. et al., 2006). The critical criteria for including respondents in the research were using ATM cards for monetary transactions.

According to one study, many customers have access to ATMs and thus use them for multi-purpose transactions. According to authorities, BDT 960000 was stolen from ATMs in both countries. The money was obtained from the Pubali Bank's three different ATM booths. They use ProxyBot, malware that executes the tasks of the middle-person worker and licenses the assailant to redirect traffic from a covered centre to a back-partner worker (Belás et al., 2016). Bangladesh's national bank was robbed of about $81 million in February. According to bank_info_USA, the funds were transferred from the Federal Reserve Bank of New York's record-holding position at the Bangladesh Bank. An illness occurred at the bank, which was used to identify potential programmers (Tham et al., 2017). By 2018, cash transfers from the Philippines had recovered more than $18 million.

Figure 1. Our analysis using a line chart for the amount of data breached from 2004 to 2021

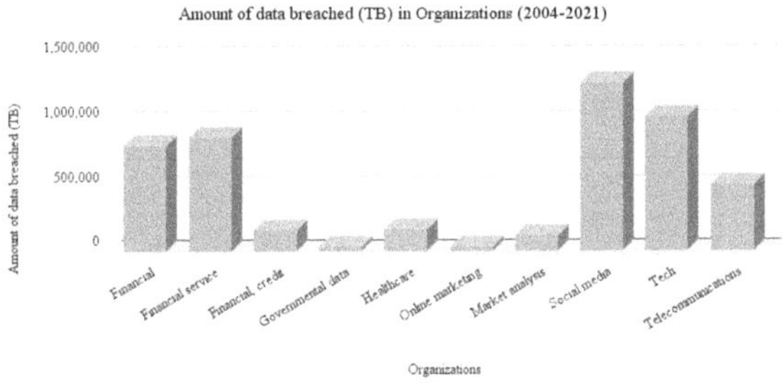

This chapter gives several examples of data breaches in various businesses. This visualization's dataset was compiled from several sources, including press releases, government news releases, and mainstream news items (The Citizen, 2021), (Mother of All Breaches Exposes 773 Million Emails, 21 Million Passwords, 2021), (Protalinski, 2021), (List of data breaches - Wikipedia, 2021). The dataset includes instances involving the theft or compromise of 30,000 or more pieces of information, although many more minor breaches happen regularly. Breach of significant businesses, the number of records of which is unknown, is also mentioned. There is also a list of the many methods used in the breaches, with hacking being the most common.

Figure 1 depicts the total quantity of data leaked between 2004 to 2021. During 2019 and 2020, most data were breached, amounting to almost 4000000 Tera Bytes, more than that of the previous years. This fluctuation in data volume has been attributed to technological developments and other factors. Nevertheless, it implies that security concerns should be prioritized in all financial sectors and other businesses. We discovered some details regarding how those data were hacked from the dataset, given in Table 1. We noticed that numerous companies were being attacked by hackers in some ways or were working for those data breaches. Figure 2 illustrates the significant businesses and the quantity of data compromised. Social media is a significant data center, and we see that most of the data were hacked from social media throughout the timeframe. There had also been a significant quantity of data leaked in the financial industry.

Table 1. Reason for data breaching in the timeline of 2004-2021 with the amount of data

Reasons and Methods	Amount of data (GB)
Accidentally exposed	900,000
Accidentally published	269822485
Accidentally uploaded	1,500,000
Data exposed by misconfiguration	250,000,000
Hacked	7,240,073,028
Improper setting	21,457,751
Inside job	76,426,105
Inside job, hacked	92,000,000
Intentionally lost	960,000
Lost / stolen computer	41,397,666
Lost / stolen media	170,434,536
Misconfiguration/poor security	100,000,000
Poor security	3,802,943,028
Poor security / hacked	412,214,295
Poor security/inside job	5,214,200
Publicly accessible Amazon Web Services (AWS) server	38,000,000
Rogue contractor	30,000
Social engineering	6,054,459
Unknown	44,77,18,889
Unprotected api	100,000,000
Unsecured S3 bucket	106,000,000

Figure 2. Our analysis showing organizations' bar chart based on the amount of data breached from 2004 to 2021

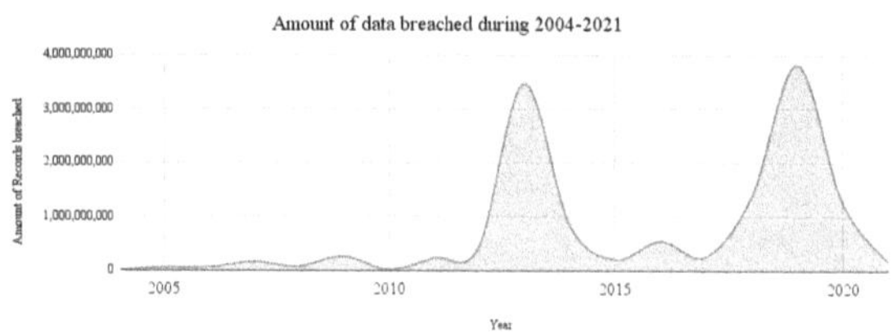

MANAGERIAL FRAMEWORK FOR BANKING SECURITY

We have provided a structure for any financial organization's management department in Figure 3. The framework outlines each organization's management's actions to ensure its security. To handle security risks and network vulnerabilities, most organizations adhere to their models for management hierarchy. All financial institutions face risks from prospective cybercriminals and the possibility of being hacked and defrauded (Elzamly et al., 2017). A financial network is regarded as one of the most popular targets for hackers and cybercriminals. If the management bodies are well-formed and structured, there may be significant results in securing the entire financial network.

Figure 3. A proposed effective managerial framework for ensuring banking network security, our own observation

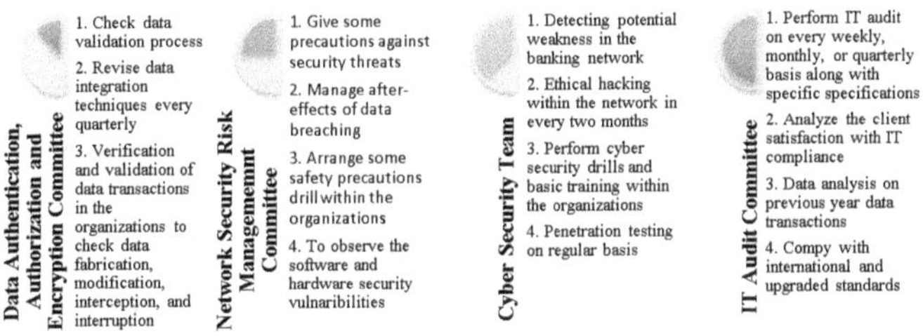

AFTER-EFFECTS OF BANK HEIST

Bangladesh's economy was severely harmed due to the National Bank blunder. In connection to the consequences of the bank heist, they explored the following topics.

- **GDP Growth:** The Bangladesh Bank Scam impacted GDP growth significantly. Data from the Bangladesh Bureau of Statistics (BBS) at the time reveal that the improvement rate in FY2016 was 7.11%, with a per capita pay of $1,465.
- **Inflation:** The central bank has triumphed by keeping the overall growth rate at approximately 5.5%. Still, food value was a prominent topic of discussion in 2017 due to the monetary gimmick.
- **Investment:** According to our sources, the Bangladesh bank is anticipated to withstand a bank heist in 2016. According to the Bangladesh Bank's quarterly report on money and currency rates, banks paid out Tk 7,97,789

crore in credits until September this year, although Tk 6,75,139 crore before the end of September 2016.

- **Poverty and Financial Effect Tricks:** The central bank has an enormous obligation to keep the economy from falling into a downturn. Regardless, the national bank blunder aggravated the situation. Speculators are also down as a result of the national bank disaster, which is generating unemployment. ATM scams can cause genuine mistrust of financial and budgetary transactions. According to Bangladesh Bank data, up to February 15, BDT 2.53 billion in exchanges were reported in February. With a typical step-by-step average of BDT 181 million, the end of February 14 saw just BDT 46 million, a two or three-day increase. Nervous customers are not to blame. It is a component of organizations, banks, or anything else to assure customer trust, especially when it comes to new paths.

IDENTIFYING ATTACKERS OR SCAMMERS

Regardless of how the attacker attempted to erase any evidence from the bank's systems, Kaspersky figured out how to access a portion of the data via structural defenses. According to the article of a report, Kaspersky maps the Lazarus bundle's actions as follows (Kaspersky, 2017): "This malware has been identified in some actual assaults, including the major data breach and record wiper assault on Sony Pictures Entertainment; in 2014 (Aggarwal, P. et al., 2014)." In its study, Kaspersky outlined the malware employed in the assault in great detail. Examining the destroyed bytecode indicates that a piece of the malware is indistinguishable from the malware utilized in some previously reported scenarios. Furthermore, regardless of how parts of the code are modified, they modify the sign of the virus and maintain up a crucial way in the area using motorized traffic analyzing equipment.

Meanwhile, Kaspersky discovered an interface with North Korea while reviewing data from a subsequent incident related to the Lazarus gathering. While criminals generally utilize VPN companies and go-betweens to hide their certified location and IP addresses, a Clutched Command and Control worker's worker records reveal that they received a North Korean IP address. Furthermore, the monitors found that a bank robbery worth around USD 1 billion was stopped because of a spelling error in the part trade, which prohibited the programmed structure from completing the deal. However, as the Fed had stated, the transaction was transferred to Srilanka (Sutherland, E., 2020). Furthermore, the value was carried out by a budgetary specialist at the bank, as the deal was startlingly large for Srilanka.

ATM CARD FRAUD AND SCAM IN BANGLADESH

ATM card extortion has become a significant problem across the world, especially in Bangladesh.

- **Card lost or stolen:** A card might be lost or stolen for criminal purposes. The scammer takes responsibility for (taking over) an accurate blue record by providing the client's record number or the card number. Tampering with an engaging strip: By executing the metallic strip with a shocking electromagnet, a scammer can alter a current card that has been illegally built up. The fraudster then manipulates the card's details to enhance the intricacies of a liberal card, which they may have done.
- **Fake card:** Using moving machinery, a scammer may create a counterfeit card with no prior preparation. Individuals use fake ATM cards to extract cash from malfunctioning ATMs.
- **Changing card details:** A scammer can alter cards by re-encoding them using PC programming that encodes the engaging stripe information on the card or re-enhancing them by providing warmth and strain to the originally decorated card's card a genuine card manufacturer.
- **Skimming:** Most occurrences are extortion disguised as skimming, a method in which secure information on a card's engagement stripe is electronically replicated on another card.

The conditions in Bangladesh are such that ATM card pressure is increasing effectively, and decreasing this issue is the critical challenge right now. To satisfy their compulsions, credit card scammers use many approaches. First, scammers place cameras above ATMs to collect client data and a Near Field Communication (NFC) device in the transaction path to duplicate cardholder data. Next, they use these tools to analyze and mold cards to put the facts into new cards with transparent strips. Then, the scammers approach ATMs as banking staff and display skimming devices as engaging stripes around the card slot, copying the card data on the device (Van Gundy et al., 2007). The PIN is tricked by directing illegally installed cameras in the ATM corner towards the button. They use the information to clone other ATM cards. Cloned cards are then used to withdraw cash in the name of a consumer. The fraudsters use fake ID cards to access ATMs at numerous banks and act as IT professionals and bank maintenance coordinators.

Customers were encouraged to swipe their cards on the NFC devices installed on the entrances as part of a security upgrade. They then used duplicate cards to withdraw cash from ATMs. As a result, ATM scams have a significant adverse effect. According to Bangladesh Bank data, up to February 15, BDT 2.53 billion in exchanges were reported in the first half of February. However, with a daily average of BDT 181 million, withdrawals on February 14 were just BDT 46 million, requiring a few days to increase to the usual number.

SECURITY VULNERABILITIES IN BANGLADESH

Most software security flaws fall into one of the following categories:

- **Bolster flood:** This defenselessness occurs when data is pushed beyond the limits of a pad. The program gets to memory dispersed through multiple means by altering information past the limitations of help which can cause a system crash, data transfers, or provide enhanced benefits.
- **Non-confirmed data:** Programs always work with data input. This data entering the program may include a harmful ingredient proposed to limit the program to continue unexpectedly.
- **Weaknesses in security procedures:** Systems and sensitive data can be secured using confirmation, endorsement, and encryption methods. However, architects should not attempt to do their security calculations since they would most certainly expose flaws.
- **Problems with access control:** Access control is the road to managing who does what, and it includes anything from limiting physical access to equipment to coordinating who moves toward an advantage, such as an archive, and what they may do with it, such as read or modify the record. The incorrect application of access restrictions leads to a variety of security vulnerabilities.

PREVENTION METHOD AND SUGGESTION

Bangladesh has a new law to stop cyber-crime. It's called the "Digital Security Act 2018. (Zaman, 2018)" This legislation was enacted by the governing body to prohibit the promotion of racism, sectarianism, extremism, terrorist propaganda, and hostility toward religious or ethnic minorities via social media, print media, or other electronic media. Any content on the internet or other media that the government deems pornographic or otherwise objectionable might result in fines or jail sentences of varying durations. Because some of its clauses are unclear, ambiguous, or open to interpretation, people thought it was used to silence people who disagreed with the government. Some journalists, activists, and criminals have been sued because of this law. Our computing devices save personal info and provide access to online life.

- **Keep the Firewall On:** Whether it is an item firewall or a hardware firewall on a switch, the firewall should be switched on and activated to prevent developers from accessing our personal or organizational data.
- **Use antivirus and anti-spyware software:** Malicious software, such as viruses, Trojan horses, worms, ransomware, and spyware, is installed on the computer without the knowledge to obtain access to the computer and data.
- **Manage Operating System and Browser:** Hackers always attempt to target loopholes in our operating systems and online applications.
- **Protect Devices:** Our registered devices, whether PCs, workstations, tablets, or mobile phones, should be in a cryptic system to protect unauthorized access. Set aside data should be blended, mainly if it is dedicated or organized.
- **Human resource training:** Giving general knowledge about technical issues to nontechnical officials in any financial institution.
- **Strict IT audit:** Both present and future clients can take their business elsewhere if we handle data that could be exposed in the event of a data breach but cannot demonstrate that it is adequately protected. If an organization's present clients are satisfied with its IT services, and IT compliance audit might help it earn more business than that before. Strict IT audits must be rolled out weekly, monthly, or quarterly basis along with specific specifications.
- **Certifications:** Certification authorities from specialized institutions should be introduced to be tested and appropriately certified before launching any system.

Even with the WPA2 encryption set, the remote foundation may be a little unstable right now. To prevent intruders from entering the personal transmit mode, modify the pre-set SSID and default password phrase for the program-based administrative interface. Of course, one should scramble remote communications by partaking in security, and the encryption is remembered for the remote switch.

- Try not to utilize any vernacular reference terms or names.
- Avoid utilizing necessary misspellings of word reference terms.
- Avoid using computers or record names on the off chance that it is feasible to utilize one-of-a-kind characters.

The data should be encoded consistently. If a rogue program corrupts any computer or mobile phone and takes potentially essential information, this may be highly hazardous. Encryption is the process of converting data into a format that an unauthorized user cannot interpret. Only an accepted authorized individual with the encryption key may decrypt and access the data. As a result, the hard disk might fail and burn. Having help may prevent the loss of essential data, such as family pictures. Users would need additional space to effectively back up data and copy the data to that region continuously and sequentially. Aside from the username and password, or individual distinguishing evidence number (PIN) or model, two-factor confirmation requires the insertion of a next token, such as material things include Master-Cards, ATM cards, phones, and collectibles, bio-metric channel - a one-of-a-kind impression, for example, a fingerprint, likely related to face or voice confirmation.

Cisco provides a threat grid for Advanced Malware Protection (AMP) that examines many records and compares them to an enormous number of other malware threats. The AMP is a customer/worker programming interface sent to endpoints, stand-alone workers, or other system security devices. Another difficulty in the ATM business is the lack of relevant IT data, such as client instructions. Therefore, when utilizing an ATM, customers must be cautious.

- They should use a feature or a specific ATM consistently.
- There are no persuasive cards.
- Install card readers only when the ATM asks for them. If we see anything strange or out of the norm and obtain a financial loan.
- Tilt the card slightly when inserting it; Examining the ATM card aperture for scratches, engravings, concrete, or other impurities.
- Keep track of developments that show how things have changed. That is, IT professionals should be updated with the latest technologies and features
- If individuals observe us, we do not accept outside assistance and avoid using the ATM. Do not leave if an ATM card becomes stuck in a machine.

The Bangladesh Bank has provided explicit directions to all banks to design and execute dynamic, contemporary security systems as many ATMs have risen. In addition, Going-to-security frameworks are being developed in Bangladesh to prevent ATM card forgeries for money-related connections.

- Install a CCTV camera: Bangladesh Bank advises all banks to install CCTV cameras inside ATM corners. As a result, if a scam is committed, the CCTV footage scammer can be traced.
- PIN-shields: Banks features a few modern measures, such as PIN-shields, to protect us from skimming situations. It can conceal the PIN fragment.
- Anti-skimming device: Installing an anti-skimming device in each ATM can help prevent skimming occurrences.
- Use EMV chip cards: EMV chip cards can be handled in the same way by banks. These provide an exciting exchange code for each transaction, whereas the engaging stripe cards do not.

- PCIDSS: Bangladesh Bank has also advised all banks to be certified by the Payment Card Industry Data Security Standard (PCIDSS). It is a financial institution data security standard that also applies to ATM card work settings.

LIMITATION AND FUTURE RESEARCH DIRECTION

Though we have a thorough analysis of the banking network, including specific observations and best practices, we have several research constraints that necessitate additional research on this issue. In this chapter, we have provided some observations based on various demographic datasets. We have discovered a limitation in the dataset's availability for this domain. A more focused dataset in this domain may be more carefully examined to provide superior insights. In the future, we hope to describe and validate our framework by presenting any model if we find many datasets related to this area. Hence, rigorous machine learning techniques may be incorporated or enforced on any financial network to detect possible risks. We are attempting to provide some observations on the banking network in Bangladesh, some possible viewpoints, and a management framework for protecting the banking network more precisely. Working with effective and efficient algorithms of security software may be a vital, challenging and emerging research area.

CONCLUSION

We have no way to compromise with financial issues, even if it is a bit. Financial organizations like banks, leasing companies, insurances, stock exchanges need to be within the limelight of our sights. Money-related foundations are the most targeted affiliations because money, information, and transparency are intimately tied with them. Collaborations must be stimulated using the most recent mechanical components and software engineering approaches to create any illegal piece of software. Academic and Industry handshaking would have happened to collaborate with those who know industrial works are whimsical at research, and there is a slight lack of technical knowledge, especially to the academic members. Massive works should be carried out in the country to avoid unexpected occurrences, and research grants should be approved for the researchers working on the subject matter. A commission or corporation may be formed in a country to deal with such kinds of issues. There should be a zero-tolerant mind with any kind of major or minor security trap doors. We should work hard and make us ready with respect to knowledge and technology to prepare ourselves for the battle of life in the future.

REFERENCES

Aggarwal, P., Arora, P., & Ghai, R. (2014). Review on cybercrime and security. *International Journal of Research in Engineering and Applied Sciences, 02*(1).

Belás, J., Korauš, M., Kombo, F., & Korauš, A. (2016). Electronic banking security and customer satisfaction in commercial banks. *Journal of Security and Sustainability Issues*.

Elzamly, A., Hussin, B., Abu-Naser, S. S., Shibutani, T., & Doheir, M. (2017). *Predicting critical cloud computing security issues using Artificial Neural Network (ANNs) algorithms in banking organizations*. Academic Press.

En.wikipedia.org. (2021). *List of data breaches - Wikipedia*. Available at: https://en.wikipedia.org/wiki/List_of_data_breaches

Fatima, A. (2011). E-banking security issues-Is there a solution in biometrics? *Journal of Internet Banking and Commerce, 16*(2), 1.

Gizmodo. (2021). *Mother of All Breaches Exposes 773 Million Emails, 21 Million Passwords*. Available at: https://gizmodo.com/mother-of-all-breaches-exposes-773-million-emails-21-m-1831833456

Hasan, A. S., Baten, M. A., Kamil, A. A., & Parveen, S. (2010). Adoption of e-banking in Bangladesh: An exploratory study. *African Journal of Business Management, 4*(13), 2718–2727.

Hofileña, J. M. G., & Sy, J. L. (2017). Gone Without a Trace: A Re-Examination of Bank Secrecy Laws and Anti-Money Laundering Laws in Light of the 2016 Bangladesh Bank Heist. *Ateneo LJ, 62*.

Hole, K. J., Moen, V., & Tjostheim, T. (2006). Case study: Online banking security. *IEEE Security and Privacy, 4*(2), 14–20. doi:10.1109/MSP.2006.36

Hossain, S., Hasan, M. M., & Hossain, T. (2020). An Analytical Study of Influencing Factors on Consumers' Behaviors in Facebook Using ANN and RF. *International Conference on Intelligent Computing & Optimization*, 744–753.

Kaspersky. (2017, April). *Lazarus Under The Hood*. https://media.kasperskycontenthub.com/wp-content/uploads/sites/43/2018/03/07180244/Lazarus_Under_The_Hood_PDF_final.pdf

Mattila, J. (2016). *The blockchain phenomenon*. Berkeley Roundtable of the International Economy.

Nurudeen, Z. B., & Nasiru, A. A. (2012). Actual and perceived consequences to improper online privacy management: A pragmatic approach. *International Journal of e-Education, e-Business, e- Management Learning*, *2*(1).

Protalinski, E. 2021. *3 million bank accounts hacked in Iran.* ZDNet. Available at: https://www.zdnet.com/article/3-million-bank-accounts-hacked-in-iran/

Rahman, S. (2016, February). *Atm frauds rattle banks, customers.* https://www.thedailystar.net/business/atm-frauds-rattle-banks-customers-510868

Rumman, M. R. H., Sarker, A., Islam, M. M., Hoque, M. I., Kuri, R., Bhuyan, M. B. A., & Bhuiyan, N. A.-T. (2015). Empirical Study of the Use of Automated Teller Machine (ATM) among Bank Customers in Dhaka City, Bangladesh. *European Journal of Business and Management*, *07*(1).

Rumman, M. R. H., Sarker, A., Islam, M. M., Hoque, M. I., Kuri, R., Bhuyan, M. B. A., & Bhuiyan, N. A.-T. (2020). ATM Shield: Analysis of Multitier Security Issues of ATM in the Context of Bangladesh. *Journal of Experimental Sciences, 11.*

Saha, A. R., & Rahman, M. M. (2018). Automated Teller Machine Card Fraud of Financial Organisations in Bangladesh. *Journal of Computer Science Applications and Information Technology*, *12*(2).

Shaw, L. (2016). *The meanings of new money: Social constructions of value in the rise of digital currencies.* University of Washington.

Siddique, N. A. (2019). *Framework for the mobilization of cyber security and risk mitigation of financial organizations in Bangladesh: A case study.* Academic Press.

Smith, R. G. (2004). Impediments to the successful investigation of transnational high-tech crime. *Trends and Issues in Crime and Criminal Justice*, 285.

Sutherland, E. (2020). The fourth industrial revolution--the case of South Africa. *Politikon, 47*(2).

Tham, J., Ab Yazid, M. S., Khatibi, A. A., & Azam, S. F. (2017). Internet and data security–understanding customer perception on trusting virtual banking security in Malaysia. *European Journal of Social Sciences Studies.*

The Citizen - It's all about you. (2021). *Analysis: Data breaches compromised 4.5bn records in half-year 2018 - Gemalto - TheCitizen - It's all about you.* Available at: https://thecitizenng.com/analysis-data-breaches-compromised-4-5bn-records-in-half-year-2018-gemalto/

Van Gundy, M., Balzarotti, D., & Vigna, G. (2007). Catch me, if you can: Evading network signatures with web-based polymorphic worms. In *Proceedings of the first USENIX workshop on Offensive Technologies*. Berkley, CA: USENIX Association.

Zaman, N. U. (2018, October 21). *Digital Security act 2018: Young generation speaks*. Retrieved April 14, 2022, from https://www.newagebd.net/article/53662/digital-security-act-2018-young-generation-speaks

KEY TERMS AND DEFINITIONS

ATM: Automated Teller Machine is the full version of the abbreviation "ATM," and it refers to a self-service banking outlet. we have the option of withdrawing money from your account, seeing our current amount, or even transferring cash. The ATM services offered by various banks are provided via cash machines that have been placed in various locations of the United States.

Cybersecurity: The protection of internet-connected systems, including their hardware, software, and data, against malicious cyberattacks is referred to as cybersecurity. To prevent unwanted access to data centers and other computerized systems, people and businesses alike engage in the practice of using two-factor authentication (2FA).

Financial Sector: The financial sector consists of businesses and institutions that provide financial services to commercial and retail consumers. This sector encompasses a vast array of businesses, including banks, financial firms, insurance organizations, and real estate corporations.

Firewall: Incoming and outgoing traffic is monitored and filtered according to an organization's specified security standards by a Firewall. An internal network's firewall acts as a barrier between it and the public Internet at its most basic.

IT Audit: A study and assessment of an organization's information technology infrastructure, applications, data usage and management, policies, procedures, and operational processes, compared to recognized standards or set norms, is what's known as an information technology audit.

Network Security: Our network and its data will be safe from invasions, breaches, and other dangers if we have adequate network security. This is a broad and all-encompassing phrase that refers to the many hardware and software solutions, as well as the procedures, policies, and settings that are associated with the usage of networks, accessibility, and overall protection against threats.

Scam: Scams might arrive in the form of text messages, real-person phone calls, or automated calls (robocalls). Callers often provide false assurances, such as chances to purchase things, invest your money, or obtain free product trials.

Chapter 10
Agile Leadership and Organization Performance in the Perspective of VUCA

Bulent Akkaya
https://orcid.org/0000-0003-1252-9334
Manisa Celal Bayar University, Turkey

Emine Sever
https://orcid.org/0000-0001-9760-7447
Istanbul Kultur University, Turkey

ABSTRACT

Agile leaders have the ability to think flexibly in changing environmental conditions to adapt an organization perfectly to these changes. These leaders can uncover the strengths of their employees, use their insights to transition the organization's intended change, and take advantage of the opportunities in change while trying to minimize their negative impact on the organization. Organizations that incorporate agile into their processes through agile leaders are better able to respond quickly to change and deliver superior business value to their stakeholders. With agile leadership, organizations will be in a better position to quickly detect developments in the business environment and achieve agility with few resources. As the volatility, uncertainty, complexity, and ambiguity (VUCA) of today's business world continues to pose great challenges for many organizations, this research examines the impact of agile leadership style on organizational performance from the perspective of VUCA world.

DOI: 10.4018/978-1-6684-3894-7.ch010

INTRODUCTION

There has been an awareness of the complexity and sustainability of the globally interconnected business world. Some will believe that this is unpredictable and that their situation is changing rapidly, causing existing models to deal with complexity and uncertainty to become obsolete (Mack & Khare, 2016). As the competitive environment of today's business world is more intense and the pace of environmental change increases, companies that can respond to these changes are more likely to produce better business outcomes (Sambamurthy et al., 2007). Therefore, in order for organizations to sustain their performance and business in the VUCA environment and to achieve better organizational performance, the need for effective leadership to transform the organization is increasing day by day. At this point, we find it useful to briefly explain the concept of VUCA. The concept of VUCA, which consists of the initials of the words Volatility, Uncertainty, Complexity and Uncertainty, has taken its foundations from the leadership theories of Warren Bennis and Burt Nanus. Later, with the end of the Cold War in 1991, it was started to be used by the US Army to reveal the multilateral world that had become volatile, uncertain, complex and ambiguous (U.S. Army Heritage and Education Center, 2021; J.Wefald & Katz, 2007).

The hard conditions brought by the VUCA environment can negatively affect business continuity and performance. Hence, organizations should be led by effective leaders when cope with change. These leaders know that the current business environment is different from what it used to be, and that due to the instability and uncertainty in the business environment, making wrong predictions can be costly. Nevertheless, organizations and leaders who fail to recognize, reject and adopt change may face difficulties in maintaining their business. There is also the possibility that these organizations will suffer huge losses and eventually leave the business sector. This reason, an effective leadership style is needed to get rid of the turbulence in the VUCA environment, to focus on the business approach to make the organization flexible, fast and agile, and to increase the performance of the organization in the long run.

All of this brings us to the concept of agility. "Agility" has become a trending word used more and more by organizations in recent years. These organizations are trying to be "agile" and implement agile organizational structures. This means that they have redesigned not only their processes but also their perspective on leadership (Greineder & Leicht, 2020). This leadership perspective will be agile leadership approach that can implement the Agile Model proposal by Horney et al. (2010), in which the VUCA environment and agility are linked, as the business environment has become more volatile, complex and uncertain. The Agile Model, five crucial areas are mentioned: anticipating change, generating confidence, initiate action, liberating thinking and evaluating results. Agile leaders will need to develop their skills by considering these five drivers in order to improve company performance.

Within this new normal, the pace of disruptive change is accelerating as a number of technological and environmental factors converge. Many organizations are struggling to survive and thrive amid these unprecedented changes in business and society (Ragasa & Ragas, 2021). Thus, in this section, we explain the concept of agile leadership and the skills that agile leaders should have in perspective of VUCA. World.

BACKGROUND

Agile Leadership

In the literature, a common definition of agile leadership and the aspects that make it different has not been established yet. Leadership researchers use a variety of names to refer to agile leadership. Definitions such as leadership agility and leadership proficiency are sometimes used by leadership researchers to denote agile leadership. Definitions such as leadership agility and leadership competence are used by leadership researchers to indicate the agility of leaders. Joiner and Joseph (2007a), who have very important studies on this subject, define agile leadership as a leader's ability to make logical and effective decisions in a complex, volatile and rapidly changing environment. According to Greineder and Leicht (2020), Agile Leadership is a way of thinking and attitude that leads agile teams with various leadership practices and processes. In addition to these definitions, according to the model proposed by Prasongko and Adianto (2019), agile leadership is a leadership approach that is quick, sensitive, decision-making, risk-taking and cope with crises. In this model, agile leaders should be who can find solutions to cope with changes, crises and pressures while allowing the organization to adapt to change. Therefore, increasing pace of market conditions and the consequent organizational flexibility show that need self-organizing teams and agile leadership (Lipman-Blumen, 2020). The definition of self-organized teams suggests that the leader should frame and guide what can be done, rather than instructions stating what needs to be done (Spreitzer et al., 1999). This is critically important for agile organizations to successfully manage teams (Alfaro, Yu, Rehman, Hysa, & & Kabeya) Flexible is quite important to adapt changes (Davidescu et al., 2020; Akkaya et al., 2022). The manager who follows these flexible and agile practices becomes an agile leader that setting the direction and encouraging continuous feedback, adaptation and collaboration.

Agile Leadership for Organizational Performance

The current VUCA world requires leaders who are strategically agile, quickly adaptable to changing situations, and with a high degree of cultural sensitivity to make them effective in rapidly changing business environments (Gerhardt, 2020).

There are many leadership definitions made by researchers in the literature. According to Stogdill (1950), leadership is goal setting and influencing the activities of a group in the organization in the process of achieving the goal. Bavelas (1969) makes a distinction between leadership as a process and leadership as individual characteristics. Leadership is also a role in groups and organizations, and when used as a collective noun it indicates is responsible for the destiny of an organization (Sadler, 2003). Therefore, leaders need to be aware of the fact that organizations live in a global economy, constantly under the pressure of change and complexity. Every year, new technologies, markets and competitors emerge at an accelerating rate. As change accelerates, so does innovation, uncertainty and ambiguity. It is getting harder to predict future threats and opportunities. In addition, organizations live in a more complex and interconnected world, with internal and external customers, all other stakeholders and business performance that can only be achieved through strategic alliances (Joiner & Josephs, 2007a).

Today's dynamic business environment has given rise to organizations adapting their structures, strategies and policies to this environment. Innovative organizational forms may adopt agile methods more easily than bureaucratic and formal ones. Organizations should carefully assess their readiness before moving forward on the agility path (Nerur et al., 2005). Leaders in different organizational sizes and industries are currently looking for ways to effectively implement the philosophy of agile thinking because of this inevitable change and its impact on all levels of the organizational hierarchy (Prange & Heracleous, 2018). Hence, agile thinking, principles, methodologies and terminologies are being adopted by an increasing number of organizations worldwide (Denning, 2018). Agile thinking fundamentally needs agile leaders as it is the framework for decision making and implementation (Tiefenbacher, 2020).

Organizations are paying more attention to improving their agility in order to maintain their performance successfully in complex and uncertain market conditions. Therefore, research in the field of change-management has been translated from a project-management-based change approach to a leadership attitude for creation, development and agility. Agile leadership is thought to play a critical and key role in the concept of Organizational Agility. This illustrates why management research has gravitated towards a leadership approach to agility and continuous change. Therefore, agile leaders must be viewed as a core component of business assets and should be given serious consideration (Chatwani, 2019).

MAIN FOCUS OF THE CHAPTER

After defining agile leadership, it is necessary to explain the required competencies. To better understand agile leadership and ways to improve it, Jack and Jones (2007a) conducted surveys, in-depth interviews, and projects spanning many years to examine the manager's thought processes and behaviors. As a result of these studies, it was found that leaders who excel in turbulent environments exhibit four leadership agility competencies: Context-setting agility, stakeholder agility, creative agility, self-leadership agility.

Context-Setting Agility: This competence includes the ability to identify new changes in the environment and clarify the steps to be taken in this context.

Stakeholder Agility: This competence includes identifying key stakeholders of an initiative and interacting with them in an optimal way.

Creative Agility: This competence includes generating creative solutions and having multiple perspectives in the face of complex and new problems.

Self-Leadership Agility: This competency includes raising self-awareness, being aware of emotions and behaviors, and self-leadership.

Agile leaders are needed in companies to achieve sustainable success and the level of corporate agility required by today's turbulent business environment. Then, the competencies we mentioned above are increasingly needed throughout the company. Research shows that leaders must progress at five different levels to advance in these vital competencies (Joiner & Josephs, 2007b): Expert, Achiever, Catalyst, Co-creator, Synergist. As the level of agility increases, managers develop leadership skills and retain skills developed at previous levels. The Figure 1 below summarizes the leadership styles found at these five agilities levels and identifies how managers at all levels engage in three types of leadership practices: leading organizational change, leading teams, and directing important conversations (discussions that contribute to results or negatively affect the achievement of important organizational goals).

Parker et al. (2015) listed the basis of agile leadership as follows:

- competence to cope with volatility
- looking at organizations as flexible and adaptable systems
- adopting a problem-solving approach that includes all stakeholders in team management
- believing in the ability of the team to take initiative as the systematic of solving problems

Figure 1. The Five Levels of Leadership Agility
(Joiner & Josephs, 2007b)

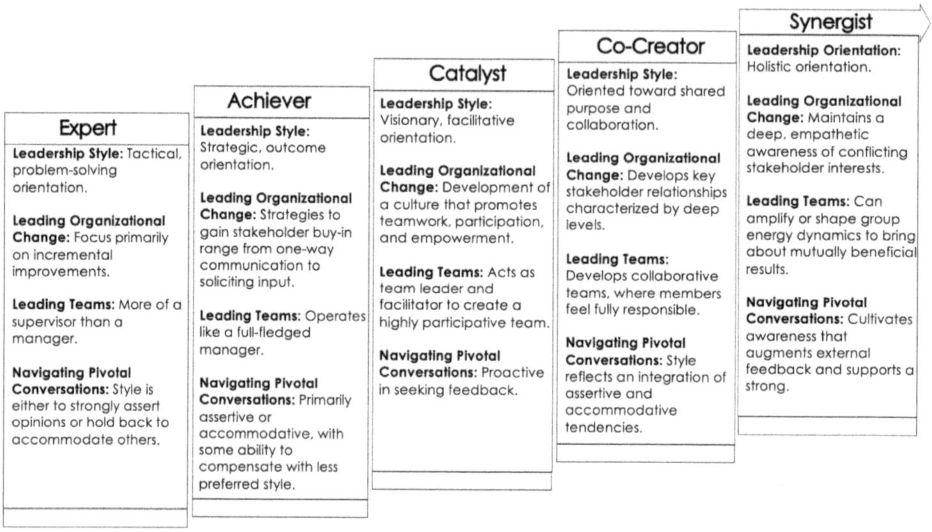

- It uses its ability to adapt to the changing conditions of the day by keeping planning to a minimum in conditions that are very difficult to foresee
- reacts according to the results produced by the self-organizing team
- manages results and removes barriers to team goals

The demand for agile skills in organizations is increasing. It's quite clear that leaders in many different organizations are increasingly using agile principles and practices to achieve their goals. Successful organizations have realized the necessity of not only agile principles but also agile leadership (Joiner, 2017).

Companies that fail to successfully deal with these disruptive changes face serious consequences, including decline or underperformance. For example, The Standard & Poor's 500 index, commonly known as the S&P 500, is a respected index of the top 500 publicly traded companies in the US based on market capitalization. The average life expectancy of a company in the S&P 500 in 1964 was 33 years (Anthony et al., 2018). The average life expectancy on this list has dropped to 24 years, by 2016. By 2027, this lifespan is predicted to decrease to just 12 years. It is estimated that about half of the companies on this list will be replaced within the next decade due to faster growing companies or acquisitions through mergers or acquisitions (Schwartz, 2019). At this point, the leadership styles that the managers of the organization will adopt can play a critical role in order to survive and be successful in an intense competitive environment (Cinnioğlu, 2020).

In this case, the important question is what skills should company leaders develop to avoid failure. The five drivers in the "Agile Model" mentioned in the introduction can contribute to this question. According to this model proposed by Horney et al. (2010), leadership in challenging conditions requires the ability to perceive and respond to changes in the business environment with focused, fast and flexible actions. The drivers and skills that the model leads are described in Figure 2.

The most important step towards building an agile organization is a leadership mindset or agility perspective. Agile leaders empower employees at all levels to serve their customers and the organization's business goals. The right leadership agility mindset will create the best momentum and cause the best technology, business systems and structures to have a greater impact on the organization. The success of an organization depends on how much importance individuals and leaders place on agility (Meyer, 2016).

An organization's resilience to dynamic environmental change and its long-term success is a matter of an agile leadership approach. Today's business environment requires leaders with continued agility to build organizations and teams that can handle unexpected turbulence. Being an agile leader means that one adopts and represents agile concepts and principles and is ready to spread them throughout the organization (Medinilla, 2012) .

Agile leaders develop strategies and provide instructions on how to make organizations agile (Akkaya, et al., 2022). To have a leadership culture that supports agility in the organization, human resource managers need a deeper understanding of the meaning of agile leadership and how it can be evaluated and developed. Agile leaders are visionary, tactical and have the ability to lead effectively in a rapidly changing business environment where success requires a wide variety of perspectives and priorities. Agile leadership is also directly related to organizational agility. An international study on organizational agility resulted in two important findings. While environmental changes often make it more difficult to compete and increase profits, companies with higher agility levels increase their competitive advantage and increase their profitability levels (Joiner, 2019). Later, these findings were reinforced with similar results by an academic study. This study of 471 North American companies shows that environmental changes can indeed be managed with agility. Companies with a higher level of agility are more competitive and profitable, even at higher levels of change. The results indicate that agility supports organizational performance (McCann, Selsky, & Lee, 2009). Other studies have confirmed the high correlation between organizational agility and business performance (Alhadid, 2016; Bazigos et al., 2015; Langley, 2017).

Figure 2. The Agile Model for Leadership and Organizational Agility
Source: Horney et al., 2010

The Agile Model		Leadership Agility Skills
Focused	**A**nticipate Change	Visioneering Sensing Monitoring
Focused / Fast	**G**enerate Confidence	Connecting Aligning Engaging
Fast	**I**nitiate Action	Bias for Action Decision Making Collaborating
Fast / Flexing	**L**iberate Thinking	Bias for Innovation Customer Focus Idea Diversity
Flexing	**E**valuate Results	Creating Expectations Real-Time Feedback Fact-Based Measurement

Agility in the VUCA World

In 2000, Stephen Hawking answered a question about how science has evolved, "I think the next century will be the century of complexity". It pointed to the growing importance of a set of scientific ideas that emerged in the 1980s and 90s that allowed us to find order in highly complex, interrelated systems. As the 21st century progresses, Hawking's prediction appears to be increasingly correct(Basios, 2017).

Today's world, where organizations try to keep up with this complex and rapid change, is defined as VUCA. Due to these newly formed environmental conditions, it has become very difficult to analyze the external environment and to plan opportunities and threats. VUCA is a concept used in the late 1990s to identify the environment in which strategic leadership was required. Although this brings with it unpredictable situations, it contains many opportunities. The key question here is what does VUCA mean and what actions are leaders and organizations taking in these situations? (Tiefenbacher, 2019). VUCA is an acronym formed from the first letters of the words Volatility, Uncertainty, Complexity and Ambiguity.

Volatility: The concept of volatility is generally used in statistical and financial theories. Volatility can be defined as a statistical measurement value that describes the fluctuations in changes and the difference between them and the uncertainty value (Hayes, 2021). An example of this situation is the fluctuations in the global raw material markets and stock markets with increasing volatility and high volatility as an indicator of the increasing pace of the environment and significant value jumps over time (Kail, 2010a).

Uncertainty: Uncertainty can also be defined as determining what threats and opportunities are, and the situation in which it is not clear enough. Predicting the future is quite difficult due to the increasing variability of the environment. In the past, statistical forecasting models that could make predictions for the future worked, but now it has become more difficult to predict the future (Kail, 2010b).

Complexity: Complexity is when a situation has many interrelated parts and variables (Bennett & Lemoine, 2014). In addition, it becomes difficult to establish the cause-and-effect connection between them. Some information is available or predictable, but its volume or nature can be very difficult to manipulate (Kail, 2010c).

Ambiguity: Ambiguity is expressed in cases where it is difficult to establish a cause-effect relationship and rule-making is uncertain (Bennett & Lemoine, 2014). Ambiguity is a type of meaning in which a statement or solution is not clearly defined, which makes various interpretations reasonable (Kail, 2011).

Figure 3 summarizes the VUCA.

Figure 3. VUCA Concept
Source: Bennett & Lemoine, 2014

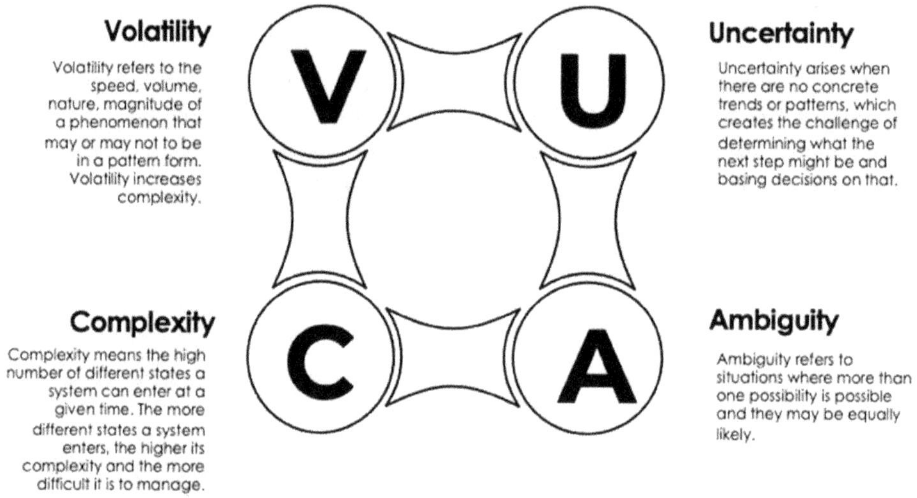

SOLUTIONS AND RECOMMENDATIONS

The performance of the organization links its success to the efficiency of the leadership, that is, the style of leadership has a significant impact on the effective management of affairs (Wang et al., 2010). The leadership styles of leaders have a significant impact on the performance of the employees of the organization. Studies show that the styles of leaders are important in organizational performance and that this also affects the performance of the organization. Leaders' styles influence the performance of the organization employees must achieve and provide practical advice and feedback (Elenkov, 2002).

As a result, the literature research we conducted in this study shows that agile leadership style has a positive and significant effect on Organizational Performance (Zehir et al., 2011; Frontiera, 2010; Kantabutra, 2006). These researches show how that agile leaders ensure that company goals are achieved through good planning. As agile leaders learn about customer expectations and market trend, improvements and innovations are made in products and services. Thus, it motivates team members to be creative and goal-oriented.

With the effect of the worldwide VUCA concept, it has become very difficult to achieve sustainable profitability and growth by gaining competitive advantage. In this case, the duty of the organization, leader and employees is to try to understand the concept of VUCA, learn the methods of coping with it, implement appropriate managerial processes and make appropriate strategic studies for the future. VUCA components, which are explained as volatility, uncertainty, complexity and ambiguity, determine the internal and external environments of organizations and affect risk management, crisis management, entrepreneurship, agile leadership, interpersonal interaction and decision-making processes.

Since today's working conditions are getting more and more complex every day, classical leadership and management approaches are no longer valid. So, managing and leading in the current working environment is to employ qualified individuals as well as dealing with complex data. Therefore, leadership and management models adopting VUCA should now be implemented. In order to deal with the challenging conditions in the VUCA world and to cope with the challenges in working life, employees need to be encouraged and supported to gain new perspectives, produce stronger ideas, be creative, gain flexibility and be challenged. To be able do this, develop responsible leadership styles that pay attention to ethical values, with business ideas and networking skills. This leadership style will be formed by applying agile leadership and its principles. Agile leaders have the ability to think flexibly in changing environmental conditions to adapt an organization perfectly to these changes. These leaders can uncover the strengths of their people, use their insights to transition the organization's intended change, and take advantage of the chance for change while striving to minimize their bad impact in the organization. Organizations that incorporate agility into their processes through agile (Attar & Abdul-Kareem, 2020).

CONCLUSION

In order to deal with the challenging conditions in the VUCA world and to cope with the challenges in working life, employees need to be encouraged and supported to gain new perspectives, produce stronger ideas, be creative, gain flexibility and be challenged. To be able do this, develop responsible leadership styles that pay attention to ethical values, with business ideas and networking skills. This leadership style will be formed by applying agile leadership and its principles. Because, agile leaders have the ability to think flexibly in changing environmental conditions to adapt an organization perfectly to these changes. These leaders can uncover the strengths of their people, use their insights to transition the organization's intended change, and take advantage of the chance for change while striving to minimize their bad impact in the organization that incorporate agility into their processes through agile (Attar & Abdul-Kareem, 2020). These studies imply that agile leadership and organizational performance are crucial components for the firm. When attention is drawn to the fact that organizations should attach importance to organizational culture and agile leadership in a challenging and competitive business environment, firms' performance will be higher.

FUTURE RESEARCH DIRECTIONS

The concept of agile leadership discussed in this chapter and how it affects firm performance will be a topic that many researchers will study in the future. It may be more meaningful to intensify these researches, especially in the conditions of Covid-19. In addition, it can be researched which organizational culture is suitable for agile leadership and its effects on firm performance. In these studies, organizational agility dimensions can be examined.

REFERENCES

Akkaya, B., Panait, M., Andreea, S., & Kaya, Y. (2022). Agile Leadership and Perceived Career Success: The Mediating Role of Job Embeddedness. *International Journal of Environmental Research and Public Health, 19*(8), 4834. doi:10.3390/ijerph19084834 PMID:35457699

Alfaro, E., Yu, F., Rehman, N. U., Hysa, E., & & Kabeya, P. K. (n.d.). Strategic management of innovation. In *The Routledge Companion to Innovation Management* (pp. 107-168). Routledge.

Alhadid, A. Y. (2016, March). The Effect of Organization Agility on Organization Performance. *International Review of Management and Business Research, 5*(1), 273–278.

Anthony, S. D., Viguerie, S. P., Schwartz, E. I., & Landeghem, J. V. (2018). *2018 corporate longevity forecast: Creative destruction is accelerating*. Innosight.

Attar, M., & Abdul-Kareem, A. (2020). *The Role of Agile Leadership in Organisational Agility. In Agile Business Leadership Methods for Industry 4.0*. Emerald Publishing Limited.

Basios, V. (2017). *The Century of Complexity*. Academic Press.

Bavelas, A. (1969). *Leadership: Man and Function, in Leadership*. Penguin.

Bazigos, M., Smet, A. D., & Gagnon, C. (2015, December 1). *Why Agility Pays.* McKinsey Quarterly. https://www.mckinsey.com/business-functions/organization/our-insigh ts/why-agility-pays# adresinden

Bennett, N., & Lemoine, G. J. (2014, Jan.). What VUCA Really Means for You. *Harvard Business Review.*

Chatwani, N. (2019). *Organisational Agility: Exploring the Impact of Identity on Knowledge Management.* Palgrave Macmillan. doi:10.1007/978-3-030-17249-7

Cinnioğlu, H. (2020). *A Review of Modern Leadership Styles in Perspective of Industry 4.0. In Agile Business Leadership Methods for Industry 4.0.* Emerald Publishing Limited.

Davidescu, A. A., Apostu, S.-A., Paul, A., & Casuneanu, I. (2020). Work Flexibility, Job Satisfaction, and Job Performance among Romanian Employees—Implications for Sustainable Human Resource Management. *Sustainability, 12*(15), 6086. doi:10.3390u12156086

Denning, S. (2018). *The Age of Agile: How Smart Companies are Transforming the Way Work Gets Done.* AMACOM.

Elenkov, D. S. (2002). Effects of Leadership on Organizational Performance in Russian Companies. *Journal of Business Research, 55*(6), 467–480. doi:10.1016/S0148-2963(00)00174-0

Frontiera, J. (2010). Leadership and Organizational Culture Transformation in Professional Sport. *Leadership and Organizational Culture Transformation in Professional Sport., 17*(1), 71–86. doi:10.1177/1548051809345253

Gerhardt, L. (2020, July 14). *Agile Leadership for Organisational Performance.* Savannah Group.

Greineder, M., & Leicht, N. (2020). *Agila Leadership - A Comparison of Agile Leadership Styles.* Enabling Technology for A Sustainable Society.

Hayes, A. (2021, August 22). *Volatility.* Investopedia: https://www.investopedia.com/terms/v/volatility.asp

Horney, N., Pasmore, B., & O'Shea, T. (2010). Leadership Agility: A Business Imperative for a VUCA World. *People & Strategy, 33*(4), 32–38.

Wefald, J. A., & Katz, J. P. (2007). Leaders: The Strategies for Taking Charge By Warren Bennis and Burt Nanus. New York: Harper & Row, 1985 (HarperCollins 2nd Edition, 2003). Academy of Management Perspectives, 21(3), 105-106.

Joiner, B. (2017). Bringing "Leadership Agility" to Agile. *Cutter Business Technology Journal, 30*(8), 1–10.

Joiner, B. (2019). Leadership Agility for Organizational Agility. *Journal of Creating Value, 5*(2), 139–149. doi:10.1177/2394964319868321

Joiner, B., & Josephs, S. (2007a, February). Developing Agile Leaders. *Industrial and Commercial Training, 39*(1), 35–42. doi:10.1108/00197850710721381

Joiner, B., & Josephs, S. (2007b). *Leadership Agility Five Levels of Mastery for Anticipating and Initiating Change*. Jossey-Bass.

Kail, E. G. (2010a, November 3). *Leading in a VUCA Environment: V Is for Volatility*. Harvard Business Review: https://hbr.org/2010/11/leading-in-a-vuca-environment

Kail, E. G. (2010b, November 10). *Leading in a VUCA Environment: U is for Uncertainty*. Harvard Business Review: https://hbr.org/2010/11/leading-in-a-vuca-environment-1

Kail, E. G. (2010c, December 3). *Leading Effectively in a VUCA Environment: C is for Complexity*. Harvard Business Review: https://hbr.org/2010/12/leading-effectively-in-a-vuca

Kail, E. G. (2011, January 6). *Leading Effectively in a VUCA Environment: A is for Ambiguity*. Harvard Business Review: https://hbr.org/2011/01/leading-effectively-in-a-vuca-1

Kantabutra, S. (2006, Spring). Relating Vision-based Leadership to Sustainable Business Performance: A Thai Perspective. *Leadership Review*, (6), 37–53.

Langley, M. A. (2017). *Achieving Greater Agility: The People and Process Drivers that Accelerate Results*. Project Management Institute.

Lipman-Blumen, J. (2020). *Connective Leadership: Managing in a Changing World*. Oxford University Press.

Mack, O., & Khare, A. (2016). Perspectives on a VUCA World. In Managing in a VUCA World (pp. 3-19). Springer.

McCann, J., Selsky, J., & Lee, J. (2009). Building Agility, Resilience and Performance in Turbulent Environments. *People & Strategy, 32*(3), 45–51.

Medinilla, A. (2012). *Agile Management: Leadership in an Agile Environment*. Springer Science & Business Media. doi:10.1007/978-3-642-28909-5

Meyer, P. (2016). *Agility Shift: Creating Agile and Effective Leaders, Teams, and Organizations*. Routledge. doi:10.4324/9781315230559

Nerur, S., Mahapatra, R., & Mangalaraj, G. (2005, May). Challenges of Migrating to Agile Methodologies. *Communications of the ACM*, *48*(5), 72–78. doi:10.1145/1060710.1060712

Parker, D. W., Holesgrove, M., & Pathak, R. (2015). Improving Productivity with Self-Organised Teams and Agile Leadership. *International Journal of Productivity and Performance Management*, *64*(1), 112–128. doi:10.1108/IJPPM-10-2013-0178

Prange, C., & Heracleous, L. (2018). *Agility. X: How Organizations Thrive in Unpredictable Times*. Cambridge University Press. doi:10.1017/9781108545884

Prasongko, A., & Adianto, T. (2019). The Role of the Agile Leadership Model as a Competitive Advantage for the Future Leader in the Era of Globalization and Industrial Revolution 4.0. *Jurnal Pertahanan*, *5*(3), 126–133. doi:10.33172/jp.v5i3.596

Ragasa, M., & Ragas, T. (2021). Understanding Agile for Strategic Communicators: Foundations, Implementations, and Implications. *International Journal of Strategic Communication*, *15*(2), 80–92. doi:10.1080/1553118X.2021.1898147

Sadler, P. (2003). *Leadership. London and Sterling*. Kogan Page.

Sambamurthy, V., Wei, K.-K., Lim, K., & Lee, D. (2007). IT-Enabled Organizational Agility and Firms ' Sustainable Competitive Advantage. ICIS 2007 Proceedings, 1-19.

Schwartz, E. I. (2019). *Corporate Longevity Update: Creative Destruction Rides High*. Onnosight.

Spreitzer, G. M., Cohen, S. G., Gerald, E., & Ledford, J. (1999, September). Developing Effective Self-Managing Work Teams in Service Organizations. *Group & Organization Management*, *24*(3), 340–366. doi:10.1177/1059601199243005

Stogdill, R. M. (1950). Leadership, Membership and Organization. *Psychological Bulletin*, *47*(1), 1–14. doi:10.1037/h0053857

Tiefenbacher, W. (2019, December 12). *Strategic management: How and why to redefine organizational strategy in today's VUCA world*. CQ Dossier: https://www.ckju.net

Tiefenbacher, W. (2020, July 12). *Agile for all: The principles of agility, agile leadership, and how to be an agile leader*. CQ Dossier: https://www.ckju.net

U.S. Army Heritage and Education Center. (2021). *Who First Originated the Term VUCA (Volatility, Uncertainty, Complexity and Ambiguity)?* Author.

Wang, F.-J., Chich-Jen, S., & Mei-Ling, T. (2010). Effect of Leadership Style on Organizational Performance as Viewed from Human Resource Management Strategy. *African Journal of Business Management*, *4*(18), 3924–3936.

Zehir, C., Ertosun, Ö. G., Zehir, S., & Müceldili, B. (2011). The Effects of Leadership Styles and Organizational Culture over Firm Performance: Multi-National Companies in İstanbul. *Procedia: Social and Behavioral Sciences*, *24*, 1460–1474. doi:10.1016/j.sbspro.2011.09.032

KEY TERMS AND DEFINITIONS

Agile Leadership: Agile leadership is a style of leadership that seeks to remove barriers to success for the purpose of enabling employees to be more successful and productive in their work. Because agile teams collaborate more effectively, agile leadership results in greater business outcomes with significantly less time and resources being spent.

Context-Setting Agility: This ability includes identifying new changes in the environment and clarifying the steps to be taken in this context.

Creative Agility: Creative Agility refers to the ability to generate creative solutions and have multiple perspectives in the face of complex and novel problems.

New Normal: A new normal is the state in which an economy, society, or other entity settles after a crisis, when it differs from the situation that existed prior to the start of the crisis.

Organizational Performance: The actual output of a corporation compared to the output that the company anticipated to produce is one definition of organizational performance. This is a vast field that examines what an organization accomplishes and what it is capable of achieving as a result of its interactions with the numerous groups that make up its constituency.

Self-Leadership Agility: This competency includes self-awareness, emotional and behavioral awareness, and self-leadership.

Stakeholder Agility: Stakeholder agility refers to the ability to identify key stakeholders of an initiative and interact with them effectively.

VUCA: VUCA is an acronym that was coined in 1987, based on Warren Bennis and Burt Nanus' leadership theories, to describe or reflect on the volatility, uncertainty, complexity, and ambiguity of general conditions and situations.

Conclusion

In myriad ways, the COVID-19 pandemic has altered global activities and people's lifestyles. Everyone had to reorient themselves to a new way of life and change the way they lived as well as the way they performed their jobs. What does this entail for a knowledge organization's talent strategies and the people who work there? The answer is the topic of debate for the remainder of the book.

The pandemic's abrupt shift from in-class to distance online education has profoundly altered the fundamental operating model of knowledge organization worldwide. This book aims to shed light on the current state of knowledge management in the post-pandemic era. As a result of technology disruption and online learning, the pandemic is driving universities to reconsider and reevaluate their classical financial models, which concentrated on the university as brick and mortar. Educational institutions have recognized the disruptive consequences of internet-enabled innovation and its role in distance teaching and learning as requiring a new paradigm.

In this book, a variety of theories and strategies are adopted by knowledge organizations to achieve sustained competitive advantages: Talent management and information technology that improve the work activities within the organization; HR practices that enhance organizational social responsibility and corporate image; leadership and organizational performance that improve overall organization performance.

INTRODUCTION OF THE BOOK

The Chief Editor of the book, Dr. Mohammad Rafiqul Islam Talukdar, authored the introduction. The introduction of the book described the philosophy and purpose of this edited volume. It is cognizant that the biggest priorities for organizational development are utilizing talent management, increasing digitization, and the organization's efforts to future emphasis and brand value. *Post-Pandemic Talent Management Models in Knowledge Organizations* is a book about human capital theory and talent management in pandemic and post-pandemic environments. The book contributes significantly to the literature on strategic human resource management, specifically talent management in modern knowledge-based organizations during and after the COVID-19 epidemic.

This work benefits from organizational change management, organizational culture, human capital theory, organizational theory and development, and leadership theory. It understands the importance of difference and innovation-focused leadership in shaping the impact-focused leadership that is sorely needed today. It also recognizes that leveraging talent management, enhanced digitalization, and the job's future direction and brand image are the highest priorities for organizational development.

Academics, researchers, professionals, and students will benefit significantly from this book's in-depth content and style. The book has an extraordinary level of author diversity, which means that male and female authors from various business schools and practitioner disciplines around the world made essential contributions from theoretical, practical, and empirical perspectives.

MODERN TALENT MANAGEMENT

Dr. Mohammad Rafiqul Islam Talukdar, Dr. Carmen Z. Lamagna, and Dulce Corazon Z. Lamagna focused on the theoretical framework of modern talent management in this chapter. The study made a significant contribution by clearly describing talent management's theoretical and conceptual foundations. According to the authors, companies must prioritize strategic aspects, change management, and future development notions. Recognizing human capital as well as managing human resources is central to accomplishing this purpose. In modern business, strategic and change management prioritize appreciating people's skills and competencies. The study employed a qualitative-focused synthesis technique to collect and document data and information from various sources.

The importance of talent management started with Drucker in 1993, who predicted that post-capitalism would not be socialist or capitalist but would be both. If capitalism had not died, society would have changed into specialized groups. In 1993, Drucker thought that the early twenty-first century would be a better time for businesses to start. In the twenty-first century, land, labor, and money are not the most important things to consider. Human capital is more important than ever to the success of a business. It has been shown by Drucker (1993) that knowledge is the new source of wealth.

According to a 1998 essay titled "The War for Talent," talent will be the future's competitive advantage. Academics and practitioners began to focus on talent management after McKinsey & Company defined talent. According to BCG and the World Federation of People Management Associations, talent management is the most important part of human resource management.

BCG and WFPMA in 2014 identified the top ambitions for organizations in several regions and industries. Most respondents cited leadership, talent management, behavior and culture, HR and people strategy, employee engagement, and strategic workforce planning as essential business needs.

The techniques used to attract, develop, and retain talented workers and contractors are referred to as talent management. Modern organizations frequently use talent management to implement personnel policies (TM). It assists businesses in achieving their strategic objectives by maximizing the potential of their employees and stakeholders. Various programs and investments have been launched to attract, retain, and develop exceptional professionals. The strategic importance of people management in modern enterprises has been boosted by skills scarcity, a talent war, an aging workforce, dropping birth rates, and cultural diversity. Organizations face new challenges due to globalization, environmental disruptions, and disruptive business paradigm shifts.

McKinsey & Co., BCG, and, most recently, Gartner have all made significant contributions. Unlike other academic disciplines, knowledge corporations, rather than individual academics, have made significant contributions to the TM concept.

Competency focus, talent pooling, talent investment, and talent orientation are the four distinct elements of human talent management—these characteristics aid in managing human resources and add value to a company. Besides, competency mapping is also an essential tool for succession planning, growth, and retention in talent management strategies. A corporation can cultivate a set of crucial characteristics in high-potential employees. This interconnectedness of TM elements generates value both within and outside the organization.

Human talent must be viewed as a significant source of commercial value creation by HR. While retaining brand image and competitive advantages, business techniques must be included in a business strategy. A talent investment policy aims to close the gap between these two loops.

Only a company's talent orientation can make external knowledge easier to understand. One group collects and distributes external knowledge, whereas another collects and distributes it. Swailes and Blackburn (2016) discovered that those left out of the talent pool feel mistreated and have fewer job opportunities. By focusing on social and organizational components such as talent culture, networks, and teams, talent orientation aids a company's success.

A theory makes assumptions and develops concepts to explain a phenomenon. Theories help us comprehend, explain, and forecast. A definition expresses the meaning and synthesis of a concept. The advancement of TM theory occurs when a learning outlook has changed. Employability, lifelong learning, and talent management are preferred over job stability and lifelong employment (Nilsson & Ellström, 2012). Globalization, technological breakthroughs, and innovation are short-lived and imitable in a competitive corporate climate (Barney, 1991). Firms need long-lasting resources (Heinen & O'Neill, 2004; Mattone & Xavier, 2012). When human resources are transformed into human capital, the firm gains a sustainable competitive advantage.

Mattone and Xavier (2012) mentioned that human capital is key to market distinctiveness, positive branding, exceptional execution, and operating success. These ideas represent a strategic shift in human resources (Boudreau & Ramstad, 2005), i.e., human capital orientation. Employability, lifelong learning, and talent management were included in the advancement of theory because individuals place a high value on these concepts. That is why most firms concentrate on attracting and retaining talent (Tetik, 2016). Organizations compete with one another to attract, develop, and retain employees. Human capital is a true competitive advantage over the long run.

Talent management (TM) is based on many theoretical foundations that are all interconnected. This claim is supported by Sparrow et al. (2014) and participant observations. TM theoretical foundations include soft models of normative and strategic human resource management perspectives; human capital theory and sustained competitive advantage; resource-based view; organizational knowledge-based view or learning organizations and organizational learning perspective; agile management view for adaptation to disruptive innovation and disruptive environments; sustainable development and impact-based management.

New institutionalism theory, Voeten's (2019) distributive rationalism-based rational-choice institutionalism, explains the given motives. Rational functionalism and distributive rationalism are the two styles of rational choice studies on institutions, according to Voeten (2019). The former sees organizations as functionally efficient answers to collective concerns, while the latter sees organizations as the result of individual and collective goals.

Frameworks link theories. It uses assumptions to explain natural phenomena (Kombo & Tromp, 2006). Talent management needs a theoretical base. Theories guide practices, assessment, and research. Human capital dominates the "theoretical base." Businesses adapt to changing conditions. Corporate strategies seek advantages, but each has a cost. "Business model canvas" is a methodical, quantitative, and strategic enterprise discussion tool. Business models govern how a company develops, adds, delivers value propositions, pays costs, and grows. It shows internal and external stakeholders' satisfaction. It reinvests to remain competitive. Thomas Kuhn's "The Structure of Scientific Revolutions" is a classic on paradigm shifts. Executives nowadays must adjust swiftly to shifting conditions (Bersin by Deloitte, 2017).

Flat hierarchies, job-based careers, and a measurable performance management system are required in knowledge-based organizations. A new employee social contract is required to address work-life balance, employment flexibility, and other relevant issues. Regarding talent management, the current framework does not allow for complacency. Evolution is thus necessary (Juneja, n.d.). Three important research questions are addressed in this section of the text: What makes talent management so crucial in 21st-century businesses? How can talent strategy be rethought to allow for digitization? What are the post-pandemic implications of the shifting landscape and rising human management concerns for knowledge organizations?

According to the current study's authors, talent management for knowledge enterprises creates additional concerns in the post-pandemic paradigm. Questions: How might knowledge organizations help post-pandemic recovery? How can knowledge organizations prepare and retain employees to confront post-pandemic challenges? How can knowledge-based firms save money using remote, contingent, and blended workers? How can switching from role-based to skills-based planning improve workforce planning, widen talent pools, and meet talent needs?

How can knowledge businesses cultivate a digitally savvy workforce? In the new setting, what sort of leadership counts for knowledge organizations? New paradigm knowledge organizations need what kind of culture? What gaps exist between talent management theory, perceptions, and actions in knowledge-based firms?

CONCEPTUAL AND THEORETICAL UNDERSTANDING

Dr. Shraddha Purandare, and Dr. Aditi Alijapurkar begin the chapter with a discussion of the history of talent management, with a particular emphasis on the conceptual and theoretical understanding. McKinsey & Company invented "the struggle for talent" in 1997. "Better talent will separate the winning organizations," McKinsey says. Talent management is a broad phrase with several definitions, which helps businesses to adapt to it. Talent management is acquiring, retaining, developing, and promoting talented people. Companies employed several strategies to find top candidates. A company's success depends on attracting a talented workforce.

They also stated that Market success depends on a company's ability to attract and retain talent. Each employee completes duties differently. Individuality is emphasized in talent management. Human capital management and competitive advantage depend on talent. Today's organizations emphasize employee skill development. It also promotes equal employment opportunities. The authors in this chapter emphasized an organization's talent management method, prerequisites, and obstacles.

The process of Talent management covers hiring and retaining employees. Talent management develops and grows people. It also involves cultivating personnel who assist the organization in success. Recruiting a talented workforce through careful planning is one of the prerequisites for talent management. Other prerequisites include training current employees to improve their performance, developing an effective interview plan, assigning skilled interviewers, and locating the ideal candidate for the position. The authors mentioned the challenges of Talent Management with the process and prerequisites. It is challenging for any organization to effectively manage employees belonging to various generations and who work in various locations. Additionally, certain companies' employees report to managers and supervisors, another challenge related to talent management.

In this age of a knowledge-based economy, when the quality of human resources as employees is of paramount importance, there are several examples of organizations that have overcome obstacles. Under the able direction of Howard Schultz, the company has consistently exhibited growth since its establishment in 1971 until 2017. Starbucks' corporate culture illustrates how HRM concerns, including rewards and incentives, should be addressed. In uncertain times, 'staff well-being' practices place a particular emphasis on 'health.'

As emphasized by the authors, a vital component of the method is approaching individuals with a clear vision and strategy in mind, then structuring internships, recruiting, and retention accordingly. Organizations that place a premium on cultivating their talent also have a leg up when designing strategies and making well-informed judgments about whether to buy or train new employees. The growing number of independent contractors and other "gig" workers has only worsened things. Recruiters must consider ways to ease these workers' transition into the workplace. Employers would hire someone with experience gained through an internship or vocational school rather than someone with a degree in the same field.

This chapter will help readers understand companies' successful strategies to improve their performance. These successful strategies include taking a proactive approach, using artificial intelligence, providing an excellent employee experience, alumni programs for employees, leadership, career opportunities, and career support. The scenario during the Covid-19 outbreak is described in this chapter, and the chapter ends with examples of effective talent management implementation. Cisco is altering its workforce positively. The company coordinated its personnel strategy during a pandemic. Kelly Jones, Cisco's Global Leader, and Senior Talent Acquisition Director, discusses the company's success. Deloitte worked on retention during Covid-19. The limited and restructured benefits to retain top employees. Profit was $1 million.

TALENT MANAGEMENT AND SUSTAINED COMPETITIVE ADVANTAGE

In this chapter, Dr. Emmanuel Imafidon focused on the connection between effective talent management and creating a sustainable competitive advantage in organizations. Specifically, he cited research that found a correlation between the two. Analyzing such a link uses the company's Resource-Based View (RBV). The RBV maintains that competitive advantage is strongly related to an organization's internal characteristics. To be more explicit, an organization will attain superior performance and a durable advantage over its competitors if it possesses and uses resources and competencies that are precious, uncommon, inimitable, and non-substitutable in the processes and operations of the company. A framework is developed that organizational leaders can use to facilitate conversations and develop talent management programs to ensure that their talent management processes are focused on honing the organization's core competencies that feed their sustainable competitive advantage and superior performance. This is done by ensuring their talent management processes focus on honing the organization's core competencies that feed their superior performance.

The nature of a company's Talent Management is acknowledged as a determinant of its long-term competitive advantage. The issue for practitioners and businesses is to figure out how to use talent management to gain a long-term competitive edge. Examples include work hybridization, internal talent mobility imperatives, and the gig economy. A company's long-term competitive advantage depends on its talent management. Long-term, people capital is the only meaningful organizational performance differentiator. RBV says internal resources help companies develop a competitive advantage that boosts market success.

Talent management must be viewed as a strategic competency that provides a competitive advantage. Using the RBV paradigm, strategic talent management can create an enduring competitive advantage by focusing on "valuable, rare, inimitable, and non-substitutable" talent. An organization's talent management method must reflect a minimal mix of variables for a lasting competitive edge. Organizations can use the framework to make their strategic talent management more "valuable," "rare," "unique," and "non-substitutable."

The author of this chapter looks at how firms can use the Resource Based View (RBV) to improve their people management strategies. He endorses Pfeffer J. (2005)'s Thirteen Practices for Managing People, which he developed for corporations based on significant research. The thirteen factors listed may not be exhaustive; their entire definition/meaning/implication and relative importance may vary by geography and labor market. A framework was recommended to help organizational executives develop obvious links between talent management strategies, key capabilities/competencies, sustainable competitive advantage, and outstanding performance.

RBV's VRIN aspects are not easily quantitative, but qualitative descriptions help frame what is valuable, rare, inimitable, and non-substitutable.

HUMAN CAPITAL DEVELOPMENT AND CREATIVE WORK BEHAVIOR

Globalization and COVID-19 have caused organizations problems. Organizations must build engaging business and HR strategies. Corporate strategy and HR link competitive advantage development (Gunnigle & Moore, 1994). This chapter describes an empirical study that used knowledge worker samples to correlate SHRM and employee creativity. The study used resource-based value, social exchange, and reciprocity norms to support chapter links.

Dr. Okechukwu Ethelbert Amah investigated the development of human resources management to position Strategic Human Resources Management (SHRM), Human Capital Development (HCD), and employee behavior, such as creative work behavior, as essential variables that are required for organizations to survive in challenging environments. It was argued that the alignment of the fits between SHRM and business strategy and between SHRM and HCD positions employees as sources of organizations' competitive advantage and drives positive and innovative employee behavior that is required in the business challenging environments by organizations. Additionally, it was argued that this alignment positions employees as sources of organizations' competitive advantage. A study that established the connection between SHRM, HCD, and creative work behavior was covered in this chapter of the book devoted to it. The study included samples from workers in the knowledge sector. The findings determined that SHRM had a direct connection to HCD and an indirect connection to CWB via HCD. No connection between SHRM and CWB could be considered direct. The findings of the study, as well as suggestions for further investigation, were presented.

TALENT MANAGEMENT FOR ACADEMIC INSTITUTIONS

In this chapter, Dr. Humayra Ferdous focuses on talent management for academic institutions during the post-pandemic era. People from many walks of life and classes come here to learn or are admitted learning. They come here to study, nurture their hidden talents, and prepare themselves to contribute to society. However, authorities face a continuing challenge in recruiting the right individuals at the right time.

The process of finding and managing resourceful people is still not well-structured. Universities are not the only companies looking for highly qualified candidates.

Conclusion

The mix and quality of academic staff are critical to the quality of educational programs, research, and university prestige. An employee value proposition can assist management in attracting and retaining key personnel (Cliffe et al., 1998). Businesses frequently mismanage talent development duties. According to a survey, executives are unaware of some of the most critical issues.

The phrase "talent management" defines effective and integrated human resource practices to attract and retain the best people for the right jobs at the right time. Academicians must keep their colleagues and fellow researchers in a healthy environment. A corporation must integrate and connect these processes with its business strategy to drive performance, deal with an increasingly rapid pace of change, and achieve long-term success. Organizations may survive and thrive in increasingly competitive marketplaces by analyzing available talent and placing the right people in the right roles.

Post Covid-19 maxim a paradigm shift that assisted academic institutions to develop rapidly in teaching and research activities. Senior academic community members will become isolated and alienated if they are not provided with regular training. University professors with a solid technical background should also take the time to hone their interpersonal communication and people skills. This cutting-edge approach to managing talent would significantly increase a company's ability to turn its human resources into productive capital. The author provided the following issues related to Talent Management for Academic Institutions During Post-Pandemic Paradigm:

- Capacity-building training to improve lecture delivery and content development. A high level of technical knowledge and competence is required for blended learning.
- Highly technical academicians need training in interpersonal skills, teaching, etc. In many cases, lab-based researchers must build legal skills, legal frameworks on any topic, strategic issues, social policy challenges, etc. A knowledge-based institution can establish a community this way. It would encourage policymakers to make beneficial changes.
- Higher education institutions should establish a link between the IQAC and HRM departments to increase the productivity of their academic and administrative staff. If the focus is not on discovering skills in academics, it will not be placed in the optimal assignment. Developing countries that want to achieve the SDGs by 2030 must put academic management first.
- Training on Legislation for STEM.
- Academics should join clubs with students depending on their respective areas of interest; as a result, their counsel will be valuable to students. In addition, these clubs have the potential to influence public opinion regarding

various government policies, techniques employed by policymakers, and stances on numerous pressing topics. Faculty members will be allowed to shape other policies. Likewise, society will value their opinions.

The author of this chapter emphasized the significance of the Human Resource Management department, which, in addition to its existing function, has the potential to place a greater emphasis on managing educational institutions' talent. Attention should be redirected to locating the best candidates for a specific academic endeavor. If this does not occur, it will result in a situation in which qualified individuals will not be assigned to the proper jobs, preventing the transformation of human resources into human capital.

TM STRATEGIES, PANACEA TO KM IIIs AND CHALLENGES

Dr. Sheikh Shamim Hasnain talked about the TM Strategies, Panacea to KM Ills, and Challenges: A Reference to COVID19. For the survival and growth of organizations, knowledge is an essential strategic resource. Knowledge utilization and transmission result in organizational outputs. Knowledge management has gained international acclaim and importance (Sandhawalia and Dalcher, 2011; Scharbrough, Robertson, and Swan, 2005). Employees' talents are skills, experiences, behavior, knowledge, and cognitive ability.

Organizations could profit significantly from correctly positioning and integrating TM tactics against KM problems. The global environment has become chaotic and complex due to the COVID 19 Pandemic. Numerous KM difficulties have arisen, necessitating the use of TM techniques.

People's hard-won knowledge could propel human civilization to its pinnacle. A thousand-year-old definition is overturned by Gettier's (1963) theory of knowledge. Because knowledge is so difficult to define, there is no widely accepted definition. In the realm of knowledge management, Polanyi's theories were pioneering. Knowledge, according to Polanyi, is socially created; it is a person's experience, which is highly tacit. It is an activity, a method of acquiring new knowledge, and a process of knowing.

Knowledge transfer is critical for an organization's existence and success. According to Mu et al. (2008), successful organizational transfer enhances trust and relationships. Knowledge transfer can occur between independent organizations (inter-organizational) or within a single organization's sub-units.

McKinsey consultants coined the expression "war for talent" in the late 1990s. Proper TM aids firms in attaining competitive advantages. In Jordan's banking sector, Al-Azzam and Al-Qura'n analyze the impact of TM tactics on customer satisfaction. The global environment has become more complex due to the pandemic, making traditional information transfer mechanisms impossible to use. According to UNICEF's World Health Organization (WHO) chief Victor Espiritu Santo Cabrera, choosing the right knowledge transfer channel is critical for all stakeholders involved in the process.

Through his research on the Chinese-Singapore Suzhou Industrial Park (SIP) and the New United Motor Manufacturing, Inc., Inkpen (2008) identifies specific methods of knowledge transfer (NUMMI). Effective techniques include personnel transfers, training programs, executive visits, a coordinating office, leadership commitments to learning, and network building.

Social media can be a valuable tool for knowledge sharing. During the COVID 19 Pandemic, the telephone comes in handy. During the curfew period, soft copies of the literature are helpful. Mobile library services and book delivery services are both beneficial. For physical publications, courier and mail services may be explored. According to Wathneet al. (1996), Face-to-face communication is the most valuable transfer mode. Face–to–face interaction is often the best option, according to Davenport and Prusak (2000).

Knowledge transmission factors fall into three primary groups. Knowledge transmission point, type, and media are evaluated. Research focuses on what hinders knowledge transfer. Tacit knowledge is visual and auditory. Perception, language, time, value, and distance impede tacit communication. Poor communities may not realize they have enough indigenous knowledge, leaving them confused about "what to offer." Virtual meetings may help create relationships and share knowledge during a COVID19 outbreak. Increased intracellular absorption capacity is dependent on absorption capacity.

The author's conclusion and recommendations stated that any organization's knowledge is a strategically important resource. By utilizing this rich resource, businesses may gain a competitive advantage. Knowledge management is the art of recognizing, obtaining, storing, managing, transferring, and applying knowledge in an organization. It is critical to pick the proper information transmission mechanisms. Knowledge Management and Talent Management each have their knowledge transfer processes. Many obstacles exist in KM; TM techniques may provide solutions. Researchers can research any organization's mechanisms, hurdles, and TM methods during unforeseen events.

VIRTUAL INTELLIGENCE IN THE POST-PANDEMIC ERA

In this chapter, Dr. Leigh Thompson focuses on Virtual Intelligence in Human Communication Challenges and Best Practices in the post-covid era. In response to the Covid19 crisis, organizations were forced to undergo the most substantial overnight organizational reform in history. In the business world, people have taken on one of three mindsets: either wait it out until it is resolved, shun virtual communication, or engage in virtual communication while employing the same methods and procedures they use in traditional face-to-face encounters.

Virtual communication refers to the capability of communicating, negotiating relationships, and achieving corporate goals while engaging with those who are not physically present in the conversation. VCQ refers to the emotional, cognitive, social, and motivational skills utilized in communicating with others through modalities that do not involve face-to-face interaction. The author highlights many advantages and disadvantages of Virtual Communication in his chapter.

Mutual gaze and directional gaze create heightened self-awareness and self-focus. On the other hand, seating configurations, back-Channel utterances, sidebar conversations, touching, gesturing, collisions, and shared context are some of the challenges that prohibit virtual communication from being effective.

Managers and enterprises must learn to thrive despite the constant threat of a pandemic. How can managers and leaders improve their teams', relationships,' and business partners' experiences? Being compassionate, understanding, and upbeat is not enough to produce a rewarding and long-lasting virtual encounter. The term "chameleon effect" refers to the ability to mimic the body language of another individual. Individuals enjoy their conversational partner better even when they know that their conversational partner mirrors their body language. The ability to accurately detect emotion in others would benefit commercial partnerships since it would allow one to adapt one's message accordingly.

Communicators with a high level of virtual intelligence are aware of the dangers of exaggerating one's abilities in communication. Leaders can set the conditions for smooth conversational turns by employing two sorts of cues: lexical and prosodic cues, respectively. The use of gaze captioning provides for a smooth transition between speakers during a conversation. Leaders with a high level of VQ try to reduce communication fear in others. Communication experts with high levels of virtual intelligence make above-the-shoulder gestures when speaking. Even in groups of fewer than ten people, the research shows significant disparities in conversational engagement levels.

The lack of shared social indicators makes building trust in virtual connections challenging. Setting the environment for trust and positive emotions requires managers to be proactive. Turning on the camera is one of the easiest and most impactful ways to improve human contact. Because videoconference users are more task-oriented, this can be an issue. Managers should go out of their way to build relationships with their employees. It has been observed that when virtual teams discuss personal and even sad experiences, they perform better.

Conclusion

Managers need to take charge of the conversation in virtual meetings. Conflict makes most individuals uncomfortable, which is why they avoid it, while highly productive teams actively participate. The leader of a virtual meeting recommended that the participants role-play by indulging in "bad norms" as an unplanned activity. Communication technologies allow people to experience others as if they were in the same room. Receivers of face-to-face communication must pay attention to both verbal and nonverbal cues. The leader must put all three of these parts in a virtual conference room.

CEO Mark Zuckerberg revealed in October 2021 that Facebook's new name would be "Meta," noting that "we are a corporation that produces technology to connect" (Lyons, 2021). The debut of Meta predicts that the future of virtual meetings will take place in a rich metaverse, where social interactants may be able to engage in reciprocal gaze, directional gaze, touch, and full-body gesture. The fundamental premise that people are at the center of technology is at the heart of meta. The virtually intelligent leader can create the metaverse in ways that promote more profitable virtual collaboration and more meaningful and rewarding relationships. The advent of Meta predicts that virtual meetings will be conducted in the future in a rich metaverse. The basic premise that people are at the center of technology is at the heart of Meta. The virtually intelligent leader will be able to mold the metaverse for more profitable virtual collaboration.

PENETRATION TESTING AND CYBER SECURITY STUDIES IN BANGLADESH

Shahadat Hossain, Lamiya Rahman, Rafat Azad, Md. Manzurul Hasan, Mehenaj Jebin, Md. Siam Mahmud, and Md. Sadman Sakib developed the concept of linking talent management with Penetration Testing and Cyber Security Studies in Bangladesh regarding Post Covid-19 Managerial Issues. The internet's growing popularity is transforming the world into a global village. Businesses can conduct their complex activities online in a couple of seconds. Likewise, Bangladesh's IT industry is becoming increasingly crucial for its economic development and progress.

With the advent of digitization, Cyber Security is becoming increasingly important. To safeguard data and systems from cyber threats, businesses are increasing their investments in cyber security. Bangladesh's government enacted the "National Cyber-Security Strategy of Bangladesh" (Azmi, R., Tibben, W., & Win, K., 2016).

With the introduction of computers, security became synonymous with information security. It is not secure if a country cannot control its cyber assets. The United States, the United Kingdom, Estonia, South Korea, Singapore, Spain, Russia, the United Arab Emirates, and Malaysia are the top-ranked countries in the Global

Cyber Security Index. Many children are exposed to basic coding as early age as 7 or 8. They provide Adventurers, Defenders, Trailblazers, Futures, and Advanced short courses. Arrange a half-day event to kick off a two-week series of entertaining and participatory seminars.

Bangladesh Bank, the country's central bank, was the target of one of the world's most heinous cyber-attacks (Fielder, A. et al., 2016). This incident warned the entire country about the scale of devastation that a cyber-attack may cause. In 2012, an international hacker group was able to move $200 million to numerous accounts in the Philippines and Sri Lanka. A transaction for $850 million to the Federal Reserve Bank of New York, on the other hand, raised suspicions. This incident served as a wake-up call to the entire country about the damage a cyber-attack may cause.

Dutch Bangla Bank was the target of a cyber-attack in June 2019 that originated in Cyprus, Russia, and Ukraine. The bank was hacked, and $1.4 million was stolen. An alert was issued to banks across the country, warning them of an impending attack. The phrase "cyber-security" is unfamiliar to a vast percentage of Bangladesh's populace. Dedicated students are making use of a variety of free and paid online courses.

Bangladesh is the most frequently targeted country for ransomware Trojan attacks. According to Kaspersky Security Bulletin 2020, there are around 34552 compromised IPs in Bangladesh. A study provided a list of Bangladeshi websites and their vulnerability to six different attack routes (BGD e-GOV CIRT, 2019). Bangladesh is a relative newbie when it comes to cyber security. Bangladesh ranked 36th among 180 countries in the recent National Cyber Security Index. The government is currently crafting the first data protection acts or laws, which is an excellent start in assuring cyber security.

The government has committed roughly 400 million BDT to the ICT division's cyber security branch. The private sector should likewise think about bolstering its security. Educational institutions should train more cyber security personnel. Public and private enterprises should periodically examine their systems' vulnerabilities and adhere to tight security measures.

To protect the security of the enterprises, a national cyber security strategy should be adopted. Cyber-attacks in Bangladesh have become a severe problem for developing countries like Bangladesh. The government must implement effective rules and regulations for improved cyber security. Private institutions must have updated security guidelines to prevent cyber-attacks. Furthermore, educational institutions must produce adequate cyber security specialists.

CONTEMPORARY SECURITY THREATS

Md. Manzurul Hasan, Shahadat Hossain, Prioty Saha Trisha, Md. Mohsin Hossain, Abu Saleh Mohammad Rajuwan, and Md. Hasibur Rahman presented Contemporary Security Threats and Some Proposals for Banking Networks in Bangladesh. The Philippines' anti-money laundering and anti-banking legislation are "absolute"; however, there are exceptions. Most firms have relocated their activities on the internet, referred to as e-commerce. Passive attacks look for information on a network that has not been altered in transit or place. Because no data is modified, this form of assault is difficult to detect.

The investigation of crimes, particularly high-tech crimes employing computing and communications technologies, has been aided and hampered by high-tech crime. Financial institutions must increase their internal security and pay attention to their security. In addition, to prevent cybercrime, businesses should hire cyber security professionals. Smith (2004) identified many roadblocks to effective cross-border investigations of high-tech crime and proposed some ideas to help future cyberspace investigations run more smoothly.

According to the governing board, access to the company's essential sectors should be restricted. Updating the switches, routers, and firewall versions will significantly lower the chances of being scammed. Employee and user training programs for online systems can significantly impact awareness.

ATMs in the Philippines and Bangladesh were robbed of more than $18 million. Pubali Bank's three ATM booths were used to obtain the funds. They utilize ProxyBot, a piece of malware that mimics the actions of a middleman and allows the attacker to divert traffic.

Financial institutions are vulnerable to potential cybercriminals and the chance of being hacked and duped. Most firms use their management hierarchy models to deal with security threats and network vulnerabilities. There may be many results in safeguarding the entire network if structures are well-formed and structured. Kaspersky investigated the malware used in the Sony hack, regardless of how the attacker attempted to wipe any evidence from the bank's computers. Examining the byte code that has been destroyed reveals that a piece of malware is indistinguishable.

Meanwhile, Clutched Command and Control worker records reveal a North Korean IP address. Because of a spelling error, a bank robbery worth roughly $1 billion was thwarted. While reviewing data from a second event related to the Lazarus gathering, Kaspersky uncovered an interface with North Korea. Furthermore, ATM card pressure is rising, and addressing this problem is a top priority right now. Scams involving ATMs have a significant negative impact. According to Bangladesh Bank data, BDT 2.53 billion in exchanges were registered in the first half of February through February 15.

The remote foundation may be a little unreliable right now, even with WPA2 encryption enabled. Modify the preset SSID and default password to prevent outsiders from entering the personal transmit mode. The process of transforming data into a format that an unauthorized user cannot understand is known as encryption. The data can only be decrypted and accessed by an authorized individual with the encryption key. Assistance may help you avoid losing important data, such as family images or photographs. To successfully back up data, users would want more space.

Cisco's Advanced Malware Protection (AMP) includes a threat grid that analyses many records and compares them to many other malware threats. Endpoints, stand-alone workers, and other system security devices receive the AMP, a customer/worker programming interface. Bangladesh is developing going-to-security frameworks to prevent ATM card forgeries for money-related connections. Anti-skimming devices installed in each ATM can assist prevent skimming.

We are hoping to make some observations about Bangladesh's financial system. A more specialized dataset in this domain could be analyzed more thoroughly to generate better insights. We believe rigorous machine learning techniques could be implemented or enforced on any financial network to detect potential hazards.

Because money, information, and transparency are all intertwined, money-related foundations are the most targeted associations. To avoid unanticipated events, massive work should be done nationwide. A country's government may establish a commission or corporation to deal with such challenges.

AGILE LEADERSHIP AND ORGANIZATION PERFORMANCE

Agile leadership is a mindset and attitude that guides agile teams via a variety of leadership strategies and processes. Agile leadership is a leadership style that is quick to react, make decisions, take risks, and deal with emergencies. Agile leaders, according to this paradigm, are those who can discover ways to deal with changes, crises, and challenges while also allowing the organization to adapt to change. As a result of the increasing pace of market conditions and the resulting organizational adaptability, self-organizing teams and agile leadership are required.

The researchers of this chapter, Dr. Bülent Akkaya, and Emine Sever, identified four leadership agility abilities in leaders who flourish in tumultuous environments: context-setting agility, takeholder agility, creative agility, and self-leadership agility. Companies need agile executives to achieve long-term success and the amount of organizational agility demanded by today's volatile business climate. Then there's the fact that the skills we discussed earlier are becoming increasingly important across the board.

Conclusion

According to research, leaders must develop through five different levels in order to advance in these critical competences (Joiner & Josephs, 2007b): expert, achiever, catalyst, co-creator, and synergist (Joiner & Josephs, 2007a). According to Parker et al. (2015), the principles of agile leadership are adaptability to change; viewing organizations as flexible and adaptive systems; adopting a problem-solving strategy that involves all team members in decision-making; believing in the team's ability to solve problems on their own as the primary mechanism; it emphasizes the ability to adapt to changing situations rather than advanced preparation; reacts according to the outcomes produced by the self-organizing team; controls results; and removes barriers that inhibit the team from accomplishing their goals.

To be effective in fast changing company environments, today's VUCA world necessitates leaders that are strategically agile, instantly adaptable to changing situations, and culturally sensitive (Gerhardt, 2020). Leaders must be conscious that their organizations operate in a global economy that is continually changing and complex. Each year, new technology, markets, and rivals arise. Change accelerates innovation, ambiguity, and uncertainty.

Enterprises need agile workers. Agile principles and techniques are being used by company executives. Successful organizations need agile leadership and agile practices (Joiner, 2017). Developing an agile organization requires a leadership mindset or agility perspective. Agile leaders enable all workers to assist customers and the organization. When CEOs are adaptable, the best technology, business systems, and structures will benefit the firm. Human resource managers must understand agile leadership and how it may be created. Agility involves insight, tact, and the capacity to lead in a changing organizational environment. Organizations with agile leaders are agile. Human resource managers must understand agile leadership and how it may be created. Agility involves insight, tact, and the capacity to lead in a changing organizational environment. Organizations with agile leaders are agile.

COVID-19 has impacted the global economy. During a pandemic, organizations needed to switch to online activities. Every organization then implemented new business strategies. Higher education institutions are regulated like other organizations. Many of the knowledge-based enterprises did not respond to a new strategic business strategy to deal with the COVID-19 pandemic. Financial problems affect talent management. Many businesses have adopted layoffs and hiring freezes.

The book's chapters stress talent management and knowledge organization in the Post-Pandemic Paradigm. Talent management is about establishing and sustaining a talented workforce to fulfill organizational goals. An organization receives a competitive advantage by setting a high standard. A company's leader and HR director can't handle talented or scholarly people like other employees. Scholarly individuals are human capital.

Pandemics promote staff safety, virtual connectedness, and stress management. Everyone can work remotely. With pandemic prevention advances, companies are reintegrating remote personnel. Post-pandemic paradigm begins. During the epidemic, executives and employees worried about how to retain competent workers, recruit high achievers, and measure adaptive performance. Post-pandemic issues are similar. Anecdotes propose a post-pandemic talent management, agile, and iterative strategy.

RECOMMENDATIONS

COVID-19 changed the way most organizations work. Employees had to adjust to working from home (with partners, children, and pets). Despite changes, skill gaps, and retrenchment threats, organizations must continue to grow. A strategic mix between external (consultants, programs, and courses) and internal (company-led efforts, and mentorship), and self-driven growth (book study, and behavior change) drives learning initiatives while managing performance of the organizations. After the epidemic, the Knowledge organization should start coordinating its talent strategy to ensure its continued success. The following is a list of effective talent management strategies for firms operating in the post-pandemic era of the knowledge organization:

- Because of the pandemic, talents were forced to adjust the duties they performed at work and in their homes. Most of the organizations that began operations during this period were digital pioneers. To strike a better balance between work and personal life, an organization can consider implementing remote work.
- Organizations can keep their most talented employees by reducing and reorganizing the benefits that talents receive.
- The four phases of the standard talent management method are obtaining, placing, developing, and keeping talent. Every knowledge-based firm should strictly adhere to these phases.
- Talent management must be viewed as a strategic competency that provides a competitive advantage. Knowledge Organizations can use the RBV paradigm, and strategic talent management can create an enduring competitive advantage by focusing on "valuable, rare, inimitable, and non-substitutable" talent.
- Creativity is valued throughout and after COVID because it helps employees tackle unanticipated obstacles. SHRM and HCD must align to give employees creative capabilities. To ensure employees have these abilities, firms must link SHRM with business strategy and HCD. Businesses must implement competency-based training and development to synergize training

and skill development. Competency-based training must track changing skill requirements.

- In the aftermath of the Covid incident, it is possible that holding regular online meetings might help develop ties and make the information exchange process easier. Absorption capacity is what determines more excellent intracellular absorption capability, which is something that needs to be improved to prevail over obstacles.
- By transforming virtual connections, a leader with virtual intelligence can influence the metaverse in ways that improve the efficiency and effectiveness of virtual teams and the quality of their relationships.
- Cyber security is supposed to be a top priority consideration. Both the government and private sectors should consider adopting measures to improve their safety. Schools must provide better cyber security education. Public and private businesses must take security seriously and perform vulnerability checks regularly. A national cyber security policy must be created to guarantee the safety of enterprises.
- To stop producing unlawful software, collaborate using the latest mechanical and software engineering techniques. Academic and industry handshaking would have occurred to collaborate with those who know industrial research is wacky and academic members lack technical understanding. Massive work should be done throughout the country to avoid unanticipated events, and researchers should be given funds. For such issues, a government may form a commission or company. Any significant or minor security holes should be considered unacceptable. Organizations must prepare themselves with knowledge and technology to encounter the future challenges.

Success-driven organizations always start working on their post-crisis strategy as soon as the essentials are handled (such as the safety of the workforce and the stability of the short-term finances). Knowledge organization should concentrate on operationalizing and achieving the main goal while navigating the short-term environment by proactive strategies.

CONCLUDING REMARKS

The COVID-19 epidemic has had a substantial effect on the worldwide economy. Organizations needed to transition from offline to online activities during a period of pandemic activity. Almost all organizations responded to the new environment by implementing new business strategies. Only few knowledge-based firms, however, became the role models for successful formation of a new strategic business model to deal with the COVID-19 pandemic situation. Notably, the financial difficulties have a substantial impact on talent management. To begin, layoffs and hiring freezes have become banal in many businesses.

This book covered many of the talent management topics that are advantageous in the post-pandemic period. This monograph investigated how effective talent management might boost innovative and creative performance levels by utilizing already-existing intellectual capital. The book's chapters emphasize the importance and strategies of talent management on knowledge organization in the Post-Pandemic Paradigm.

During a pandemic, businesses placed a priority on employee safety, virtual connectivity, and stress management. Corporate entities were then attempting to reintegrate remote workers considering evolving situations in the pandemic. The post-pandemic paradigm has now started. Organizational leaders and HR professionals are concerned now about how to keep talented people, attract high performers, and integrate a sustainable brand-image-focused business model and a high-performing as well as a learning culture. Considering the concerns, anecdotes point to an iterative approach, agile management, and a post-pandemic talent management attitude.

To accomplish organizational goals that are in line with the organization's vision and mission, talent management aims to create and keep a talented, winning staff. The ability to establish such a standard gives a corporation a long-lasting competitive edge over competing business. Talented or academically accomplished individuals cannot be managed by an organization's CEO or director of strategic human resource management in the same manner applied to managing other human resources. Human capital management is central to managing scholarly individuals.

Rezbin Nahar
American International University-Bangladesh, Bangladesh

Sultana Parvin
Quantum Foundation, Bangladesh

Farheen Hassan
American International University-Bangladesh, Bangladesh

REFERENCES

Azmi, R., Tibben, W., & Win, K. (2016). *Motives behind Cyber Security Strategy Development: A Literature Review of National Cyber Security Strategy*. *Australasian Conference on Information Systems*, Wollongong, Australia.

Barney, J. B. and Wright, P. M. (1998). On becoming a strategic partner: The role of human resources in gaining competitive advantage. *Human Resource Management, 37*(1), 31–46. doi:10.1002/(SICI)1099-050X(199821)37:1<31::AID-HRM4>3.0.CO;2-W

Bersin by Deloitte. (2017). *High-Impact Leadership: The New Leadership Maturity Model.* Retrieved on February 2, 2021, from https://www2.deloitte.com/content/dam/Deloitte/ca/Documents/audit/ca-audit-abm-scotia-high-impact-leadership.pdf

BGD e-GOV CIRT | Bangladesh e-Government Computer Incident Response Team. (n.d.). *Statistics development – BGD e-GOV CIRT: Bangladesh e-government computer incident response team.* BGD eGOV CIRT Bangladesh eGovernment Computer Incident Response Team. Retrieved October 13, 2021, from https://www.cirt.gov.bd/statistics-development/

Boudreau, J. W., & Ramstad, P. M. (2005). Talentship, talent segmentation, and sustainability: A new HR decision science paradigm for a new strategy definition. *Human Resource Management, 44*(2), 129-136. doi:10.1002/hrm.20054

Cliffe, S. (1998). Human resources: Winning the war for talent. *Harvard Business Review, 76*(5), 18–19.

Davenport, T. H., & Prusak, L. (1998). *Working Knowledge: How Organizations Manage What They Know*. Harvard Business School Press.

Drucker, P. (1993). *Post Capitalist Society*. Routledge.

Fielder, A., Panaousis, E., Malacaria, P., Hankin, C., & Smeraldi, F. (2016). Decision support approaches for cyber security investment. *Decision Support Systems, 86*, 13–23.

Gerhardt, L. (2020, July 14). *Agile Leadership for Organisational Performance*. Savannah Group.

Gettier, E. L. (1963). Is justified true belief knowledge? *Analysis, 23*, 121–123.

Gunnigle, P., & Moore, S. (1994). Linking Business Strategy and Human Resource Management: Issues and Implications. *Personnel Review, 23*(1), 63–84.

Heinen, J. S., & O'Neill, C. (2004). Managing talent to maximize performance. *Employment Relations Today, 31*(2), 67–82. doi:10.1002/ert.20018

Inkpen, A. C. (1998). Learning and knowledge acquisition through international strategic alliances. *Academy of Management ExecutiVaus, 12*(4), 69–80.

Joiner, B. (2017). Bringing "Leadership Agility" to Agile. *Cutter Business Technology Journal, 30*(8), 1–10.

Joiner, B., & Josephs, S. (2007a). Developing Agile Leaders. *Industrial and Commercial Training, 39*(1), 35–42.

Joiner, B., & Josephs, S. (2007b). *Leadership Agility Five Levels of Mastery for Anticipating and Initiating Change.* Jossey-Bass.

Juneja, P. (n.d.). *Talent Management for the New Generation.* Retrieved on February 3, 2022, from https://www.managementstudyguide.com/talent-management-new-generation.htm

Kombo, K. D., & Tromp, L. A. D. (2006). *Proposal and Thesis Writing: An Introduction.* Paulines Publications.

Mattone, J., & Xavier, L. (2012). *Talent Leadership: A Proven Method for Identifying and Developing High-Potential Employees.* AMACOM.

Nilsson, S., & Ellström, P. (2012). Employability and talent management: challenges for HRD practices. *European Journal of Training and Development, 36*(1), 26–45. doi:10.1108/03090591211192610

Parker, D. W., Holesgrove, M., & Pathak, R. (2015). Improving Productivity with Self-Organised Teams and Agile Leadership. *International Journal of Productivity and Performance Management, 64*(1), 112–128.

Pfeffer, J. (2005). Producing sustainable competitive advantage through the effective management of people. *The Academy of Management Executive, 19*(4), 95–106. https://doi.org/10.5465/AME.2005.19417910

Sandhawalia, B. S., & Dalcher, D. (2011). Developing knowledge management capabilities: A structured approach. *Journal of Knowledge Management, 15*(2), 313–328.

Scarbrough, H., Robertson, M., & Swan, J. (2005). Professional media and management fasion: The case of knowledge management. *Scandinavian Journal of Management, 2*(21), 197–208.

Smith, R. G. (2004). Impediments to the successful investigation of transnational high-tech crime. *Trends and Issues in Crime and Criminal Justice*, 285.

Sparrow, P., Scullion, H., & Tarique, I. (2014). Multiple lenses on talent management: Definitions and contours of the field. In P. Sparrow, H. Scullion, & I. Tarique (Eds.), *Strategic Talent Management.* Cambridge University Press. doi:10.1017/CBO9781139424585.004

Swailes, S., & Blackburn, M. (2016). Employee reactions to talent pool membership. *Employee Relations, 38*(1), 112-128. doi:10.1108/ER-02-2015-0030

Tetik, S. (2016). Talent Management: A Review of Theoretical Perspectives and a Guideline for Practitioners. *Nile Journal of Business and Economics*, *4*, 40-56. doi:10.20321/nilejbe.v2i4.77

Voeten, E. (2019). Making Sense of the Design of International Institutions. *Annual Review of Political Science, 22*, 147–163. doi:10.1146/annurev-polisci-041916-021108

Wathne, K., Roos, J., & von Krogh, G. (1996). Towards a theory of knowledge transfer in a cooperative context. In Managing Knowledge: Perspectives on Cooperation and Competition. SAGE Publications Ltd.

Compilation of References

Aadne, J., Krogh, G., & Roos, J. (1996). Representationism: The traditional approach to cooperative strategies. In G. Krogh & J. Roos (Eds.), *Managing Knowledge: Perspectives on Cooperation and Competition* (pp. 9–31). Sage Publications. doi:10.4135/9781446280195.n2

Abraham, A. (2015). Gender & creativity: An overview of psychological and neuroscientific literature. *Brain Imaging and Behavior*. Advance online publication. doi:10.100711682-015-9410-8 PMID:26051636

Aggarwal, D. (2006). *Strategic approach of HR – Managing the Talent Pipe line*. Netkode Solution Pvt. Ltd. https://ww.netkode.com/whitepapers/Strategic_Approach.pdf

Aggarwal, P., Arora, P., & Ghai, R. (2014). Review on cybercrime and security. *International Journal of Research in Engineering and Applied Sciences*, *02*(1).

Agrawal, De Smet, Lacroix, & Reich. (2020). To emerge stronger from the COVID-19 crisis, companies should start re-skilling their workforces now. *McKinsey Insights*. https://www.mckinsey.com/

Agrawal, A. M. K., Bolli, D. B., Teja, C., Budhwani, T. P., Sehgal, L., Dharia, J. N., & Aggarwal, A. (2021). Offensive Web Application Security Framework. *Design Engineering (London)*, (9), 17334–17342.

Aguinis, H., & Burgi-Tian, J. (2021). Talent management challenges during COVID-19 and beyond: Performance management to the rescue. *BRQ Business Research Quarterly*, *24*(3), 233–240. doi:10.1177/23409444211009528

Ahmad, S., & Schroeder, R. G. (2003). The impact of human resource management practices on operational performance: Recognizing country and industry differences. *Journal of Operations Management*, *21*(1), 19–43. doi:10.1016/S0272-6963(02)00056-6

Ahmed, N., Kulsum, U., Azad, I., Momtaz, A., Haque, M., & Rahman, M. (2017). *Cybersecurity awareness survey: An analysis from Bangladesh perspective. 2017 IEEE Region 10 Humanitarian Technology Conference (R10-HTC).*

Akkaya, B., Panait, M., Andreea, S., & Kaya, Y. (2022). Agile Leadership and Perceived Career Success: The Mediating Role of Job Embeddedness. *International Journal of Environmental Research and Public Health*, *19*(8), 4834. doi:10.3390/ijerph19084834 PMID:35457699

Akunda, D., Chen, Z., & Gikiri, S. N. (2018). Role of HRM in talent retention with evidence. *Journal of Management and Strategy*, *9*(2), 8–19. doi:10.5430/jms.v9n2p8

Al Shebli, H., & Beheshti, B. (2018). A study on penetration testing process and tools. In *2018 IEEE Long Island Systems, Applications and Technology Conference (LISAT)* (pp. 1–7). 10.1109/LISAT.2018.8378035

Alam, M. (2012). E-governance in Bangladesh: Present problems and possible suggestions for future development. *International Journal of Applied Information Systems*, *4*(8), 21–25. doi:10.5120/ijais12-450804

Alavi, M., & Leidner, D. E. (2001). Knowledge management and knowledge management systems: Conceptual foundations and research issues. *Management Information Systems Quarterly*, *25*(1), 107–136. doi:10.2307/3250961

Al-Azzam, Z.F., & Al-Qura'a. (2018). How knowledge management mediates the strategic role of talent management in enhancing customer satisfaction. *Pacific Business Review, 11*(1), 30-42. https://ssrn.com/abstract=3364693

Albino, V., Claudio, G. A., & Schiuma, G. (1999). Knowledge transfer and inter-firm relationships in industrial districts: The role of the leader firm. *Technovation*, *19*(1), 53–63. doi:10.1016/S0166-4972(98)00078-9

Alfaro, E., Yu, F., Rehman, N. U., Hysa, E., & & Kabeya, P. K. (n.d.). Strategic management of innovation. In *The Routledge Companion to Innovation Management* (pp. 107-168). Routledge.

Alhadid, A. Y. (2016, March). The Effect of Organization Agility on Organization Performance. *International Review of Management and Business Research*, *5*(1), 273–278.

Ali, M. M. (2019). Grim situation of the world due to COVID19: economic perspective. *Geopolitics under Globalization, 3*(1), 24-29. . doi:10.21511/gg.03(1).2020.03

Ali, M. M. (2017). Quality Enhancement in Teaching-Learning Strategies of Bangladesh: A qualitative Assessment. *International Journal of Advanced Trends in Technology, Management & Applied Sciences, 3*(1), 121–147.

Ali, M. M. (2017). Testing hypothesis on theory of social networking, community banking and empowerment of people: A conceptual view. *Psychology and Behavioral Sciences.*, *6*(5), 96–104. doi:10.11648/j.pbs.20170605.14

Ali, M. M. (2019). The Strategic Role of Human Resources Planning to Achieve Sustainable Competitive Advantage. *Електронно списание. Dialog*, (2), 1–13.

Ali, M. M. (2020). Digitization of Emerging Economy: An exploratory and explanatory case study. *Journal of Governance and Regulation*, *9*(4), 25–36. doi:10.22495/jgrv9i4art2

Ali, M. M. (2021). Digital opportunities in the healthcare enterprises during COVID-19: An empirical analysis of the developing country. *Corporate Governance and Organizational Behavior Review*, *5*(2), 44–55. doi:10.22495/cgobrv5i2p4

Ali, M. M., Rattanawiboonsom, V., & Hasan, F. (2018). Knowledge Management at Higher Educational Institutes in Bangladesh: The Case Study of Self-assessed Processes of Two Educational Institutes. *International Journal of Trade and Commerce-IIARTC*, *7*(2), 514–535.

Almaaitah, M. A., Al-Shalabi, F. S., & Aljamal, W. H. (2013). Talent management and competitive advantage: The moderating effect of knowledge integration. *International Journal of Computer Applications*, *66*(11), 19-27. https://research.ijcaonline.org/volume66/number11/pxc3886202.pdf

Amabile, T. M., Barsade, S. G., Mueller, J. S., & Staw, B. M. (2005). Affect and creativity at work. *Administrative Science Quarterly*, *50*(3), 367–403. doi:10.2189/asqu.2005.50.3.367

Ambrosini, V., & Bowman, C. (2001). Tacit knowledge: Some suggestions for operationalisation. *Journal of Management Studies*, *38*(6), 811–829. doi:10.1111/1467-6486.00260

Amr, G. (2020). Kaspersky security. *Bulletin*.

Anku, A., & Farnand, S. P. (2021). Preferred white balance for applications using virtual backgrounds. *Color Research and Application*, *46*(6), 1227–1244. doi:10.1002/col.22694

Ankur, G. (2021). *The 7 Steps to build a great Talent Management Process*. https://www.peoplestrong.com/

Anthony, S. D., Viguerie, S. P., Schwartz, E. I., & Landeghem, J. V. (2018). *2018 corporate longevity forecast: Creative destruction is accelerating*. Innosight.

Appleyard, M. M. (1996). How does Knowledge flow? Interfirm patterns in the semiconductor industry. *Strategic Management Journal*, *17*, 137-154. https://www.jstor.org/stable/2486996

April Chang, W., & Huang, C. T. (2005). Relationship between strategic human resource management and firm performance: A contingency perspective. *International Journal of Manpower*, *26*(5), 434–449. doi:10.1108/01437720510615125

Ardichvili, A., Maurer, M., Li, W., Wentling, T., & Stuedemann, R. (2006). Cultural influences on knowledge sharing through online communities of practice. *Journal of Knowledge Management*, *10*(1), 94–107. doi:10.1108/13673270610650139

Argote, L. (1999). *Organizational Learning: Creating, Retaining and Transferring Knowledge*. Kluwer Academic Publishers.

Argote, L., & Ingram, P. (2000). Knowledge transfer: A basis for competitive advantage in Firms. *Organizational Behavior and Human Decision Processes*, *82*(1), 150–169. doi:10.1006/obhd.2000.2893

Argote, L., Ingram, P., Levine, J. M., & Moreland, R. L. (2000). Knowledge transfer in organizationns: Learning from the experience of others. *Organizational Behavior and Human Decision Processes*, *82*(1), 1–8. doi:10.1006/obhd.2000.2883

Argote, L., McEvily, B., & Reagans, R. (2003). Managing knowledge in organizations: An integrative framework and review of emerging themes. *Management Science*, *49*(4), 571–582. doi:10.1287/mnsc.49.4.571.14424

Ariss, A. A., Cascio, W. F., & Paauwe, J. (2014). Talent management: Current theories and future research directions. *Journal of World Business*, *49*(2), 173–179. doi:10.1016/j.jwb.2013.11.001

Arkin, B., Stender, S., & McGraw, G. (2005). Software penetration testing. *IEEE Security and Privacy*, *3*(1), 84–87. doi:10.1109/MSP.2005.23

Aryanto, R., Fontana, A., & Afiff, A. Z. (2015). Strategic human resource management, innovation Capability and performance: An empirical study in Indonesia software industry. *Procedia-Social and Behavioral Sciences*, *211*, 874-879. 10.1016/j.sbspro.2015.11.115

Attar, M., & Abdul-Kareem, A. (2020). *The Role of Agile Leadership in Organisational Agility. In Agile Business Leadership Methods for Industry 4.0.* Emerald Publishing Limited.

Ausubel, D. P. (1968). *Educational psychology: a cognitive view*. Holt, Rinehart and Winston.

Azmi, F. (2011). Strategic human resource management and its linkage with HRM effectiveness and organizational performance: Evidence from India. *International Journal of Human Resource Management*, *22*(18), 3888–3912. doi:10.1080/09585192.2011.561245

Azmi, R., Tibben, W., & Win, K. (2016). Motives behind Cyber Security Strategy Development: A Literature Review of National Cyber Security Strategy. *Australasian Conference on Information Systems.*

Bailenson, J. N., Beall, A. C., Loomis, J., Blascovich, J., & Turk, M. (2005). Transformed social interaction, augmented gaze, and social influence in immersive virtual environments. *Human Communication Research*, *31*(4), 511–537. doi:10.1111/j.1468-2958.2005.tb00881.x

Bailenson, J. N., & Yec, N. (2005). Digital chameleons: Automatic assimilation of nonverbal gestures in immersive virtual environments. *Psychological Science*, *16*(10), 814–819. doi:10.1111/j.1467-9280.2005.01619.x PMID:16181445

Barachini, F. (2009). Cultural and social issues for knowledge sharing. *Journal of Knowledge Management*, *13*(1), 98–110. doi:10.1108/13673270910931198

Barney, J. (1991). Firm Resources and Sustained Competitive Advantage. *Journal of Management*, *17*(1), 99–120. doi:10.1177/014920639101700108

Barney, J. B. and Wright, P. M. (1998). On becoming a strategic partner: The role of human resources in gaining competitive advantage. *Human Resource Management*, *37*(1), 31–46. doi:10.1002/(SICI)1099-050X(199821)37:1<31::AID-HRM4>3.0.CO;2-W

Barney, J. B. (2001). Is the Resource-Based 'View' A Useful Perspective for Strategic Management Research? Yes. *Academy of Management Review*, *26*(1), 41–56. doi:10.2307/259393

Basios, V. (2017). *The Century of Complexity*. Academic Press.

Bavelas, A. (1969). *Leadership: Man and Function, in Leadership*. Penguin.

Bayyoud, M., & Sayyad, N. (2015). The role of talent management on companies' performance listed in Palestine: Literature Review. *American Journal of Business, Economics and Management, 3*(4), 234-240. http://www.openscienceonline.com/journal/archive2?journalId=709&paperId=2470

Bazigos, M., Smet, A. D., & Gagnon, C. (2015, December 1). *Why Agility Pays*. McKinsey Quarterly. https://www.mckinsey.com/business-functions/organization/our-insigh ts/why-agility-pays# adresinden

Beattie, G., Webster, K., & Ross, J. (2010). The fixation and processing of the iconic gestures that accompany talk. *Journal of Language and Social Psychology*, *29*(2), 194–213. doi:10.1177/0261927X09359589

Belás, J., Korauš, M., Kombo, F., & Korauš, A. (2016). Electronic banking security and customer satisfaction in commercial banks. *Journal of Security and Sustainability Issues*.

Bell, D. G., Giordano, R., & Putz, P. (2002). Inter-firm sharing of process knowledge: Exploring knowledge markets. *Knowledge and Process Management*, *9*(1), 12–22. doi:10.1002/kpm.131

Bennett, N., & Lemoine, G. J. (2014, Jan.). What VUCA Really Means for You. *Harvard Business Review*.

Benson, J., & Brown, M. (2011). Generations at work: are there differences and do they matter? *The International Journal of Human Resource Management, 22*(9), 1843-1865. doi:10.1080/09585192.2011.573966

Berger, L., & Berger, D. (2010). *The Talent Management Handbook: Creating a Sustainable Competitive Advantage by Selecting, Developing, and Promoting the Best People*. McGraw-Hill Publication.

Berman, M. (1981). *The re-enchantment of the world*. Cornell University Press.

Bersin by Deloitte. (2017). *High-Impact Leadership: The New Leadership Maturity Model.* Retrieved on February 2, 2021, from https://www2.deloitte.com/content/dam/Deloitte/ca/Documents/audit/ca-audit-abm-scotia-high-impact-leadership.pdf

Bersin, J., & Chamorro-Premuzic, T. (2019). New ways to gauge talent and potential. *MIT Sloan Management Review*, *60*(2), 7–10.

BGD e-GOV CIRT | Bangladesh e-Government Computer Incident Response Team. (n.d.). *Statistics development – BGD e-GOV CIRT: Bangladesh e-government computer incident response team.* BGD eGOV CIRT Bangladesh eGovernment Computer Incident Response Team. Retrieved October 13, 2021, from https://www.cirt.gov.bd/statistics-development/

Bhalla, A. (2020). *Talent Engineering For Tomorrow*. https://www.forbes.com/sites/forbestechcouncil/2020/12/14/talent-engineering-for-tomorrow/?sh=9449d75271c4

Bishop, M. (2007). About penetration testing. *IEEE Security and Privacy*, *5*(6), 84–87. doi:10.1109/MSP.2007.159

Blau, P. M. (1986). *Exchange and Power in Social Life* (2nd ed.). Routledge.

Bolden, R., Gosling, J., & O'Brien, A. (2014). Citizens of the academic community? A societal perspective on leadership in UK higher education. *Studies in Higher Education, 39*(5), 754-770. doi:10.1080/03075079.2012.754855

Borkenau, P., Mauer, N., Riemann, R., Spinath, F. M., & Angleitner, A. (2004). Thin slices of behavior as cues of personality and intelligence. *Journal of Personality and Social Psychology*, *86*(4), 599–614. doi:10.1037/0022-3514.86.4.599 PMID:15053708

Bossler, A. M., & Berenblum, T. (2019). Introduction: New directions in cybercrime research. *Journal of Criminal Justice*, *42*(5), 495–499.

Boston Consulting Group & World Federation of People Management Association. (2010). *Creating People Advantage 2010: How companies can adapt their HR practices for volatile times.* Author.

Boston Consulting Group & World Federation of People Management Association. (2014). Creating people advantage 2014-2015: How to set up great HR functions - Connect, prioritize, impact. Author.

Boston Consulting Group and World Federation of People Management Association. (2021). *Creating People Advantage 2021: The Future of People Management Priorities.* Author.

Boston Consulting Group. (2007). *Aligning Talent for Global Advantage: How top companies develop the right talent in the right places.* Author.

Boudreau, J. W., & Ramstad, P. M. (2005). Talentship, talent segmentation, and sustainability: A new HR decision science paradigm for a new strategy definition. *Human Resource Management*, *44*(2), 129–136.

Boudreau, J. W., & Ramstad, P. M. (2005). Talentship, talent segmentation, and sustainability: A new HR decision science paradigm for a new strategy definition. *Human Resource Management*, *44*(2), 129-136. doi:10.1002/hrm.20054

Boudreau, J. W., & Ramstad, P. M. (2005). *Talentship, talent segmentation, and sustainability: A new HR decision science paradigm for a new strategy definition.* Human Resource.

Boxall, P., Steenveld, M. (1999). Human Resource Strategy and Competitive Advantage: A Longitudinal Study of Engineering Consultancies. *Journal of Management Studies, 36*(4), 443–463.

Boxall, P. (1998). Achieving competitive advantage through human resource strategy: Towards a theory of industry dynamics. *Human Resource Management Review*, *8*(3), 265–288. doi:10.1016/S1053-4822(98)90005-5

Boxall, P., & Purcell, J. (2000). Strategic human resource management: Where have we come from, and where should we be going? *International Journal of Management Reviews*, *2*(2), 183–203. doi:10.1111/1468-2370.00037

Boxall, P., & Purcell, J. (2003). *Strategy and human resource management*. Palgrave Macmillan.

Brechbühl, H., Bruce, R., Dynes, S., & Johnson, M. (2010). Protecting critical information infrastructure: Developing cybersecurity policy. *Information Technology for Development*, *20*(2), 122–139. doi:10.1002/itdj.20096

Brett, J. (2014). *Negotiating globally: How to negotiate deals, resolve disputes, and make decisions across cultural boundaries* (3rd ed.). John Wiley & Sons.

Bruce-Lockhart, A. (2021). What Is Human Capital? Everything You Need told. *Economic Forum*. https://www.weforum.org/agenda/2019/06/what-isital-know/

Brucks, M. S., & Levav, J. (2022, April 27). Virtual communication curbs creative idea generation. *Nature*, *605*(7908), 108–112. doi:10.103841586-022-04643-y PMID:35477754

Buchan, N. R., Chen, X.-P., Zhang, Y., & Adair, W. L. (2021). *Teamwork during a global pandemic* [Manuscript in preparation]. CIBER, University of South Carolina.

Buck, R. (1980). Nonverbal behavior and the theory of emotion: The facial feedback hypothesis. *Journal of Personality and Social Psychology*, *38*(5), 811–824. doi:10.1037/0022-3514.38.5.811 PMID:7381683

Bukth, T., & Huda, S. (2017). *The soft threat: The story of the Bangladesh bank reserve heist*. SAGE Publications.

Burke, A. (2013, November 15). Why Zappos CEO Hsieh wants to enable more collisions in Vegas. *Forbes*.

Burton-Jones, A. (2001). The Knowledge Supply Model: A Framework for Education and Training in the New Economy. *Education and Training*, *43*(4-5), 225-232. https://eric.ed.gov/?id=EJ630485

Cappelli, P. (2008). Talent Management for the Twenty-First Century. *Harvard Business Review*, *86*(3), 74-81.

Cappelli, P., & Singh, H. (1992). Integrating strategic human resources and strategic management. In O. S. Mitchell & P. D. Sherer (Eds.), *Research frontiers in industrial relations and human resources* (pp. 165–192). IRRA.

Capra, F. (1983). *The turning point: Science, society, and the rising culture*. Bantam Books.

Cartwright, S., & Cooper, C. L. (2002). *HR Know-how in mergers and acquisitions*. Cromwell Press.

Chambers, E. G., Foulon, M., Handfield-jones, H., Hankin, S. M., & Michaels, E. G. (1998). The War for Talent. *McKinsey Quarterly*, *3*(3). 44-57. https://www.researchgate.net/publication/284689712_The_War_for_Talent

Chang, S., Van Witteloostuijn, A., & Eden, L. (2010). Common method variance in international business research. *Journal of International Business Studies*, *41*(2), 178–184. doi:10.1057/jibs.2009.88

Chartrand, T. L., & Bargh, J. A. (1999). The chameleon effect: The perception-behavior link and social interaction. *Journal of Personality and Social Psychology*, *76*(6), 893–910. doi:10.1037/0022-3514.76.6.893 PMID:10402679

Chaturvedi, S., & Singh, T. (2021). Knowledge Management Initiatives for Tackling th COVID19 Pandemic. *Metamorphosis*, *20*(1), 25–34. doi:10.1177/09726225211023677

Chatwani, N. (2019). *Organisational Agility: Exploring the Impact of Identity on Knowledge Management*. Palgrave Macmillan. doi:10.1007/978-3-030-17249-7

Chen, L., & Harper, M. P. (2009, November 2-4). Multimodal floor control shift detection. *Proceedings of the 2009 International Conference on Multimodal Interfaces*, 15-22.

Cheung, P. C., & Lau, S. (2010). Gender differences in the creativity of Hong Kong, school children: Comparison by using the new electronic Wallach–kogan creativity tests. *Creativity Research Journal*, *22*(2), 194–199. doi:10.1080/10400419.2010.481522

Choden, C., Zangmo, G., & Dem, K. (2021). Universalism in Human Resource Management. *Academia Letters. Article*, *1580*. Advance online publication. doi:10.20935/AL1580

Chowdhury, D. (2009). *The Determinants of Knowledge Transfer in Turkish Textile Apparel Industry* (PhD Thesis). University of Plymouth.

Chowdhury, D., & Butel, L. (2007). Knowledge transfer-A network approach to Turkey's Small and Medium Sized Enterprises (SMEs). *Journal of Global Strategy Management*, *1*(2), 142–151. doi:10.20460/JGSM.2007118707

Chowdhury, D., Butel, L., Hakki, E., & Ismail, B. (2009). Knowledge transfer (KT) practices in Small and Medium Enterprises (SME's) of Turkish textile and apparel industry. *Journal of Global Strategy Management*, *JSGM-6*(3), 52–66. doi:10.20460/JGSM.2009318460

Chromium. The Chromium Projects. (n.d.). Retrieved October 13, 2021, from https://www.chromium.org/Home

Cinnioğlu, H. (2020). *A Review of Modern Leadership Styles in Perspective of Industry 4.0. In Agile Business Leadership Methods for Industry 4.0*. Emerald Publishing Limited.

Cliffe, S. (1998). Human resources: Winning the war for talent. *Harvard Business Review*, *76*(5), 18–19.

Clulow, V., Gerstman, J., & Barry, C. (2003). The resource-based view and sustainable competitive advantage: The case of a financial services firm. *Journal of European Industrial Training*, *27*(5), 220–232. doi:10.1108/03090590310469605

Collings, D.G., & Mellahi, K. (2009). Strategic talent management: A review and research agenda. *Human Resource Management Review, 19*(4), 304-313. doi:10.1016/j.hrmr.2009.04.001

Connell, N. A. D., Klein, J. H., & Powell, P. L. (2003). It's tacit knowledge but not as we know it: Redirecting the search for knowledge. *The Journal of the Operational Research Society, 54*(2), 140–152. doi:10.1057/palgrave.jors.2601444

Conner, J., & Ulrich, D. (1996). Human resource roles: Creating value, not rhetoric. *Human Resource Planning, 19*(3), 1–10.

Crossman, A. (2020). *The Major Theoretical Perspectives of Sociology: An Overview of Four Key Perspectives.* Posted in ThoughtCo on January 22, 2020. Retrieved on February 6, 2022, from https://www.thoughtco.com/theoretical-perspectives-3026716

Cyber threat report - cirt.gov.bd. (n.d.). Retrieved October 13, 2021, from https://www.cirt.gov.bd/wp-content/uploads/2021/04/HAFNIUM.pdf

Darr, E. D., Argote, L., & Epple, D. (1995). The acquisition, transfer and deprecation of knowledge in service organization s: Productivity in franchises. *Management Science, 41*(11), 1750–1762. https://www.jstor.org/stable/2632871. doi:10.1287/mnsc.41.11.1750

Darr, E. D., & Kurtzberg, T. R. (2000). An investigation of partner similarity dimensions of knowledge transfer. *Organizational Behavior and Human Decision Processes, 82*(1), 28–44. doi:10.1006/obhd.2000.2885 PMID:10631067

Davenport, T. H. (2005). *Thinking for a living: how to get better performance and results from knowledge workers.* Harvard Business Publishing.

Davenport, T. H., & Prusak, L. (1998). *Working Knowledge: How Organizations Manage What They Know.* Harvard Business School Press.

David, F. R., & David, F. R. (2015). Strategic Management: Concepts and Cases (15th ed.). Harlow.

Davidescu, A. A., Apostu, S.-A., Paul, A., & Casuneanu, I. (2020). Work Flexibility, Job Satisfaction, and Job Performance among Romanian Employees—Implications for Sustainable Human Resource Management. *Sustainability, 12*(15), 6086. doi:10.3390u12156086

Dawson, R. (2000). *Developing Knowledge-Based Client Relationships: The Future of Professional Services.* Butterworth-Heinemann.

de Mio, R. R. (2002, June 6-8). *On defining virtual emotion intelligence* [Conference session]. European Conference on Information Systems, Gdansk, Poland.

Debowski, S. (2006). *Knowledge Management.* John Wiley & Sons Australia Ltd.

Degutyte, Z., & Astell, A. (2021). The role of eye gaze in regulating turn taking in conversations: A systematized review of methods and findings. *Frontiers in Psychology, 12*, 616471. doi:10.3389/fpsyg.2021.616471 PMID:33897526

Delery, J. E., & Doty, D. H. (1996). Theoretical frameworks in strategic human resource management: Universalistic, contingency, and configurational perspectives. *Academy of Management Journal*, *39*(4), 802–835.

Deloitte. (2005). *Becoming a Magnet for Talent*. Global Talent Pulse Survey Results.

Denning, S. (2018). *The Age of Agile: How Smart Companies are Transforming the Way Work Gets Done*. AMACOM.

Dessler, G. (2011). *Human resource management* (12th ed.). Pearson.

Dewhurst, M., Hancock, B., & Ellsworth, D. (2013). Redesigning knowledge work: How to free-up high-end experts to do what they do best. *Harvard Business Review*, *91*(1), 58–64.

DocuSign (n.d.). *Building Sustainability into the Modern Business: Landscape Reducing waste and emissions with powerful digital workflows*. DocuSign eBook.

Donnellan, J., & Rutledge, W. L. (2019). A case for resource-based view and competitive advantage in banking. *Managerial and Decision Economics*, *40*(6), 728–737. doi:10.1002/mde.3041

Dovidio, J. F., & Ellyson, S. L. (1982). Decoding visual dominance: Attributions of power based on relative percentages of looking while speaking and looking while listening. *Social Psychology Quarterly*, *45*(2), 106–113. doi:10.2307/3033933

Dowling, P., & Roots, A. (2009). 'Review of Boudreau, P. and Ramstad, A. (2009) Beyond HR: The new science of human capital. In *Research and Practice in Human Resource Management* (p. 268). HBS Press.

Draganidis, F., & Mentzas, G. (2006). Competency Based Management: a review of systems and approaches. *Information Management & Computer Security, 14*(1), 51-64. doi:10.1108/09685220610648373

Dries, N. (2013). The psychology of talent management: A review and research agenda. *Human Resource Management Review, 23*(4), 272-285. doi:10.1016/j.hrmr.2013.05.001

Drucker, P. (1999). Knowledge-Worker Productivity: The Biggest Challenge. *California Management Review*, *41*(2), 79-94. doi:10.2307/41165987

Drucker, P. (1993). *Post Capitalist Society*. Routledge.

Duke, I. I. J. II, & Udono, E. N. (2012). A new paradigm in traditional human resource management practices. *Journal of Management and Sustainability*, *2*(2), 146–159. doi:10.5539/jms.v2n2p158

Dyer, J. H., & Nobeoka, K. (2000). Creating and managing a high performance knowledge sharing network: The Toyota case. *Strategic Management Journal*, *21*(3), 345–367. doi:10.1002/(SICI)1097-0266(200003)21:3<345::AID-SMJ96>3.0.CO;2-N

Eadeh, F., Ostrowski, B., & Woolley, A.W. (2021, October). *Misery loves company: The implications of mood for affiliation and collective intelligence in remote collaboration* [Paper presentation]. Interdisciplinary Network for Group Research (INGRoup) Virtual Conference.

Easterby-Smith, M., Lyles, M. A., & Tsang, E. W. K. (2008). Inter-organizational knowledge transfer: Current themes and future prospects. *Journal of Management Studies*, *45*(4), 677–690. doi:10.1111/j.1467-6486.2008.00773.x

Easterby-Smith, M., Thorpe, R., & Lowe, A. (2002). *Management Research: An Introduction*. Sage Publications.

Economist Intelligence Unit. (2006). The CEO 's role in talent management: How top executives from ten countries are nurturing the leaders of tomorrow. *The Economist.* http://graphics.eiu.com/files/ad_pdfs/eiu_DDI_talent_Management_WP.pdf

Edelman, M. S., Omark, D. R., & Freedman, D. G. (1973). Dominance hierarchies in young children. *Social Sciences Information. Information Sur les Sciences Sociales*, *12*(1), 103–110. doi:10.1177/053901847301200105

Edmondson, A. (1999). Psychological safety and learning behavior in work teams. *Administrative Science Quarterly*, *44*(2), 350–383. doi:10.2307/2666999

Edvardsson, I. R. (2006). Knowledge management and SMEs: The case of Icelandic firms. *Knowledge Management Research and Practice*, *4*(4), 275–282. doi:10.1057/palgrave.kmrp.8500111

Edwards, J. (2014). *Mastering Strategic Management*. BCcampus. https://opentextbc.ca/strategicmanagement/

Edwards, D., & Smith, T. F. (2010). 'Supply issues for science academics in Australia: Now and in the future. *Higher Education*, *60*(1), 19–32. doi:10.100710734-009-9283-0

Egbunike, C. F., & Okerekeoti, C. U. (2018). Macroeconomic factors, firm characteristics, and financial performance: A study of selected quoted manufacturing firms in Nigeria. *Asian Journal of Accounting Research*, *3*(2), 142–168. doi:10.1108/AJAR-09-2018-0029

Eichhorn, B. R. (2014). *Common method variance techniques*. https://www.lexjansen.com/mwsug/2014/AA/MWSUG-2014-AA11.pdf

Ekman, P., & Friesen, W. V. (2003). *Unmasking the face: A guide to recognizing emotions from facial clues*. Malor Books.

Elbanna, S., & Abdel-Maksoud, A. (2020). Organizational resources and performance: The case of an oil-rich country. *Public Performance & Management Review*, *43*(3), 713–739. doi:10.1080/15309576.2019.1660187

Elenkov, D. S. (2002). Effects of Leadership on Organizational Performance in Russian Companies. *Journal of Business Research*, *55*(6), 467–480. doi:10.1016/S0148-2963(00)00174-0

Elzamly, A., Hussin, B., Abu-Naser, S. S., Shibutani, T., & Doheir, M. (2017). *Predicting critical cloud computing security issues using Artificial Neural Network (ANNs) algorithms in banking organizations*. Academic Press.

Emeagwal, L., & Ogbonmwan, K. O. (2018). Mapping the perceived role of strategic human resource management practices in sustainable competitive advantage. *Academy of Strategic Management Journal*, *17*(2), 1–19.

En.wikipedia.org. (2021). *List of data breaches - Wikipedia*. Available at: https://en.wikipedia.org/wiki/List_of_data_breaches

Epling, L., Hinkel, B., & Hu, Y. (2015, October). Penetration testing in a box. In *Proceedings of the 2015 information security curriculum development conference* (pp. 1-4). Academic Press.

Exline, R. V., Ellyson, S. L., & Long, B. (1975). Visual behavior as an aspect of power role relationships. In P. Pliner, L. Krames, & T. Alloway (Eds.), *Nonverbal communication of aggression: Advances in the study of communication and affect* (Vol. 2, pp. 21–52). Springer. doi:10.1007/978-1-4684-2835-3_2

Farah, T., Alam, D., Kabir, M., & Bhuiyan, T. (2015). SQLi penetration testing of financial Web applications: Investigation of Bangladesh region. In *2015 World Congress on Internet Security (WorldCIS)* (pp. 146–151). Academic Press.

Fareed, M., Noor, W. S., Isa, M. F., & Salleh, S. S. (2016). Developing human capital for sustainable competitive advantage: The roles of organizational culture and high-performance work system. *Journal of Economic & Management Perspectives*, *10*(4), 655–673.

Farndale, E., Scullion, H., & Sparrow, P. (2010). The role of the corporate HR function in global talent management. *Journal of World Business*, *45*(2), 161–168. doi:10.1016/j.jwb.2009.09.012

Fatima, A. (2011). E-banking security issues-Is there a solution in biometrics? *Journal of Internet Banking and Commerce*, *16*(2), 1.

Felin, T., & Hesterly, W. S. (2007). The Knowledge-Based View, Nested Heterogeneity, and New Value Creation: Philosophical Considerations on the Locus of Knowledge. *The Academy of Management Review, 32*(1), 195-218. doi:10.5465/amr.2007.23464020

Ferreira, J. J., Fernandes, C. I., & Ferreira, F. A. (2019). To be or not to be digital, that is the question: Firm innovation and performance. *Journal of Business Research*, *101*, 583–590. doi:10.1016/j.jbusres.2018.11.013

Fielder, A., Panaousis, E., Malacaria, P., Hankin, C., & Smeraldi, F. (2016). Decision support approaches for cyber security investment. *Decision Support Systems*, *86*, 13–23.

Firefox: About your rights. Mozilla. (n.d.). Retrieved October 13, 2021, from https://www.mozilla.org/en-US/about/legal/terms/firefox/

Fitz-enz, J. (2002). *How to measure human resource selection* (3rd ed.). McGraw Hill.

Fleming, J. H., Darley, J. M., Hilton, J. L., & Kojetin, B. A. (1990). Multiple audience problem: A strategic communication perspective on social perception. *Journal of Personality and Social Psychology*, *58*(4), 593–609. doi:10.1037/0022-3514.58.4.593 PMID:2348361

Flink, C., Leslie, J., & Mehta, S. (2022). *Talent leaders can help emerging leaders manage the challenges of virtual leadership with three key tools.* Retrieved on February 4, 2022, from https://www.talentmgt.com/articles/2022/01/31/equipping-emerging-leaders-for-success-in-a-virtual-world/

Foote, E., Hancock, B., Jeffery, B., & Malan, R. (2021). *The key role of dynamic talent allocation in shaping the future of work.* https://www.mckinsey.com/

Ford, J. (2021). *What are the four criteria of sustainable competitive advantage?* https://answerstoall.com/technolgownt-are-the-four-criteria-of-sustainable-

Fox, J. (2022, January 18). Work from home is becoming a permanent part of how jobs are done. *Bloomberg Businessweek.* https://www.bloomberg.com/news/articles/2022-01-18/work-from-home-is-becoming-a-permanent-part-of-how-jobs-are-done

Frankiewicz, B., & Chamorro-Premuzic, T. (2020). The Post-Pandemic Rules of Talent Management. *Harvard Business Review.*

Frontiera, J. (2010). Leadership and Organizational Culture Transformation in Professional Sport. *Leadership and Organizational Culture Transformation in Professional Sport.*, *17*(1), 71–86. doi:10.1177/1548051809345253

Fulk, J., Steinfield, C. W., Schmitz, J., & Power, J. G. (1987, October). A social information processing model of media use in organizations. *Communication Research, 14*(5), 529–552. doi:10.1177/009365087014005005

Fung, M. K. (2019). Fraudulent financial reporting and technological capability in the information technology sector: A resource-based perspective. *Journal of Business Ethics, 156*(2), 577–589. doi:10.100710551-017-3605-4

Gahlawat, N., & Kundu, S. (2019). Progressive human resource management and firm Performance. *The International Journal of Organizational Analysis, 27*(3), 471–493. doi:10.1108/IJOA-05-2017-1159

Gallardo-Gallardo, E., Dries, N., & González-Cruz, T. F. (2013). What is the meaning of 'talent' in the world of work? *Human Resource Management Review, 23*(4), 290–300. doi:10.1016/j.hrmr.2013.05.002

Gamble, P., & Blackwell, J. (2001). *Knowledge Management: A State of the Art Guide*. Kogan Page Limited.

Ganaie, M. U., & Haque, M. I. (2017). Talent management and value creation: A conceptual framework. *Academy of Strategic Management Journal, 16*(2), 1-9.

Garaventa, E. (1998). Drama: A tool for teaching business ethics. *Business Ethics Quarterly, 8*(3), 535–545. doi:10.2307/3857436

Gartner. (2019). *Gartner for HR - Reinvent Talent Strategies: The digital-age mandate for HR.* https://www.gartner.com/en/confirmation/human-resources/trends/reinvent-talent-strategies?msclkid=75a00348645716bee27862bc54bbe601

Gartner. (n.d.). *3 Workforce-Planning Imperatives That Drive Business Outcomes.* Retrieved on February 4, 2022, from https://www.gartner.com/en/human-resources/research/talentneuron/3-key-hr-workforce-planning-challenges

Gartner. (n.d.a). *The Unbounded Workforce: Design a data-driven talent strategy that aligns with today's shifting workforce trends.* Retrieved on February 3, 2022, from https://www.gartner.com/en/human-resources/research/talentneuron/unbounded-workforce-ebook?

George, J. M., & Zhou, J. (2002). Understanding when bad moods foster creativity and good ones do not: The role of context and clarity feelings. *The Journal of Applied Psychology, 87*(4), 687–697. doi:10.1037/0021-9010.87.4.687 PMID:12184573

George, J. S., Schwager, S., & Canavan, F. (1998). A guide to drama-based training. *Employment Relations Today, 25*(4), 15–19. doi:10.1002/ert.3910250408

Gerhardt, L. (2020, July 14). *Agile Leadership for Organisational Performance*. Savannah Group.

Gettier, E. L. (1963). Is justified true belief knowledge? *Analysis, 23*(6), 121–123. doi:10.1093/analys/23.6.121

Ghosh, P. (2021). What is Human Capital Management (HCD)? Definition, Process, Platforms (tools) with Examples. *Performance Management.* https://www.toolbox.com/hr/performancemanagement/articles/what-is-human-capital-management/

Gilliot, D., Overlaet, B., & Verdin, P. (2002). 'Managing academic personnel flow at universities. *Tertiary Education and Management, 8*(4), 277–295. doi:10.1080/13583883.2002.9967085

Gizmodo. (2021). *Mother of All Breaches Exposes 773 Million Emails, 21 Million Passwords.* Available at: https://gizmodo.com/mother-of-all-breaches-exposes-773-million-emails-21-m-1831833456

Glaser, J. E. (2014). *Conversational intelligence: How great leaders build trust & get extraordinary results.* Taylor and Francis Group.

Global cybersecurity index 2020. My ITU. (n.d.). Retrieved October 13, 2021, from https://www.itu.int/en/myitu/Publications/2021/06/28/13/22/Global-Cybersecurity-Index-2020

Goethe, O., Sørum, H., & Johansen, J. (2022). The effect or non-effect of virtual versus non-virtual backgrounds in digital learning. In T. Ahram, & R. Taiar (Eds.), *IHIET 2021: Human Interaction, Emerging Technologies and Future Systems V* (Vol. 319, pp. 274-281). Springer.

Goh, S. C. (2002). Managing effective knowledge transfer: An integrative framework and some practice implications. *Journal of Knowledge Management, 6*(1), 23–30. doi:10.1108/13673270210417664

Gold, J., Oldroyd, T., Chesters, E., Booth, A., & Waugh, A. (2016). Exploring talenting: Talent management as a collective endeavor. *European Journal of Training and Development, 40*(7), 513-533. https://www.emerald.com/insight/content/doi/10.1108/EJTD-11-2015-0091/full/html

Goleman, D., Boyatis, R., & McKee, A. (2013). *Primal leadership: Unleashing the power of emotional intelligence*. Harvard Business Review Press.

Goutam, R. K. (2015). Importance of cyber security. *International Journal of Computers and Applications, 111*(7).

Grant, R. M. (1996). Toward a knowledge-based theory of the firm. *Strategic Management Journal, 17*(S2), 109-122. doi:10.1002/smj.4250171110

Grant, R. M. (1997). The knowledge-based view of the firm: Implications for management practice. *Long Range Planning, 30*(3), 450–454. https://www.jstor.org/stable/2486994. doi:10.1016/S0024-6301(97)00025-3

Gratton, L., Hailey, V. H., & Truss, C. (2000). *Strategic human resource management*. Oxford University.

Greineder, M., & Leicht, N. (2020). *Agila Leadership - A Comparison of Agile Leadership Styles*. Enabling Technology for A Sustainable Society.

Griffiths, K., Birdi, K., & Alsina, V. (2016). Knowledge sharing practices and issues in policing contexts: A systematic review of the literature. *European Journal of Policing Studies, 3*(3), 267–291. www.maklu-online.eu/en/tijdschrift/ejps/volume-3/issue-3/

Groves, K. S. (2007). Integrating leadership development and succession planning best practices. *Journal of Management Development, 26*(3), 239–260. doi:10.1108/02621710710732146

Guest, D. (1987). Human resource management and industrial relations. *Journal of Management Studies, 24*(5), 503–521. doi:10.1111/j.1467-6486.1987.tb00460.x

Gunnigle, P., & Moore, S. (1994). Linking Business Strategy and Human Resource Management: Issues and Implications. *Personnel Review, 23*(1), 63–84. doi:10.1108/00483489410053038

Habeck, M. M., Kroger, F., & Tram, M. R. (2000). *After The Merger. Seven Rules For Successful Post-Merger Integration*. Pearson Education Limited.

Hacking alert: Banks in Bangladesh limit atms, cards and online transactions to avoid risks. Dhaka Tribune. (2020, September 7). Retrieved October 13, 2021, from https://www.dhakatribune.com/business/banks/2020/09/07/hacking-alert-banks-in-bangladesh-limit-atms-cards-and-online-transactions-to-avoid-risks

Haines, R., Kramer, M., & Vehring, N. (2011). Activity awareness as a means to promote connectedness, willingness to do additional work, and congeniality: An experimental study. *Proceedings of the 32nd International Conference on Information Systems*.

Hair, J. F. Jr, Black, W. C., & Babin, B. J. (2010). *Multivariate data analysis* (7th ed.). Pearson Prentice-Hall.

Haldin-Herrgard, T. (2000). Difficulties in diffusion of tacit knowledge in organizations. *Journal of Intellectual Capital, 1*(4), 357–365. https://doi.org/10.1108/14691930010359252

Halfond, W., Viegas, J., Orso, A., & ... (2006). A classification of SQL-injection attacks and countermeasures. In *Proceedings of the IEEE international symposium on secure software engineering* (pp. 13–15). IEEE.

Hall, B. P. (2001). Values development and learning organization s of knowledge. *Journal of Management, 1*(5), 19–32. doi:10.1108/13673270110384374

Hanafi, M., Wibisono, D., Mangkusubroto, K., Siallagan, M., & Badriyah, M. J. K. (2017). Modelling competitive advantage of nation: A literature review. *Competitiveness Review, 27*(4), 335–365. doi:10.1108/CR-06-2016-0031

Hanif, R., Masood, A., & Azhar, S. (2013). Strategic Talent Management as Source of Competitive Advantage Talent Competitiveness Framework. SSRN *2240400 Electronic Journal* doi:10.2139/ssrn.2240400

Hans, S. (2021). Strategic Human Resource Management and Employee Relationship Management: An Approach for Realizing Sustainable Competitive Advantage. *IUP Journal of Organizational Behavior, 20*(4).

Hansen, M. T., Nohria, N., & Tierney, T. (1999). What's your strategy for managing knowledge? *Harvard Business Review*, (March-April), 106–116.

Haque, A. (2019). *Need for Critical Cyber Defence, Security Strategy and Privacy Policy in Bangladesh–Hype or Reality? International Journal of Managing Information Technology*, 11.

Hasan, A. S., Baten, M. A., Kamil, A. A., & Parveen, S. (2010). Adoption of e-banking in Bangladesh: An exploratory study. *African Journal of Business Management, 4*(13), 2718–2727.

Hasan, A., & Meva, D. (2018). Web application safety by penetration testing. *International Journal of Advanced Studies of Scientific Research, 3*(9).

Hasnain, S. S. (2015). Organizational knowledge: The Panacea to NGO-operations. *Procedia: Social and Behavioral Sciences, 195*, 197–201. https://doi.org/10.1016/j.sbspro.2015.06.350

Hasnain, S. S. (2016). *Knowledge Management: Towards a New Horizon*. IISTE.

Hasnain, S. S., Jasimuddin, S. M., & Fuller-Love, N. (2016). Exploring causes, taxonomies, mechanisms and barriers influencing knowledge transfer: Empirical studies in NGOs. *Information Resources Management Journal, 29*(1), 39–56. doi:10.4018/IRMJ.2016010103

Hayes, A. (2021, August 22). *Volatility*. Investopedia: https://www.investopedia.com/terms/v/volatility.asp

Heavin, C., & Neville, K. (2006). Mentoring knowledge workers. In D. G. Schwartz (Ed.), *Encyclopedia of Knowledge Management* (pp. 621–626). Idea Group Reference.

Heinen, J. S., & O'Neill, C. (2004). Managing talent to maximize performance. *Employment Relations Today*, *31*(2), 67–82. doi:10.1002/ert.20018

Henderson, H. (2009). *Encyclopedia of computer science and technology*. Infobase Publishing.

Hendriks, P. H. J. (1999). Why share knowledge? The influence of ICT on the motivation for knowledge sharing. *Knowledge and Process Management*, *6*(2), 91–100. https://doi.org/10.1002/(SICI)1099-1441(199906)6:2%3C91::AID-KPM54%3E3.0.CO;2-M

He, W., & Wong, W. (2011). Gender differences in creative thinking revisited: Findings from analysis of variability. *Personality and Individual Differences*, *51*(7), 807–811. doi:10.1016/j.paid.2011.06.027

Hislop, D. (2005). *Knowledge Management in Organizations-A Critical Introduction*. Oxford University Press.

Hofer-Alfeis, J., & van der Spek, R. (2002). The knowledge strategy process: An Instrument for business owners. In T. H. Davenport & G. J. B. Probst (Eds.), *Knowledge Management Case Book: Siemens Best Practices* (pp. 24–39). Policies Corporate Publishing & John Wiley & Sons.

Hofileña, J. M. G., & Sy, J. L. (2017). Gone Without a Trace: A Re-Examination of Bank Secrecy Laws and Anti-Money Laundering Laws in Light of the 2016 Bangladesh Bank Heist. *Ateneo LJ*, *62*.

Hogberg, C., & Edvinsson, L. (1998). A design for futurizing knowledge networking. *Journal of Knowledge Management*, *2*(2), 81–92. https://doi.org/10.1108/13673279810249404

Holdsworth, R., & Lundgaard, W. (2009). An HR intervention. *HR Monthly*, (May), 32.

Hole, K. J., Moen, V., & Tjostheim, T. (2006). Case study: Online banking security. *IEEE Security and Privacy*, *4*(2), 14–20. doi:10.1109/MSP.2006.36

Home. Indeed.com. (n.d.). Retrieved October 13, 2021, from https://www.indeed.com/career/salaries/Cyber%20Security

Horney, N., Pasmore, B., & O'Shea, T. (2010). Leadership Agility: A Business Imperative for a VUCA World. *People & Strategy*, *33*(4), 32–38.

Hossain, M., Hassan, R., Amjad, M., & Rahman, M. (2021). Web Performance Analysis: An Empirical Analysis of E-Commerce Sites in Bangladesh. *International Journal of Information Engineering & Electronic Business*, *13*(4).

Hossain, S., Hasan, M. M., & Hossain, T. (2020). An Analytical Study of Influencing Factors on Consumers' Behaviors in Facebook Using ANN and RF. *International Conference on Intelligent Computing & Optimization*, 744–753.

Hsiao, R., & Ormerod, R. (1999). *The dynamics of knowledge transfer: a discovery-oriented framework*. Warwick Business School Research Paper, No.307.

Hsu, L. C., & Wang, C. H. (2012). Clarifying the effect of intellectual capital on performance: The mediating role of dynamic capability. *British Journal of Management, 23*(2), 179–205. doi:10.1111/j.1467-8551.2010.00718.x

Huang, T. C. (2001). The effects of linkage between business and human resource management strategies. *Personnel Review, 30*(2), 132–151. doi:10.1108/00483480110380316

Huber, G. (2001). Transfer of knowledge in knowledge management systems: Unexplored issues and suggested studies. *European Journal of Information Systems, 10*, 72–79. https://doi.org/10.1057/palgrave.ejis.3000399

Huisman, J., Weert, E., & Bartelse, J. (2002). Academic careers from a European perspective: The declining desirability of the faculty position. *The Journal of Higher Education, 73*(1), 141–160. doi:10.1080/00221546.2002.11777134

Hu, L. T., & Bentler, P. M. (1999). Cutoff criteria for fit indexes in covariance structure analysis: Conventional criteria versus new alternatives. *Structural Equation Modeling, 6*(1), 1–55. doi:10.1080/10705519909540118

Hu, Y. (1995). The international transferability of the firm's advantage. *California Management Review, 37*, 73–88. https://doi.org/10.2307%2F41165811

Iles, P., Preece, D., & Chuai, X. (2010). Talent management as a management fashion in HRD: Towards a research agenda. *Human Resource Development International, 13*(2), 125–145. doi:10.1080/13678861003703666

Inkpen, A. C. (1998). Learning and knowledge acquisition through international strategic alliances. *Academy of Management Executives, 12*(4), 69-80. https://www.jstor.org/stable/4165495

Inyang, B. J. (2010). Strategic human resource management (SHRM): A paradigm shift for achieving sustained competitive advantage in an organization. *International Bulletin of Business Administration, 7*(23), 215–243.

Ipe, M. (2003). Knowledge sharing in organizations: A conceptual framework. *Human Resource Development Review, 2*(4), 337–359. https://doi.org/10.1177%2F1534484303257985

Iverson, J. M., & Goldin-Meadow, S. (1998, November 19). Why people gesture when they speak. *Nature, 396*(6708), 228. doi:10.1038/24300 PMID:9834030

Jackson, S. E., Schuler, R. S., & Carlos Rivero, J. (1989). Organizational characteristics as to predictors of personnel practices. *Personnel Psychology, 42*(4), 727–786. doi:10.1111/j.1744-6570.1989.tb00674.x

Jackson, S. E., Schuler, R. S., & Jiang, K. (2014). An aspirational framework for strategic human resource management. *The Academy of Management Annals, 8*(1), 1–56. doi:10.5465/19416520.2014.872335

Jacobs, G. M., & Farrell, T. (2001). Paradigm shift: Understanding and implementing change in second language education. *TESL-EJ, 5*(1). https://files.eric.ed.gov/fulltext/ED574144.pdf

Jagamogan, R. S., Ismail, S. A., Hafizah, N., & Abas, H. H. (2021, October). A Review: Penetration Testing Approaches on Content Management System (CMS). In *2021 7th International Conference on Research and Innovation in Information Systems (ICRIIS)* (pp. 1-6). IEEE.

Jashapara, A. (2004). *Knowledge Management-An Integrated Approach*. Pearson Education Limited.

Jasimuddin, S. M. (2007). Exploring knowledge transfer mechanisms: The case of a UK-based group within a high-tech global corporation. *International Journal of Information Management*, *27*, 294–300. https://doi.org/10.1016/j.ijinfomgt.2007.03.003

Jasimuddin, S. M., Connell, N. A. D., & Klein, J. H. (2005). The paradox of using tacit and explicit knowledge: Strategies to face dilemmas. *Management Decision*, *43*(1), 102–112. https://doi.org/10.1108/00251740510572515

Jasimuddin, S. M., Connell, N. A. D., & Klein, J. H. (2006). Understanding organizational memory. In D. G. Schwartz (Ed.), *Encyclopedia of Knowledge Management* (pp. 870–875). Idea Group Reference.

Jofre, S. (2011). *Strategic management: The theory and practice of strategy in (business) organizations.* DTU Management: Kgs. Lyngby. https://orbit.dtu.dk/en/publications/strategic-management-the-theory-and-practice-of-strategy-in-busin

Johnson, M. W., Christensen, C. M., & Kagermann, H. (2008). Reinventing Your Business Model: One secret to maintaining a thriving business is recognizing when it needs a fundamental change. *Harvard Business Review*. https://hbr.org/2008/12/reinventing-your-business-model

Joiner, B. (2017). Bringing “Leadership Agility” to Agile. *Cutter Business Technology Journal*, *30*(8), 1–10.

Joiner, B. (2019). Leadership Agility for Organizational Agility. *Journal of Creating Value*, *5*(2), 139–149. doi:10.1177/2394964319868321

Joiner, B., & Josephs, S. (2007a, February). Developing Agile Leaders. *Industrial and Commercial Training*, *39*(1), 35–42. doi:10.1108/00197850710721381

Joiner, B., & Josephs, S. (2007b). *Leadership Agility Five Levels of Mastery for Anticipating and Initiating Change*. Jossey-Bass.

Jorch, U. (2019). *Develop these 6 skills for impactful leadership.* Posted in WorkAlchemy on November 12, 2019. Retrieved on February 2, 2021, from https://www.workalchemy.com/impactful-leadership-skills

Jovanovic, N., Kirda, E., & Kruegel, C. (2006). Preventing cross site request forgery attacks. In 2006 Securecomm and Workshops. Academic Press.

Joveda, N., Khan, M., Pathak, A., & Chattogram, B. (2019). Cyber laundering: a threat to banking industries in bangladesh: in quest of effective legal framework and cyber security of financial information. *International Journal of Economics and Finance*, *11*(10), 54–65.

Joy, R. J., & Howes, P. (2001). Globalization and HR. In M. Effron, R. Gandossy, & M. Goldsmith (Eds.), *Human Resources in the 21st Century* (pp. 169–175). John Wiley & Sons Inc.

Juneja, P. (n.d.). *Talent Management for the New Generation.* Retrieved on February 3, 2022, from https://www.managementstudyguide.com/talent-management-new-generation.htm

Kabwe, C., & Okorie, C. (2019). The efficacy of talent management in international business: The case of European multinationals. *Thunderbird International Business Review, 61*(6), 857–872. doi:10.1002/tie.22090

Kadir, A. R. A., Aminallah, A., Ibrahim, A., Sulaiman, J., Yusoff, M. F. M., Idris, M. M., Bahar, M. R., Hasanordin, R., Rahim, S. S. A., & Abd Malek, Z. (2018). The influence of intellectual capital and corporate entrepreneurship towards small and medium enterprises' (SMEs) sustainable competitive advantage: building a conceptual framework. *Proceedings of the 2nd Advances in Business Research International Conference.* 10.1007/978-981-10-6053-3_7

Kail, E. G. (2010a, November 3). *Leading in a VUCA Environment: V Is for Volatility.* Harvard Business Review: https://hbr.org/2010/11/leading-in-a-vuca-environment

Kail, E. G. (2010b, November 10). *Leading in a VUCA Environment: U is for Uncertainty.* Harvard Business Review: https://hbr.org/2010/11/leading-in-a-vuca-environment-1

Kail, E. G. (2010c, December 3). *Leading Effectively in a VUCA Environment: C is for Complexity.* Harvard Business Review: https://hbr.org/2010/12/leading-effectively-in-a-vuca

Kail, E. G. (2011, January 6). *Leading Effectively in a VUCA Environment: A is for Ambiguity.* Harvard Business Review: https://hbr.org/2011/01/leading-effectively-in-a-vuca-1

Kalling, T. (2003). Organization-internal transfer of knowledge and the role of motivation: A qualitative case study. *Knowledge and Process Management, 10*(2), 115–126. https://doi.org/10.1002/kpm.170

Kantabutra, S. (2006, Spring). Relating Vision-based Leadership to Sustainable Business Performance: A Thai Perspective. *Leadership Review*, (6), 37–53.

Kaspersky. (2017, April). *Lazarus Under The Hood.* https://media.kasperskycontenthub.com/wp-content/uploads/sites/43/2018/03/07180244/ Lazarus_Under_The_Hood_PDF_final.pdf

Kazemian, S., & Grant, S. B. (2022). The impact of the COVID-19 pandemic on knowledge sharing in UK higher education. *VINE Journal of Information and Knowledge Management Systems.* doi:10.1108/VJIKMS-06-2021-0096

Kazlauskaite, R., & Buciuniene, I. (2008). The role of human resources and their management in the establishment of sustainable competitive advantage. *Inžinerinė ekonomika*, (5), 78–84.

Kenton, W. (2020). Human capital. *Investopedia.* https://www.investopedia.com/terms/h/humancapital.asp

Khan, M. A. (2010). Effects of human resource management practices on organizational performance. An empirical study of the oil and gas industry in Pakistan. *European Journal of Economics, Financial and Administrative Sciences*, *24*(158), 1450–2275.

Khan, S. Z., Yang, Q., & Waheed, A. (2019). Investment in intangible resources and capabilities spurs sustainable competitive advantage and firm performance. *Corporate Social Responsibility and Environmental Management*, *26*(2), 285–295. doi:10.1002/csr.1678

Khavul, S., Benson, G. S., & Datta, D. K. (2010). Is internationalization associated with investments in HRM? A study of entrepreneurial firms in emerging markets. *Human Resource Management*, *49*(4), 693–713. doi:10.1002/hrm.20367

Khoreva, V., Vaiman, V., & VanZalk, M. (2017). Talent management practice effectiveness: investigating employee perspective. *Employee Relations, 39*(1), 19-33. https://www.emerald.com/insight/content/doi/10.1108/ER-01-2016-0005/full/html

Knudsen, E. S., Lien, L. B., Timmermans, B., Belik, I., & Pandey, S. (2021). Stability in turbulent times? The effect of digitalization on the sustainability of competitive advantage. *Journal of Business Research*, *128*, 360–369. doi:10.1016/j.jbusres.2021.02.008

Kombo, K. D., & Tromp, L. A. D. (2006). *Proposal and Thesis Writing: An Introduction.* Paulines Publications.

Kontoghiorghes, C. (2016). Linking high-performance organizational culture and talent management: Satisfaction/motivation and organizational commitment as mediators. *International Journal of Human Resource Management*, *27*(16), 1833–1853. doi:10.1080/09585192.2015.1075572

Kortjan, N., & Solms, R. (2012). Cyber security education in developing countries: A South African perspective. In *International conference on e-Infrastructure and e-Services for developing countries* (pp. 289–297). Academic Press.

Koufteros, X. A., Vonderembse, M. A., & Doll, W. J. (2002). Examining the competitive capabilities of manufacturing firms. *Structural Equation Modeling*, *9*(2), 256–282. doi:10.1207/S15328007SEM0902_6

Krishnan, K. (2019). *3 Vital Skills for the Age of Disruption.* World Economic Forum. https://www.weforum.org/agenda/2019/09/3-vital-skills-for-the-age-of-disruption/

Kubler, J., & DeLuca, C. (2006). *Trends in Academic Recruitment and Retention: A Commonwealth Perspective*. The Association of Commonwealth Universities.

Kuhn, T. S. (1962). *The Structure of Scientific Revolutions*. University of Chicago Press.

Lado, A. A., & Wilson, M.C. (1994). Human Resource Systems and Sustained Competitive Advantage: A Competency-Based Perspective. *The Academy of Management Review, 19*(4), 699-727. doi:10.5465/amr.1994.9412190216

Lam, W. (2005). Successful knowledge management requires a knowledge culture: A case study. *Knowledge Management Research and Practice*, *3*, 206–217. https://doi.org/10.1057/palgrave.kmrp.8500068

Langley, M. A. (2017). *Achieving Greater Agility: The People and Process Drivers that Accelerate Results*. Project Management Institute.

Latukha, M. (2015). Talent management in Russian companies: Domestic challenges and international experience. *The International Journal of Human Resource Management, 26*(8), 1051–1075. doi:.2014.922598 doi:10.1080/09585192

Latukha, M. O. (2018). Can talent management practices be considered as a basis for sustainable competitive advantages in emerging-market firms? Evidence from Russia. *Thunderbird International Business Review*, *60*(1), 69–87. doi:10.1002/tie.21778

Lawler, E. E. (2008). *Make human capital a source of competitive advantage.* Marshall School of Business Working Paper No. MOR, 16–09. doi:10.1016/j.orgdyn.2008.10.007

Leach, B. (2018). Sustainable competitive advantage and demographic change. *Canadian Manager*, *43*(2), 19–21.

Lee, J. D., Regan, M. A., & Young, K. L. (2009). What drives distraction? Distraction as a breakdown of multilevel control. In M.A. Regan, J.D. Lee, & K. Young (Eds.), Driver distraction: Theory, effects, and mitigation (1st ed., pp. 41-56). CRC Press, Taylor and Francis Group.

Lee, S. (2015). A concept analysis of 'meaning in work' and its implications for nursing. *Journal of Advanced Nursing*, *71*(10), 2258–2267. doi:10.1111/jan.12695 PMID:26010379

Lemerle, M., Rudisuli, R., & Steinert, M. (2019). *Talent in wholesale banking: Building a sustainable competitive advantage*. McKinsey Insights. https://www.mckinsey.com/industries/financial-services/our-insights/talent-in-wholesale-banking-building-a-sustainable-competitive-advantage

Lestrange, G. (2019). *The evolution of Talent Management*. HRD Connect. https://www.hrdconnect.com/2019/10/17/the-evolution-of-talent-management/

Lewin, D. (2001). Human resources management and performance: Lessons from the 21st Century. In M. Effron, R. Gandossy, & M. Goldsmith (Eds.), *Human Resources in the 21st Century* (pp. 91–98). John Wiley & Sons Inc.

Lewis, R. E., & Heckman, R. J. (2006). Talent management: A critical review. *Human Resource Management Review, 16*(2), 139–154. doi:10.1016/j.hrmr.2006.03.001

Lewis, R. E., & Heckman, R. J. (2006). Talent Management: A critical review. *Human Resource Management Review*, *16*, 139–154. https://doi.org/10.1016/j.hrmr.2006.03.001

Liao, Y. (2005). Business strategy and performance: The role of human resource management control. *Personnel Review*, *34*(3), 294–309. doi:10.1108/00483480510591444

Lipman-Blumen, J. (2020). *Connective Leadership: Managing in a Changing World.* Oxford University Press.

Lisbeth, C. (2019). HR disruption- Time already to reinvent talent management. *BRQ Business Research Quarterly, 22*(3), 207–215. doi:10.1016/j.brq.2019.04.002

Liu, S. (2019, September 13). *Open-Source Services Market Revenue Worldwide 2017-2022.* Statista. Retrieved October 13, 2021, from https://www.statista.com/statistics/270805/projected-revenue-of-open-source-software-since-2008/

Lojeski, K. S., Reilly, R., & Dominick, P. (2007, January 3-6). *Multitasking and innovation in virtual teams* [Conference session]. 2007 40th Annual Hawaii International Conference on System Sciences, Waikoloa, HI, United States.

Lorange, P. (2006). 'A performance based, minimalist human resource management approach in business schools. *Human Resource Management, 45*(4), 649–658. doi:10.1002/hrm.20136

Loscos, F. (2022). *The 15 Big Challenges Facing Talent Management In 2022.* https://www.forbes.com/sites/esade/2022/01/10/the-15-big-challenges-facing-talent-management-in-2022/?sh=1b382c5d5d60

Lubbe, V., & Larsen, V. (2008). *Quick-Scan Jong Talent in De Wetenschap. Probleemanalyse Ten Behoeve Van Het Programma 'Loopbaanperspectief Jong Talent.* VSNU.

Lyons, K. (2021). *Facebook just revealed its new name: Meta.* The Verge.

Mack, O., & Khare, A. (2016). Perspectives on a VUCA World. In Managing in a VUCA World (pp. 3-19). Springer.

Madhani, P. M. (2010). *Resource based view of competitive advantage: an overview. ICFAI business school.* Icfai University Press. http://www.researchgate.net

Mahapatra & Dash. (2022). Talent development in a changing world of work. *IIMB Management Review.*

Mahmood, B. S. (2021, September 13). Bangladesh's New Data Protection Act: Brittle shield or blunt sword? *The Daily Star.* Retrieved October 13, 2021, from https://www.thedailystar.net/views/in-focus/news/bangladeshs-new-data-protection-act-brittle-shield-or-blunt-sword-2174371

Makarius, E. E., & Larson, B. Z. (2017). Changing the perspective of virtual work: Building virtual intelligence at the individual level. *The Academy of Management Perspectives, 31*(2), 159–178. doi:10.5465/amp.2014.0120

Manashree, C. (2021). *Evolution of human resource management (HRM).* https://www.economicsdiscussion.net/human-resource-management/evolution-of-human-resource-management-hrm/31460

Marbun, D. S., Juliandi, A., & Effendi, S. (2020). The effect of social media culture and knowledge transfer on performance. *BIRCI Journal, 3*(3), 2513-2530. doi:10.33258/birci.v3i3.1234

Margherita, A., Elia, G., & Klein, M. (2021). Managing the COVID-19 emergency: A coordination framework to enhance response practices and actions. *Technological Forecasting and Social Change*, *166*, 120656. doi:10.1016/j.techfore.2021.120656 PMID:33551496

Markson, L., & Paterson, K. B. (2009). Effects of gaze-aversion on visual-spatial imagination. *British Journal of Psychology*, *100*(3), 553–563. doi:10.1348/000712608X371762 PMID:19021925

Marquardt, M. J. (1996). *Building the Learning Organization: A Systems Approach to Quantum Improvement and Global Success*. McGraw-Hill.

Maruf, A., Islam, M., & Ahamed, B. (2010). Emerging Cyber Threats in Bangladesh: In quest of effective legal remedies. *Northern University Journal of Law*, *1*, 112–124.

Masters in Information Systems Security (MISS). Bangladesh University of Professionals (BUP). (n.d.). Retrieved October 13, 2021, from https://bup.edu.bd/programs/22/details-academics?department_id=17%7D%2C+journal

Mattila, J. (2016). *The blockchain phenomenon*. Berkeley Roundtable of the International Economy.

Mattone, J., & Xavier, L. (2012). *Talent Leadership: A Proven Method for Identifying and Developing High-Potential Employees*. AMACOM.

Mayhew, R. (2018). *Employee turnover definitions & calculations*. Retrieved from https://smallbusiness.chron.com/employee-turnover-Definitions-calculations-11611.h

McCann, J., Selsky, J., & Lee, J. (2009). Building Agility, Resilience and Performance in Turbulent Environments. *People & Strategy*, *32*(3), 45–51.

McLean and Company HR Trends Report. (2021). https://hr.mcleanco.com/

Medinilla, A. (2012). *Agile Management: Leadership in an Agile Environment*. Springer Science & Business Media. doi:10.1007/978-3-642-28909-5

Mellahi, K., & Collings, D.G. (2010). The barriers to effective global talent management: The example of corporate élites in MNEs. *Journal of World Business*, *45*(2), 143 149. doi:10.1016/j.jwb.2009.09.018

Merchant, C. (1992). *Radical ecology: The search for a livable world*. Routledge.

Metcalf, H., Rolfe, H., Stevens, P., & Weale, M. (2005). *Recruitment and Retention of Academic Staff in Higher Education*. National Institute of Economic and Social Research.

Meyer, P. (2016). *Agility Shift: Creating Agile and Effective Leaders, Teams, and Organizations*. Routledge. doi:10.4324/9781315230559

Meyers, M. C., VanWoerkom, M., & Dries, N. (2013). Talent—innate or acquired? Theoretical considerations and their implications for talent management. *Human Resource Management Review*, *23*(4), 305–321. https://www.sciencedirect.com/science/article/abs/pii/S1053482213000314

Michaels, E., Handfield-Jones, H., & Axelrod, B. (2001). *The War for Talent*. Harvard Business Press.

Minbaeva, D. B. (2018). Building credible human capital analytics for organizational competitive advantage. *Human Resource Management*, *57*(3), 701–713. doi:10.1002/hrm.21848

Mintzberg, H., Ahlstrand, B., & Lampel, J. (1998). *Strategy Safari: A Guided Tour through the Wilds of Strategic Management*. The Free Press.

Mngqibisa, S. (2017). Theoretical Framework of the Talent Management. *Talent Management*. Retrieved on January 30, 2022, from https://www.academia.edu/38102731/Chapter_1_THEORETICAL_FRAMEWORK_OF_TALENT_MANAGEMENT

Moczydłowska, J. (2012). Talent Management: Theory and Practice of Management - The Polish Experience. *International Journal of Bossiness Management and Economic Research*, *3*(1), 432-438.

Mohaimein, M. A. (2013). Talent Management: Three new Perceptions intended for managing and retaining Talent in Bangladesh. *Asian Business Review*, *3*(5).

Mohammad, A. A., Gururajan, R., & Hafeez-Baig. (2017). Knowledge Management in Business Environment. *Proceeding WI '17*.

Mohrman, S. A. (2007). Designing organizations for growth: The human resource contribution. *Human Resource Planning*, *30*(4), 1–11.

Momtazian, M. (2021). What is talent management, and why is it important? *EXPERT360*. https://expert360.com/articles/talent-management-important

Moniruzzaman, M., Chowdhury, F., & Ferdous, M. (2019). Measuring vulnerabilities of Bangladeshi websites. In *2019 International Conference on Electrical, Computer and Communication Engineering (ECCE)* (pp. 1–7). Academic Press.

Moore, D. A., Kurtzberg, T. R., Thompson, L. L., & Morris, M. W. (1999). Long and short routes to success in electronically mediated negotiations: Group affiliations and good vibrations. *Organizational Behavior and Human Decision Processes*, *77*(1), 22–43. doi:10.1006/obhd.1998.2814 PMID:9924140

Morris, M., Nadler, J., Kurtzberg, T., & Thompson, L. (2002). Schmooze or lose: Social friction and lubrication in e-mail negotiations. *Group Dynamics*, *6*(1), 89–100. doi:10.1037/1089-2699.6.1.89

Moşteanu, N. R. (2020). Challenges for Organizational Structure and design as a result of digitalization and cybersecurity. *The Business & Management Review*, *11*(1), 278–286.

Moton, L., & Ashton, C. (2005). Managing talent for competitive advantage. *Strategic HR Review*, *5*(4), 28–31. https://doi.org/10.1108/14754390580000819

Mugayar-BaldocchM.SchaningerB.SharmaK. (2021). https://www.mckinsey.com/business-functions/people-and-organizational-performance/our-insights/the-organization-blog/the-future-of-work-the-now-the-how-and-the-why

Mu, J., Peng, G., & Love, E. (2008). Interfirm networks, social capital, and knowledge flow. *Journal of Knowledge Management, 12*(4), 86–100. https://dx.doi.org/10.1108/13673270810884273

Muller, L. (2015). *Cyber security capacity building in developing countries: Challenges and opportunities*. Norwegian Institute of International Affairs.

Mysirlaki, S., & Paraskeva, E. (2020). Emotional intelligence and transformational leadership in virtual teams: Lessons from MMOGs. *Leadership and Organization Development Journal, 41*(4), 551–566. doi:10.1108/LODJ-01-2019-0035

Nahapiet, J., & Ghosal, S. (1998). Social capital, intellectual capital, and the organizational advantage. *Academy of Management Review, 23*(2), 242–266. https://doi.org/10.2307/259373

Nair, P. J. (2012). Is talent management accentuated by competency mapping? With special reference to educational sector. *International Journal of Social Science & Interdisciplinary Research, 1*(11), 132-147. www.indianresearchjournals.com/pdf/ijssir/2012/november/14.pdf

Nankervis, A., Chatterjee, S., & Coffey, J. (2007). *Perspectives of human resource management in the Asia Pacific*. Pearson Education Australia.

Nerur, S., Mahapatra, R., & Mangalaraj, G. (2005, May). Challenges of Migrating to Agile Methodologies. *Communications of the ACM, 48*(5), 72–78. doi:10.1145/1060710.1060712

Nilsson, S., & Ellström, P. (2012). Employability and talent management: challenges for HRD practices. *European Journal of Training and Development, 36*(1), 26–45. doi:10.1108/03090591211192610

Nonaka, I. (1994). A dynamic theory of organizational knowledge creation. *Organization Science, 5*(1), 14–37.

Nonaka, I., & Konno, N. (1998). The concept of "Ba": Building a foundation for knowledge creation. *California Management Review, 40*(3), 40–45. https://doi.org/10.2307%2F41165942

Nonaka, I., & Takeuchi, H. (1995). *The Knowledge Creating Company*. Oxford University Press.

Novick, D. G., Hansen, B., & Ward, K. (1996, October 3-6). *Coordinating turn-taking with gaze* [Conference session]. Fourth International Conference on Spoken Language Processing, ICSLOP, Philadelphia, PA, United States.

Nunnally, J. (1978). *Psychometric theory*. McGraw-Hill.

Nurudeen, Z. B., & Nasiru, A. A. (2012). Actual and perceived consequences to improper online privacy management: A pragmatic approach. *International Journal of e-Education, e-Business, e- Management Learning, 2*(1).

Oben, B., & Brone, G. (2015). What you see if what you do: On the relationship between gaze and gesture in multimodal alignment. *Language and Cognition*, *7*(4), 546–562. doi:10.1017/langcog.2015.22

Ogbu Edeh, F., & Mlanga, S. (2019). Talent management and workers' commitment to oil & gas firms in Nigeria. *Journal of Management*, *2*(3), 1–15.

Osterwalder, A. (2013). *A Better Way to Think About Your Business Model.* Posted in Harvard Business Review on May 06, 2013. Retrieved on February 7, 2022, from https://hbr.org/2013/05/a-better-way-to-think-about-yo

Osterwalder, A., & Pigneur, Y. (2010). *Business Model Generation: A Handbook for Visionaries, Game Changers, and Challengers* (1st ed.). John Wiley & Sons.

Palanica, A., & Fossat, Y. (2022). Effects of nature virtual background on creativity during videoconferencing. *Thinking Skills and Creativity*, *43*, 100976. doi:10.1016/j.tsc.2021.100976

Pan, S. L., & Scarbrough, H. (1998). A Socio-technical view of knowledge-sharing at Buckman Laboratories. *Journal of Knowledge Management*, *2*(1), 55–66. https://doi.org/10.1108/EUM0000000004607

Parker, D. W., Holesgrove, M., & Pathak, R. (2015). Improving Productivity with Self-Organised Teams and Agile Leadership. *International Journal of Productivity and Performance Management*, *64*(1), 112–128. doi:10.1108/IJPPM-10-2013-0178

Payal, J. (2019). Talent management: Opportunities & challenges for industry 4.0. *Journal of Management Development*, *38*, 1–15.

Pellegrini, R. J. (1971). Some effects of seating position on social perception. *Psychological Reports*, *28*(3), 887–893. doi:10.2466/pr0.1971.28.3.887

Penetration Testing. (2018). *Office of Chief Information Officer, U.S. Department of the Interior.* Retrieved December 18, 2018. https://www.doi.gov/ocio/customers/penetration-testing

Pentland, A. (2008). *Honest signals: How they shape our world.* MIT Press. doi:10.7551/mitpress/8022.001.0001

Peters, T. J., & Waterman, R. (1982). *In search of excellence.* Harper and Row.

Pfeffer, J. (1995). Producing sustainable competitive advantage through the effective management of people. *Academy of Management Executive, 9*(1), 55–69. 10.5465/AME.2005.19417910

Pitts, V. E., Wright, N. A., & Harkabus, L. C. (2012). Communication in virtual teams. The role of emotional intelligence. *Journal of Organizational Psychology*, *12*(3/4), 21–34.

Podsakoff, P. M., & Organ, D. W. (1986). Self-report in organizational research: Problems and Prospects. *Journal of Management*, *12*(4), 545–560. doi:10.1177/014920638601200408

Polanyi, M. (1962). *Personal Knowledge: Towards a Post-Critical Philosophy.* University of Chicago Press.

Polanyi, M. (1966). *The Tacit Dimension*. Routledge.

Popper, K. (1963). *Conjectures and refutations*. Routledge & Kegan Paul.

Popper, K. (1968). *The Logic of Scientific Discovery*. Harper & Row.

Popper, K. (1972). *Objective knowledge: An evolutionary approach*. Oxford University Press.

Porter, M. E. (1980). *Competitive strategy*. New York Free Press.

Porter, M. E. (1990). The Competitive Advantage of Nations. (Cover story). *Harvard Business Review*, *68*(2), 73–93.

Prabhu, T. N. (2019, August 10). *List of countries by number of internet users*. Kaggle. Retrieved April 14, 2022, from https://www.kaggle.com/datasets/tanuprabhu/list-of-countries-by-number-of-internet-users

Prahalad, C. K., & Hamel, G. (1990). The core competition of the corporation. *Harvard Business Review*, *68*(3), 79–91.

Prange, C., & Heracleous, L. (2018). *Agility. X: How Organizations Thrive in Unpredictable Times*. Cambridge University Press. doi:10.1017/9781108545884

Prasongko, A., & Adianto, T. (2019). The Role of the Agile Leadership Model as a Competitive Advantage for the Future Leader in the Era of Globalization and Industrial Revolution 4.0. *Jurnal Pertahanan*, *5*(3), 126–133. doi:10.33172/jp.v5i3.596

Protalinski, E. 2021. *3 million bank accounts hacked in Iran*. ZDNet. Available at: https://www.zdnet.com/article/3-million-bank-accounts-hacked-in-iran/

Purwanto, E., & Purwanto, A. D. B. (2020). An investigative study on sustainable competitive advantage of manufacture companies in Indonesia. *Business: Theory and Practice*, *21*(2), 633–642. doi:10.3846/btp.2020.12256

Quintanilla, K., & Mallard, J. (2008). Understanding the role of communication bravado: An important issue for trainers/educators. *Texas Speech Communication Journal*, *33*(1), 44–49.

Ragasa, M., & Ragas, T. (2021). Understanding Agile for Strategic Communicators: Foundations, Implementations, and Implications. *International Journal of Strategic Communication*, *15*(2), 80–92. doi:10.1080/1553118X.2021.1898147

Rahman, S. (2016, February). *Atm frauds rattle banks, customers*. https://www.thedailystar.net/business/atm-frauds-rattle-banks-customers-510868

RE100. (2020). *Growing renewable power: companies seizing leadership opportunities*. RE100 Annual Progress and Insights Report 2020, Released in December 2020 by RE100, a global initiative led by the Climate Group in partnership with CDP. Retrieved on February 5, 2022, from https://www.there100.org/growing-renewable-power-companies-seizing-leadership-opportunities

Ready, D. A., Hill, L. A., & Thomas, R. J. (2014). Building a Game-Changing Talent Strategy. *Harvard Business Review*, (January–February), 2014.

Real, A. D. (2022). *How to retain your top talent amid the Great Resignation.* Posted in TM on January 27, 2022. Retrieved on February 5, 2022, from https://www.talentmgt.com/articles/2022/01/27/how-to-retain-your-top-talent-amid-the-great-resignation/

Reynolds, C. J., Knighten, K. R., & Conway, P. (2019). Mirror, mirror, on the wall, who is deontological? Completing moral dilemmas in front of mirrors increases deontological but not utilitarian response tendencies. *Cognition*, *192*, 103993. doi:10.1016/j.cognition.2019.06.005 PMID:31229738

Rice, G. (2006). Individual values, organizational context, and self-perceptions of employee creativity: Evidence from Egyptian organizations. *Journal of Business Research*, *59*(2), 233–241. doi:.jbusres.2005.08.001 doi:10.1016/j

Ringo, T., Schweyer, A., DeMarco, M., Jones, R., & Lesser, E. (2010). *Integrating talent management-turning talent management into a competitive advantage-an industry view*. IBM Global Business Services.

Rogers, M. (2014). Job resources, employees' creativity, and firm performance of commercial Banks in Uganda. *International Journal of Economics, Commerce, and Management*, *11*(9), 1–14.

Rothwell, W. J. (2008). Next-generation talent management. *HRM Review*, *8*(10), 10–16.

Rotich, K. J. (2015). History, evolution, and development of human resources management: A contemporary perspective. *Global Journal of Human Resource Management*, *3*(3), 58–73.

Rubin, Z. (1970). Measurement of romantic love. *Journal of Personality and Social Psychology*, *16*(2), 265–273. doi:10.1037/h0029841 PMID:5479131

Rumman, M. R. H., Sarker, A., Islam, M. M., Hoque, M. I., Kuri, R., Bhuyan, M. B. A., & Bhuiyan, N. A.-T. (2020). ATM Shield: Analysis of Multitier Security Issues of ATM in the Context of Bangladesh. *Journal of Experimental Sciences, 11*.

Rumman, M. R. H., Sarker, A., Islam, M. M., Hoque, M. I., Kuri, R., Bhuyan, M. B. A., & Bhuiyan, N. A.-T. (2015). Empirical Study of the Use of Automated Teller Machine (ATM) among Bank Customers in Dhaka City, Bangladesh. *European Journal of Business and Management*, *07*(1).

Ryder, B. (2021). *Solving Talent Management Challenges Today And For The Future.* https://www.forbes.com/sites/ryder/2021/06/01/solving-talent-management-challenges-today-and-for-the-future/?sh=3d094956739f

Sadler, P. (2003). *Leadership. London and Sterling*. Kogan Page.

Saha, A. R., & Rahman, M. M. (2018). Automated Teller Machine Card Fraud of Financial Organisations in Bangladesh. *Journal of Computer Science Applications and Information Technology*, *12*(2).

Salovey, P., & Mayer, J. (1990). Emotional Intelligence. *Imagination, Cognition and Personality*, *9*(3), 185–211. doi:10.2190/DUGG-P24E-52WK-6CDG

Sambamurthy, V., Wei, K.-K., Lim, K., & Lee, D. (2007). IT-Enabled Organizational Agility and Firms ' Sustainable Competitive Advantage. ICIS 2007 Proceedings, 1-19.

Sandhawalia, B. S., & Dalcher, D. (2011). Developing knowledge management capabilities: A structured approach. *Journal of Knowledge Management*, *15*(2), 313–328. https://doi.org/10.1108/13673271111119718

Saravanan, K. (2017). Sources of Sustainable Competitive Advantage: A Study & Industry Outlook. *St. Theresa. Journal of the Humanities and Social Sciences*, *3*(1).

Sawalha, L. (2021). Measuring Human Capital: Why and How to Measure it. *Atman Co*. https://atmanco.com/resources/blog/measuring-human-capital/

Sayed, E. M., & Mohamed, A. H. H. (2013). Gender differences in divergent thinking: Use of the test of creative thinking-drawing production on an Egyptian sample. *Creativity Research Journal*, *25*(2), 222–227. doi:10.1080/10400419.2013.783760

Scarbrough, H., Robertson, M., & Swan, J. (2005). Professional media and management fashion: The case of knowledge management. *Scandinavian Journal of Management*, *2*(21), 197–208. https://doi.org/10.1016/j.scaman.2005.02.011

Schiemann, W.A. (2006). People Equity: A New Paradigm for Measuring and Managing Human Capital. *Human Resource Planning, 29*(1), 34-44.

Schiemann, W. A., Seibert, J. H., & Blankenship, M. H. (2018). Putting human capital analytics to work: Predicting and driving business success. *Human Resource Management*, *57*(3), 795–807. doi:10.1002/hrm.21843

Schroeder, J., Risen, J., Gino, F., & Norton, M. I. (2019). Handshaking promotes deal-making by signaling cooperative intent. *Journal of Personality and Social Psychology: Interpersonal Relations and Group Processes*, *116*(5), 743–768. doi:10.1037/pspi0000157 PMID:30550327

Schuler, R. S., & Jackson, S. E. (1989). Determinants of human resource management priorities and implications for industrial relations. *Journal of Management*, *15*(1), 89–99. doi:10.1177/014920638901500108

Schwartz, E. I. (2019). *Corporate Longevity Update: Creative Destruction Rides High*. Onnosight.

Scott, S., & Palincsar, A. (2013). *Sociocultural theory*. http://dr-hatfield.com/theorists/resources/sociocultural_theory.pdf

Scullion, H., Collings, D.G., & Caligiuri, P. (2010). Global talent management. *Journal of World Business, 45*(2), 105-108. doi:10.1016/j.jwb.2009.09.011

Shahid, S., Krahmer, E., Neerincx, M. A., & Swerts, M. (2013). Positive affective interactions: The role of repeated exposure and presence. *IEEE Transactions on Affective Computing, PP, 4*(99), 1–13. doi:10.1109/T-AFFC.2012.39

Shahid, S., Krahmer, E., & Swerts, M. (2012). Video-mediated and co-present gameplay: Effects of mutual gaze on game experience, expressiveness and perceived social presence. *Interacting with Computers, 24*(4), 292–305. doi:10.1016/j.intcom.2012.04.006

Shah, S., & Mehtre, B. M. (2015). An overview of vulnerability assessment and penetration testing techniques. *Journal of Computer Virology and Hacking Techniques, 11*(1), 27–49.

Shaw, L. (2016). *The meanings of new money: Social constructions of value in the rise of digital currencies*. University of Washington.

Shiomi, M., Nakata, A., Kanbara, M., & Hagita, N. (2017, August 28 – September 1). *A hug from a robot encourages prosocial behavior* [Paper presentation]. *26th IEEE International Symposium on Robot and Human Interactive Communication*, Lisbon, Portugal.

Short, J., Williams, E., & Christie, B. (1976). *The social psychology of telecommunications*. John Wiley & Sons.

Shravan, K., Neha, B., & Pawan, B. (2014). Penetration testing: A Review. *Compusoft, 3*(4), 752.

Shukla, R. (2008). *Talent Management: Process of Developing and Integrating Skilled Workers*. Global India Publications.

Siddique, N. A. (2019). *Framework for the mobilization of cyber security and risk mitigation of financial organizations in Bangladesh: A case study*. Academic Press.

Sigalas, C., Economou, V. P., & Georgopoulos, N. B. (2013). Developing a measure of competitive advantage. *Journal of Strategy and Management, 6*(4), 320–334. doi:10.1108/JSMA-03-2013-0015

Sikora, D. M., Thompson, K. W., Russell, Z. A., & Ferris, G. R. (2016). Reimagining overqualified human resources to promote organizational effectiveness and competitive advantage. *Journal of Organizational Effectiveness: People and Performance, 3*(1), 23–42. doi:10.1108/JOEPP-03-2015-0012

Silvia, P. J., & Duval, T. S. (2001). Objective self-awareness theory: Recent progress and enduring problems. *Personality and Social Psychology Review, 5*(3), 230–241. doi:10.1207/S15327957PSPR0503_4

Simmel, G. (1969). Soziologie der Geselligkeit. In Deutscher Soziologentag" Wege und Ziele der Soziologie" (pp. 1-16). Sauer u. Auvermann.

Simon, A., & Bartle, C. (2012). Resources, Capabilities, and Business Success. In Service Science Research, Strategy and Innovation: Dynamic Knowledge Management Methods (pp. 304-324). IGI Global. doi:10.4018/978-1-4666-0077-5.ch018

Singh, S. K. (2008). Role of leadership in knowledge management. *Journal of Knowledge Management, 12*(4), 1367–3270. https://doi.org/10.1108/13673270810884219

Sinha, R. (2014). *What is strategic human resource management?* https://Ezine Articles.com/expert

Skuza, A., Scullion, H., & McDonnel, A. (2013). An analysis of the talent management challenges in a post-communist country: The case of Poland. *International Journal of Human Resource Management, 24*(3), 453–470. doi:10.1080/09585192.2012.694111

Smilansky, J. (2006). *Developing Executive Talent: Best Practices from Global Leaders*. John Wiley & Sons Ltd. https://onlinelibrary.wiley.com/doi/pdf/10.1002/9781119202370.fmatter

Smith, R. G. (2004). Impediments to the successful investigation of transnational high-tech crime. *Trends and Issues in Crime and Criminal Justice*, 285.

Sousa, M. J., & Rocha, Á. (2019). Strategic knowledge management in the digital age: JBR special issue editorial. *Journal of Business Research, 94,* 223–226. 10.1016/j.jbusres.2018.10.016

Sparrow, P., Scullion, H., & Tarique, I. (2014). Multiple lenses on talent management: Definitions and contours of the field. In P. Sparrow, H. Scullion, & I. Tarique (Eds.), *Strategic Talent Management*. Cambridge University Press. doi:10.1017/CBO9781139424585.004

Spender, J.C. (1996). Making knowledge the basis of a dynamic theory of the firm. *Strategic Management Journal, 17*(S2), 45–62. doi:10.1002/smj.4250171106

Spreitzer, G. M., Cohen, S. G., Gerald, E., & Ledford, J. (1999, September). Developing Effective Self-Managing Work Teams in Service Organizations. *Group & Organization Management, 24*(3), 340–366. doi:10.1177/1059601199243005

Srivastava, M., Franklin, A., & Martinette, L. (2013). Building a sustainable competitive advantage. *Journal of Technology Management & Innovation, 8*(2), 47–60. doi:10.4067/S0718-27242013000200004

Stahl, G. K., Björkman, I., Farndale, E., Morris, S. S., Paauwe, J., Stiles, P., Trevor, J., & Wright, P. M. (2007). *Global Talent Management: How Leading Multinationals Build and Sustain Their Talent Pipeline*. INSEAD Working Paper Series, INSEAD. file:///C:/Users/Teacher/Downloads/Globaltalentmanagement.pdf

Stenmark, D. (2000). Leveraging tacit Organizational knowledge. *Journal of Management Information Systems, 17*(3), 9–24. https://doi.org/10.1080/07421222.2000.11045655

Stogdill, R. M. (1950). Leadership, Membership and Organization. *Psychological Bulletin, 47*(1), 1–14. doi:10.1037/h0053857

Stoian, C. A., & Tohanean, D. (2019, November). BMI in the digital era: Competitive advantage through human capital analytics. In *ECMLG 2019 15th European Conference on Management, Leadership & Governance* (p. 366). Academic Conferences and Publishing Limited. 10.34190/MLG.19.075

Suler, J. (2004). The online disinhibition effect. *Cyberpsychology & Behavior*, *7*(3), 321–326. doi:10.1089/1094931041291295 PMID:15257832

Sullivan, J. (2005). *Clarifying the strategic role of HR*. https//www.drjohnsullivan.com

Sun, P. Y., & Scott, J. L. (2005). An investigation of barriers to knowledge transfer. *Journal of Knowledge Management*, *9*(2), 75–90. https://doi.org/10.1108/13673270510590236

Susanna, V. (2022). *Morning Brew*. Retrieved July 28, 2022, from https://www.morningbrew.com/series/the-years-ahead/stories/2022/01/05/happy-new-year-recruiting-and-retaining-employees-in-2022-won-t-get-any-%20easier?%2BUtm%2B_%2Bcampaign%2B=%2Bhrb%2B&%2Butm_medium=newsletter&utm_source=morning_brew&mid=8c47bac00786b49a5ebabb2258b3ae22%2B%5Baccessed%2Bon%2B15th%2BJan%2B2021%5D

Sutherland, E. (2020). The fourth industrial revolution--the case of South Africa. *Politikon, 47*(2).

Sveiby, K. E. (1996). Transfer of knowledge and information processing professions. *European Management Journal*, *14*(4), 379–388. https://doi.org/10.1016/0263-2373(96)00025-4

Swailes, S., & Blackburn, M. (2016). Employee reactions to talent pool membership. *Employee Relations, 38*(1), 112-128. doi:10.1108/ER-02-2015-0030

Szulanski, G. (1996). Exploring internal stickiness: Impediments to the transfer of best practice within the firm. *Strategic Management Journal, 17*, 27-43. doi:10.1002/smj.4250171105

Szulanski, G. (2000). The process of knowledge transfer: A diachronic analysis of stickiness. *Organizational Behavior and Human Decision Processes*, *82*(1), 9–27. https://doi.org/10.1006/obhd.2000.2884

Tajuddin, D., Ali, R., & Kamaruddin, B.H. (2015). Developing Talent Management Crisis Model for Quality Life of Bank Employees in Malaysia. *Procedia-Social and Behavioral Sciences, 201*, 80-84. doi:10.1016/j.sbspro.2015.08.133

Talaja, A. (2012). Testing VRIN framework: Resource value and rareness as sources of competitive advantage and above average performance. *Management*, *17*(2), 51–64.

Talukdar, M. R. I., Hasan, F., & Nahar, R. (2021). Necessity of blended learning Bangladesh's higher education institutions, *The Independent*, 1.

Talukdar, M. R. I., Hassan, F., & Nahar, R. (2021). Virtual, Blended, and Dual System Teaching-Learning: Fitness and Relevance for Universities. In *Proceedings, AICBM-2021*. FBA-AIUB.

Talukdar, M.R.I. (2020). Uncertain time calls for agile management and adaptation of contingency plan: Lessons from HEIs in Bangladesh. *AIUB Journal of Business and Economics*, *17*(2), 219-238.

Talukdar, M.R.I. (2021). The emergence of new strategic business models for HEIs: Evidence from Bangladesh. *Academy of Entrepreneurship Journal, 27*(S2), 1-16.

Talukdar, M. R. I. (2012). Mobile communications and fighting corruption. In V. Kumar & J. Sevensson (Eds.), *M4D 2012. Karlstad University Studies.*

Talukdar, M. R. I. (2018). Partners and priorities for Bangladesh: Development aid effectiveness. *The International Journal of Social Sciences (Islamabad), 7*(4), 435–446. https://doi.org/10.34190/ejkm.19.3.2102

Tammy, E. (2008). Today's Top 10 Talent-Management Challenges. *Harvard Business Review.*

Tammy. (2008). Today's Top 10 Talent-Management Challenges. *Harvard Business Review, 86.*

Tansley, C., Turner, P., Foster, C. J., Harris, L., Stewart, J., Sempik, A., & Williams, H. (2007). *Talent: strategy, management, measurement.* CIPD. http://hdl.handle.net/10545/621011

Tatoglu, E., Glaister, A.J., & Demirbag, M. (2016) Talent management motives and practices in an emerging market: A comparison between MNEs and local firms. *Journal of World Business, 51*(2), 278–293. doi:10.1016/j.jwb.2015.11.001

Team, C. I. R. T. (n.d.). *Common vulnerabilities in cyber space of Bangladesh.* BGD e-GOV CIRT |Bangladesh e-Government Computer Incident Response Team. Retrieved October 13, 2021, from https://www.cirt.gov.bd/common-vulnerabilities-in-cyber-space-of-bangladesh/

Ten, C. W., Liu, C. C., & Manimaran, G. (2008). Vulnerability assessment of cybersecurity for SCADA systems. *IEEE Transactions on Power Systems, 23*(4), 1836–1846.

Tenten, D., & Allen, S. (2005). *The virtual handshake: Opening doors and closing deals online.* American Management Association.

Tetik, S. (2016) Talent Management: A Review of Theoretical Perspectives and a Guideline for Practitioners. *Nile Journal of Business and Economics, 4*, 40-56. doi:10.20321/nilejbe.v2i4.77

Tham, J., Ab Yazid, M. S., Khatibi, A. A., & Azam, S. F. (2017). Internet and data security–understanding customer perception on trusting virtual banking security in Malaysia. *European Journal of Social Sciences Studies.*

Thayer, S. (1969). The effect of interpersonal looking duration on dominance judgments. *The Journal of Social Psychology, 79*(2), 285–286. doi:10.1080/00224545.1969.9922427 PMID:5810641

The Citizen - It's all about you. (2021). *Analysis: Data breaches compromised 4.5bn records in half-year 2018 - Gemalto - TheCitizen - It's all about you.* Available at: https://thecitizenng.com/analysis-data-breaches-compromised-4-5bn-records-in-half-year-2018-gemalto/

The Citizen. (2018, October 17). *Analysis: Data breaches compromised 4.5bn records in half year 2018 - gemalto - thecitizen - it's all about you.* TheCitizen. Retrieved April 14, 2022, from https://thecitizenng.com/analysis-data-breaches-compromised-4-5bn-records-in-half-year-2018-gemalto/ [Accessed 11 October 2021].

Third Eye Blind Productions. (2021). *What is talent management and why is it important?* Posted in Talent Management on June 12, 2021. Retrieved on January 30, 2022, from https://thirdeyeblindproductions.com/what-is-talent-management-and-why-is-it-important/

Thompson, L. (2021, December). Virtual collaboration won't be the death of creativity. *MIT Sloan Management Review*, *62*(2), 42–46.

Thompson, L. (2022). *Leading High Impact Teams* [Executive Education program]. Kellogg School of Management.

Thumiki, V. R. R., & Jurcic, A. (2021). Impact of COVID-19 Crisis on Knowledge Management Practices in Sultanate of Oman. *Electronic Journal of Knowledge Management*, *19*(3), 213–225. https://doi.org/10.34190/ejkm.19.3.2102

Tickle-Degnen, L., & Rosenthal, R. (1990). The nature of rapport and its nonverbal correlates. *Psychological Inquiry*, *1*(4), 285–293. doi:10.120715327965pli0104_1

Tiefenbacher, W. (2019, December 12). *Strategic management: How and why to redefine organizational strategy in today's VUCA world.* CQ Dossier: https://www.ckju.net

Tiefenbacher, W. (2020, July 12). *Agile for all: The principles of agility, agile leadership, and how to be an agile leader.* CQ Dossier: https://www.ckju.net

Tome, E., Gromara, E., & Hatch, A. (2021). Knowledge management and COVID 19. *Knowledge and Process Management*, *29*, 70–78. https://doi.org/10.1002/kpm.1699

Tomprou, M., Kim, Y. J., Chikersal, P., Williams Wooley, A., & Dabbish, L. A. (2021). Speaking out of turn: How video conferencing reduces vocal synchrony and collective intelligence. *PLoS One*, *16*(3), e0247655. doi:10.1371/journal.pone.0247655 PMID:33735258

Truss, C., & Gratton, L. (1994). Strategic human resource management: A conceptual approach. *International Journal of Human Resource Management*, *5*(3), 663–686. doi:10.1080/09585199400000053

Tuccio, M. (2020). *OECD Social, Employment and Migration Working Papers No. 229*. OECD Report. https://www.oecd-ilibrary.org/social-issues-migration-health/measuring-and-assessing-talent-attractiveness-in-oecd-countries_b4e677ca-en

U.S. Army Heritage and Education Center. (2021). *Who First Originated the Term VUCA (Volatility, Uncertainty, Complexity and Ambiguity)?* Author.

Uddin, R., & Arif, A. A. (2016). Talent management and organizational performance: An empirical study in the retail sector in Sylhet City, Bangladesh. *IOSR Journal of Business and Management*, *18*(10), 11–18. doi:10.9790/487X-1810041118

Ulrich, D. (2007). *The Talent Trifecta.* Posted in workforce.com under Staffing Management on September 17, 2007. Retrieved on February 5, 2022, from https://workforce.com/news/the-talent-trifecta

Ulrich, D., Brockbank, W., Johnson, D., & Younger, J. (2007). Human resource competencies: Responding to increased expectations. *Employment Relations Today*, *34*(3), 1-12. doi:10.1002/ert.20159

Unsworth, K. (2001). Unpacking creativity. *Academy of Management Review, 26*(2), 289–297. doi:10.5465/amr.2001.4378025

VALAMIS. (2021). *Talent Management.* Posted in valamis.com. on April 9, 2021. Retrieved on February 2, 2022, from https://www.valamis.com/hub/talent-management

Van Balen, B., & van den Besselaar, P. (2007). Universitaire Onderzoeksloopbanen. Een Verkenning Van Problemen En Oplossingen [Academic Careers. An Exploration of Problems and Solutions]. Rathenau Instituut SciSa rapport 0702. Den Haag: Rathenau Instituut.

Van Durme. (2019). *Talent mobility: Winning the war on the home front.* Global Human Capital Trends. https://www2.deloitte.com/us/en/insights/focus/human-capital-trends/2019/internal-talent-mobility.html

Van Gundy, M., Balzarotti, D., & Vigna, G. (2007). Catch me, if you can: Evading network signatures with web-based polymorphic worms. In *Proceedings of the first USENIX workshop on Offensive Technologies*. Berkley, CA: USENIX Association.

Van Wijk, R., Jansen, J. J. P., & Lyles, M. A. (2008). Inter- and intra-organizational knowledge transfer: A meta-analytic review and assessment of its antecedents and consequences. *Journal of Management Studies, 45*(4), 830–853. https://doi.org/10.1111/j.1467-6486.2008.00771.x

Vertegaal, R., Slagter, R., van der Veer, G., & Nijholt, A. (2001, March 31 – April 5th). Eye gaze patterns in conversations: There is more to conversational agents than meets the eyes. *Proceedings of the SIGCHI Conference on Human Factors on Computing Systems.*

Vinayan, G., Jayashree, S., & Marthandan, G. (2012). Critical success factors of sustainable competitive advantage: A study in Malaysian manufacturing industries. *International Journal of Business and Management, 7*(22), 29–45. doi:10.5539/ijbm.v7n22p29

VincentN. (2010). A Constructive Model for Performance Evaluation in Higher Education Institutions. Available at https://ssrn.com/abstract=1877598 doi:10.2139/ssrn.1877598

Voeten, E. (2019). Making Sense of the Design of International Institutions. *Annual Review of Political Science, 22*, 147–163. doi:10.1146/annurev-polisci-041916-021108

Volberda, H. W., Morgan, R. E., Reinmoeller, P., Hitt, M. A., Ireland, R. D., & Hoskisson, R. E. (2011). *Strategic Management: Competitiveness and Globalization (Concepts & Cases).* Cengage Learning.

Waber, B., Magnolfi, J., & Lindsay, G. (2014). Workspaces that move people. *Harvard Business Review, 92*(10), 68–77. PMID:25509577

Wall, T., & Knights, J. (2013). Leadership Assessment for Talent Development. Kogan Page.

Wang, F.-J., Chich-Jen, S., & Mei-Ling, T. (2010). Effect of Leadership Style on Organizational Performance as Viewed from Human Resource Management Strategy. *African Journal of Business Management, 4*(18), 3924–3936.

Wang, J., Ashleigh, M., & Meyer, E. (2006). Knowledge sharing and team trustworthiness: It's all about social ties. *Knowledge Management Research and Practice*, *4*, 175–186. https://doi.org/10.1057/palgrave.kmrp.8500098

Wassermann, G., & Su, Z. (2008). Static detection of cross-site scripting vulnerabilities. In *2008 ACM/IEEE 30th International Conference on Software Engineering* (pp. 171–180). ACM.

Wathne, K., Roos, J., & von Krogh, G. (1996). Towards a theory of knowledge transfer in cooperative context. In G. Krogh & J. Roos (Eds.), *Managing Knowledge: Perspectives on Cooperation and Competition* (pp. 55–81). SAGE Publications Ltd.

Wefald, J. A., & Katz, J. P. (2007). Leaders: The Strategies for Taking Charge By Warren Bennis and Burt Nanus. New York: Harper & Row, 1985 (HarperCollins 2nd Edition, 2003). Academy of Management Perspectives, 21(3), 105-106.

Weiss, C. (2018). When gaze-selected next speakers do not take the turn. *Journal of Pragmatics*, *133*, 28–44. doi:10.1016/j.pragma.2018.05.016

Wernerfelt, B. (1984). A resource-based view of the firm. *Strategic Management Journal*, *5*(2), 171–180. doi:10.1002mj.4250050207

Westacott, E. (2019). *What is a paradigm shift?* Posted in ThoughtCo on October 12, 2019. Retrieved on February 1, 2021, from https://www.thoughtco.com/what-is-a-paradigm-shift-2670671

West, M. A., & Farr, J. L. (1989). Innovation at Work: Psychological Perspectives. *Social Behaviour*, *4*, 15–30.

Wheelan, S. A. (2009). Group size, group development, and group productivity. *Small Group Research*, *40*(2), 247–262. doi:10.1177/1046496408328703

Whelan, E., Collings, D. G., & Donnellan, B. (2010). Managing talent in knowledge-intensive settings. *Journal of Knowledge Management, 14*(3), 486-504. doi:10.1108/13673271011050175

Whelan, E., & Carcary, M. (2011). Integrating talent and knowledge management: Where are the benefits? *Journal of Knowledge Management*, *15*(4), 675–687. https://ssrn.com/abstract=1694455

Whitaker, A., & Newman, D. (2005). *Penetration Testing and Network Defense: Penetration Testing*. Cisco Press.

Wiederhold, B. K. (2020, July). Connecting through technology during the Coronavirus disease 2019 pandemic: Avoiding "Zoom Fatigue". *Cyberpsychology, Behavior, and Social Networking*, *23*(7), 437–438. doi:10.1089/cyber.2020.29188.bkw PMID:32551981

Wijenayaka, G. A. U. (2021). HR strategy is necessary to underline the interactive relationship between business strategy and human resource management. *Academia Letters*. Advance online publication. doi:10.20935/AL4316

Williams, M. (2000). *The war for talent: Getting the best from the best*. CIPD House.

Wilson, P. (2009). True north. *HR Monthly*, (May), 16–18.

Wilson, T. L., Lindbergh, L., & Graff, J. (2014). The Competitive Advantage of Nations 20 Years Later: The Cases of Sweden, South Korea and the USA. *Competitiveness Review*, *24*(4), 306. doi:10.1108/CR-11-2012-0027

Wright, P. M., & McMahan, G. C. (1992). Theoretical perspectives for strategic human resource management. *Journal of Management*, *18*(2), 295–320. doi:10.1177/014920639201800205

Wright, P. M., & Snell, S. A. (1998). Toward a unifying framework for exploring fit and flexibility in strategic human resources. *Academy of Management Review*, *23*(4), 756–772. doi:10.5465/amr.1998.1255637

Yoganathan, V., Osburg, V. S., & Bartikowski, B. (2021). Building better employer brands through employee social media competence and online social capital. *Psychology and Marketing*, *38*(3), 524–536. doi:10.1002/mar.21451

Yoyo, T., Daryanto, A., Gumbira-Sa'id, E., & Hasan, M. F. (2014). Competitiveness model and gap analysis of Indonesian palm oil-based fatty acid and fatty alcohol industry. *Journal of Economics and Finance*, *6*(2), 218–225.

Zaman, N. U. (2018, October 21). *Digital Security act 2018: Young generation speaks*. Retrieved April 14, 2022, from https://www.newagebd.net/article/53662/digital-security-act-2018-young-generation-speaks

Zehir, C., Ertosun, Ö. G., Zehir, S., & Müceldili, B. (2011). The Effects of Leadership Styles and Organizational Culture over Firm Performance: Multi-National Companies in İstanbul. *Procedia: Social and Behavioral Sciences*, *24*, 1460–1474. doi:10.1016/j.sbspro.2011.09.032

Zica, R. M. F., Gonçalves, C. A., Cordeiro Martins, H., & Gonçalves, M. A. (2016). The resource-based theory and its adherence to a superior performance strategy: An analysis in small companies in Brazil. *Corporate Ownership & Control*, *13*(3-3), 434-444. . doi:10.22495/cocv13i3c3p2

Related References

To continue our tradition of advancing information science and technology research, we have compiled a list of recommended IGI Global readings. These references will provide additional information and guidance to further enrich your knowledge and assist you with your own research and future publications.

Abdul Razak, R., & Mansor, N. A. (2021). Instagram Influencers in Social Media-Induced Tourism: Rethinking Tourist Trust Towards Tourism Destination. In M. Dinis, L. Bonixe, S. Lamy, & Z. Breda (Eds.), *Impact of New Media in Tourism* (pp. 135-144). IGI Global. https://doi.org/10.4018/978-1-7998-7095-1.ch009

Abir, T., & Khan, M. Y. (2022). Importance of ICT Advancement and Culture of Adaptation in the Tourism and Hospitality Industry for Developing Countries. In C. Ramos, S. Quinteiro, & A. Gonçalves (Eds.), *ICT as Innovator Between Tourism and Culture* (pp. 30–41). IGI Global. https://doi.org/10.4018/978-1-7998-8165-0.ch003

Abir, T., & Khan, M. Y. (2022). Importance of ICT Advancement and Culture of Adaptation in the Tourism and Hospitality Industry for Developing Countries. In C. Ramos, S. Quinteiro, & A. Gonçalves (Eds.), *ICT as Innovator Between Tourism and Culture* (pp. 30–41). IGI Global. https://doi.org/10.4018/978-1-7998-8165-0.ch003

Abtahi, M. S., Behboudi, L., & Hasanabad, H. M. (2017). Factors Affecting Internet Advertising Adoption in Ad Agencies. *International Journal of Innovation in the Digital Economy*, *8*(4), 18–29. doi:10.4018/IJIDE.2017100102

Afenyo-Agbe, E., & Mensah, I. (2022). Principles, Benefits, and Barriers to Community-Based Tourism: Implications for Management. In I. Mensah & E. Afenyo-Agbe (Eds.), *Prospects and Challenges of Community-Based Tourism and Changing Demographics* (pp. 1–29). IGI Global. doi:10.4018/978-1-7998-7335-8.ch001

Agbo, V. M. (2022). Distributive Justice Issues in Community-Based Tourism. In I. Mensah & E. Afenyo-Agbe (Eds.), *Prospects and Challenges of Community-Based Tourism and Changing Demographics* (pp. 107–129). IGI Global. https://doi.org/10.4018/978-1-7998-7335-8.ch005

Agrawal, S. (2017). The Impact of Emerging Technologies and Social Media on Different Business(es): Marketing and Management. In O. Rishi & A. Sharma (Eds.), *Maximizing Business Performance and Efficiency Through Intelligent Systems* (pp. 37–49). Hershey, PA: IGI Global. doi:10.4018/978-1-5225-2234-8.ch002

Ahmad, A., & Johari, S. (2022). Georgetown as a Gastronomy Tourism Destination: Visitor Awareness Towards Revisit Intention of Nasi Kandar Restaurant. In M. Valeri (Ed.), *New Governance and Management in Touristic Destinations* (pp. 71–83). IGI Global. https://doi.org/10.4018/978-1-6684-3889-3.ch005

Alkhatib, G., & Bayouq, S. T. (2021). A TAM-Based Model of Technological Factors Affecting Use of E-Tourism. *International Journal of Tourism and Hospitality Management in the Digital Age*, *5*(2), 50–67. https://doi.org/10.4018/IJTHMDA.20210701.oa1

Altinay Ozdemir, M. (2021). Virtual Reality (VR) and Augmented Reality (AR) Technologies for Accessibility and Marketing in the Tourism Industry. In C. Eusébio, L. Teixeira, & M. Carneiro (Eds.), *ICT Tools and Applications for Accessible Tourism* (pp. 277-301). IGI Global. https://doi.org/10.4018/978-1-7998-6428-8.ch013

Anantharaman, R. N., Rajeswari, K. S., Angusamy, A., & Kuppusamy, J. (2017). Role of Self-Efficacy and Collective Efficacy as Moderators of Occupational Stress Among Software Development Professionals. *International Journal of Human Capital and Information Technology Professionals*, *8*(2), 45–58. doi:10.4018/IJHCITP.2017040103

Aninze, F., El-Gohary, H., & Hussain, J. (2018). The Role of Microfinance to Empower Women: The Case of Developing Countries. *International Journal of Customer Relationship Marketing and Management*, *9*(1), 54–78. doi:10.4018/IJCRMM.2018010104

Antosova, G., Sabogal-Salamanca, M., & Krizova, E. (2021). Human Capital in Tourism: A Practical Model of Endogenous and Exogenous Territorial Tourism Planning in Bahía Solano, Colombia. In V. Costa, A. Moura, & M. Mira (Eds.), *Handbook of Research on Human Capital and People Management in the Tourism Industry* (pp. 282–302). IGI Global. https://doi.org/10.4018/978-1-7998-4318-4.ch014

Arsenijević, O. M., Orčić, D., & Kastratović, E. (2017). Development of an Optimization Tool for Intangibles in SMEs: A Case Study from Serbia with a Pilot Research in the Prestige by Milka Company. In M. Vemić (Ed.), *Optimal Management Strategies in Small and Medium Enterprises* (pp. 320–347). Hershey, PA: IGI Global. doi:10.4018/978-1-5225-1949-2.ch015

Aryanto, V. D., Wismantoro, Y., & Widyatmoko, K. (2018). Implementing Eco-Innovation by Utilizing the Internet to Enhance Firm's Marketing Performance: Study of Green Batik Small and Medium Enterprises in Indonesia. *International Journal of E-Business Research, 14*(1), 21–36. doi:10.4018/IJEBR.2018010102

Asero, V., & Billi, S. (2022). New Perspective of Networking in the DMO Model. In M. Valeri (Ed.), *New Governance and Management in Touristic Destinations* (pp. 105–118). IGI Global. https://doi.org/10.4018/978-1-6684-3889-3.ch007

Atiku, S. O., & Fields, Z. (2017). Multicultural Orientations for 21st Century Global Leadership. In N. Baporikar (Ed.), *Management Education for Global Leadership* (pp. 28–51). Hershey, PA: IGI Global. doi:10.4018/978-1-5225-1013-0.ch002

Atiku, S. O., & Fields, Z. (2018). Organisational Learning Dimensions and Talent Retention Strategies for the Service Industries. In N. Baporikar (Ed.), *Global Practices in Knowledge Management for Societal and Organizational Development* (pp. 358–381). Hershey, PA: IGI Global. doi:10.4018/978-1-5225-3009-1.ch017

Atsa'am, D. D., & Kuset Bodur, E. (2021). Pattern Mining on How Organizational Tenure Affects the Psychological Capital of Employees Within the Hospitality and Tourism Industry: Linking Employees' Organizational Tenure With PsyCap. *International Journal of Tourism and Hospitality Management in the Digital Age, 5*(2), 17–28. https://doi.org/10.4018/IJTHMDA.2021070102

Ávila, L., & Teixeira, L. (2018). The Main Concepts Behind the Dematerialization of Business Processes. In M. Khosrow-Pour, D.B.A. (Ed.), Encyclopedia of Information Science and Technology, Fourth Edition (pp. 888-898). Hershey, PA: IGI Global. https://doi.org/ doi:10.4018/978-1-5225-2255-3.ch076

Ayorekire, J., Mugizi, F., Obua, J., & Ampaire, G. (2022). Community-Based Tourism and Local People's Perceptions Towards Conservation: The Case of Queen Elizabeth Conservation Area, Uganda. In I. Mensah & E. Afenyo-Agbe (Eds.), *Prospects and Challenges of Community-Based Tourism and Changing Demographics* (pp. 56–82). IGI Global. https://doi.org/10.4018/978-1-7998-7335-8.ch003

Baleiro, R. (2022). Tourist Literature and the Architecture of Travel in Olga Tokarczuk and Patti Smith. In R. Baleiro & R. Pereira (Eds.), *Global Perspectives on Literary Tourism and Film-Induced Tourism* (pp. 202-216). IGI Global. https://doi.org/10.4018/978-1-7998-8262-6.ch011

Barat, S. (2021). Looking at the Future of Medical Tourism in Asia. *International Journal of Tourism and Hospitality Management in the Digital Age*, *5*(1), 19–33. https://doi.org/10.4018/IJTHMDA.2021010102

Barbosa, C. A., Magalhães, M., & Nunes, M. R. (2021). Travel Instagramability: A Way of Choosing a Destination? In M. Dinis, L. Bonixe, S. Lamy, & Z. Breda (Eds.), *Impact of New Media in Tourism* (pp. 173-190). IGI Global. https://doi.org/10.4018/978-1-7998-7095-1.ch011

Bari, M. W., & Khan, Q. (2021). Pakistan as a Destination of Religious Tourism. In E. Alaverdov & M. Bari (Eds.), *Global Development of Religious Tourism* (pp. 1-10). IGI Global. https://doi.org/10.4018/978-1-7998-5792-1.ch001

Bartens, Y., Chunpir, H. I., Schulte, F., & Voß, S. (2017). Business/IT Alignment in Two-Sided Markets: A COBIT 5 Analysis for Media Streaming Business Models. In S. De Haes & W. Van Grembergen (Eds.), *Strategic IT Governance and Alignment in Business Settings* (pp. 82–111). Hershey, PA: IGI Global. doi:10.4018/978-1-5225-0861-8.ch004

Bashayreh, A. M. (2018). Organizational Culture and Organizational Performance. In W. Lee & F. Sabetzadeh (Eds.), *Contemporary Knowledge and Systems Science* (pp. 50–69). Hershey, PA: IGI Global. doi:10.4018/978-1-5225-5655-8.ch003

Bechthold, L., Lude, M., & Prügl, R. (2021). Crisis Favors the Prepared Firm: How Organizational Ambidexterity Relates to Perceptions of Organizational Resilience. In A. Zehrer, G. Glowka, K. Schwaiger, & V. Ranacher-Lackner (Eds.), *Resiliency Models and Addressing Future Risks for Family Firms in the Tourism Industry* (pp. 178–205). IGI Global. https://doi.org/10.4018/978-1-7998-7352-5.ch008

Bedford, D. A. (2018). Sustainable Knowledge Management Strategies: Aligning Business Capabilities and Knowledge Management Goals. In N. Baporikar (Ed.), *Global Practices in Knowledge Management for Societal and Organizational Development* (pp. 46–73). Hershey, PA: IGI Global. doi:10.4018/978-1-5225-3009-1.ch003

Bekjanov, D., & Matyusupov, B. (2021). Influence of Innovative Processes in the Competitiveness of Tourist Destination. In J. Soares (Ed.), *Innovation and Entrepreneurial Opportunities in Community Tourism* (pp. 243–263). IGI Global. https://doi.org/10.4018/978-1-7998-4855-4.ch014

Bharwani, S., & Musunuri, D. (2018). Reflection as a Process From Theory to Practice. In M. Khosrow-Pour, D.B.A. (Ed.), Encyclopedia of Information Science and Technology, Fourth Edition (pp. 1529-1539). Hershey, PA: IGI Global. doi:10.4018/978-1-5225-2255-3.ch132

Bhatt, G. D., Wang, Z., & Rodger, J. A. (2017). Information Systems Capabilities and Their Effects on Competitive Advantages: A Study of Chinese Companies. *Information Resources Management Journal, 30*(3), 41–57. doi:10.4018/IRMJ.2017070103

Bhushan, M., & Yadav, A. (2017). Concept of Cloud Computing in ESB. In R. Bhadoria, N. Chaudhari, G. Tomar, & S. Singh (Eds.), *Exploring Enterprise Service Bus in the Service-Oriented Architecture Paradigm* (pp. 116–127). Hershey, PA: IGI Global. doi:10.4018/978-1-5225-2157-0.ch008

Bhushan, S. (2017). System Dynamics Base-Model of Humanitarian Supply Chain (HSCM) in Disaster Prone Eco-Communities of India: A Discussion on Simulation and Scenario Results. *International Journal of System Dynamics Applications, 6*(3), 20–37. doi:10.4018/IJSDA.2017070102

Binder, D., & Miller, J. W. (2021). A Generations' Perspective on Employer Branding in Tourism. In V. Costa, A. Moura, & M. Mira (Eds.), *Handbook of Research on Human Capital and People Management in the Tourism Industry* (pp. 152–174). IGI Global. https://doi.org/10.4018/978-1-7998-4318-4.ch008

Birch Freeman, A. A., Mensah, I., & Antwi, K. B. (2022). Smiling vs. Frowning Faces: Community Participation for Sustainable Tourism in Ghanaian Communities. In I. Mensah & E. Afenyo-Agbe (Eds.), *Prospects and Challenges of Community-Based Tourism and Changing Demographics* (pp. 83–106). IGI Global. https://doi.org/10.4018/978-1-7998-7335-8.ch004

Biswas, A., & De, A. K. (2017). On Development of a Fuzzy Stochastic Programming Model with Its Application to Business Management. In S. Trivedi, S. Dey, A. Kumar, & T. Panda (Eds.), *Handbook of Research on Advanced Data Mining Techniques and Applications for Business Intelligence* (pp. 353–378). Hershey, PA: IGI Global. doi:10.4018/978-1-5225-2031-3.ch021

Boragnio, A., & Faracce Macia, C. (2021). "Taking Care of Yourself at Home": Use of E-Commerce About Food and Care During the COVID-19 Pandemic in the City of Buenos Aires. In M. Korstanje (Ed.), *Socio-Economic Effects and Recovery Efforts for the Rental Industry: Post-COVID-19 Strategies* (pp. 45–71). IGI Global. https://doi.org/10.4018/978-1-7998-7287-0.ch003

Borges, V. D. (2021). Happiness: The Basis for Public Policy in Tourism. In A. Perinotto, V. Mayer, & J. Soares (Eds.), *Rebuilding and Restructuring the Tourism Industry: Infusion of Happiness and Quality of Life* (pp. 1–25). IGI Global. https://doi.org/10.4018/978-1-7998-7239-9.ch001

Bücker, J., & Ernste, K. (2018). Use of Brand Heroes in Strategic Reputation Management: The Case of Bacardi, Adidas, and Daimler. In A. Erdemir (Ed.), *Reputation Management Techniques in Public Relations* (pp. 126–150). Hershey, PA: IGI Global. doi:10.4018/978-1-5225-3619-2.ch007

Buluk Eşitti, B. (2021). COVID-19 and Alternative Tourism: New Destinations and New Tourism Products. In M. Demir, A. Dalgıç, & F. Ergen (Eds.), *Handbook of Research on the Impacts and Implications of COVID-19 on the Tourism Industry* (pp. 786–805). IGI Global. https://doi.org/10.4018/978-1-7998-8231-2.ch038

Bureš, V. (2018). Industry 4.0 From the Systems Engineering Perspective: Alternative Holistic Framework Development. In R. Brunet-Thornton & F. Martinez (Eds.), *Analyzing the Impacts of Industry 4.0 in Modern Business Environments* (pp. 199–223). Hershey, PA: IGI Global. doi:10.4018/978-1-5225-3468-6.ch011

Buzady, Z. (2017). Resolving the Magic Cube of Effective Case Teaching: Benchmarking Case Teaching Practices in Emerging Markets – Insights from the Central European University Business School, Hungary. In D. Latusek (Ed.), *Case Studies as a Teaching Tool in Management Education* (pp. 79–103). Hershey, PA: IGI Global. doi:10.4018/978-1-5225-0770-3.ch005

Camillo, A. (2021). *Legal Matters, Risk Management, and Risk Prevention: From Forming a Business to Legal Representation.* IGI Global. doi:10.4018/978-1-7998-4342-9.ch004

Căpusneanu, S., & Topor, D. I. (2018). Business Ethics and Cost Management in SMEs: Theories of Business Ethics and Cost Management Ethos. In I. Oncioiu (Ed.), *Ethics and Decision-Making for Sustainable Business Practices* (pp. 109–127). Hershey, PA: IGI Global. doi:10.4018/978-1-5225-3773-1.ch007

Chan, R. L., Mo, P. L., & Moon, K. K. (2018). Strategic and Tactical Measures in Managing Enterprise Risks: A Study of the Textile and Apparel Industry. In K. Strang, M. Korstanje, & N. Vajjhala (Eds.), *Research, Practices, and Innovations in Global Risk and Contingency Management* (pp. 1–19). Hershey, PA: IGI Global. doi:10.4018/978-1-5225-4754-9.ch001

Charlier, S. D., Burke-Smalley, L. A., & Fisher, S. L. (2018). Undergraduate Programs in the U.S: A Contextual and Content-Based Analysis. In J. Mendy (Ed.), *Teaching Human Resources and Organizational Behavior at the College Level* (pp. 26–57). Hershey, PA: IGI Global. doi:10.4018/978-1-5225-2820-3.ch002

Chumillas, J., Güell, M., & Quer, P. (2022). The Use of ICT in Tourist and Educational Literary Routes: The Role of the Guide. In C. Ramos, S. Quinteiro, & A. Gonçalves (Eds.), *ICT as Innovator Between Tourism and Culture* (pp. 15–29). IGI Global. https://doi.org/10.4018/978-1-7998-8165-0.ch002

Dahlberg, T., Kivijärvi, H., & Saarinen, T. (2017). IT Investment Consistency and Other Factors Influencing the Success of IT Performance. In S. De Haes & W. Van Grembergen (Eds.), *Strategic IT Governance and Alignment in Business Settings* (pp. 176–208). Hershey, PA: IGI Global. doi:10.4018/978-1-5225-0861-8.ch007

Damnjanović, A. M. (2017). Knowledge Management Optimization through IT and E-Business Utilization: A Qualitative Study on Serbian SMEs. In M. Vemić (Ed.), *Optimal Management Strategies in Small and Medium Enterprises* (pp. 249–267). Hershey, PA: IGI Global. doi:10.4018/978-1-5225-1949-2.ch012

Daneshpour, H. (2017). Integrating Sustainable Development into Project Portfolio Management through Application of Open Innovation. In M. Vemić (Ed.), *Optimal Management Strategies in Small and Medium Enterprises* (pp. 370–387). Hershey, PA: IGI Global. doi:10.4018/978-1-5225-1949-2.ch017

Daniel, A. D., & Reis de Castro, V. (2018). Entrepreneurship Education: How to Measure the Impact on Nascent Entrepreneurs. In A. Carrizo Moreira, J. Guilherme Leitão Dantas, & F. Manuel Valente (Eds.), *Nascent Entrepreneurship and Successful New Venture Creation* (pp. 85–110). Hershey, PA: IGI Global. doi:10.4018/978-1-5225-2936-1.ch004

David, R., Swami, B. N., & Tangirala, S. (2018). Ethics Impact on Knowledge Management in Organizational Development: A Case Study. In N. Baporikar (Ed.), *Global Practices in Knowledge Management for Societal and Organizational Development* (pp. 19–45). Hershey, PA: IGI Global. doi:10.4018/978-1-5225-3009-1.ch002

De Uña-Álvarez, E., & Villarino-Pérez, M. (2022). Fostering Ecocultural Resources, Identity, and Tourism in Inland Territories (Galicia, NW Spain). In G. Fernandes (Ed.), *Challenges and New Opportunities for Tourism in Inland Territories: Ecocultural Resources and Sustainable Initiatives* (pp. 1-16). IGI Global. https://doi.org/10.4018/978-1-7998-7339-6.ch001

Delias, P., & Lakiotaki, K. (2018). Discovering Process Horizontal Boundaries to Facilitate Process Comprehension. *International Journal of Operations Research and Information Systems*, *9*(2), 1–31. doi:10.4018/IJORIS.2018040101

Denholm, J., & Lee-Davies, L. (2018). Success Factors for Games in Business and Project Management. In *Enhancing Education and Training Initiatives Through Serious Games* (pp. 34–68). Hershey, PA: IGI Global. doi:10.4018/978-1-5225-3689-5.ch002

Deshpande, M. (2017). Best Practices in Management Institutions for Global Leadership: Policy Aspects. In N. Baporikar (Ed.), *Management Education for Global Leadership* (pp. 1–27). Hershey, PA: IGI Global. doi:10.4018/978-1-5225-1013-0.ch001

Deshpande, M. (2018). Policy Perspectives for SMEs Knowledge Management. In N. Baporikar (Ed.), *Knowledge Integration Strategies for Entrepreneurship and Sustainability* (pp. 23–46). Hershey, PA: IGI Global. doi:10.4018/978-1-5225-5115-7.ch002

Dezdar, S. (2017). ERP Implementation Projects in Asian Countries: A Comparative Study on Iran and China. *International Journal of Information Technology Project Management*, *8*(3), 52–68. doi:10.4018/IJITPM.2017070104

Domingos, D., Respício, A., & Martinho, R. (2017). Reliability of IoT-Aware BPMN Healthcare Processes. In C. Reis & M. Maximiano (Eds.), *Internet of Things and Advanced Application in Healthcare* (pp. 214–248). Hershey, PA: IGI Global. doi:10.4018/978-1-5225-1820-4.ch008

Dosumu, O., Hussain, J., & El-Gohary, H. (2017). An Exploratory Study of the Impact of Government Policies on the Development of Small and Medium Enterprises in Developing Countries: The Case of Nigeria. *International Journal of Customer Relationship Marketing and Management*, *8*(4), 51–62. doi:10.4018/IJCRMM.2017100104

Durst, S., Bruns, G., & Edvardsson, I. R. (2017). Retaining Knowledge in Smaller Building and Construction Firms. *International Journal of Knowledge and Systems Science*, *8*(3), 1–12. doi:10.4018/IJKSS.2017070101

Edvardsson, I. R., & Durst, S. (2017). Outsourcing, Knowledge, and Learning: A Critical Review. *International Journal of Knowledge-Based Organizations*, *7*(2), 13–26. doi:10.4018/IJKBO.2017040102

Edwards, J. S. (2018). Integrating Knowledge Management and Business Processes. In M. Khosrow-Pour, D.B.A. (Ed.), Encyclopedia of Information Science and Technology, Fourth Edition (pp. 5046-5055). Hershey, PA: IGI Global. doi:10.4018/978-1-5225-2255-3.ch437

Eichelberger, S., & Peters, M. (2021). Family Firm Management in Turbulent Times: Opportunities for Responsible Tourism. In A. Zehrer, G. Glowka, K. Schwaiger, & V. Ranacher-Lackner (Eds.), *Resiliency Models and Addressing Future Risks for Family Firms in the Tourism Industry* (pp. 103–124). IGI Global. https://doi.org/10.4018/978-1-7998-7352-5.ch005

Eide, D., Hjalager, A., & Hansen, M. (2022). Innovative Certifications in Adventure Tourism: Attributes and Diffusion. In R. Augusto Costa, F. Brandão, Z. Breda, & C. Costa (Eds.), *Planning and Managing the Experience Economy in Tourism* (pp. 161-175). IGI Global. https://doi.org/10.4018/978-1-7998-8775-1.ch009

Ejiogu, A. O. (2018). Economics of Farm Management. In *Agricultural Finance and Opportunities for Investment and Expansion* (pp. 56–72). Hershey, PA: IGI Global. doi:10.4018/978-1-5225-3059-6.ch003

Ekanem, I., & Abiade, G. E. (2018). Factors Influencing the Use of E-Commerce by Small Enterprises in Nigeria. *International Journal of ICT Research in Africa and the Middle East, 7*(1), 37–53. doi:10.4018/IJICTRAME.2018010103

Ekanem, I., & Alrossais, L. A. (2017). Succession Challenges Facing Family Businesses in Saudi Arabia. In P. Zgheib (Ed.), *Entrepreneurship and Business Innovation in the Middle East* (pp. 122–146). Hershey, PA: IGI Global. doi:10.4018/978-1-5225-2066-5.ch007

El Faquih, L., & Fredj, M. (2017). Ontology-Based Framework for Quality in Configurable Process Models. *Journal of Electronic Commerce in Organizations, 15*(2), 48–60. doi:10.4018/JECO.2017040104

Faisal, M. N., & Talib, F. (2017). Building Ambidextrous Supply Chains in SMEs: How to Tackle the Barriers? *International Journal of Information Systems and Supply Chain Management, 10*(4), 80–100. doi:10.4018/IJISSCM.2017100105

Fernandes, T. M., Gomes, J., & Romão, M. (2017). Investments in E-Government: A Benefit Management Case Study. *International Journal of Electronic Government Research, 13*(3), 1–17. doi:10.4018/IJEGR.2017070101

Figueira, L. M., Honrado, G. R., & Dionísio, M. S. (2021). Human Capital Management in the Tourism Industry in Portugal. In V. Costa, A. Moura, & M. Mira (Eds.), *Handbook of Research on Human Capital and People Management in the Tourism Industry* (pp. 1–19). IGI Global. doi:10.4018/978-1-7998-4318-4.ch001

Gao, S. S., Oreal, S., & Zhang, J. (2018). Contemporary Financial Risk Management Perceptions and Practices of Small-Sized Chinese Businesses. In I. Management Association (Ed.), Global Business Expansion: Concepts, Methodologies, Tools, and Applications (pp. 917-931). Hershey, PA: IGI Global. doi:10.4018/978-1-5225-5481-3.ch041

Garg, R., & Berning, S. C. (2017). Indigenous Chinese Management Philosophies: Key Concepts and Relevance for Modern Chinese Firms. In B. Christiansen & G. Koc (Eds.), *Transcontinental Strategies for Industrial Development and Economic Growth* (pp. 43–57). Hershey, PA: IGI Global. doi:10.4018/978-1-5225-2160-0.ch003

Gencer, Y. G. (2017). Supply Chain Management in Retailing Business. In U. Akkucuk (Ed.), *Ethics and Sustainability in Global Supply Chain Management* (pp. 197–210). Hershey, PA: IGI Global. doi:10.4018/978-1-5225-2036-8.ch011

Gera, R., Arora, S., & Malik, S. (2021). Emotional Labor in the Tourism Industry: Strategies, Antecedents, and Outcomes. In V. Costa, A. Moura, & M. Mira (Eds.), *Handbook of Research on Human Capital and People Management in the Tourism Industry* (pp. 73–91). IGI Global. https://doi.org/10.4018/978-1-7998-4318-4.ch004

Giacosa, E. (2018). The Increasing of the Regional Development Thanks to the Luxury Business Innovation. In L. Carvalho (Ed.), *Handbook of Research on Entrepreneurial Ecosystems and Social Dynamics in a Globalized World* (pp. 260–273). Hershey, PA: IGI Global. doi:10.4018/978-1-5225-3525-6.ch011

Glowka, G., Tusch, M., & Zehrer, A. (2021). The Risk Perception of Family Business Owner-Manager in the Tourism Industry: A Qualitative Comparison of the Intra-Firm Senior and Junior Generation. In A. Zehrer, G. Glowka, K. Schwaiger, & V. Ranacher-Lackner (Eds.), *Resiliency Models and Addressing Future Risks for Family Firms in the Tourism Industry* (pp. 126–153). IGI Global. https://doi.org/10.4018/978-1-7998-7352-5.ch006

Glykas, M., & George, J. (2017). Quality and Process Management Systems in the UAE Maritime Industry. *International Journal of Productivity Management and Assessment Technologies*, *5*(1), 20–39. doi:10.4018/IJPMAT.2017010102

Glykas, M., Valiris, G., Kokkinaki, A., & Koutsoukou, Z. (2018). Banking Business Process Management Implementation. *International Journal of Productivity Management and Assessment Technologies*, *6*(1), 50–69. doi:10.4018/IJPMAT.2018010104

Gomes, J., & Romão, M. (2017). The Balanced Scorecard: Keeping Updated and Aligned with Today's Business Trends. *International Journal of Productivity Management and Assessment Technologies*, *5*(2), 1–15. doi:10.4018/IJPMAT.2017070101

Gomes, J., & Romão, M. (2017). Aligning Information Systems and Technology with Benefit Management and Balanced Scorecard. In S. De Haes & W. Van Grembergen (Eds.), *Strategic IT Governance and Alignment in Business Settings* (pp. 112–131). Hershey, PA: IGI Global. doi:10.4018/978-1-5225-0861-8.ch005

Goyal, A. (2021). Communicating and Building Destination Brands With New Media. In M. Dinis, L. Bonixe, S. Lamy, & Z. Breda (Eds.), *Impact of New Media in Tourism* (pp. 1-20). IGI Global. https://doi.org/10.4018/978-1-7998-7095-1.ch001

Grefen, P., & Turetken, O. (2017). Advanced Business Process Management in Networked E-Business Scenarios. *International Journal of E-Business Research*, *13*(4), 70–104. doi:10.4018/IJEBR.2017100105

Guasca, M., Van Broeck, A. M., & Vanneste, D. (2021). Tourism and the Social Reintegration of Colombian Ex-Combatants. In J. da Silva, Z. Breda, & F. Carbone (Eds.), *Role and Impact of Tourism in Peacebuilding and Conflict Transformation* (pp. 66-86). IGI Global. https://doi.org/10.4018/978-1-7998-5053-3.ch005

Haider, A., & Saetang, S. (2017). Strategic IT Alignment in Service Sector. In S. Rozenes & Y. Cohen (Eds.), *Handbook of Research on Strategic Alliances and Value Co-Creation in the Service Industry* (pp. 231–258). Hershey, PA: IGI Global. doi:10.4018/978-1-5225-2084-9.ch012

Hajilari, A. B., Ghadaksaz, M., & Fasghandis, G. S. (2017). Assessing Organizational Readiness for Implementing ERP System Using Fuzzy Expert System Approach. *International Journal of Enterprise Information Systems*, *13*(1), 67–85. doi:10.4018/IJEIS.2017010105

Haldorai, A., Ramu, A., & Murugan, S. (2018). Social Aware Cognitive Radio Networks: Effectiveness of Social Networks as a Strategic Tool for Organizational Business Management. In H. Bansal, G. Shrivastava, G. Nguyen, & L. Stanciu (Eds.), *Social Network Analytics for Contemporary Business Organizations* (pp. 188–202). Hershey, PA: IGI Global. doi:10.4018/978-1-5225-5097-6.ch010

Hall, O. P. Jr. (2017). Social Media Driven Management Education. *International Journal of Knowledge-Based Organizations, 7*(2), 43–59. doi:10.4018/IJKBO.2017040104

Hanifah, H., Halim, H. A., Ahmad, N. H., & Vafaei-Zadeh, A. (2017). Innovation Culture as a Mediator Between Specific Human Capital and Innovation Performance Among Bumiputera SMEs in Malaysia. In N. Ahmad, T. Ramayah, H. Halim, & S. Rahman (Eds.), *Handbook of Research on Small and Medium Enterprises in Developing Countries* (pp. 261–279). Hershey, PA: IGI Global. doi:10.4018/978-1-5225-2165-5.ch012

Hartlieb, S., & Silvius, G. (2017). Handling Uncertainty in Project Management and Business Development: Similarities and Differences. In Y. Raydugin (Ed.), *Handbook of Research on Leveraging Risk and Uncertainties for Effective Project Management* (pp. 337–362). Hershey, PA: IGI Global. doi:10.4018/978-1-5225-1790-0.ch016

Hass, K. B. (2017). Living on the Edge: Managing Project Complexity. In Y. Raydugin (Ed.), *Handbook of Research on Leveraging Risk and Uncertainties for Effective Project Management* (pp. 177–201). Hershey, PA: IGI Global. doi:10.4018/978-1-5225-1790-0.ch009

Hawking, P., & Carmine Sellitto, C. (2017). Developing an Effective Strategy for Organizational Business Intelligence. In M. Tavana (Ed.), *Enterprise Information Systems and the Digitalization of Business Functions* (pp. 222–237). Hershey, PA: IGI Global. doi:10.4018/978-1-5225-2382-6.ch010

Hawking, P., & Sellitto, C. (2017). A Fast-Moving Consumer Goods Company and Business Intelligence Strategy Development. *International Journal of Enterprise Information Systems, 13*(2), 22–33. doi:10.4018/IJEIS.2017040102

Hawking, P., & Sellitto, C. (2017). Business Intelligence Strategy: Two Case Studies. *International Journal of Business Intelligence Research, 8*(2), 17–30. doi:10.4018/IJBIR.2017070102

Hee, W. J., Jalleh, G., Lai, H., & Lin, C. (2017). E-Commerce and IT Projects: Evaluation and Management Issues in Australian and Taiwanese Hospitals. *International Journal of Public Health Management and Ethics, 2*(1), 69–90. doi:10.4018/IJPHME.2017010104

Hernandez, A. A. (2018). Exploring the Factors to Green IT Adoption of SMEs in the Philippines. *Journal of Cases on Information Technology, 20*(2), 49–66. doi:10.4018/JCIT.2018040104

Hollman, A., Bickford, S., & Hollman, T. (2017). Cyber InSecurity: A Post-Mortem Attempt to Assess Cyber Problems from IT and Business Management Perspectives. *Journal of Cases on Information Technology*, *19*(3), 42–70. doi:10.4018/JCIT.2017070104

Ibrahim, F., & Zainin, N. M. (2021). Exploring the Technological Impacts: The Case of Museums in Brunei Darussalam. *International Journal of Tourism and Hospitality Management in the Digital Age*, *5*(1), 1–18. https://doi.org/10.4018/IJTHMDA.2021010101

Igbinakhase, I. (2017). Responsible and Sustainable Management Practices in Developing and Developed Business Environments. In Z. Fields (Ed.), *Collective Creativity for Responsible and Sustainable Business Practice* (pp. 180–207). Hershey, PA: IGI Global. doi:10.4018/978-1-5225-1823-5.ch010

Iwata, J. J., & Hoskins, R. G. (2017). Managing Indigenous Knowledge in Tanzania: A Business Perspective. In P. Jain & N. Mnjama (Eds.), *Managing Knowledge Resources and Records in Modern Organizations* (pp. 198–214). Hershey, PA: IGI Global. doi:10.4018/978-1-5225-1965-2.ch012

Jain, P. (2017). Ethical and Legal Issues in Knowledge Management Life-Cycle in Business. In P. Jain & N. Mnjama (Eds.), *Managing Knowledge Resources and Records in Modern Organizations* (pp. 82–101). Hershey, PA: IGI Global. doi:10.4018/978-1-5225-1965-2.ch006

James, S., & Hauli, E. (2017). Holistic Management Education at Tanzanian Rural Development Planning Institute. In N. Baporikar (Ed.), *Management Education for Global Leadership* (pp. 112–136). Hershey, PA: IGI Global. doi:10.4018/978-1-5225-1013-0.ch006

Janošková, M., Csikósová, A., & Čulková, K. (2018). Measurement of Company Performance as Part of Its Strategic Management. In R. Leon (Ed.), *Managerial Strategies for Business Sustainability During Turbulent Times* (pp. 309–335). Hershey, PA: IGI Global. doi:10.4018/978-1-5225-2716-9.ch017

Jean-Vasile, A., & Alecu, A. (2017). Theoretical and Practical Approaches in Understanding the Influences of Cost-Productivity-Profit Trinomial in Contemporary Enterprises. In A. Jean Vasile & D. Nicolò (Eds.), *Sustainable Entrepreneurship and Investments in the Green Economy* (pp. 28–62). Hershey, PA: IGI Global. doi:10.4018/978-1-5225-2075-7.ch002

Joia, L. A., & Correia, J. C. (2018). CIO Competencies From the IT Professional Perspective: Insights From Brazil. *Journal of Global Information Management*, *26*(2), 74–103. doi:10.4018/JGIM.2018040104

Juma, A., & Mzera, N. (2017). Knowledge Management and Records Management and Competitive Advantage in Business. In P. Jain & N. Mnjama (Eds.), *Managing Knowledge Resources and Records in Modern Organizations* (pp. 15–28). Hershey, PA: IGI Global. doi:10.4018/978-1-5225-1965-2.ch002

K., I., & A, V. (2018). Monitoring and Auditing in the Cloud. In K. Munir (Ed.), *Cloud Computing Technologies for Green Enterprises* (pp. 318-350). Hershey, PA: IGI Global. https://doi.org/ doi:10.4018/978-1-5225-3038-1.ch013

Kabra, G., Ghosh, V., & Ramesh, A. (2018). Enterprise Integrated Business Process Management and Business Intelligence Framework for Business Process Sustainability. In A. Paul, D. Bhattacharyya, & S. Anand (Eds.), *Green Initiatives for Business Sustainability and Value Creation* (pp. 228–238). Hershey, PA: IGI Global. doi:10.4018/978-1-5225-2662-9.ch010

Kaoud, M. (2017). Investigation of Customer Knowledge Management: A Case Study Research. *International Journal of Service Science, Management, Engineering, and Technology*, *8*(2), 12–22. doi:10.4018/IJSSMET.2017040102

Katuu, S. (2018). A Comparative Assessment of Enterprise Content Management Maturity Models. In N. Gwangwava & M. Mutingi (Eds.), *E-Manufacturing and E-Service Strategies in Contemporary Organizations* (pp. 93–118). Hershey, PA: IGI Global. doi:10.4018/978-1-5225-3628-4.ch005

Khan, M. Y., & Abir, T. (2022). The Role of Social Media Marketing in the Tourism and Hospitality Industry: A Conceptual Study on Bangladesh. In C. Ramos, S. Quinteiro, & A. Gonçalves (Eds.), *ICT as Innovator Between Tourism and Culture* (pp. 213–229). IGI Global. https://doi.org/10.4018/978-1-7998-8165-0.ch013

Kinnunen, S., Ylä-Kujala, A., Marttonen-Arola, S., Kärri, T., & Baglee, D. (2018). Internet of Things in Asset Management: Insights from Industrial Professionals and Academia. *International Journal of Service Science, Management, Engineering, and Technology*, *9*(2), 104–119. doi:10.4018/IJSSMET.2018040105

Klein, A. Z., Sabino de Freitas, A., Machado, L., Freitas, J. C. Jr, Graziola, P. G. Jr, & Schlemmer, E. (2017). Virtual Worlds Applications for Management Education. In L. Tomei (Ed.), *Exploring the New Era of Technology-Infused Education* (pp. 279–299). Hershey, PA: IGI Global. doi:10.4018/978-1-5225-1709-2.ch017

Kővári, E., Saleh, M., & Steinbachné Hajmásy, G. (2022). The Impact of Corporate Digital Responsibility (CDR) on Internal Stakeholders' Satisfaction in Hungarian Upscale Hotels. In M. Valeri (Ed.), *New Governance and Management in Touristic Destinations* (pp. 35–51). IGI Global. https://doi.org/10.4018/978-1-6684-3889-3.ch003

Kożuch, B., & Jabłoński, A. (2017). Adopting the Concept of Business Models in Public Management. In M. Lewandowski & B. Kożuch (Eds.), *Public Sector Entrepreneurship and the Integration of Innovative Business Models* (pp. 10–46). Hershey, PA: IGI Global. doi:10.4018/978-1-5225-2215-7.ch002

Kumar, J., Adhikary, A., & Jha, A. (2017). Small Active Investors' Perceptions and Preferences Towards Tax Saving Mutual Fund Schemes in Eastern India: An Empirical Note. *International Journal of Asian Business and Information Management, 8*(2), 35–45. doi:10.4018/IJABIM.2017040103

Latusi, S., & Fissore, M. (2021). Pilgrimage Routes to Happiness: Comparing the Camino de Santiago and Via Francigena. In A. Perinotto, V. Mayer, & J. Soares (Eds.), *Rebuilding and Restructuring the Tourism Industry: Infusion of Happiness and Quality of Life* (pp. 157–182). IGI Global. https://doi.org/10.4018/978-1-7998-7239-9.ch008

Lavassani, K. M., & Movahedi, B. (2017). Applications Driven Information Systems: Beyond Networks toward Business Ecosystems. *International Journal of Innovation in the Digital Economy, 8*(1), 61–75. doi:10.4018/IJIDE.2017010104

Lazzareschi, V. H., & Brito, M. S. (2017). Strategic Information Management: Proposal of Business Project Model. In G. Jamil, A. Soares, & C. Pessoa (Eds.), *Handbook of Research on Information Management for Effective Logistics and Supply Chains* (pp. 59–88). Hershey, PA: IGI Global. doi:10.4018/978-1-5225-0973-8.ch004

Lechuga Sancho, M. P., & Martín Navarro, A. (2022). Evolution of the Literature on Social Responsibility in the Tourism Sector: A Systematic Literature Review. In G. Fernandes (Ed.), *Challenges and New Opportunities for Tourism in Inland Territories: Ecocultural Resources and Sustainable Initiatives* (pp. 169–186). IGI Global. https://doi.org/10.4018/978-1-7998-7339-6.ch010

Lederer, M., Kurz, M., & Lazarov, P. (2017). Usage and Suitability of Methods for Strategic Business Process Initiatives: A Multi Case Study Research. *International Journal of Productivity Management and Assessment Technologies, 5*(1), 40–51. doi:10.4018/IJPMAT.2017010103

Lee, I. (2017). A Social Enterprise Business Model and a Case Study of Pacific Community Ventures (PCV). In V. Potocan, M. Üngan, & Z. Nedelko (Eds.), *Handbook of Research on Managerial Solutions in Non-Profit Organizations* (pp. 182–204). Hershey, PA: IGI Global. doi:10.4018/978-1-5225-0731-4.ch009

Leon, L. A., Seal, K. C., Przasnyski, Z. H., & Wiedenman, I. (2017). Skills and Competencies Required for Jobs in Business Analytics: A Content Analysis of Job Advertisements Using Text Mining. *International Journal of Business Intelligence Research, 8*(1), 1–25. doi:10.4018/IJBIR.2017010101

Levy, C. L., & Elias, N. I. (2017). SOHO Users' Perceptions of Reliability and Continuity of Cloud-Based Services. In M. Moore (Ed.), *Cybersecurity Breaches and Issues Surrounding Online Threat Protection* (pp. 248–287). Hershey, PA: IGI Global. doi:10.4018/978-1-5225-1941-6.ch011

Levy, M. (2018). Change Management Serving Knowledge Management and Organizational Development: Reflections and Review. In N. Baporikar (Ed.), *Global Practices in Knowledge Management for Societal and Organizational Development* (pp. 256–270). Hershey, PA: IGI Global. doi:10.4018/978-1-5225-3009-1.ch012

Lewandowski, M. (2017). Public Organizations and Business Model Innovation: The Role of Public Service Design. In M. Lewandowski & B. Kożuch (Eds.), *Public Sector Entrepreneurship and the Integration of Innovative Business Models* (pp. 47–72). Hershey, PA: IGI Global. doi:10.4018/978-1-5225-2215-7.ch003

Lhannaoui, H., Kabbaj, M. I., & Bakkoury, Z. (2017). A Survey of Risk-Aware Business Process Modelling. *International Journal of Risk and Contingency Management, 6*(3), 14–26. doi:10.4018/IJRCM.2017070102

Li, J., Sun, W., Jiang, W., Yang, H., & Zhang, L. (2017). How the Nature of Exogenous Shocks and Crises Impact Company Performance?: The Effects of Industry Characteristics. *International Journal of Risk and Contingency Management, 6*(4), 40–55. doi:10.4018/IJRCM.2017100103

Lopez-Fernandez, M., Perez-Perez, M., Serrano-Bedia, A., & Cobo-Gonzalez, A. (2021). Small and Medium Tourism Enterprise Survival in Times of Crisis: "El Capricho de Gaudí. In D. Toubes & N. Araújo-Vila (Eds.), *Risk, Crisis, and Disaster Management in Small and Medium-Sized Tourism Enterprises* (pp. 103–129). IGI Global. doi:10.4018/978-1-7998-6996-2.ch005

Mahajan, A., Maidullah, S., & Hossain, M. R. (2022). Experience Toward Smart Tour Guide Apps in Travelling: An Analysis of Users' Reviews on Audio Odigos and Trip My Way. In R. Augusto Costa, F. Brandão, Z. Breda, & C. Costa (Eds.), *Planning and Managing the Experience Economy in Tourism* (pp. 255-273). IGI Global. https://doi.org/10.4018/978-1-7998-8775-1.ch014

Malega, P. (2017). Small and Medium Enterprises in the Slovak Republic: Status and Competitiveness of SMEs in the Global Markets and Possibilities of Optimization. In M. Vemić (Ed.), *Optimal Management Strategies in Small and Medium Enterprises* (pp. 102–124). Hershey, PA: IGI Global. doi:10.4018/978-1-5225-1949-2.ch006

Malewska, K. M. (2017). Intuition in Decision-Making on the Example of a Non-Profit Organization. In V. Potocan, M. Ünğan, & Z. Nedelko (Eds.), *Handbook of Research on Managerial Solutions in Non-Profit Organizations* (pp. 378–399). Hershey, PA: IGI Global. doi:10.4018/978-1-5225-0731-4.ch018

Maroofi, F. (2017). Entrepreneurial Orientation and Organizational Learning Ability Analysis for Innovation and Firm Performance. In N. Baporikar (Ed.), *Innovation and Shifting Perspectives in Management Education* (pp. 144–165). Hershey, PA: IGI Global. doi:10.4018/978-1-5225-1019-2.ch007

Marques, M., Moleiro, D., Brito, T. M., & Marques, T. (2021). Customer Relationship Management as an Important Relationship Marketing Tool: The Case of the Hospitality Industry in Estoril Coast. In M. Dinis, L. Bonixe, S. Lamy, & Z. Breda (Eds.), Impact of New Media in Tourism (pp. 39-56). IGI Global. https://doi.org/doi:10.4018/978-1-7998-7095-1.ch003

Martins, P. V., & Zacarias, M. (2017). A Web-based Tool for Business Process Improvement. *International Journal of Web Portals*, *9*(2), 68–84. doi:10.4018/IJWP.2017070104

Matthies, B., & Coners, A. (2017). Exploring the Conceptual Nature of e-Business Projects. *Journal of Electronic Commerce in Organizations*, *15*(3), 33–63. doi:10.4018/JECO.2017070103

Mayer, V. F., Fraga, C. C., & Silva, L. C. (2021). Contributions of Neurosciences to Studies of Well-Being in Tourism. In A. Perinotto, V. Mayer, & J. Soares (Eds.), *Rebuilding and Restructuring the Tourism Industry: Infusion of Happiness and Quality of Life* (pp. 108–128). IGI Global. https://doi.org/10.4018/978-1-7998-7239-9.ch006

McKee, J. (2018). Architecture as a Tool to Solve Business Planning Problems. In M. Khosrow-Pour, D.B.A. (Ed.), Encyclopedia of Information Science and Technology, Fourth Edition (pp. 573-586). Hershey, PA: IGI Global. doi:10.4018/978-1-5225-2255-3.ch050

McMurray, A. J., Cross, J., & Caponecchia, C. (2018). The Risk Management Profession in Australia: Business Continuity Plan Practices. In N. Bajgoric (Ed.), *Always-On Enterprise Information Systems for Modern Organizations* (pp. 112–129). Hershey, PA: IGI Global. doi:10.4018/978-1-5225-3704-5.ch006

Meddah, I. H., & Belkadi, K. (2018). Mining Patterns Using Business Process Management. In R. Hamou (Ed.), *Handbook of Research on Biomimicry in Information Retrieval and Knowledge Management* (pp. 78–89). Hershey, PA: IGI Global. doi:10.4018/978-1-5225-3004-6.ch005

Melian, A. G., & Camprubí, R. (2021). The Accessibility of Museum Websites: The Case of Barcelona. In C. Eusébio, L. Teixeira, & M. Carneiro (Eds.), *ICT Tools and Applications for Accessible Tourism* (pp. 234–255). IGI Global. https://doi.org/10.4018/978-1-7998-6428-8.ch011

Mendes, L. (2017). TQM and Knowledge Management: An Integrated Approach Towards Tacit Knowledge Management. In D. Jaziri-Bouagina & G. Jamil (Eds.), *Handbook of Research on Tacit Knowledge Management for Organizational Success* (pp. 236–263). Hershey, PA: IGI Global. doi:10.4018/978-1-5225-2394-9.ch009

Menezes, V. D., & Cavagnaro, E. (2021). Communicating Sustainable Initiatives in the Hotel Industry: The Case of the Hotel Jakarta Amsterdam. In F. Brandão, Z. Breda, R. Costa, & C. Costa (Eds.), *Handbook of Research on the Role of Tourism in Achieving Sustainable Development Goals* (pp. 224-234). IGI Global. https://doi.org/10.4018/978-1-7998-5691-7.ch013

Menezes, V. D., & Cavagnaro, E. (2021). Communicating Sustainable Initiatives in the Hotel Industry: The Case of the Hotel Jakarta Amsterdam. In F. Brandão, Z. Breda, R. Costa, & C. Costa (Eds.), *Handbook of Research on the Role of Tourism in Achieving Sustainable Development Goals* (pp. 224-234). IGI Global. https://doi.org/10.4018/978-1-7998-5691-7.ch013

Mitas, O., Bastiaansen, M., & Boode, W. (2022). If You're Happy, I'm Happy: Emotion Contagion at a Tourist Information Center. In R. Augusto Costa, F. Brandão, Z. Breda, & C. Costa (Eds.), *Planning and Managing the Experience Economy in Tourism* (pp. 122-140). IGI Global. https://doi.org/10.4018/978-1-7998-8775-1.ch007

Mnjama, N. M. (2017). Preservation of Recorded Information in Public and Private Sector Organizations. In P. Jain & N. Mnjama (Eds.), *Managing Knowledge Resources and Records in Modern Organizations* (pp. 149–167). Hershey, PA: IGI Global. doi:10.4018/978-1-5225-1965-2.ch009

Mokoqama, M., & Fields, Z. (2017). Principles of Responsible Management Education (PRME): Call for Responsible Management Education. In Z. Fields (Ed.), *Collective Creativity for Responsible and Sustainable Business Practice* (pp. 229–241). Hershey, PA: IGI Global. doi:10.4018/978-1-5225-1823-5.ch012

Monteiro, A., Lopes, S., & Carbone, F. (2021). Academic Mobility: Bridging Tourism and Peace Education. In J. da Silva, Z. Breda, & F. Carbone (Eds.), *Role and Impact of Tourism in Peacebuilding and Conflict Transformation* (pp. 275-301). IGI Global. https://doi.org/10.4018/978-1-7998-5053-3.ch016

Muniapan, B. (2017). Philosophy and Management: The Relevance of Vedanta in Management. In P. Ordóñez de Pablos (Ed.), *Managerial Strategies and Solutions for Business Success in Asia* (pp. 124–139). Hershey, PA: IGI Global. doi:10.4018/978-1-5225-1886-0.ch007

Murad, S. E., & Dowaji, S. (2017). Using Value-Based Approach for Managing Cloud-Based Services. In A. Turuk, B. Sahoo, & S. Addya (Eds.), *Resource Management and Efficiency in Cloud Computing Environments* (pp. 33–60). Hershey, PA: IGI Global. doi:10.4018/978-1-5225-1721-4.ch002

Mutahar, A. M., Daud, N. M., Thurasamy, R., Isaac, O., & Abdulsalam, R. (2018). The Mediating of Perceived Usefulness and Perceived Ease of Use: The Case of Mobile Banking in Yemen. *International Journal of Technology Diffusion, 9*(2), 21–40. doi:10.4018/IJTD.2018040102

Naidoo, V. (2017). E-Learning and Management Education at African Universities. In N. Baporikar (Ed.), *Management Education for Global Leadership* (pp. 181–201). Hershey, PA: IGI Global. doi:10.4018/978-1-5225-1013-0.ch009

Naidoo, V., & Igbinakhase, I. (2018). Opportunities and Challenges of Knowledge Retention in SMEs. In N. Baporikar (Ed.), *Knowledge Integration Strategies for Entrepreneurship and Sustainability* (pp. 70–94). Hershey, PA: IGI Global. doi:10.4018/978-1-5225-5115-7.ch004

Naumov, N., & Costandachi, G. (2021). Creativity and Entrepreneurship: Gastronomic Tourism in Mexico. In J. Soares (Ed.), *Innovation and Entrepreneurial Opportunities in Community Tourism* (pp. 90–108). IGI Global. https://doi.org/10.4018/978-1-7998-4855-4.ch006

Nayak, S., & Prabhu, N. (2017). Paradigm Shift in Management Education: Need for a Cross Functional Perspective. In N. Baporikar (Ed.), *Management Education for Global Leadership* (pp. 241–255). Hershey, PA: IGI Global. doi:10.4018/978-1-5225-1013-0.ch012

Nedelko, Z., & Potocan, V. (2017). Management Solutions in Non-Profit Organizations: Case of Slovenia. In V. Potocan, M. Üngan, & Z. Nedelko (Eds.), *Handbook of Research on Managerial Solutions in Non-Profit Organizations* (pp. 1–22). Hershey, PA: IGI Global. doi:10.4018/978-1-5225-0731-4.ch001

Nedelko, Z., & Potocan, V. (2017). Priority of Management Tools Utilization among Managers: International Comparison. In V. Wang (Ed.), *Encyclopedia of Strategic Leadership and Management* (pp. 1083–1094). Hershey, PA: IGI Global. doi:10.4018/978-1-5225-1049-9.ch075

Nedelko, Z., Raudeliūnienė, J., & Črešnar, R. (2018). Knowledge Dynamics in Supply Chain Management. In N. Baporikar (Ed.), *Knowledge Integration Strategies for Entrepreneurship and Sustainability* (pp. 150–166). Hershey, PA: IGI Global. doi:10.4018/978-1-5225-5115-7.ch008

Nguyen, H. T., & Hipsher, S. A. (2018). Innovation and Creativity Used by Private Sector Firms in a Resources-Constrained Environment. In S. Hipsher (Ed.), *Examining the Private Sector's Role in Wealth Creation and Poverty Reduction* (pp. 219–238). Hershey, PA: IGI Global. doi:10.4018/978-1-5225-3117-3.ch010

Obicci, P. A. (2017). Risk Sharing in a Partnership. In *Risk Management Strategies in Public-Private Partnerships* (pp. 115–152). Hershey, PA: IGI Global. doi:10.4018/978-1-5225-2503-5.ch004

Obidallah, W. J., & Raahemi, B. (2017). Managing Changes in Service Oriented Virtual Organizations: A Structural and Procedural Framework to Facilitate the Process of Change. *Journal of Electronic Commerce in Organizations*, *15*(1), 59–83. doi:10.4018/JECO.2017010104

Ojo, O. (2017). Impact of Innovation on the Entrepreneurial Success in Selected Business Enterprises in South-West Nigeria. *International Journal of Innovation in the Digital Economy*, *8*(2), 29–38. doi:10.4018/IJIDE.2017040103

Okdinawati, L., Simatupang, T. M., & Sunitiyoso, Y. (2017). Multi-Agent Reinforcement Learning for Value Co-Creation of Collaborative Transportation Management (CTM). *International Journal of Information Systems and Supply Chain Management*, *10*(3), 84–95. doi:10.4018/IJISSCM.2017070105

Olivera, V. A., & Carrillo, I. M. (2021). Organizational Culture: A Key Element for the Development of Mexican Micro and Small Tourist Companies. In J. Soares (Ed.), *Innovation and Entrepreneurial Opportunities in Community Tourism* (pp. 227–242). IGI Global. doi:10.4018/978-1-7998-4855-4.ch013

Ossorio, M. (2022). Corporate Museum Experiences in Enogastronomic Tourism. In R. Augusto Costa, F. Brandão, Z. Breda, & C. Costa (Eds.), Planning and Managing the Experience Economy in Tourism (pp. 107-121). IGI Global. https://doi.org/doi:10.4018/978-1-7998-8775-1.ch006

Ossorio, M. (2022). Enogastronomic Tourism in Times of Pandemic. In G. Fernandes (Ed.), *Challenges and New Opportunities for Tourism in Inland Territories: Ecocultural Resources and Sustainable Initiatives* (pp. 241–255). IGI Global. https://doi.org/10.4018/978-1-7998-7339-6.ch014

Özekici, Y. K. (2022). ICT as an Acculturative Agent and Its Role in the Tourism Context: Introduction, Acculturation Theory, Progress of the Acculturation Theory in Extant Literature. In C. Ramos, S. Quinteiro, & A. Gonçalves (Eds.), *ICT as Innovator Between Tourism and Culture* (pp. 42–66). IGI Global. https://doi.org/10.4018/978-1-7998-8165-0.ch004

Pal, K. (2018). Building High Quality Big Data-Based Applications in Supply Chains. In A. Kumar & S. Saurav (Eds.), *Supply Chain Management Strategies and Risk Assessment in Retail Environments* (pp. 1–24). Hershey, PA: IGI Global. doi:10.4018/978-1-5225-3056-5.ch001

Palos-Sanchez, P. R., & Correia, M. B. (2018). Perspectives of the Adoption of Cloud Computing in the Tourism Sector. In J. Rodrigues, C. Ramos, P. Cardoso, & C. Henriques (Eds.), *Handbook of Research on Technological Developments for Cultural Heritage and eTourism Applications* (pp. 377–400). Hershey, PA: IGI Global. doi:10.4018/978-1-5225-2927-9.ch018

Papadopoulou, G. (2021). Promoting Gender Equality and Women Empowerment in the Tourism Sector. In F. Brandão, Z. Breda, R. Costa, & C. Costa (Eds.), Handbook of Research on the Role of Tourism in Achieving Sustainable Development Goals (pp. 152-174). IGI Global. https://doi.org/ doi:10.4018/978-1-7998-5691-7.ch009

Papp-Váry, Á. F., & Tóth, T. Z. (2022). Analysis of Budapest as a Film Tourism Destination. In R. Baleiro & R. Pereira (Eds.), *Global Perspectives on Literary Tourism and Film-Induced Tourism* (pp. 257-279). IGI Global. https://doi.org/10.4018/978-1-7998-8262-6.ch014

Patiño, B. E. (2017). New Generation Management by Convergence and Individual Identity: A Systemic and Human-Oriented Approach. In N. Baporikar (Ed.), *Innovation and Shifting Perspectives in Management Education* (pp. 119–143). Hershey, PA: IGI Global. doi:10.4018/978-1-5225-1019-2.ch006

Patro, C. S. (2021). Digital Tourism: Influence of E-Marketing Technology. In M. Dinis, L. Bonixe, S. Lamy, & Z. Breda (Eds.), *Impact of New Media in Tourism* (pp. 234-254). IGI Global. https://doi.org/10.4018/978-1-7998-7095-1.ch014

Pawliczek, A., & Rössler, M. (2017). Knowledge of Management Tools and Systems in SMEs: Knowledge Transfer in Management. In A. Bencsik (Ed.), *Knowledge Management Initiatives and Strategies in Small and Medium Enterprises* (pp. 180–203). Hershey, PA: IGI Global. doi:10.4018/978-1-5225-1642-2.ch009

Pejic-Bach, M., Omazic, M. A., Aleksic, A., & Zoroja, J. (2018). Knowledge-Based Decision Making: A Multi-Case Analysis. In R. Leon (Ed.), *Managerial Strategies for Business Sustainability During Turbulent Times* (pp. 160–184). Hershey, PA: IGI Global. doi:10.4018/978-1-5225-2716-9.ch009

Perano, M., Hysa, X., & Calabrese, M. (2018). Strategic Planning, Cultural Context, and Business Continuity Management: Business Cases in the City of Shkoder. In A. Presenza & L. Sheehan (Eds.), *Geopolitics and Strategic Management in the Global Economy* (pp. 57–77). Hershey, PA: IGI Global. doi:10.4018/978-1-5225-2673-5.ch004

Pereira, R., Mira da Silva, M., & Lapão, L. V. (2017). IT Governance Maturity Patterns in Portuguese Healthcare. In S. De Haes & W. Van Grembergen (Eds.), *Strategic IT Governance and Alignment in Business Settings* (pp. 24–52). Hershey, PA: IGI Global. doi:10.4018/978-1-5225-0861-8.ch002

Pérez-Uribe, R. I., Torres, D. A., Jurado, S. P., & Prada, D. M. (2018). Cloud Tools for the Development of Project Management in SMEs. In R. Perez-Uribe, C. Salcedo-Perez, & D. Ocampo-Guzman (Eds.), *Handbook of Research on Intrapreneurship and Organizational Sustainability in SMEs* (pp. 95–120). Hershey, PA: IGI Global. doi:10.4018/978-1-5225-3543-0.ch005

Petrisor, I., & Cozmiuc, D. (2017). Global Supply Chain Management Organization at Siemens in the Advent of Industry 4.0. In L. Saglietto & C. Cezanne (Eds.), *Global Intermediation and Logistics Service Providers* (pp. 123–142). Hershey, PA: IGI Global. doi:10.4018/978-1-5225-2133-4.ch007

Pierce, J. M., Velliaris, D. M., & Edwards, J. (2017). A Living Case Study: A Journey Not a Destination. In N. Silton (Ed.), *Exploring the Benefits of Creativity in Education, Media, and the Arts* (pp. 158–178). Hershey, PA: IGI Global. doi:10.4018/978-1-5225-0504-4.ch008

Pipia, S., & Pipia, S. (2021). Challenges of Religious Tourism in the Conflict Region: An Example of Jerusalem. In E. Alaverdov & M. Bari (Eds.), *Global Development of Religious Tourism* (pp. 135-148). IGI Global. https://doi.org/10.4018/978-1-7998-5792-1.ch009

Poulaki, P., Kritikos, A., Vasilakis, N., & Valeri, M. (2022). The Contribution of Female Creativity to the Development of Gastronomic Tourism in Greece: The Case of the Island of Naxos in the South Aegean Region. In M. Valeri (Ed.), *New Governance and Management in Touristic Destinations* (pp. 246–258). IGI Global. https://doi.org/10.4018/978-1-6684-3889-3.ch015

Radosavljevic, M., & Andjelkovic, A. (2017). Multi-Criteria Decision Making Approach for Choosing Business Process for the Improvement: Upgrading of the Six Sigma Methodology. In J. Stanković, P. Delias, S. Marinković, & S. Rochhia (Eds.), *Tools and Techniques for Economic Decision Analysis* (pp. 225–247). Hershey, PA: IGI Global. doi:10.4018/978-1-5225-0959-2.ch011

Radovic, V. M. (2017). Corporate Sustainability and Responsibility and Disaster Risk Reduction: A Serbian Overview. In M. Camilleri (Ed.), *CSR 2.0 and the New Era of Corporate Citizenship* (pp. 147–164). Hershey, PA: IGI Global. doi:10.4018/978-1-5225-1842-6.ch008

Raghunath, K. M., Devi, S. L., & Patro, C. S. (2018). Impact of Risk Assessment Models on Risk Factors: A Holistic Outlook. In K. Strang, M. Korstanje, & N. Vajjhala (Eds.), *Research, Practices, and Innovations in Global Risk and Contingency Management* (pp. 134–153). Hershey, PA: IGI Global. doi:10.4018/978-1-5225-4754-9.ch008

Raman, A., & Goyal, D. P. (2017). Extending IMPLEMENT Framework for Enterprise Information Systems Implementation to Information System Innovation. In M. Tavana (Ed.), *Enterprise Information Systems and the Digitalization of Business Functions* (pp. 137–177). Hershey, PA: IGI Global. doi:10.4018/978-1-5225-2382-6.ch007

Rao, Y., & Zhang, Y. (2017). The Construction and Development of Academic Library Digital Special Subject Databases. In L. Ruan, Q. Zhu, & Y. Ye (Eds.), *Academic Library Development and Administration in China* (pp. 163–183). Hershey, PA: IGI Global. doi:10.4018/978-1-5225-0550-1.ch010

Ravasan, A. Z., Mohammadi, M. M., & Hamidi, H. (2018). An Investigation Into the Critical Success Factors of Implementing Information Technology Service Management Frameworks. In K. Jakobs (Ed.), *Corporate and Global Standardization Initiatives in Contemporary Society* (pp. 200–218). Hershey, PA: IGI Global. doi:10.4018/978-1-5225-5320-5.ch009

Rezaie, S., Mirabedini, S. J., & Abtahi, A. (2018). Designing a Model for Implementation of Business Intelligence in the Banking Industry. *International Journal of Enterprise Information Systems, 14*(1), 77–103. doi:10.4018/IJEIS.2018010105

Richards, V., Matthews, N., Williams, O. J., & Khan, Z. (2021). The Challenges of Accessible Tourism Information Systems for Tourists With Vision Impairment: Sensory Communications Beyond the Screen. In C. Eusébio, L. Teixeira, & M. Carneiro (Eds.), *ICT Tools and Applications for Accessible Tourism* (pp. 26–54). IGI Global. https://doi.org/10.4018/978-1-7998-6428-8.ch002

Rodrigues de Souza Neto, V., & Marques, O. (2021). Rural Tourism Fostering Welfare Through Sustainable Development: A Conceptual Approach. In A. Perinotto, V. Mayer, & J. Soares (Eds.), *Rebuilding and Restructuring the Tourism Industry: Infusion of Happiness and Quality of Life* (pp. 38–57). IGI Global. https://doi.org/10.4018/978-1-7998-7239-9.ch003

Romano, L., Grimaldi, R., & Colasuonno, F. S. (2017). Demand Management as a Success Factor in Project Portfolio Management. In L. Romano (Ed.), *Project Portfolio Management Strategies for Effective Organizational Operations* (pp. 202–219). Hershey, PA: IGI Global. doi:10.4018/978-1-5225-2151-8.ch008

Rubio-Escuderos, L., & García-Andreu, H. (2021). Competitiveness Factors of Accessible Tourism E-Travel Agencies. In C. Eusébio, L. Teixeira, & M. Carneiro (Eds.), *ICT Tools and Applications for Accessible Tourism* (pp. 196–217). IGI Global. https://doi.org/10.4018/978-1-7998-6428-8.ch009

Rucci, A. C., Porto, N., Darcy, S., & Becka, L. (2021). Smart and Accessible Cities?: Not Always – The Case for Accessible Tourism Initiatives in Buenos Aries and Sydney. In C. Eusébio, L. Teixeira, & M. Carneiro (Eds.), *ICT Tools and Applications for Accessible Tourism* (pp. 115–145). IGI Global. https://doi.org/10.4018/978-1-7998-6428-8.ch006

Ruhi, U. (2018). Towards an Interdisciplinary Socio-Technical Definition of Virtual Communities. In M. Khosrow-Pour, D.B.A. (Ed.), Encyclopedia of Information Science and Technology, Fourth Edition (pp. 4278-4295). Hershey, PA: IGI Global. doi:10.4018/978-1-5225-2255-3.ch371

Ryan, L., Catena, M., Ros, P., & Stephens, S. (2021). Designing Entrepreneurial Ecosystems to Support Resource Management in the Tourism Industry. In V. Costa, A. Moura, & M. Mira (Eds.), *Handbook of Research on Human Capital and People Management in the Tourism Industry* (pp. 265–281). IGI Global. https://doi.org/10.4018/978-1-7998-4318-4.ch013

Sabuncu, I. (2021). Understanding Tourist Perceptions and Expectations During Pandemic Through Social Media Big Data. In M. Demir, A. Dalgıç, & F. Ergen (Eds.), *Handbook of Research on the Impacts and Implications of COVID-19 on the Tourism Industry* (pp. 330–350). IGI Global. https://doi.org/10.4018/978-1-7998-8231-2.ch016

Safari, M. R., & Jiang, Q. (2018). The Theory and Practice of IT Governance Maturity and Strategies Alignment: Evidence From Banking Industry. *Journal of Global Information Management, 26*(2), 127–146. doi:10.4018/JGIM.2018040106

Sahoo, J., Pati, B., & Mohanty, B. (2017). Knowledge Management as an Academic Discipline: An Assessment. In B. Gunjal (Ed.), *Managing Knowledge and Scholarly Assets in Academic Libraries* (pp. 99–126). Hershey, PA: IGI Global. doi:10.4018/978-1-5225-1741-2.ch005

Saini, D. (2017). Relevance of Teaching Values and Ethics in Management Education. In N. Baporikar (Ed.), *Management Education for Global Leadership* (pp. 90–111). Hershey, PA: IGI Global. doi:10.4018/978-1-5225-1013-0.ch005

Sambhanthan, A. (2017). Assessing and Benchmarking Sustainability in Organisations: An Integrated Conceptual Model. *International Journal of Systems and Service-Oriented Engineering, 7*(4), 22–43. doi:10.4018/IJSSOE.2017100102

Sambhanthan, A., & Potdar, V. (2017). A Study of the Parameters Impacting Sustainability in Information Technology Organizations. *International Journal of Knowledge-Based Organizations, 7*(3), 27–39. doi:10.4018/IJKBO.2017070103

Sánchez-Fernández, M. D., & Manríquez, M. R. (2018). The Entrepreneurial Spirit Based on Social Values: The Digital Generation. In P. Isaias & L. Carvalho (Eds.), *User Innovation and the Entrepreneurship Phenomenon in the Digital Economy* (pp. 173–193). Hershey, PA: IGI Global. doi:10.4018/978-1-5225-2826-5.ch009

Sanchez-Ruiz, L., & Blanco, B. (2017). Process Management for SMEs: Barriers, Enablers, and Benefits. In M. Vemić (Ed.), *Optimal Management Strategies in Small and Medium Enterprises* (pp. 293–319). Hershey, PA: IGI Global. doi:10.4018/978-1-5225-1949-2.ch014

Sanz, L. F., Gómez-Pérez, J., & Castillo-Martinez, A. (2018). Analysis of the European ICT Competence Frameworks. In V. Ahuja & S. Rathore (Eds.), *Multidisciplinary Perspectives on Human Capital and Information Technology Professionals* (pp. 225–245). Hershey, PA: IGI Global. doi:10.4018/978-1-5225-5297-0.ch012

Sarvepalli, A., & Godin, J. (2017). Business Process Management in the Classroom. *Journal of Cases on Information Technology, 19*(2), 17–28. doi:10.4018/JCIT.2017040102

Saxena, G. G., & Saxena, A. (2021). Host Community Role in Medical Tourism Development. In M. Singh & S. Kumaran (Eds.), *Growth of the Medical Tourism Industry and Its Impact on Society: Emerging Research and Opportunities* (pp. 105–127). IGI Global. https://doi.org/10.4018/978-1-7998-3427-4.ch006

Saygili, E. E., Ozturkoglu, Y., & Kocakulah, M. C. (2017). End Users' Perceptions of Critical Success Factors in ERP Applications. *International Journal of Enterprise Information Systems, 13*(4), 58–75. doi:10.4018/IJEIS.2017100104

Saygili, E. E., & Saygili, A. T. (2017). Contemporary Issues in Enterprise Information Systems: A Critical Review of CSFs in ERP Implementations. In M. Tavana (Ed.), *Enterprise Information Systems and the Digitalization of Business Functions* (pp. 120–136). Hershey, PA: IGI Global. doi:10.4018/978-1-5225-2382-6.ch006

Schwaiger, K. M., & Zehrer, A. (2021). The COVID-19 Pandemic and Organizational Resilience in Hospitality Family Firms: A Qualitative Approach. In A. Zehrer, G. Glowka, K. Schwaiger, & V. Ranacher-Lackner (Eds.), *Resiliency Models and Addressing Future Risks for Family Firms in the Tourism Industry* (pp. 32–49). IGI Global. https://doi.org/10.4018/978-1-7998-7352-5.ch002

Scott, N., & Campos, A. C. (2022). Cognitive Science of Tourism Experiences. In R. Augusto Costa, F. Brandão, Z. Breda, & C. Costa (Eds.), Planning and Managing the Experience Economy in Tourism (pp. 1-21). IGI Global. https://doi.org/ doi:10.4018/978-1-7998-8775-1.ch001

Seidenstricker, S., & Antonino, A. (2018). Business Model Innovation-Oriented Technology Management for Emergent Technologies. In M. Khosrow-Pour, D.B.A. (Ed.), Encyclopedia of Information Science and Technology, Fourth Edition (pp. 4560-4569). Hershey, PA: IGI Global. doi:10.4018/978-1-5225-2255-3.ch396

Selvi, M. S. (2021). Changes in Tourism Sales and Marketing Post COVID-19. In M. Demir, A. Dalgıç, & F. Ergen (Eds.), *Handbook of Research on the Impacts and Implications of COVID-19 on the Tourism Industry* (pp. 437–460). IGI Global. doi:10.4018/978-1-7998-8231-2.ch021

Senaratne, S., & Gunarathne, A. D. (2017). Excellence Perspective for Management Education from a Global Accountants' Hub in Asia. In N. Baporikar (Ed.), *Management Education for Global Leadership* (pp. 158–180). Hershey, PA: IGI Global. doi:10.4018/978-1-5225-1013-0.ch008

Sensuse, D. I., & Cahyaningsih, E. (2018). Knowledge Management Models: A Summative Review. *International Journal of Information Systems in the Service Sector*, *10*(1), 71–100. doi:10.4018/IJISSS.2018010105

Seth, M., Goyal, D., & Kiran, R. (2017). Diminution of Impediments in Implementation of Supply Chain Management Information System for Enhancing its Effectiveness in Indian Automobile Industry. *Journal of Global Information Management*, *25*(3), 1–20. doi:10.4018/JGIM.2017070101

Seyal, A. H., & Rahman, M. N. (2017). Investigating Impact of Inter-Organizational Factors in Measuring ERP Systems Success: Bruneian Perspectives. In M. Tavana (Ed.), *Enterprise Information Systems and the Digitalization of Business Functions* (pp. 178–204). Hershey, PA: IGI Global. doi:10.4018/978-1-5225-2382-6.ch008

Shaqrah, A. A. (2018). Analyzing Business Intelligence Systems Based on 7s Model of McKinsey. *International Journal of Business Intelligence Research*, *9*(1), 53–63. doi:10.4018/IJBIR.2018010104

Sharma, A. J. (2017). Enhancing Sustainability through Experiential Learning in Management Education. In N. Baporikar (Ed.), *Management Education for Global Leadership* (pp. 256–274). Hershey, PA: IGI Global. doi:10.4018/978-1-5225-1013-0.ch013

Shetty, K. P. (2017). Responsible Global Leadership: Ethical Challenges in Management Education. In N. Baporikar (Ed.), *Innovation and Shifting Perspectives in Management Education* (pp. 194–223). Hershey, PA: IGI Global. doi:10.4018/978-1-5225-1019-2.ch009

Sinthupundaja, J., & Kohda, Y. (2017). Effects of Corporate Social Responsibility and Creating Shared Value on Sustainability. *International Journal of Sustainable Entrepreneurship and Corporate Social Responsibility*, *2*(1), 27–38. doi:10.4018/IJSECSR.2017010103

Škarica, I., & Hrgović, A. V. (2018). Implementation of Total Quality Management Principles in Public Health Institutes in the Republic of Croatia. *International Journal of Productivity Management and Assessment Technologies*, *6*(1), 1–16. doi:10.4018/IJPMAT.2018010101

Skokic, V. (2021). How Small Hotel Owners Practice Resilience: Longitudinal Study Among Small Family Hotels in Croatia. In A. Zehrer, G. Glowka, K. Schwaiger, & V. Ranacher-Lackner (Eds.), *Resiliency Models and Addressing Future Risks for Family Firms in the Tourism Industry* (pp. 50–73). IGI Global. doi:10.4018/978-1-7998-7352-5.ch003

Smuts, H., Kotzé, P., Van der Merwe, A., & Loock, M. (2017). Framework for Managing Shared Knowledge in an Information Systems Outsourcing Context. *International Journal of Knowledge Management*, *13*(4), 1–30. doi:10.4018/IJKM.2017100101

Sousa, M. J., Cruz, R., Dias, I., & Caracol, C. (2017). Information Management Systems in the Supply Chain. In G. Jamil, A. Soares, & C. Pessoa (Eds.), *Handbook of Research on Information Management for Effective Logistics and Supply Chains* (pp. 469–485). Hershey, PA: IGI Global. doi:10.4018/978-1-5225-0973-8.ch025

Spremic, M., Turulja, L., & Bajgoric, N. (2018). Two Approaches in Assessing Business Continuity Management Attitudes in the Organizational Context. In N. Bajgoric (Ed.), *Always-On Enterprise Information Systems for Modern Organizations* (pp. 159–183). Hershey, PA: IGI Global. doi:10.4018/978-1-5225-3704-5.ch008

Steenkamp, A. L. (2018). Some Insights in Computer Science and Information Technology. In *Examining the Changing Role of Supervision in Doctoral Research Projects: Emerging Research and Opportunities* (pp. 113–133). Hershey, PA: IGI Global. doi:10.4018/978-1-5225-2610-0.ch005

Stipanović, C., Rudan, E., & Zubović, V. (2022). Reaching the New Tourist Through Creativity: Sustainable Development Challenges in Croatian Coastal Towns. In M. Valeri (Ed.), *New Governance and Management in Touristic Destinations* (pp. 231–245). IGI Global. https://doi.org/10.4018/978-1-6684-3889-3.ch014

Tabach, A., & Croteau, A. (2017). Configurations of Information Technology Governance Practices and Business Unit Performance. *International Journal of IT/Business Alignment and Governance*, *8*(2), 1–27. doi:10.4018/IJITBAG.2017070101

Talauc, G. M., & Iqbal, T. (2017). Assessment of e-Business Mode of Selected Private Universities in the Philippines and Pakistan. *International Journal of Online Marketing*, *7*(4), 63–77. doi:10.4018/IJOM.2017100105

Tam, G. C. (2017). Project Manager Sustainability Competence. In *Managerial Strategies and Green Solutions for Project Sustainability* (pp. 178–207). Hershey, PA: IGI Global. doi:10.4018/978-1-5225-2371-0.ch008

Tambo, T. (2018). Fashion Retail Innovation: About Context, Antecedents, and Outcome in Technological Change Projects. In I. Management Association (Ed.), Fashion and Textiles: Breakthroughs in Research and Practice (pp. 233-260). Hershey, PA: IGI Global. https://doi.org/ doi:10.4018/978-1-5225-3432-7.ch010

Tantau, A. D., & Frăţilă, L. C. (2018). Information and Management System for Renewable Energy Business. In *Entrepreneurship and Business Development in the Renewable Energy Sector* (pp. 200–244). Hershey, PA: IGI Global. doi:10.4018/978-1-5225-3625-3.ch006

Teixeira, N., Pardal, P. N., & Rafael, B. G. (2018). Internationalization, Financial Performance, and Organizational Challenges: A Success Case in Portugal. In L. Carvalho (Ed.), *Handbook of Research on Entrepreneurial Ecosystems and Social Dynamics in a Globalized World* (pp. 379–423). Hershey, PA: IGI Global. doi:10.4018/978-1-5225-3525-6.ch017

Teixeira, P., Teixeira, L., Eusébio, C., Silva, S., & Teixeira, A. (2021). The Impact of ICTs on Accessible Tourism: Evidence Based on a Systematic Literature Review. In C. Eusébio, L. Teixeira, & M. Carneiro (Eds.), *ICT Tools and Applications for Accessible Tourism* (pp. 1–25). IGI Global. doi:10.4018/978-1-7998-6428-8.ch001

Trad, A., & Kalpić, D. (2018). The Business Transformation Framework, Agile Project and Change Management. In M. Khosrow-Pour, D.B.A. (Ed.), Encyclopedia of Information Science and Technology, Fourth Edition (pp. 620-635). Hershey, PA: IGI Global. https://doi.org/ doi:10.4018/978-1-5225-2255-3.ch054

Trad, A., & Kalpić, D. (2018). The Business Transformation and Enterprise Architecture Framework: The Financial Engineering E-Risk Management and E-Law Integration. In B. Sergi, F. Fidanoski, M. Ziolo, & V. Naumovski (Eds.), *Regaining Global Stability After the Financial Crisis* (pp. 46–65). Hershey, PA: IGI Global. doi:10.4018/978-1-5225-4026-7.ch003

Trengereid, V. (2022). Conditions of Network Engagement: The Quest for a Common Good. In R. Augusto Costa, F. Brandão, Z. Breda, & C. Costa (Eds.), *Planning and Managing the Experience Economy in Tourism* (pp. 69-84). IGI Global. https://doi.org/10.4018/978-1-7998-8775-1.ch004

Turulja, L., & Bajgoric, N. (2018). Business Continuity and Information Systems: A Systematic Literature Review. In N. Bajgoric (Ed.), *Always-On Enterprise Information Systems for Modern Organizations* (pp. 60–87). Hershey, PA: IGI Global. doi:10.4018/978-1-5225-3704-5.ch004

Vargas-Hernández, J. G. (2017). Professional Integrity in Business Management Education. In N. Baporikar (Ed.), *Management Education for Global Leadership* (pp. 70–89). Hershey, PA: IGI Global. doi:10.4018/978-1-5225-1013-0.ch004

Varnacı Uzun, F. (2021). The Destination Preferences of Foreign Tourists During the COVID-19 Pandemic and Attitudes Towards: Marmaris, Turkey. In M. Demir, A. Dalgıç, & F. Ergen (Eds.), *Handbook of Research on the Impacts and Implications of COVID-19 on the Tourism Industry* (pp. 285–306). IGI Global. https://doi.org/10.4018/978-1-7998-8231-2.ch014

Vasista, T. G., & AlAbdullatif, A. M. (2017). Role of Electronic Customer Relationship Management in Demand Chain Management: A Predictive Analytic Approach. *International Journal of Information Systems and Supply Chain Management, 10*(1), 53–67. doi:10.4018/IJISSCM.2017010104

Vieru, D., & Bourdeau, S. (2017). Survival in the Digital Era: A Digital Competence-Based Multi-Case Study in the Canadian SME Clothing Industry. *International Journal of Social and Organizational Dynamics in IT*, *6*(1), 17–34. doi:10.4018/IJSODIT.2017010102

Vijayan, G., & Kamarulzaman, N. H. (2017). An Introduction to Sustainable Supply Chain Management and Business Implications. In M. Khan, M. Hussain, & M. Ajmal (Eds.), *Green Supply Chain Management for Sustainable Business Practice* (pp. 27–50). Hershey, PA: IGI Global. doi:10.4018/978-1-5225-0635-5.ch002

Vlachvei, A., & Notta, O. (2017). Firm Competitiveness: Theories, Evidence, and Measurement. In A. Vlachvei, O. Notta, K. Karantininis, & N. Tsounis (Eds.), *Factors Affecting Firm Competitiveness and Performance in the Modern Business World* (pp. 1–42). Hershey, PA: IGI Global. doi:10.4018/978-1-5225-0843-4.ch001

Wang, C., Schofield, M., Li, X., & Ou, X. (2017). Do Chinese Students in Public and Private Higher Education Institutes Perform at Different Level in One of the Leadership Skills: Critical Thinking?: An Exploratory Comparison. In V. Wang (Ed.), *Encyclopedia of Strategic Leadership and Management* (pp. 160–181). Hershey, PA: IGI Global. doi:10.4018/978-1-5225-1049-9.ch013

Wang, J. (2017). Multi-Agent based Production Management Decision System Modelling for the Textile Enterprise. *Journal of Global Information Management, 25*(4), 1–15. doi:10.4018/JGIM.2017100101

Wiedemann, A., & Gewald, H. (2017). Examining Cross-Domain Alignment: The Correlation of Business Strategy, IT Management, and IT Business Value. *International Journal of IT/Business Alignment and Governance*, *8*(1), 17–31. doi:10.4018/IJITBAG.2017010102

Wolf, R., & Thiel, M. (2018). Advancing Global Business Ethics in China: Reducing Poverty Through Human and Social Welfare. In S. Hipsher (Ed.), *Examining the Private Sector's Role in Wealth Creation and Poverty Reduction* (pp. 67–84). Hershey, PA: IGI Global. doi:10.4018/978-1-5225-3117-3.ch004

Yablonsky, S. (2018). Innovation Platforms: Data and Analytics Platforms. In *Multi-Sided Platforms (MSPs) and Sharing Strategies in the Digital Economy: Emerging Research and Opportunities* (pp. 72–95). Hershey, PA: IGI Global. doi:10.4018/978-1-5225-5457-8.ch003

Yaşar, B. (2021). The Impact of COVID-19 on Volatility of Tourism Stocks: Evidence From BIST Tourism Index. In M. Demir, A. Dalgıç, & F. Ergen (Eds.), *Handbook of Research on the Impacts and Implications of COVID-19 on the Tourism Industry* (pp. 23–44). IGI Global. https://doi.org/10.4018/978-1-7998-8231-2.ch002

Yusoff, A., Ahmad, N. H., & Halim, H. A. (2017). Agropreneurship among Gen Y in Malaysia: The Role of Academic Institutions. In N. Ahmad, T. Ramayah, H. Halim, & S. Rahman (Eds.), *Handbook of Research on Small and Medium Enterprises in Developing Countries* (pp. 23–47). Hershey, PA: IGI Global. doi:10.4018/978-1-5225-2165-5.ch002

Zacher, D., & Pechlaner, H. (2021). Resilience as an Opportunity Approach: Challenges and Perspectives for Private Sector Participation on a Community Level. In A. Zehrer, G. Glowka, K. Schwaiger, & V. Ranacher-Lackner (Eds.), *Resiliency Models and Addressing Future Risks for Family Firms in the Tourism Industry* (pp. 75–102). IGI Global. https://doi.org/10.4018/978-1-7998-7352-5.ch004

Zanin, F., Comuzzi, E., & Costantini, A. (2018). The Effect of Business Strategy and Stock Market Listing on the Use of Risk Assessment Tools. In *Management Control Systems in Complex Settings: Emerging Research and Opportunities* (pp. 145–168). Hershey, PA: IGI Global. doi:10.4018/978-1-5225-3987-2.ch007

Zgheib, P. W. (2017). Corporate Innovation and Intrapreneurship in the Middle East. In P. Zgheib (Ed.), *Entrepreneurship and Business Innovation in the Middle East* (pp. 37–56). Hershey, PA: IGI Global. doi:10.4018/978-1-5225-2066-5.ch003

About the Contributors

Mohammad Rafiqul Islam Talukdar is a Professor of Business Administration at American International University-Bangladesh (AIUB), Dhaka, Bangladesh. The International Education Summit & Awards, 2020 Bangkok, selected Dr. Talukdar as an Outstanding Trained Graduate Teacher for his significant contributions in teaching, research, and curriculum development. Political economy, gender-responsive budgeting and planning, gender and development, decentralization and governance, sustainable development, performance management, talent management, strategic and change management, and leadership and entrepreneurship development are among his research interests. He has authored 2 internationally published books, 2 nationally published books, 5 internationally published book chapters, 15 internationally published scholarly journal articles, 6 nationally published peer-reviewed journal articles, 2 working papers, and 100 OP-ED pieces. He undertook several assignments in Bangladesh, Thailand, the Philippines, and Vietnam.

Carmen Z. Lamagna is a Professor and the Vice Chancellor at American International University-Bangladesh (AIUB), Dhaka, Bangladesh. Her achievements as an educator and manager may be gleaned from the positions she has held in prestigious international bodies. She was the Treasurer (2011-2014) and Board member (2017-present) of the International Association of University Presidents (IAUP), Administrative Board Member (2017-present) of the International Association of Universities (IAU), with the Association of Universities of Asia and the Pacific (AUAP) as an ex-official board member (2010-2018), having served as the first female President from 2008 to 2010, and AUAP Advisory Council member for 2021. She was one of the awardees of the 2006 Presidential Award for Overseas Filipinos, was selected as one of the top 100 women in the world by the International Alliance for Women in 2012 and was awarded as one of the 100 most influential Filipinas in 2014 by the Filipina Women Network. She has inspired women to act in support of women's empowerment and advancement in society as Bangladesh's first female Vice Chancellor. Her extraordinary accomplishments in promoting women through education-based programs, initiatives, or personal action in a developing country like Bangladesh have earned her the most coveted recognition.

Charles Carillo Villanueva is a Professor and the Dean of Business Administration at American International University-Bangladesh (AIUB), Dhaka, Bangladesh. He is also the Director of the University's Quality Assurance Cell/Center. He held various managerial and technical positions in the Philippine government for 31 years, including Chief Educational Planning Analyst, Chief Educational Researcher, and first Director IV, CESO III, of the Office of Planning, Policy, Research, and Information of the Commission on Higher Education, Manila, Philippines. UNESCO hired him as an educational consultant in Bangladesh, Thailand, Myanmar, Pakistan, Vietnam, China, South Korea, Kazakhstan, Tajikistan, Uzbekistan, Armenia, Syria, and Paris, France because of his pioneering work in establishing EMIS and HEMIS in the Philippines and other Southeast Asian countries. After his early retirement in 2000, he was Vice President for Academic Affairs at Aklan Catholic College, Philippines. He has authored Training Manuals on EMIS (English and Russian), Training Modules on Educational Planning and Management, Quality Assurance, professional papers in journals, national and international papers, locally and internationally sponsored research, projects, trainers, and more. He's been a speaker at worldwide and national quality assurance conferences and seminars. He's won national and international awards for his excellent work in education, civics, and social work.

Rezbin Nahar is an Associate Professor in the Department of Management and Human Resources Management at the Faculty of Business Administration of American International University Bangladesh (AIUB), Dhaka, Bangladesh. Previously, she taught at Southeast Business School of Southeast University. Her professional experiences provided her with a range of insights that, over the years, have proven useful in guiding students with projects and assignments. Throughout her career, she devoted herself to various research activities, which have been published in the form of research articles in numerous scholarly journals and proceedings of national and international conferences. Her research interests are broadly concentrated within the fields of management, human resources management, education, and organizational behavioral contexts. development issues.

Farheen Hassan is a Professor and Director of the BBA Program, as well as the Department Head of Management and Human Resources in the Faculty of Business Administration at American International University-Bangladesh (AIUB), Dhaka, Bangladesh. She is also the Additional Director of AIUB's Institutional Quality Assurance Cell. She also works as an External Peer Reviewer, Trainer, and Resource

Speaker as a QA Practitioner in Higher Education (HE). She is an educator of Business Studies with 24 years of teaching and consulting experience in the education, NGO, development, and service sectors. Having taught as a course instructor at the University of Madras, India; and in the BBA & MBA programs of the University of Gavle, Sweden as a visiting lecturer, she has also worked as a consultant on QA with IIEP-UNESCO, Paris; ISAS-IAU-UNESCO; MTC Global, India; and participated in research projects with the British Council.

* * *

Aditi Vijaysingh Aljapurkar has a decade of experience in teaching management programs across various institutes and universities. Her areas of interest are in the fields of organizational behavior and human resource management, which she has developed through extensive research, teaching, and extension activities. She has keenly worked on her writings by publishing research papers, books, and case studies on her record. She is actively engaged in role-based training. She holds a vivid interest in corporate networking in different sectors and startups for entrepreneurial activities.

Bülent Akkaya works as a Lecturer in the Department of Office Management-Executive Assistant at Manisa Celal Bayar University in Turkey. He holds a PhD in Business Administration Management with a specialization in Management, Leadership, and Agility in Science Parks. His research interests comprise networks and partnerships in diverse disciplines. He has been working on questions of dynamic capabilities, agile leadership, and the quality of management in contemporary enterprises.

Okechukwu Ethelbert Amah is a full-time faculty at Lagos Business School, Pan Atlantic University, where he facilitates sessions in organizational behavior and human resources management. He is the author of the book "Globalization and Leadership in Africa: Developments and Challenges for the Future."

Rafat Azad has completed his undergraduate thesis at American International University-Bangladesh (AIUB), Bangladesh under the supervision of Md. Manzurul Hasan, Assistant Professor, Department of Computer Science and Engineering.

Humayra Ferdous an academician. She advocates for investment on human resources to achieve higher standard in education. She believes the leadership quality among the citizens of a country would flourish if human resources were converted into human capital. She also has a keen interest in public health and health policy of a country to have better and affordable healthcare for all. She has been conducting research in the field of Biomedical Physics and Technology for the last ten years. Her research area includes lung impedance measurement, electrical propertied of living bodies, low-cost instrumentation etc. Upon completion of her doctoral studies from the University of Oslo, Norway in 2014, Dr. Ferdous continued her academic career in the Department of Physics of Faculty of Science and Technology (FST), American International University' Bangladesh (AIUB). Currently, she has been serving there as an Associate Professor. She received her Master of Science and Bachelor Science (Hons) degree in Physics from the University of Dhaka, Bangladesh in 2009 (session 2005-06). She has conducted several research projects in the field of Physics Education too.

Manzurul Hasan obtained his B. Sc. Engg. in Computer Science and Engineering (CSE) and M. Sc. Engg. in CSE from Chittagong University of Engineering & Technology (CUET) and Bangladesh University of Engineering & Technology (BUET), respectively. He is now a Ph.D. applicant from the department of CSE, BUET, Bangladesh. Mr. Hasan is currently serving at the Department of Computer Science as Assistant Professor at American International University-Bangladesh (AIUB). He served at different reputed professional organizations and teaching positions with a service length near about 16 years. He is an active member of different professional bodies like the Institute of Engineers (IEB), Bangladesh Computer Society, etc. Depending on the research activity at his young age, he was invited to attend the 12th HOPE Meeting with Nobel Laureates funded by JSPS, Japan. Mr. Hasan has a good number of prestigious publications in different journals and different conference proceedings like Springer, ACM, IEEE Xplore, Taylor and Francis etc.

Sheikh Shamim Hasnain works at British University in Egypt as a Senior Lecturer (Associate Professor). Hasnain has taught at numerous universities in the UK, Egypt, and Bangladesh. Besides many academic papers, he has also written a book titled "Knowledge Management in Non-Governmental Organizations: Towards a New Horizon," which tackles current knowledge management issues.

Md. Mohsin Hossain has completed his undergraduate thesis at American International University-Bangladesh (AIUB), Bangladesh under the supervision of Md. Manzurul Hasan, Assistant Professor, Department of Computer Science and Engineering.

Shahadat Hossain is a Lecturer at the Faculty of Science and Engineering, City University. Prior to entering City University, he was a Lecturer at the Department of Computer Science and Engineering at the University of South Asia. His research focuses are on addressing the effect of human behaviors on various digital platforms by integrating data visualization and behavior analysis with machine learning. More precisely, he is interested in exploring new aspects of behavioral analysis by analyzing real-time datasets and by considering the usefulness and possible trade-offs of such approaches from the perspectives of real-world users. Under the supervision of Md. Manzurul Hasan, He earned his master's in computer science from American International University-Bangladesh (AIUB). He has published papers in the prestigious Proceedings of the world-famous publisher Springer, Taylor & Francis, and the CRC Press of Taylor & Francis. Many of his papers are currently under review.

Emmanuel Ogbeide **Imafidon** is a Senior Fellow at the Lagos Business School where he facilitates learning in the Organizational Behavior & Human Resource Management Department. Prior to joining Lagos Business School, he had worked for over three decades in the education, manufacturing, and energy sectors in Nigeria. He was the Director of Human Resources & Medical in Chevron Nigeria Limited for seven years and subsequently, the Director of Business Services for nine years in the same company. He has a bachelor's degree in Education (Political Science) from the University of Benin, an M. Sc. in Industrial Relations and Personnel Management from the University of Lagos, an MBA from IESE Business School, Barcelona and a PhD in International Business Management from the International School of Management, Paris. He is an alumnus of the Harvard Business School Advanced Management Program (AMP), a Fellow of the Chartered Institute of Personnel Management of Nigeria and member of the Society for Human Resource Management (SHRM).

Mehenaj Jebin has completed her undergraduate thesis at American International University-Bangladesh (AIUB), Bangladesh under the supervision of Md. Manzurul Hasan, Assistant Professor, Department of Computer Science and Engineering.

Dulce Corazon Z. Lamagna earned her Bachelor of Business Administration in Human Resource Management from American International University-Bangladesh. She obtained her Master of Business Administration in Finance and Accounting degree also from American International University-Bangladesh and her second Master of Business Admiration Degree in Commerce from Royal Melbourne Institute of Technology. She is currently pursuing her Doctor of Education in Organizational Leadership from California Coast University. She is a Senior Assistant Professor in the Faculty of Business Administration at American International University-Bangladesh. Her achievements as a teacher may be obtained from the experiences she had in the university in different capacities in several departments in addition to her academic responsibility. As an academician and a researcher, she has been an example in supporting women's empowerment and advancement in society through initiatives or personal action in the country. Her interest in the fields of teaching and research are in Human Resource, Women Empowerment and Organizational Behavior. She has contributed many articles for newspapers and is involved in various research being conducted in the university.

Md. Siam Mahmud has completed his undergraduate thesis at American International University-Bangladesh (AIUB), Bangladesh under the supervision of Md. Manzurul Hasan, Assistant Professor, Department of Computer Science and Engineering.

Sultana Parvin is an Assistant Program Organizer at Quantum Foundation, a well-known non-profit organization in Bangladesh, where her main responsibilities include program organizing and teaching accounting to both high school and college students. Besides this, she also performs a job as a consultant. She completed her graduation from International Islamic University Malaysia (IIUM) with the 2nd highest CGPA. She was also awarded a scholarship for her undergraduate degree. Her working areas are knowledge management, spiritual intelligence, strategic management, economics, neuro-economics, and so on.

Shraddha Purandare has over a decade of experience in academic, corporate training, and consulting activities. She brings insightful, hands-on expertise in the areas of business strategy, HR, and organizational development to implement pragmatic and high-impact solutions to business challenges. She has an inclination toward writing research papers and developing business cases. She has several research papers, and cases to her credit. Her areas of interest are talent management, employee wellbeing, employee relations, and employee engagement.

Lamiya Rahman has completed her undergraduate thesis at American International University-Bangladesh (AIUB), Bangladesh under the supervision of Md. Manzurul Hasan, Assistant Professor, Department of Computer Science and Engineering.

Md. Hasibur Rahman has completed his undergraduate thesis at American International University-Bangladesh (AIUB), Bangladesh under the supervision of Md. Manzurul Hasan, Assistant Professor, Department of Computer Science and Engineering.

Abu Saleh Mohammad Rajuwan has completed his undergraduate thesis at American International University-Bangladesh (AIUB), Bangladesh under the supervision of Md. Manzurul Hasan, Assistant Professor, Department of Computer Science and Engineering.

Md. Sadman Sakib has completed his undergraduate thesis at American International University-Bangladesh (AIUB), Bangladesh under the supervision of Md. Manzurul Hasan, Assistant Professor, Department of Computer Science and Engineering.

Emine Sever currently works in the Department of Economics and Administrative Sciences at Kultur University. Emine does research in organizational behavior. Her current projects are organizational agility, organizational culture, and firm performance.

Leigh Thompson is the J. Jay Gerber Distinguished Professor of Dispute Resolution and Organizations at the Kellogg School of Management, Northwestern University. An acclaimed researcher, author, and speaker, Thompson's research focuses on negotiation, creativity, and teamwork. His books include Negotiating the Sweet Spot: The Art of Leaving Nothing on the Table, Creative Conspiracy: The New Rules of Breakthrough Collaboration, Making the Team, The Mind and Heart of the Negotiator, The Truth about Negotiations, and Stop Spending, Start Managing. Thompson directs several executive education programs, including Leading High-Impact Teams; High Performance Negotiation Skills; Constructive Collaboration; Negotiating in a Virtual World; and Creativity as a Competitive Edge: Inspiration, Ideation, and Implementation.

Prioty Saha Trisha has completed her undergraduate thesis at American International University-Bangladesh (AIUB), Bangladesh under the supervision of Md. Manzurul Hasan, Assistant Professor, Department of Computer Science and Engineering.

Index

H

I

K

L

M

N

O

P

R

S

T

V

Z

www.ingramcontent.com/pod-product-compliance
Lightning Source LLC
LaVergne TN
LVHW081343300926
849161LV00008B/2052